Bringing up a Boy

Bringing up a Boy

The Nature and Nurture of Male Character

Eli H. Newberger, M.D.

BLOOMSBURY

C. P. Cavafy, "Ithaka," in C. P. Cavafy, *Collected Poems*, trans. E. Keeley
and P. Sherrard (Princeton: Princeton University Press, 1992), 36.
Reprinted by permission of Princeton University Press. Copyright 1992
by Edmund Keeley and Philip Sherrard.

First published as 'The Men They Will Become' in Great Britain 2000
This edition published 2001

First published by Perseus Books, Perseus Books Group, New
York

Bloomsbury Publishing Plc, 38 Soho Square, London W1D 3HB

The moral right of the author has been asserted

A CIP catalogue record for this book
is available from the British Library

ISBN 0 7475 3967 7

10 9 8 7 6 5 4 3 2 1

Printed in Great Britain by Clays Limited, St Ives Plc

For Noah

Contents

ACKNOWLEDGMENTS

First, I acknowledge with deep gratitude the boys and parents who shared their lives with me. Their identities are necessarily masked, but their stories will always sing in my mind.

I am grateful for comments on various drafts of the manuscript from Peter Gorski, Barbara Meltz, Rob Perkins, Carol Schraft, Kirk Smith, Amy Tishelman, and Robert Weintraub. James Carroll and Robie Harris gave me wise advice on my first book proposals. Merloyd Lawrence, my editor at Perseus Books, provided the kind of thoughtful, line-by-line appraisal that I needed and wanted.

Several colleagues at Children's Hospital in Boston contributed to my thought and knowledge. Alison Clapp, the Hospital librarian, guided my initial computer searches of professional literature on raising boys. Tina Nappi, a social worker, and Jennifer Robertson, director of the AWAKE program for battered women, and colleagues Kim McNamara and Maria Prodromou from the Family Development Clinic contributed to case discussions that addressed issues I've treated. Maria and her counterpart, Molly Benson, in the psychiatry department transcribed interviews for me on evenings and weekends. Psychologists Amy Tishelman, Laura Bencov, Maureen O'Brien, and Janice Ware loaned me books and vouched for me to friends when I was looking for families to interview. Janice recommended Troy Carr and Phoebe Fulton as research assistants. They brought to our work a magical combination of enthusiasm and intelligence; our weekly meetings yielded many paths to explore. Phoebe recruited her teacher friends, Amy Walker, George Noble, and Trina Saltonstall, for a memorable evening's discussion of school-age boys from teachers' perspectives. Phoebe's friend Nan Dewing, a nurse clinician, put me in touch with several families.

One of my former postdoctoral fellows, Katherine White Malley of Boston University, recommended my first research assistant, Kyra Kulik Johnson, a developmental psychologist. Kyra arranged with her sister-in-law, Sharon Kulik, the director of an inspiring family day-care program, for me to interview several mothers and fathers of infants and toddlers. Kyra also recommended a Boston College student, Kara Graziano, who located books and articles for me. Amanda Sonis, a student at Tufts University, searched the Internet for pertinent stories about parenting boys. Susan Heilman, the executive director of the Horizons Initiative in Boston, arranged for my first group meeting with parents. Through Bunny Meyer, a school principal, I met several articulate boys and their families.

In the course of my work, I benefited from discussing my observations with John Adams, Laura Broad, Virginia Davies, Joel Hirsch, Christopher Lydon, Claire Sylvia, Philip and Linda Stubblefield, and Willard Taylor.

When I mentioned in the fall of 1997 that there were many professional interruptions when I wrote at home, Donald Cutler and Pamela Hartford, my agents at Bookmark, said "Come and work here." I welcomed being able to discuss my work with them on a daily basis.

Through all their travails, my parents, Helen Newberger and Joseph Newberger, always let me know of their love and commitment. My brother, Henry, and my sister, Bett, read a semifinal draft, checking the facts about our family story, and approving how I told it.

No one helped me as much as did my wife, Carolyn Moore Newberger, a developmental and clinical child psychologist. Her research and deep understanding of parents and children has always profoundly influenced my work as a physician, and humanized my research and writing. Her contributions to this book included offering essential guidance on its approach and organization, sharing her comprehension of psychological theory and clinical practice, commenting on multiple drafts, and listening with patience and affection to the ruminations of a husband attempting his first book for a general readership.

With unerring timing, our daughter, Mary Helen Newberger Nsangou, and her husband, Usmanou Nsangou, produced Noah, the grandson to whom this book is dedicated. Usmanou reminded me gently to be aware of culture-bound opinions and advice. When Noah was two weeks old, M.H. said to me over dinner: "Dad, you're writing a book on raising boys. Teach me something!" I hope I have done so, in reciprocation for all she has taught me.

Eli H. Newberger, M.D.

Bringing up a Boy

1

WHAT IS CHARACTER?

This is a book about how to understand and influence the character of boys so that they have every opportunity to become admirable men. I have wrestled with the issue of character for a long time. As a pediatrician specializing in the treatment and prevention of family violence, I have dealt with urgent situations where one person—usually a man—has hurt others emotionally, and often physically, too. Daily I see expressions of masculinity we all deplore—power-obsessed, controlling, self-indulgent, belligerent, insensitive, foolishly risk-taking. Yet I have not met a single man in whom I could not find some point of connection with his better self; I've always been able to find a side of him that loves his children, or that yearns for a better relationship with their mother, or that knows violence is wrong. No one is just a "bad" man.

Throughout my life I've enjoyed the companionship of boys and men who personify the qualities of masculinity we admire—courage, good humor, flexibility, dependability, sociability, protectiveness of others. Some of these friends I first met during childhood and in high school, others were contemporaries at college, or have become professional colleagues. My life as a musician has also generated a rich variety of associations. None of us is perfect. We've all behaved in ways we regret, have all done things we wish we could do over with a clearer conscience and more careful choice. No one is just a "good" man.

So I need to define what I mean by character very carefully. First of all, since character is a subject as relevant to girls as to boys, why am I writing a book devoted exclusively to boys? I have two reasons. First, heredity bestows a different body and mind on a boy than on a girl. Not totally different, but distinctive enough to provide a unique biological starting point for a boy's development through childhood and adolescence.

A boy's environment adds a second powerful influence on his character formation. Ours has been called a gender-polarizing society. From the moment of birth, we raise boys differently from girls. We have different ways of relating to them, different expectations for them, different goals for them, different roles for them. While these are not totally different from our ways of raising girls, they are distinctive enough to provide a unique cultural environment with problems specific to males and their character.

The Role of Character

To define what I mean by character as it relates to boys and men, I shall begin by telling a story about a second cousin of mine. The names and places are fictional; the events are actual.

Sam Greenfield

Sam was a senior in high school in the 1950s when a developer bought a large, wooded tract of land adjacent to his family's secluded home on Long Island, New York, and began to clear it off and fill it up with look-alike houses. The invasion of the Greenfields' wooded privacy was as bothersome as a chronic toothache. Laments about the new development dominated family conversations; there seemed little to be done about the new houses except gradually to screen them off with border plantings. Other neighbors were equally unhappy.

But Sam was not content to accept the intrusion passively. Exploring the construction site one evening, he found where the construction crew had hidden the keys to the bulldozer they used to build access roads and dig foundations. After a little experimentation, Sam got the bulldozer in motion. He didn't damage any existing foundations or frames, but he plowed up the access roads to make them temporarily unusable, then put the bulldozer and keys back where he had found them. He carried out this and other mischievous acts several times.

Eventually, on one of his prowls, Sam was throwing rocks into an empty foundation to create nuisance work when a guard jumped out of hiding to confront him. "So you're the one who has been doing all the damage!" the guard shouted. Sam kept his composure. He identified himself truthfully. But he denied having done anything other than the petty vandalism the guard had just witnessed. Sam removed the rocks he'd thrown into the foundation and left the site scolded by the guard's parting words, "If we catch you again on this property, you'll be in plenty of trouble! You haven't heard the last of this!"

Some boys would deal with the threat of investigation and arrest by worrying in private. Others might boast about the mischief to friends.

Sam went home and told his parents what he had done to upset the construction schedule, and what he feared if the local police investigated.

"I feel partly responsible for what you've done, Sam," said his father. "We've all groused about the damned housing development without making it clear that we have to live with it, whether we like it or not." "But Sam," interjected his mother, "didn't it occur to you that if you got caught, Haverford College might learn of it and withdraw your acceptance for this fall?" Stella Greenfield's quick thought of Sam's month-old admission to Haverford was surely related to the fact that she had had to leave college herself in the midst of the Great Depression to help support her family; she knew the pain of lost opportunity.

My parents thought of Sam as a model of adolescent respectability. He was president of his high school class and an outstanding student. How did he come to initiate a one-man campaign to sabotage a housing development? One clue lies in his capacity for initiative and leadership. Sam wasn't one to sit around and mope. I suspect that he had a bit of the impulse to challenge authority that almost every adolescent has. He sincerely believed that the new housing subdivision was a bad thing for the community as well as his family.

I don't believe Sam thought what he was doing was anything worse than engaging in mischief. Many relatives who eventually heard of the episode thought of it as a humorous prank. Years later, at family reunions, someone would invariably say, "Do you remember the time Sam . . . ?" and everyone would share a laugh over his nerve and imagination.

But what Sam had done amounted to trespass, temporary theft of a bulldozer, and property damage. These acts constituted at least a serious misdemeanor, perhaps even a felony offense. An irritated public prosecutor might have chosen to exploit the case to Sam's and his family's embarrassment; an angry contractor might have initiated a civil suit for reimbursement of the damage Sam had caused. Stella Greenfield was properly concerned that public knowledge of Sam's actions might jeopardize his college acceptance.

The Greenfields were never put in the position of having to decide whether to acknowledge what they knew of Sam's escapades. No policeman ever came to the door to ask questions. Sam went to Haverford, and from there on to a distinguished career in public service.

Looking back at this family legend, it is clear that Sam was raised in an environment that stressed his ability—and responsibility—to make his own choices, and that emphasized the values of honesty, hard work, and positive action to benefit others. Sam exercised this responsibility by bringing the situation to his parents. He knew that he could trust them to help him work through the problem he had created for himself. They, in turn, made sure he understood the wrongfulness of what he had done, and its potential consequences, but not in such a way as to squelch his confidence in himself. After all, there are other, lawful ways to oppose housing sprawl, as many enterprising activists have found.

Sam was eighteen. His character was still being formed—as part of a process that began when he was an infant and would continue throughout his adulthood. The bulldozer was a blip on the screen, not the full picture of his personality. Like all adolescents, he was a work in progress, and Sam was blessed with a family that knew it. His admirable qualities, cultivated with care, weren't changed by one set of bad choices, although the consequences, had he been caught and punished, could have been devastating for him and his future. Sam—and his family—grew from this experience. Not least, it gave all the participants a frightening, penetrating sense of our human capacity for error, correction, and better judgment in the future. A good glimpse into what character is all about.

In *For Kings and Planets*, the novelist Ethan Canin says about his protagonist, who has undergone rigorous tests of character: "Hardship *made* character; hardship *broke* character; that was the paradox. Character to him was kindness and diligence and a certain social egalitarianism that was fundamental to society, and he still believed somehow that all three were instinctive. This, perhaps, was his unbending core."

We wouldn't have any way of discerning character if it weren't tested by hard circumstances. The testing often comes from outside as a challenge. It can also come from inside as a boy deliberately tests his own limits. But where does character come from in the first place?

At the beginning of his life, a boy scarcely has a self. He has a temperament, which I shall discuss later, but not a character. His world is microcosmic—consisting of himself and the principal people who take care of him. His strongest social instinct is to bond very closely to his mother. Very quickly he experiences tension between what he wants and what he is being given. In the course of infancy and early childhood, every one of his desires will be tested.

Depending on how he is treated, an infant boy develops fundamental attitudes about himself and his surroundings. He may develop trustfulness because his physical and emotional needs are met reasonably adequately and reliably; or he may develop distrustfulness because they are not. He may develop a capacity for intimacy because he is held and stroked and talked to lovingly a lot; or he may become accustomed to detachment from others because his first principal caregivers were somewhat distant toward him.

At every step of childhood and adolescence, the needs and wishes of the self get further crystallized, and more consciously in tension with the perceived interests of others. Eventually, in day care and school and in community activities, a boy's experience will become broad enough for him to deal conceptually with conflicts of interest. He begins to appreciate that there are needs that *everyone* can claim as worthy of fulfillment and protection. We call such universally justifiable interests "rights."

Though people argue with one another as to which needs are worthy of being called rights, most agree that everyone has some basic ones that deserve to be protected. The most challenging tension of the lifelong process of character formation arises when my wishes run headlong into the rights of others, or, just as importantly, when the wishes of others run headlong into my rights. There are plenty of occasions when our wishes conflict with the wishes of others, but those situations are not as significant as when rights are involved. As the following story shows, even five-year-old boys can develop friction that involves a human right.

Peter and Larry

Peter Nilsson and Larry Wyden, each five years old, live in a small New Hampshire town. The two boys are not buddies, but they meet each other regularly when children of the neighborhood get together to play. Peter's parents, especially his dad, Erik, have raised their only son to be self-sufficient and well-mannered. Erik practices self-sufficiency himself. He rarely has to call for the services of a tradesman or technician to solve a problem at his house; he has learned how to maintain and repair everything without help. He believes Peter ought to be able to solve *his* problems with minimal adult intervention.

Already this story alludes to an aspect of character. The larger subject of character gets broken down frequently into subcategories we call "values." Erik highly values self-sufficiency. He wants his son to internalize this value and then express it in the way he behaves.

There are two methods Erik could use to recommend self-sufficiency to Peter. He could teach him with little instructions—and he has done that; or he could model self-sufficiency in such a way that Peter might choose to follow his example—and he has done that, too. Values can be taught and they can be caught. I think they're just as often caught as taught, but both methods can be successful. What doesn't work well is for a dad to try to teach his son a value that the father hasn't himself internalized and exemplified, but thinks he has. The result is a son confused about that value, a son whose respect for his father may be diminished. I believe, however, that it's appropriate for a parent to recommend values to a son even while the parent acknowledges that he himself doesn't perfectly embody them. He expresses the hope that his son will surpass his parental example.

Every adult in his neighborhood has a good word to say about Peter Nilsson; his respectful manners (reflecting another value his parents teach: deference to elders), together with his outgoing temperament, make him the kind of boy that other parents might envy. Larry Wyden, however, proved immune to Peter's friendliness.

One day, over lunch, Peter said to his mom, Jiffy, "Larry is always hitting me." It was an accurate statement. Larry had begun to hit Peter without provocation almost every time they met at play. He had also been observed to hit his sitter or his mother if he became frustrated with them.

"Do you like it when he hits you?" Jiffy asked.

"Of course not," Peter replied.

"Well, then, you say 'I don't like it when you hit me,' and you walk away."

Jiffy was tempted to speak to Larry's mother, Sara, about Larry's aggressiveness, but she felt constrained. Larry's behavior was upsetting to Peter, but there was little chance that Larry would physically injure him. Jiffy fully endorsed Erik's wish to have Peter, with parental guidance and support, solve problems by himself. She also felt constrained because she didn't know Larry's mother very well and didn't want to make her defensive or irritated.

A couple of days later, Larry hit Peter again at the local playground. Sara happened to be there at the time, but didn't see her son deliver the punch. Peter responded to the blow by saying, "I hate you. You're not my friend, because you hurt me." Peter didn't walk away then. He spoke his mind and stood his ground.

The comparative lack of sophistication in a five-year-old boy actually helps us to see the workings of character here. If Peter had followed his mother's suggestion exactly, said "I don't like your hitting me," and walked away, Larry might not have felt really confronted. What Peter did was stronger, more confrontational than his mother had advised.

Probably to Peter's surprise, his response to Larry's punch touched a point of insecurity in Larry, who began to cry. What happened next shows just how unpredictable life can be, and why we can't ever eliminate the element of choice. Sara, seeing Larry in tears, rushed over and, without inquiring into the cause of her son's unhappiness, told Peter to apologize for making Larry cry. Peter was now caught between competing values. He had followed his mother's advice about how to respond to Larry's aggressiveness (self-sufficiency), but now Larry's mother was telling him to apologize (respect and deference to elders). The adult-respect rule won out, and Peter apologized to Larry for making him cry!

Both of his parents were home when Peter reported his confusing experience. "If it happens again," Erik told his son, "you say as *respectfully* as you can to Larry's mother, 'I'm sorry I hurt his feelings, but *he* hit *me*, and I'm the one who deserves the apology.'"

As might be expected, the same scenario was played out during the next weekend. Larry punched Peter, and Peter told him off in the same terms he had used before. Larry again broke into tears. Both mothers were at the playground. Again Sara rushed over and told Peter to apologize. Peter looked to Jiffy for reassurance, then delivered the message suggested by his dad. Sara dropped her demand that Peter apologize, but she didn't respond to his suggestion that Larry was the one who should offer an apology.

Both boys wandered off in separate directions to play, and the mothers had a chance to discuss the situation. Sara said that she and her husband were experiencing difficulty getting Larry to acknowledge that he couldn't always do as he pleased. She said she much preferred Larry's infancy when punishment was not an issue.

Later the same day, after a talk with his mom, Larry came over to Peter's house and promised not to hit Peter again. Jiffy was less than confident of the reliability of the truce. The next time the two boys were at the playground, Jiffy noted that Larry was in a bad mood. She thought he might well hit Peter again. Larry appeared to think about it, reconsidered, and punched a five-year-old girl from the neighborhood instead.

Peter, in many ways, is a five-year-old version of my cousin Sam. He already displays a temperamental outgoingness that could make him a born leader at an older age. His parents are teaching and modeling a coherent set of values, and he is comfortable discussing problems with them, trying their proposed solutions, coming back home for further consultation, and returning to the playground with a revised game plan. His mother is carefully calibrating her involvement, letting Peter work things out for himself, but staying close enough to be protective if the need should arise. She and Peter's dad could be counted on to protect Peter's right—the right not to be assaulted.

I don't know the causes of Larry's moodiness. Why did he embark on a pattern of hitting other children? His parents are said to be very mild-mannered in public. I have no reason to think Larry is copying aggressiveness he has witnessed at home, although in my medical practice I have many times met men whose public behavior was reasonable but who raged out of control in the privacy of their own homes.

Sara and Larry were at a neighborhood tea when the hostess left the dining room for a few minutes. Larry immediately shifted over to the hostess's chair and began to eat cake from her plate. Sara said, "Larry, please ask before you take something next time, okay?" Then, as if to reassure everyone, including herself, she asked, "Isn't he cute?" Her way is to follow every hesitant public correction of Larry with an immediate assertion of his adorableness, a disarming tactic that no one has the nerve to challenge.

Another neighbor found it disconcerting that Larry would come into her house without knocking, with the intention of playing with her children's toys. She was quite firm with Larry, telling him that it alarmed her when she was on the second floor and heard the door open and an unknown person walk through the downstairs rooms. Larry accepted the correction amiably, and abided by it; to the neighbor's surprise, Sara herself, after Larry had been taught to knock, walked into the same neighbor's house one day unannounced.

Larry's parents' insecurity and inconsistency have left him confused and anxious. He wields more power, without their loving restraint, than a five-year-old boy can feel comfortable with. He knows he's small and relatively defenseless. His hitting behavior may be a way of reassuring himself of his power in an environment where his parents are so weak they can't control him.

The Force of the Environment

Responsible parents begin to give their children structure and guidelines early in life so that the building blocks for resiliency, strength, and respect for others are laid. In other words, the building blocks of character. The only way to tell what a boy is absorbing from this tutelage is to observe how he behaves, particularly in a situation where there is some tension that pulls him between alternative choices.

In situations where the choices are familiar and undemanding, a boy may behave as if on automatic pilot. But stressful situations will make him weigh the alternatives more carefully and try to make a choice that is acceptable to him and others. His temperament will be a factor. Peter isn't even tempted to hit others without provocation. Larry might find it difficult to give up this outlet for his moodiness.

I think of character always as something that develops and is influenced, but not acquired. "Acquired" suggests that one can go out and get it, or that it can be indoctrinated into a child. The process of making character involves not only the outside world pushing on the boy but also his inner self working actively to integrate his own desires with these outside pressures. Parents, neighbors, and others (the human environment) can encourage certain kinds of boyish behavior and restrain others. Sometimes external demands are so strong that a boy feels overwhelmed. Then his masculine impulses of "fight or flight" cut in. He may submerge his own desires and attempt to escape the demands (flight) or he may become aggressive (fight).

Character thus consists of a constantly evolving balance between a boy's inner desires and ideals and the forces of his environment. The balance can shift in an instant. The dynamic quality of character formation means that sterling character can develop out of unlikely family histories—as the story of Pascal amply demonstrates.

Pascal

Pascal's mother grew up in a Moslem family in Southeast Asia, and came to the United States to go to college. "I was like a bird that had never flown before," Lani says now. "I was crazy about the freedom. I never neglected my education, but otherwise I tried everything. I met my first husband, a foreign student like me, but from the Balkans, and I had sex for the first time; and it was like Pascal's 'spirit' said, 'Oop, this is what I want, coming in,' and there I was: pregnant from my first sexual experience. I came from a family with very strong values, which included getting married when you were pregnant. So I did, but it was a tempestuous relationship, and Alex and I soon separated. When Pascal was nine months old, and I was still nursing him, Alex kidnapped Pascal and took him back to his native country."

"How did you get him back?" I asked, sitting spellbound in Lani's living room in a suburb of Boston. "The United States Embassy and my father hired the best lawyer," she replied. I asked whether the local authorities co-operated in the effort to repatriate Pascal. "No," Lani said, "but my father was a military officer and he had some paramilitary connections. I was asked whether I wanted Alex killed or just hurt. I said I didn't want him hurt at all. In five weeks I had Pascal back."

Lani returned to the United States as a graduate student and she met Joe Lehman when Pascal was three years old. She works as a school counselor, he as a newspaper reporter. They have had two more children together. Pascal is a sophomore in high school. I asked how they manage three kids and two careers with little outside help. "It's tough," Joe said. "We pray at five o'clock in the morning, before dawn. I converted to Islam, so we all pray together as a family. That's the one time of day we are always all to-gether: from prayers until we leave for school and work. I work very long days, but the children are in after-school programs and sports until Lani gets home to pick them up."

The relationship between Pascal and his stepfather was cemented when Pascal was five. Alex, the biological father, came to the Lehman's apartment building for a parental visit and tried to abduct Pascal again. "We were in the lobby," Pascal recalls, "and the next minute my father was walking out the door with me in his arms. And my dad (stepfather Joe) was like, 'Wait a minute, where are you going?' I struggled out of my father's arms and ran back into the elevator. My father ran after me, but my dad blocked him. My dad was like, 'Give me your best shot,' but my father didn't do anything. Then my mother called the police. I'll never forget that. From that day on, I knew my dad was going to protect me, so I didn't need to be scared. I used to be scared of robbers and stuff, but after that I wasn't. I was fine after that."

"I don't want to put you on the spot," I said to Pascal at one point, "but have you ever faced a situation where you saw violence or the possibility of danger, and there was a decision to be made by you with regard to what to do and whether to tell your parents?" There was such a situation, it turned out, and it concerned high school wrestling. Joe Lehman had been an enthusiastic wrestler in his youth, and he had transmitted his enthusiasm to Pascal.

"When I was a freshman wrestler," Pascal said, "the captains were great. They didn't believe in freshman initiation. They'd maybe give you a hard time once in a while, but not enough to make kids quit the team. I've never told my parents about this, but the captains this year started freshman initiation again. The juniors and seniors would beat up the freshmen, push them into lockers, turn out the lights, and start to shake the lockers. Kids were quitting the team.

"I didn't say anything during practice because I didn't feel it was my place. But after practice I went to one of the captains and said, 'Our program's not so strong. I don't feel that initiation is a smart thing to do because we're losing kids. They're quitting.' The captain called me names, 'pussy' and stuff like that, but he didn't do any more hazing either. But later there was another heated discussion, and I said to him, 'If you want to hurt these kids, then you're going to have to hurt me first.'"

"Pascal has gifts that some other students don't have," Joe Lehman interjected. "It's a rarity, for example, for a freshman to make varsity as he did last year. We believe these gifts are given from God, because we're a religious family, and that we have to do more. It's important to take a stand like that, to show courage, to stand up when you see injustice, especially among your own. I'm glad that he does it and I don't even know about it."

"When you challenged the captain," I asked Pascal, "did you have any fallback plan in mind? Would you have told your parents or someone at the school?" "If he'd gone against me," Pascal said, "I would've told my dad and we would've gone to see the athletic director or something like that."

"Star athletes are often revered by other kids," I said, "and they have a tremendous amount of power. If they behave toward others as they did toward the freshman wrestlers, that could be dangerous. How did these athletes behave toward girls?"

"The captain couldn't stop talking about sex," Pascal said. "It's all he can think about. And, ah, he'll lie because he doesn't really have a lot of friends. I guess it's normal to have locker-room talk about girls, but he would talk about them nonstop. Some kids thought he was serious, but I didn't take him seriously."

After we had discussed the fact that the wrestling captain dropped out of school midway through his senior year, Pascal said, "I still respect his parents a lot. His mom was always nice to me; and his dad would show me how to improve some of my wrestling moves. You know, constructive criticism. He helped me a lot."

"So it must have been difficult for them when their son dropped out of school," I suggested. "Yeah," Pascal agreed. "But his parents kind of let him do what he wants. They're sort of afraid of him."

"I know what he's talking about," Joe concurred. "The wrestling captain's confused about things. The way his parents treat him is not the way we would treat our son. We would expect more of our son. His parents are in some ways too nice. We believe that most people, especially children, are basically good. We try to pay attention and encourage that goodness."

Joe's way of expressing the Lehman family's structure of conduct and discipline occasionally sounds slightly authoritarian. But that is a misleading impression. It was Pascal who caught the dynamic balance of his family by stating two things:

First, his parents have given him considerable responsibility for his own behavior. "My parents have taught me how to make my own decisions about what's right and what's wrong. They haven't tried to tell me exactly what to do and what not to do in every situation." This significant degree of moral autonomy is balanced, secondly, with a close relationship between Pascal and his mother and stepfather. "I'm actually lucky because my parents are there for me. Some of my friends' parents aren't there for them, so they actually tell me their stuff, and I feel really bad. Their parents aren't there because they're working or because there isn't a relationship or connection between them and their kids. They let things go. It's tough. I feel bad for them. Most of my friends are in that predicament. Some of the parents that are around just don't care. The kids will smoke dope in the house and stuff like that. One kid says his parents don't even know when he does it; if he does get caught, he gets grounded for a week, and that's it."

My friend and fellow pediatrician, Peter Gorski, stated the interdependence of Pascal's two points in a conversation we had about the strengths, or "virtues," one hopes parents will bring to their child-rearing—a subject I take up at the end of this chapter. In speaking about love and trust he pointed out that "Many children feel loved but not trusted—I mean, not trusted to be reasonable, competent, and resilient. They grow up with a hole at their center, a basic distrust of themselves. This loss imposes limitations on their own abilities to feel faith and hope, to take initiatives, to value intimacy, and to be generous toward others."

Joe and Lani Lehman, coming from profoundly different cultures—Joe from an American family in which his parents were largely inattentive, giving him little parental guidance, Lani from a very authoritarian Asian family with rigid roles for everyone—nevertheless exhibit a fusion of love and trust toward their children. They love their kids extravagantly; they also trust them to an increasing degree, as they grow up, to work things out for themselves.

In a later chapter in the book, I shall describe a particularly challenging behavioral crisis that the headmaster of our local high school had to handle while I was writing this book. I went to see him to learn more about the crisis, but I also asked him for some general comments on nurturing character in boys. What did he think I should keep in mind?

"Three things," Bob Weintraub said. Point number one was not to underestimate the power of popular culture in kids' heads. "They have a whole language that circulates through the music and television and movies they listen to and watch. The language of their media pays about equal attention to sex and to disrespect for adults. I like to say that once upon a time Ozzie Nelson was the role model for Dad, and now Homer Simpson is."

The second factor Bob cited is the diminished adult presence in many kids' homes. "Whether it's because both parents are working, or because there's only one parent in the household, there's not a lot of nights when dinner is cooked and everyone sits down at the table together to eat and talk. There's a loss of adult influence in boys' lives. That's huge. It's not because parents are bad people, it's just what's happening. It's reality. Adults are stretched, they're stressed. Just as *Friends* is reality and Homer Simpson is reality, the loss of the adult presence and voice is reality.

"And then,"—Bob moved into his third point—"going along with that is the nature of the adolescent boy. He's seeking his identity. He's trying to figure out what's okay and what's not okay. Right now I strongly believe that peer influence is much stronger than adult influence. The adults aren't there for a variety of reasons that cut across class lines, cut across everything.

"Parents want to raise thoughtful, successful, respectful kids, right? I don't think anybody wants not to do that. And teachers want to do the same thing: raise thoughtful, successful, respectful kids. I don't know if it's simplistic or not, but in the face of the things I mentioned—popular culture, and the demands and reality of adult life today—there's just not a strong and unified adult voice. There's a great line from James Comer, a psychiatrist at Yale. He said, 'When I grew up, there was a conspiracy of adults to make me a responsible person.' And there is not that conspiracy today, or at least it's weakened. So kid's decisions are based on the influences of popular culture and peer influences more than they are on the adult voice."

Despite the challenging circumstances of our time, a great many boys are growing up to superb manhood. There are Pascals everywhere. The success stories are not defined by social class, race, ethnicity, or religion. Nor are they defined by the composition of the household. Married couples, single parents, gay couples—all types, as I shall show—are raising fine young men.

The fact also remains that some boys from all walks of life and all manner of households crash. There is no such thing as perfect childhood. Everyone stumbles along the way. The stumbles often serve a profound, positive purpose, enabling boys to integrate their achievements and their failures into a personality with a balance of confidence and humility. Often, in the midst of disappointments over their own efforts, boys learn that they are loved for themselves and their character, not just for their achievements.

Temperament

But what leverage, parents may justifiably ask, do we actually have? How much of our son is the personality he was born to be, and what part can we influence?

Every boy is born with an innate temperament and other inherited characteristics that will be his for a lifetime, and that influence the way he behaves in any situation. Winifred Gallagher put it this way:

> While we may be born equal, we're not born the same, and can be very broadly distinguished by our expression of a few basic traits, or abiding behavioral tendencies. According to our capacities for anxiety, aggression, and involvement in the world, some of us fear the challenges that thrill others; some of us look for the fights that others duck; some of us are the life of the party that others observe.

Stella Chess and Alexander Thomas, two child psychiatrists, contributed significantly to our understanding of temperament in their writings from the 1980s:

> It was clear from the parents' descriptions that babies did differ in many ways, even in the first few months of life. Some infants cried softly while others tended to cry loudly. Some fussed or cried a great deal, others only a lit-

tle. Some babies developed regular sleep and feeding schedules quickly and easily; others got hungry and sleepy at different times from day to day. Some moved their arms and legs and twisted their necks and bodies actively; others moved much less and lay quietly most of the time.

Two child psychologists I've worked with are each the mother of fraternal male twins. Both mothers are professionally trained to be observant of behavior. Both were conscious of intending to treat their twins exactly the same after birth. Both were astonished by how quickly they were aware of the strikingly different temperaments of their twin boys. One of the mothers had a difficult pregnancy that was closely monitored. She discovered, for example, that one of the fetuses was much more active than the other, a difference that held up after the twin boys were born.

Some elements of a boy's temperament are pretty impervious to outside influence; they are referred to as the "hardwired" part. Other elements are more malleable; they are the "softwired" part. Specialists in neuroscience and child development have many disagreements about distinguishing the two parts, so the best resolution is to say that both elements are involved more or less equally in what we call temperament.

As soon as a boy is born, his innate temperament begins to interact with the outside environment, human and otherwise. His parents have temperaments, too! In fact, pediatricians report that parents frequently complain about their children's temperaments even in the absence of behavioral problems: their sons are shyer or more intense or more stubborn or more frequently tearful than their parents wish they were.

A core of temperament in every person, said Chess and Thomas, holds up over time:

> Two children may dress and feed themselves equally well, ride a bicycle with the same skill, and have the same motives for engaging in these activities. Two adolescents may have similar academic interests, learn equally quickly, and have similar ambitions. Two adults may have the same technical expertise and motivation on their jobs. Yet these two children, adolescents, or adults may differ markedly in the quickness with which they move, the ease with which they approach a new physical environment, social situation, or task, the intensity and character of their mood expression, and the effort it takes to distract them when they are absorbed in an activity.

Just as assessments of character may (usually misguidedly) stress a single virtue or fault—he's a liar—assessments of temperament may (equally misguidedly) stress a single trait—he's shy, or he's hyperactive. Chess and Thomas concluded that temperament has nine irreducible components. I list them, cast in masculine terms, to encourage readers to look at temperament broadly:

1. Activity Level. How intense is his activity, and what is the proportion of active to inactive periods in his day?
2. Regularity. How predictable or unpredictable is he in the timing of basic biological functions such as eating and sleeping?
3. Approach or Withdrawal. How does he react initially to new situations?
4. Adaptability. How does he respond over time to new or altered situations?
5. Sensory Threshold. How much stimulus does he need before he responds?
6. Mood. How pleasant and friendly, or unfriendly, is he?
7. Intensity of Reaction. How energetic is his response, positively or negatively?
8. Distractibility. How easily does a new stimulus interfere with ongoing activity?
9. Persistence and Attention Span. Does he continue activities in the face of obstacles? How long will he pursue an activity before abandoning it?

Chess and Thomas went on to describe three clusters of temperament traits that many pediatricians and child psychologists still use as a rough guide to evaluating temperament: the "easy" child (gregarious, cooperative, focused—everyone wants one of these); the "difficult" child; and the "slow-to-warm-up" child. There has been much theorizing and research on temperament since Chess and Thomas did their pioneering work. Stanley Greenspan, for example, has profiled five distinguishable types of "difficult" or "challenging" children: the highly sensitive child, the self-absorbed child, the defiant child, the inattentive child, and the active/aggressive child. These profiles appear to cover in an expanded way the "difficult" and the "slow-to-warm-up" categories of Chess and Thomas. But I'm not sure that the five profiles rebut the criticism of William Carey and some other writers on child development—directed at the three profiles of Chess and Thomas—that such profiles can lead to hasty and unhelpful typing and labeling of children, particularly by people untrained in the disciplined observation of behavior.

Greenspan, whose work I admire, acknowledges that his five personality patterns "appear in different proportions in many individuals. . . . Some of us are combinations, so we fall into more than one of these five profiles." Thus we should all the more resist using the profiles as labels to justify unsympathetic caregiving. Their usefulness lies in promoting behavior by parents and other caregivers that takes these personality patterns into account: "For each characteristic, certain ways that parents behave enhance the flexibility, creativity, and potential of a child showing that pattern of behavior. Others are almost certain to compound the problems presented by a given characteristic."

In the end, I think, the three-part classification by Chess and Thomas is too simple, too easily misused, and the five-part system of Greenspan is more helpful as a list of themes to be aware of than as a classification system. Five-part systems will probably always lose out to three-part systems if only for utility purposes. For describing a child's temperament, I find myself returning to something like the Chess and Thomas list of nine irreducible components.

But we are all indebted to Greenspan for a very clear statement on the relationship between nature and nurture:

> Whenever you hear that a child's temperament or traits may be fixed, remember that not only are these traits not fixed, the personality characteristics we are most concerned with are 'bigger' than any one trait. The capacity to love, to empathize with others, to be confident and assertive, and to think creatively are complex products of many of our traits; indeed, they are the result of our relationships and experience over many years. . . . A child's personality, therefore, is not simply a product of both 'nature' and 'nurture,' or even a product of how nature adjusts to nurture. It is a product of the unique and continuous interplay between nature and nurture. . . . In the last ten years, we have learned a great deal more about this interplay. It operates a little like a lock and key. Finding the right key creates new patterns of interaction. Out of this new relationship, a child can often develop the warmth and confidence he or she needs.

Jerome Kagan has also refined the subject of temperament in significant ways. He pointed out that the nine irreducible categories of Chess and Thomas, abstract and universal as they may sound, were not drawn from a value-free investigation. They were extracted from interviews with urban, middle-class parents and reflected those parents' predominant concerns with their infants' "fussiness, ease of feeding, regularity of sleep, fearfulness, and reciprocity with others." This insight doesn't invalidate the work of Chess and Thomas; it simply reminds us to notice what presuppositions a scientist brings to his or her interests, methods, and findings. "All such temperamental qualities can be changed by experience," Kagan noted, "and all require certain experiences in order to be actualized."

Kagan paid particular attention to the difference between timid or inhibited children and outgoing, comparatively fearless children. About 10 percent of two-year-olds, he reported, display pronounced inhibition toward unthreatening but unfamiliar situations; one longitudinal study has shown this temperamental quality enduring stably through childhood and adolescence and on into adulthood.

Parents, at least initially, may be pleased to have shy or inhibited children—although American parents in general prefer a bold to a timid child—because they tend to be obedient, display caution about rushing into dangerous situations, and may be more attentive to academic mastery than some outgoing kids. The inhibited children often get along better with parents and other adults than with peers. However, even this temperamental quality can be deeply influenced by a parent who wants a different kind of child than he or she got genetically.

Kagan tells of a mother who wanted a bold, fearless son. Just before he turned two, her child fit the description of an inhibited youngster. By age four he appeared to be an uninhibited child. He was playful and sociable and laughed heartily. Yet there were little signs to suggest that the transformation was far from complete. When the boy was observed being assertive, he seemed more mean-spirited than playful. Put into a play situation with an unfamiliar boy, he seemed hostile rather than relaxed, and quickly scurried to his mother's side when his playmate became dominating. This little boy seems mainly to have been encouraged to be outgoing, and the tension between his natural inhibition and his parentally influenced style showed in the edge of anger in his sociability. If an inhibited child is born to parents who feel deeply threatened by this characteristic and react to it with hostility, they might drive him into being an aggressively disobedient child. Thus may nurture create a very different surface appearance than nature intended for a child.

Nurturing Character

Temperament and character each affect the other. Temperament influences how receptive the child will be to life experiences, and how life experiences will be absorbed by the child. Character, as it develops over the years, becomes a resource for shaping the part of temperament that is malleable.

We might agree in principle that it is desirable for a boy to develop the quality of courage as part of his character; but it will involve one kind of effort for an inherently gregarious or combative boy to develop courage, and quite another, perhaps more arduous, effort for a naturally shy boy to become courageous. Similarly, it may be easy for a naturally agreeable boy to develop that most demanding of virtues, patience, while a naturally intense or hyperactive boy will find it excruciatingly difficult.

What qualities do parents and teachers need to have to cope with the long and complex task of raising a boy to be a man of admirable character? Certainly attentiveness is a prerequisite to everything else. Pascal Lehman and Bob Weintraub have each given eloquent testimony already to the plight of boys growing up in the custody of parents who are either too busy with other things or too uninterested in parenting to pay attention.

When I began thinking about this book, I thought that the cardinal virtue for child-raisers might be patience. A passage from Robert Coles's *The Moral Intelligence of Children* seemed to confirm my hunch. Midway through an open letter to parents and teachers, Coles recalls trying to elicit specific child-raising advice in a conversation with Erik Erikson, the renowned theorist of personality. Coles wrote:

> Our sons were becoming school-age children and every once in a while I wanted to scream, I was made so frustrated and anxious by something one of them did, or didn't do—get into a fight, dress like a slob, leave his room messy every day, swear like a trooper, forget and forget to say 'please' and 'thank you'! He saw my impatience, Erikson clearly did, as I knew when I heard him say, 'It's a long haul, bringing up children to be good; you have to keep doing that, bring them up, and that means bringing things up with them: asking; telling; sounding them out; sounding off yourself. . . . You have to learn where you stand—and, by God, you won't budge from there. You have to make sure your kids learn that (where you stand), understand why, and soon, you hope, they'll be standing there beside you, with you, and it'll be patience that gets them there, day-by-day work, the patience to do it: moral work, based upon speaking those moral sentences that you hope your kids will learn from you, for themselves—their own version, though!'

One emphasis in Erikson's spontaneous but eloquent statement gave me slight pause. All of us will probably have thought some issues of childcare through to Eriksonian decisiveness for ourselves—although it's humbling how often we change our minds as we wrestle with actual situations. But there are many gray areas about which we may not be fully prepared to "take a stand"; we haven't yet resolved them for ourselves. So we must keep on searching, looking for truths, keeping open to others' perspectives, having the patience to tolerate uncertainty, having the will to explore and question. Sometimes the truth comes down to the fact that different people see things in different ways, and there will be different—but reasonable—stands taken from person to person. I view the gray areas as ideal subjects for sharing tentative thoughts with boys as they grow up. As much as they need the security of our convictions, they also need the experience of seeing and sharing the way we explore unresolved character issues. Not that we shouldn't also share with boys how we came to our convictions, but since they will be in the process of exploring issues, they will be especially attracted to our grappling with the gray areas.

Despite Erikson's repeated references to patience, there was something else in his words that caught my attention most of all. He was repeatedly emphasizing how active the parent or teacher should be. A very passive person can display great patience, but in raising boys that kind of patience isn't enough. Erikson's counsel reminded me of another of Bob Weintraub's comments. "As a teacher," he said, "you have to be tenacious about kids being there on time, tenacious about helping a kid when he's not being as responsible as he should. Tenacity takes energy. Some parents don't want to be tenacious, and take the easy way out." He might have added, tenacity in believing in, protecting, and celebrating every boy's inner sense of worth.

Urie Bronfenbrenner, the Cornell child psychologist, emphasizes the importance of such tenacious support. He argues that a boy can survive all manner of childhood disappointments and sufferings if there is at least one person in his life who is crazy about him, is deeply invested and protective of him, advocates for him when it is needed. That person might not be a parent; a grandparent or other relative, a neighbor, a teacher, a family friend: what matters is the quality, consistency, and dependability of the attention.

There you have it. Patience is immensely valuable, but tenacity, with its implications of energetic engagement with a boy, and a refusal to give up on him, may be the greatest child-raising virtue of all.

2

THE ROOTS OF
CHARACTER

My goal in this chapter is to put forth a framework for understanding the relationships between adults and the boys they care for—and for understanding how those relationships provide a foundation for the development of boys' character. All of us, whether parents or grandparents, teachers, coaches, or counselors, would like to develop such relationships. To do so, we need first to observe ourselves: to become aware of our beliefs and actions, their effects on our children, and our children's effects on us.

For each of us, such a search can begin with an exploration, as probing as possible, of how we were raised by our own parents and other influential caregivers. How were we treated? What are the most vivid mental snapshots we have of those relationships? We may well have adopted their best ways of nurturing, but we may also have adopted some of their less desirable ways, simply because their having so treated us gives those ways a certain legitimacy. Unless we have consciously modified the mindsets and methods of the most influential nurturing we received, we will probably default often to those ways when we nurture children ourselves. A default position is what one falls back on without thinking when circumstances have overwhelmed one's conscious philosophy and methods. If a parent can become mindful of his or her default positions, choices can be made about whether these fallback positions are sufficiently responsive to a son's needs and behavior.

Levels of Parental Awareness

In her research and writing, my wife, Carolyn Moore Newberger, has identified four distinct levels of awareness that parents may realize in their relationships with their children. This work was influenced by the approaches to moral development at Harvard's Laboratory of Human Development, most notably by Lawrence Kohlberg, Robert Selman, and later, Carol Gilligan. Between the first or lowest level of what Carolyn calls "parental awareness," and the fourth or highest level, there is a growing mindfulness of the child's world and of the parent's place in that world. As we will see later in this chapter, the levels of awareness are equally relevant to all relationships, and to the stages of a boy's moral development.

Level One: Me First

At this level, an adult is aware of a child always through the lens of his or her own adult needs. Parents functioning at Level One, if asked to define a child's needs, may describe their own needs as though those needs were the child's, confusing one with the other.

For example, imagine an eight-month-old boy who one evening keeps playfully pushing his food off his high-chair tray. He is toying with what happens to things that disappear over the edge of the tray, and enjoying the small chaos he has created. It's all a hilarious game to him.

At Level One, a parent may view the child's behavior only as the creation of a mess the parent will have to clean up, unmindful that it is also an innocent and playful exploration that might be enjoyed so long as the mess doesn't get out of hand. The parent focuses on the behavior's impact on the parent rather than on its meaning to the child. An annoyed parent functioning at this level will probably interrupt the little boy's play by firmly saying "No!" or by removing all the remaining food from the tray, or by striking the boy's hands as punishment. The message to the infant is: Don't do this to me!

The parent of a teenager arrested for drinking alcohol in a public park, to give another example, may be concerned principally with whether public knowledge of the episode will adversely affect the parent's reputation in the community, downplaying the evidence that a son has shown a need for thoughtful and sensitive intervention to discover what is awry in his life. A parent functioning at Level One isn't by definition a bad person; he or she is, however, a parent with a very limited appreciation of the child's world for its own sake and with its own agenda, and therefore has a somewhat limited grasp of the opportunities of parenthood. So long as the parent's needs and the child's needs are reasonably congruent, the relationship between the two can be satisfactory to both. The more starkly those needs diverge, the more a parent guided by "Me First" will ignore or suppress the child's needs.

Level Two: Follow the Rules

Those functioning on Level Two apply to child care a set of traditions and rules that they themselves believe in. These standards for good parenting/good children may have been acquired from traditional family practices, or from religious teachings, or from acceptance of a child-care authority's views, or from prevailing community standards, or from some combination of these sources. The standards are not tailored to the individuality of any child; they are rules that adherents believe all children and caregivers should be governed by.

A parent applying rules might also reprimand the eight-month-old boy who is pushing his food off his tray, or slap his hands—not because the parent feels inconvenienced by the mess but because the infant is not behaving as the parent believes children of that age should behave. On the other hand, if the boy's messiness is viewed as what a child of that age should be doing (exploring whatever materials he can get his hands on), the parent may handle the situation without blaming the boy, or even delight in his play. Some rules-oriented parents might be content to let the boy play with his food; many others would take away the smashed peas and smeared peaches, clean him off, and give him something less messy to play with.

The central idea at Level Two is that there are hard and fast rules that tell us what makes a good parent and what makes a good child. A rules orientation may favor order and neatness, and obedience by children to parental authority, or it might favor some other style of child-rearing, such as permissiveness. The parent, in effect, strives to know and follow a "manual" for being and creating a good child.

Every household has to have a basic set of understandings that stand between a secure, reasonably orderly family life and utter chaos, but I think you will see that there is a vast difference between a rules manual as the principal organizer of family life, and family interactions at Levels Three and Four where rules are tempered by a regard for individual personalities.

Level Three: We Are Individuals

At Level Three, an adult can move beyond the self-perspective of Level One and the manual of Level Two, and view each boy as a person with individual needs and potentiality. The boy may be seen to have much in common with every other child, but will also be seen as a person who is in important respects unique.

To understand a boy's world from his own point of view means trying to identify and meet his particular needs rather than operating within a set of rules and expectations held to apply to every well-brought-up child. A corollary to this way of understanding a boy is that the adult also views himself or herself as a unique person whose needs and responses can't be defined merely by following a rule book.

A parent on Level Three watching an infant push food off his tray would see the game the boy is playing, and his delight with it. Parental response would take into account this particular boy's needs and likely responses. Sharing the boy's delight might be enough to make the mess tolerable. But if not, the parent would likely remove the food and substitute some other nonbreakable objects the infant could push over the edge with comparable enjoyment but less mess.

Another example: a three-year-old boy who gets easily overexcited. Shortly before bedtime, still wound up and on the verge of becoming irritable, he dashes to his wooden train, grabs its engine, and runs around the bedroom pretending the engine is an airplane. A parent functioning at Level One or Two might ignore this activity if it didn't bother the parent or break a rule. A parent functioning at Level Three, knowing that this child's overexcited bursts of activity precede crashes, would be better able to tune into the boy's underlying need for a firm and calming hand; the parent's strategy might be to divert the boy into a quiet game together, in preparation for a bath, story time, and a happy bedtime.

Level Four: Living and Growing Together

On Level Four, adults have the same regard for the preciousness of individuality as those at Level Three. But this appreciation is set in a different context. The adult now sees that he or she and the child are in a mutual and reciprocal relationship that continually develops and changes. Adults at this level are more self-aware; part of this awareness is a recognition of the mutual influence of adult and child. Sometimes the process of living together is supremely happy for both, sometimes it is difficult for one or the other, and occasionally it is miserable for both.

There is tolerance at Level Four for the conflict and ambivalence all self-aware persons come to recognize in themselves and in their relationships. I don't want to fall into the trap of overinterpreting every moment of a boy's behavior—sometimes, as they say, a cigar is just a cigar—but the game of pushing food off the tray might possibly be seen as exhibiting more than casual child's play. The infant is already grappling with an inarticulate wish to master his world; but his control is threatened by the fact that the persons and objects he is most attached to regularly disappear in anxiety-provoking ways. An insightful parent understands this anxiety and loves to play little games with him in which things disappear and, to his immense satisfaction, quickly reappear.

One of the cornerstones of Carolyn's concept of parental awareness is that each higher level builds from the lower levels. Parents don't abandon their own needs as they move from Me First to Follow the Rules; they incorporate their needs into a larger worldview, and draw upon the child-care rules embedded in it. Parents with an individualized perspective (We are Individuals) may very well also draw on the advice of grandma or of a particular child-care authority, but will evaluate advice and rules from that authority in relation to the needs of their own child.

Barry Zuckerman and Steven Parker recently gave an example of how parental awareness may differ along gender lines:

> The separation anxiety that usually becomes apparent at the 9-month visit is another opportunity for learning about normal development. If parents don't mention it, the clinician can easily elicit separation protest by asking the mother to leave the room for 10 to 20 seconds. When the baby cries, ask the parents whether the same thing happens at home, and how they explain it. A common misinterpretation of separation protest at this age is the father who, in a somewhat scolding tone, explains that the infant cries every time the mother leaves because she 'spoils' him. The father's view may be due in part to feeling displaced following the birth of the child, or to holding different opinions on child rearing from his wife's. Concerns about how to discipline children and the management of anger for everyone in the family are just under the surface in such a discussion.

The father who complains in this case that his wife is spoiling the baby is in effect using a Level Two argument (she is breaking the rules) to assuage a Level One feeling (it hurts my feelings that the baby cries when she leaves the room but doesn't cry when I leave the room). A father functioning at Level Four might acknowledge the envy he feels when his son's attachment to his wife seems to exclude him from the circle of intimacy, yet he can also understand that this is a normal step in infant development and doesn't mean that his son doesn't love him, too.

A mother described to me her consternation when her eighteen-month-old fretting son, whom she was carrying as she made her way though a supermarket checkout, suddenly hauled off and struck her forcefully in the face, something he had never done before. What should she have done, she asked.

In my clinic and elsewhere over the years, I've seen many mothers I would characterize as functioning at the Me First level reflexively return the favor: strike the child, bite the child, pull the child's hair, or yell intemperately at the child. A mother functioning at Follow the Rules level will try to ignore her hurt or embarrassment and do what she feels is the socially appropriate thing. She might verbalize the rule, perhaps in a reprimanding tone: "Joey, it's not right to hit someone. We don't do that." By speaking of "we," the mother is showing that she and Joey live under the same rules.

A mother functioning at the We are Individuals level would try to understand why Joey hit her, and respond to Joey's motive. If Joey said, "Mama, home," she might commiserate with him that he has had to endure a long wait; but she would also tell him that even if he wants to go home, he shouldn't hit Mommy. Perhaps she would offer him some reward if he can hang on for just a few minutes until the groceries are paid for. Or perhaps she would distract him with some food.

At Level Four (Living and Growing Together) a mother would also reinforce the no-hitting rule and use some of the diversionary tactics of the mother reacting at Level Three. But she might also feel that she should express both her pain and embarrassment to her son—"Oh, Joey, that really hurt Mommy"—which might enable Joey to transfer his attention from his own discomfort to the hurt he has caused.

If the hitting persisted, she would look at what is going on in Joey's relationship with her and others, and what he may have witnessed in real life or on television that might contribute to this behavior. (I think that any violence by a preschooler should stimulate this kind of reflection, by the way. Many parents, after making it known that they won't tolerate being hit again, write this sort of thing off under the exonerating statement, "Boys will be boys.")

The Growth of Parental Awareness

People are not born with an innate capacity for high levels of awareness of relationships. The higher levels are learned, beginning to some extent in childhood. As boys grow, they have many opportunities to become aware of their feelings toward others, and of others' feelings toward them. They may begin to grasp the dynamics of human interaction. Whatever they've learned about relationships through childhood, adolescence, and early adulthood is what they have first to offer to a relationship with a new child of their own. As a father and his child grow together, the father's capacity to understand the child and the parent-child relationship grows as well.

Carolyn once stated the challenge of parenting as follows:

Parenthood is often thought of as a natural or instinctive process. With the birth of a baby, the parent is expected somehow to be fully equipped to raise a child with love and skill. Yet increasing awareness of the magnitude of such problems as child abuse and neglect, emotional disturbances in children, and adolescent pregnancies and runaways has forced the realization that parenthood is at best a difficult process and at worst an experience of failure and a source of stress and disability for many families.

In the same essay, Carolyn pointed out the gritty, practical environment in which the parent operates:

Parental action is to a great extent a process of negotiating conflicting claims. The introduction into the family of each new member brings new demands and a necessary redistribution of finite physical and emotional resources. Many of the issues with which parents must deal directly involve areas of conflicting claims, such as resolving conflict between family members, changing children's behavior, and meeting needs. The needs and claims of the child come in conflict with those of the parent or siblings, yet the parent must make decisions about what he or she ought to do—decisions that may affect the parent's own resources or contradict the child's will.

Much of what we do as parents is intuitive and positive, drawn from our basic love for our children and from the reservoir of knowledge and common sense we bring to our parental roles. There are times in every parent's life, however, when conflicts arise, our efforts fail, or we respond in ways we later regret. These are opportunities to examine ourselves, to test our own characters: Are we acting out of our own needs alone? Are we defaulting to patterns that are hurtful or ineffective? Are we stuck with rules that don't apply to our son?

Learning Through Crisis

Sometimes, parental awareness is jolted to another level by a crisis that makes a mother or father view parenthood in a sharply different light. One day in my clinic I interviewed Betsy Keenan while one of our volunteers played with her children, Billy, aged four, and Katie, aged eighteen months. She had recently separated from her husband.

"I was a trophy wife," Betsy said. "Ken was already president of the computer company when I became a management trainee assigned to assist him on presentations at international conferences. One night, toward the end of a weeklong meeting in London, we went to the hotel bar after an interminable dinner with too many toasts, and a long after-dinner speech. Ken is twenty years older than I. He said the European engineers and their wives bored him, but I made him feel young again. He pulled me close to him and said he wanted to spend the night with me.

"I quit my job when we moved in together, but things were still fun because I traveled with him and had a luxurious house and unlimited budget for clothes. Looking back on it, though, I'm amazed at myself for sacrificing my life that way.

"It was Billy who opened my eyes. After his fourth-birthday party had ended, and the nanny and I had tucked the kids into bed, Ken and I drove over to Saporito's for dinner. As usual, he had too much to drink, but he insisted on driving when we returned home. I made the mistake of gripping the driver's side of the bucket seat as we came around the curve to our house because we were going too fast and there was a dangerous drop-off to the ocean on our right. It was a reflex action.

"Ken stopped the car at the foot of the driveway, reached over, grabbed my neck, and shouted, 'Don't you play games with me!' He pulled the car into the garage and went inside while I sat in the semidarkness pulling myself together. About thirty seconds later he came back out. Without saying a word—the nanny's room is off the corridor to the garage—he grabbed me by the hair and pulled me out of the car onto the garage floor. Then he left again. Not another word was spoken that night. I brushed myself off and slept in a guest bedroom.

"The next night was the nanny's off, and Ken was at a dinner meeting. I was bathing both kids in one tub before bedtime. Billy splashed some soapy water on Katie, just in fun, but some got in her eyes and she began to cry. And I simply 'lost it.' I was overcome with rage and sadness.

"In a voice I don't think I ever used before, and know I haven't used since, I yelled, 'Can't you see how hard this is for me? I can't stand this! Billy, hold on to Katie. Don't let her go!' And I pulled the bathtub plug and ran out of the room to my bedroom. I fell on the bed in tears. Two images flooded my mind. One was the look of dismay on Billy's face moments before. The other was how the undercarriage of the BMW looked from the garage floor the night before. I knew for the sake of the kids I had to get out.

"Two days later, I was driving Billy to preschool when he said, out of the blue, 'Mommy, I'm so sad I'm thinking of jumping out of the car right here.' I pulled over to the curb and hugged him close. 'Billy, why would you say such a thing?' I asked. 'Mommy, I don't know,' he said. We sat there and cried together a long time."

Over the years I've known of many children who drowned or nearly drowned in bathtubs because of parental negligence. Betsy was doing a risky thing when she pulled the plug and left Billy to watch over Katie while the tub emptied. But she was also, I believe, interrupting her strong impulse to strike Billy, a male, for causing discomfort to Katie, a female.

A child psychologist I recommended for Billy ascertained, after winning his confidence, that Billy had, from the stairs and unbeknownst to his parents, witnessed at least two instances of Ken's angrily assaulting Betsy. "Billy's the kind of boy who has always let me know what he needs," Betsy said of him. "When he was younger, he often deliberately pushed me to test limits—when the light had to be turned out at bedtime, for example. But what he said to me on the way to school was different. He was telling me that he was desperate about life at home, and that I had to do something to make things better.

"My feeling was that I had to get out of this marriage for my sake and for Katie's, but most of all for Billy's. He was hurting the most. He shouldn't have to grow up miserable, thinking that this is what family life is all about. And he should have a relationship with his parents that doesn't involve his mother's suffering abuse."

Betsy's awareness of the implications of her marriage for the children, set off by a spontaneous commotion in the bathtub and Billy's confession of sadness, triggered a leap of awareness that spousal abuse hadn't provoked. It forced her to step outside her own shoes and view her parental responsibility in a substantially new light. She didn't reach the highest level of parental awareness in one leap, but she showed a new capacity to think of her children's individual needs.

Gradual Growth of Awareness

The degree of pressure Betsy felt is extremely common. In other families the pressure might be caused by financial or health factors, by addiction, by sexual infidelity, or by heavy parental workloads, but the challenge to children's welfare and the need for greater awareness remains the same. Betsy handled her crisis well when she became aware of it. But crises don't always bring out strength and upward leaps of awareness. In the heat of the moment, some parents lose their ability to analyze what's going on. They may fail to call on their better instincts or their common sense. Their default position may be more destructive than beneficial. In desperation, they may protect just their own interests. In short, they lose their awareness.

Rather than relying on crises to promote leaps of parental awareness, gradual steps can be taken. Child-care discussions can be a weekly item in the household schedule, beginning in pregnancy and continuing after childbirth. Counseling or mediation may be needed when basic differences in conceptions of parenting within the household don't resolve themselves in friendly but frank conversation. Weekly discussions between parents can be precursors of regular family meetings as children grow old enough to participate in democratic negotiation of family issues.

Discuss (not lecture about) your parenting philosophy with grandparents and other relatives whom you will see frequently—before a child is born, and as you revise your views in the course of parenting. Don't wait for situations that reveal disagreement and disapproval. Within the bounds of honesty, praise the basics of how you were cared for even if you are not planning to replicate all of them. Describe how you believe the context of child care has changed from your childhood to the situation your son lives in.

Another good way to enlarge your perspective as a parent, and to give and receive help from others, is to join or form a parenting group. I recommend it to every parent. Inevitably, such groups focus on problems shared in common. Such groups need to meet at least once a month. Six to eight adults is an ideal size—larger groups begin to break down into the overtalkatives and the oversilents; smaller groups begin to limit too much the range of experience brought to the group. Discussion of child-care periodicals and books can be woven into conversations about the group's experiences. A significant portion of the discussion should focus not just on the children and their behavior but on the experiences and feelings of the adults as they practice child care.

Ideally, a parenting group will include a mix of married and single parents, and a degree of cultural diversity. The need to stimulate parents' awareness of levels of relationships is matched by the need for them to be aware of the diverse environments in which boys are growing up.

In such a group, two things happen. Participants are usually surprised by some of the perspectives others bring to common problems—ways of thinking about parenting that hadn't occurred to them. How and why did he or she think of that subject that way? Why haven't I thought about it like that? Then, when seen against the ways others articulate their viewpoints, parents see their own more clearly—both the strengths and the weaknesses. Most parents who reach the two higher levels of awareness have employed some such method to catch reflections of themselves—if not a parents' group, then perhaps regular sharing of parent talk with a good and wise friend.

The Changing Family Context

In the United States in 1998, only half of the approximately 36 million boys lived with both biological parents. Another one-fifth lived with one biological parent and a stepparent, and often also with stepbrothers and stepsisters. That left almost a third of boys who lived with a single parent or no parent.

Of the roughly 10 million boys who live with one parent, over 8 million live with their mothers. Divorce might be thought to account for most of the single mother households, but in 1996 unwed-mother households outnumbered divorced-mother households by a ratio of three to one.

In 1995, mothers of more than 3.5 million boys under age six were employed thirty-five or more hours per week. About 40 percent of these boys were in day-care centers for large portions of their waking hours; the others were being cared for in a variety of ways—by babysitters or by relatives and friends. Between 1 and 1.5 million boys live with relatives other than their parents. Over a million boys are being raised by single fathers, and more than half a million live in foster homes or other institutions. The implication of these few statistics is that boys are being raised in a great variety of situations—far more variety than can be addressed by any approach to child care that assumes a common context. What we know about the context of boys' lives makes it all the more urgent that their caregivers rise to the highest level of awareness they possibly can—to a level where they have the capacity to see each boy's individual needs, and to understand how a boy and his caregiver are interacting and could better interact.

Boys of good character are being raised by single mothers (unwed or divorced), single fathers, lesbian mothers and their partners, gay men and their partners, grandparents, other relatives, guardians, foster parents— and, of course, by both biological parents. The question remains whether enough boys are getting the attention they deserve in their particular situations. On the whole, are we giving them enough attention? The best kind of attention?

In an essay entitled "Family," Marilynne Robinson has argued that the work situations alone of millions of American men and women raise troubling questions as to whether these caregivers can give boys the amount of character-building time they deserve:

> An employed American today works substantially longer hours than he or she did twenty-five years ago, when only one adult in an average household was employed and many more households had two adults. The recent absence of parents from the home has first of all to do with how much time people spend at work. Some of them are ambitious businesspeople or professionals, but many more patch together a living out of two or three part-time jobs, or work overtime as an employer's hedge against new hiring . . . work can demand always more of our time, and our families can claim always less of it.

Encouraging Father's Involvement

These statistics, including reference to the several hundred thousand single fathers raising boys, suggest that men have increased roles in parenting today compared to the general situation only a few decades ago. Do men have any advantages or disadvantages compared to women in reaching higher levels of parental awareness?

From my point of view, women have four distinct parenting advantages over men. The first is that females are expected culturally to be enthusiastic about parenting. The society begins to plant that expectation as early as girls begin to play with dolls and dollhouses. It is virtually an assignment that a female should express interest in parenting; women who don't want the assignment often feel guilty about their reluctance. Men who resist parenting are less criticized.

Secondly, women share their parenting knowledge and problems with one another more readily than men do.

Thirdly, women are more apt to consult books and other sources of knowledge and advice about parenting than men are. A number of the mothers I've talked to in the past year indicated how much they wanted their husbands to read some of the literature about parenting before the birth of their first child, but found it difficult to get them to read more than a few chapters.

Finally, women are more comfortable than men with the language and reality of relationships. There are plenty of factual matters to be dealt with in child care—diet, safe environment, symptoms of illness, etc.—but the areas where women have a cultural advantage are emotional and behavioral.

As you will see throughout this book, the kinds of adjustments that need to be made in the lives of boys to nurture them toward good character in their adult life are coherent with—sometimes identical with—the adjustments that will make men more highly aware and nurturant fathers. Boys need to become more familiar with feelings and with the vocabulary of feelings, if only to be men of excellent character. This "emotional literacy" will make them better fathers, and better husbands and professionals, too.

Cultural adjustments need to be made so that boys learn very early in life that playing parent is not just for girls; they are likely going to have to participate actively in raising children later in their lives, so best to begin playing daddy as toddlers and preschoolers. A concerted effort should be made to make parenting groups inclusive of men and women, because they represent the best opportunity for men to learn from others about parenting.

The literature of child care could also be tailored to speak more directly to men than much of it does now. The audience for it is largely female at this time. The nature of the known audience affects what is written and how it is written. It is obvious when books are written with female readers in mind. Lest there be any doubt about this book, let me say that when I refer to the reader, I have a father or male teacher or male caregiver of some kind as vividly in mind as a mother or other female caregiver.

Stephanie Coontz, a sociologist who has specialized in the history of the American family, says there is plenty of evidence that men did much more parenting earlier in our society's history; so we are concerned with a recovery of an awareness and a skill, not the introduction of something unprecedented:

History also demonstrates that men do *not* need their wives to teach them how to relate to their children. Men have both the ability and the motivation to care for children at their own initiative. English and American fathers in the seventeenth and eighteenth centuries, historian John Gillis reports, were active in all aspects of domestic life, from monitoring their wives' pregnancies to taking responsibility for the daily socialization of children. . . . Prior to the nineteenth century, fathers, not mothers, 'carried on the bulk of family correspondence and were the masters of ceremonies for baptisms, weddings, and funerals.' The idea that fathers are 'junior partners' in domestic matters and that women have unique, irreplaceable roles in nurturing infants has 'no precedent in earlier notions of parenthood.' . . . The memoirs of Cotton Mather, the most famous Puritan clergyman in colonial America, reveal that when he or his siblings got sick during the night, they went to their father, not their mother, for comfort and relief . . . . Many children raised in the eighteenth and early nineteenth centuries recalled that their fathers were their primary nurturers, even when their mothers were around. . . . In the nineteenth century, fathers were displaced from the center of the family circle, their parenting skills were disparaged, and they lost the direct emotional access to their children that colonial fathers had possessed. The nurturing of husbands and fathers only came to be recognized when expressed in a paycheck. . . . But the historical evidence from earlier coprovider families demonstrates that fathers can take a much larger share of child rearing and mothers a much larger share of economic support without needing to feel inadequate or guilty.

Equal responsibility may be unrealizable for many marriages (just as shared responsibility is out of the question for many single parents of both genders). A more reasonable—and highly satisfactory—goal is that a husband and wife have a clearly articulated collaboration for their parenting that is satisfying to both partners and responsive to their child's needs. However, men need to be reassured that their gender doesn't automatically disqualify them from having the capacity to be excellent, engaged parents—doing it by themselves if their situations require it.

To judge from the number of diaper-changing stations proliferating on the walls of public restrooms for men, restoration of a more equal gender balance in child care is well under way. I've talked to many men about their commitment to child care, and I invariably ask mothers I meet to comment on the quality and quantity of child care provided by their husbands or male partners. Both genders confirm, on the whole, that where child care is shared between men and women, women are still expected to take the initiative in negotiating with their male partners, sometimes on a daily basis, what responsibilities the male will undertake.

An episode related by one father I interviewed caught the transitional moment we are in perfectly. He and a friend, each pushing a stroller holding a male toddler, were riding an elevator during a weekend excursion. The two men remarked to each other that diapers obviously needed to be changed. They lamented what a trying task it was, whereupon a woman, a stranger, riding the same elevator said, "Would you like me to do it for you?" They accepted the offer.

Several mothers told me that they were bothered by their husbands' comparative slowness to respond to their infants' cries for food or comfort. Or by a father's not thinking to lower the volume of his voice when he walked into the nursery where his son was sleeping. Or by a father's impatiently ignoring the questions his sons were asking during bedtime storybook time, so eager was the father to get the story (and his chore) completed.

Differing Views of Risk

Males are more prone to risk-taking behavior than females, though it isn't clear how much of this tendency is conveyed biologically and how much is induced by learning generation after generation. Jay Belsky, a professor of human development, has described this small-scale risk-taking: "Dads like to toss their babies in the air. And I guarantee you, wait long enough and the tossing gets higher, and pretty soon, the wife is saying, 'Honey, that's enough.' She'll stop him. If you look at emergency room statistics I suspect you'd see more children injured on Dad's watch than on Mom's. Dads don't watch in the same way; they're more willing to take risks, even with their children."

The mothers I've talked to confirmed Belsky's opinion. For example, one mother told me of a situation that made her so angry she wouldn't speak to her husband for days. The family lives in the North End of Boston, an area with narrow streets and lots of traffic. When the mother went out to watch her husband finish packing his car for a daylong business trip, she found him with his head deep in the trunk, while their two-year-old son played in the middle of the street. The father didn't understand her reaction. "I would have seen any car coming down the street," he argued.

Another mother, listening in a group discussion to the mother just reported on, said that she and her husband each take responsibility for one of their two young sons during family shopping excursions. She takes the three-year-old on foot, and her husband takes the eighteen-month-old in a stroller. But she tries to keep an eye on everyone, and recently she returned from shopping in another section of the store to find her husband engrossed in racks of CDs while the stroller stood untended about thirty feet away. Casually she walked up and moved the stroller—not completely out of his field of vision, but far enough that it wouldn't be where he expected to see it when he finally looked around. "It was quite a long time before he looked for the stroller," she said, "and when he did, his face turned absolutely white. I was so struck by his response that I apologized for giving him a fright. But he realized how negligent he had been, and how easy it would have been for someone to walk off with Ricky."

One mother related the kind of experience that makes one optimistic that males can regain the nurturing touch they've lost over the past century. In this instance, the man was her father. Her son was just five months old, and she had taken him for an overnight visit to his grandparents' house.

"My father asked if he could put Sam to bed. It was a remarkable request because my father is uncertain of himself around babies. As soon as they cry, he immediately hands them off to my mother. I was touched by his request because he knew the chances of Sam's crying were high. I explained my routine at Sam's bedtime—what music to play, when to put him in the crib, etc.—kissed Sam good night, and waved as he went off with my dad.

"Five minutes later, I heard Sam crying. I desperately wanted to go and comfort him, but I knew it would shatter Dad's confidence. I did go and stand outside the door, praying he would quiet down. And he did, and I tiptoed away. Ten minutes later, Dad emerged from the bedroom, trying to look nonchalant but beaming with pride. He shrugged his shoulders as if to say it was no big deal, but the size of his grin betrayed him.

"Later, around three o'clock in the morning, I heard Sam crying and knew he needed his pacifier. Just as I was about to leave my room, I saw my father dash out of his room and across the hall into Sam's. He swiftly gave Sam a pacifier and began to rock him back to sleep. I happily turned around and went back to bed."

The Moral Basis of Character

A recent story in the *Boston Globe* with a wryly humorous slant reminded me how naturally the levels of parental awareness we have just seen can be applied to the stages of moral development of a boy. Police officers investigating a report of a man behaving suspiciously at a public parking deck encountered a Mr. Clifton and his son. Mr. Clifton told the officers he was just passing through, but his son piped up to say that his father had tried to break a window on a Jeep Cherokee. The boy led everyone to the Jeep and showed officers the piece of concrete his father used, leaving scratches on the car window. Mr. Clifton, police said, angrily denied trying to break into the car, but his son said, "Yes, you did, Daddy. Don't lie to the police." The story didn't say who taught the five-year-old boy not to lie, but it may not have been his dad, who was arrested for attempted auto theft.

This car theft story is a perfect example of a boy functioning at Level Two, Follow the Rules. Little boys who have moved from the Me First level of awareness to the Follow the Rules level can exhibit a certain kind of innocent purity about rules. It is as though they believe that if everyone follows the rules, everything will be perfect. They have yet to learn the complexity and ambiguity of life that rules can never eliminate. This story is an exaggerated version of an experience almost every parent has had of doing something that breaks a house rule or a general social rule, often with justification in the circumstances, only to be reminded by a child of the violation and of the importance of keeping to the rules.

Every boy is born with a Me First outlook. He isn't aware of it at all, but he's totally concerned with his own needs. Since he is totally dependent on others to provide for his needs, the quality of how they are provided for is his first step in moral development. He doesn't himself contribute much to this process at first. He learns from it. The moral responsibility lies squarely with his caregivers to provide for his needs consistently and lovingly. Every want doesn't have to be satisfied, but the satisfaction of basic needs can be seen as a right. A civilized society owes him that, even though he may not always receive his rightful due.

Morality begins with respect for the wholeness or integrity of everyone. The way we respect helpless infants is to respect their needs. No one questions the significance of the basic physical needs of food, clothing, shelter. I believe the basic emotional needs for love and respect are equally a human right.

When his needs, physical and emotional, are well and truly met, an infant begins early in life to view his world as protected, safe, and loving. His outlook is influenced in the direction of being optimistic and hopeful. His temperament figures in this equation, but even if his temperament is an obstacle to the natural development of trust and optimism, he can be nurtured in that direction by sensitive caregivers.

On the other hand, if his needs are met inconsistently, he is bound to have a degree of apprehensiveness. There is a long continuum here on which each infant finds his place. No male infant escapes a degree of inconsistent care, and few, if any, receive only abuse. It is a matter of degree. Does his experience tilt predominantly toward trust and optimism, or does it tilt toward apprehensiveness and distrust? Some lifelong Me Firsters are created in the first years of life.

As a boy grows through his first year and into toddlerhood, he comes more and more into contact with the inevitability of conflicting claims. He wants his mother to be always in the same room with him, but she has to go off to work. He wants the toy his older brother is playing with, but his older brother won't share it. How a boy deals with these conflicts is his second moral challenge after that of developing a basic outlook of trust or distrust, optimism or pessimism.

Rules are one of the ways we have of dealing with conflicting claims. We can't quite imagine such a human condition, but if there weren't any conflicting claims, we wouldn't need rules. Rules organize the resolution of conflict by saying that in certain kinds of situations certain kinds of resolutions should prevail. I don't know why, but rules are often talked about through extreme examples that rarely occur—when the passenger ship sinks, women and children should get the lifeboats before the men, and crew should get them last, for example—but it's equally true and more often invoked that if one wishes to have a high degree of decorum at the dinner table, family members shouldn't eat everything with their fingers (an activity once tolerated in the high chair).

I certainly believe unequivocally in some child-care rules. For example, I've dealt with more than enough battered infants to believe in this rule for everyone: never strike a child, whether in frustration or anger, or as a way of teaching a lesson or as punishment. (Actually, the rule should be generalized further: don't ever hit anyone for those reasons.) To me, this is a moral principle that should be accepted as a prerequisite to child care of any kind.

Hitting is disrespectful of the bodily integrity of the person hit. It escalates disagreement about behavior and lessens everyone's capacity to work through the disagreement to an unresentful conclusion. Boys have natural inclinations to please their caregivers; hitting them violates that inclination. Hitting boys also shows that the hitter doesn't acknowledge the imbalance of power between an adult and a child. To a boy it means that it's okay to hit someone if you're bigger and stronger and angry. Establishing no-hitting of siblings in a household is also essential. Parents who themselves hit others have no basis other than their superior power for establishing such a household rule for children.

Many rules are influential in a male infant's environment before he becomes aware of them; and rules will continue to be a prominent part of his moral universe for his entire life. There is no getting away from them. They are always there, even when we break them. But as a boy grows up, he will gradually learn that there isn't just one set of rules. There are many systems of them, and he will continually have to decide which set has priority in a situation, and which rules within that system most apply, and whether he will follow the rules, or bend them, or break them.

Rules, in a word, indispensable as they are much of the time, often conflict with individual needs and sensibilities. A male infant may well have had very early, if unconscious, experience with the disjunction between rules and individual needs; parenting is as subject to competing systems of rules as any other human activity. A boy's parents may have understood their responsibilities mainly as the imposition of one or another set of rules of "good parenting" that in fact ignored some of the infant's deeply felt needs.

While there may be glimpses of it earlier in his behavior and speech, I think a boy can't begin to function at Level Three, We Are Individuals, in a major way until he is aware of his own individuality. That is a main task of adolescence as he detaches from his parents and siblings and establishes his own identity. One sign of his eagerness to establish emotional and moral individuality is an adolescent boy's increasing impatience with rules, especially the rules commended or commanded by parents and other elders. He wants passionately to be recognized as an individual.

Likewise, while there may be glimpses of it in his adolescent behavior and speech, a very young man doesn't usually function at Level Four, Living and Growing Together, until adulthood. This is the level of awareness a young man would best carry into a marriage of his own. But many husbands don't ever function at Level Four with its subtle interactions, or even at Level Three with its respect for everyone's individual needs.

In the Beginning

So there the newborn male infant lies in the bassinet. How should we begin to think about his first moral development as an infant, then a toddler, then a preschooler? How can we encourage good character from the very beginning?

First, we should treat him with great respect. He has no intellectual grasp of what we are doing, but from the beginning he has a capacity to perceive in some inchoate way that he is the recipient of loving care. He also has a not-yet-conscious sense of whether he is living in a culture of mutual respect in his home. So he will be influenced not just by the relationships between him and his parents, but by the quality of other relationships that are swirling around him.

In this connection, I'd like to express disagreement with the argument recently advanced by Judith Rich Harris in her book, *The Nurture Assumption: Why Children Turn Out the Way They Do*, that the most important social influences on children come from peers, with parents having little or no effect. Howard Gardner, the Harvard psychologist who developed the theory of multiple intelligences in children, demolished Harris's argument most eloquently in his review in the November 5, 1998, *New York Review of Books*.

> Parental attitudes and efforts will determine to a significant extent how a child resolves the conflicting messages of the home and the wider community as well as the kind of parent the child one day becomes. I would give much weight to the hundreds of studies pointing toward parental influence and to the folk wisdom accumulated by hundreds of societies over thousands of years. And I would, accordingly, be skeptical of a perspective such as Ms. Harris's, that relies too heavily on heritability statistics and manages to reanalyze numerous studies and practices so that they all somehow point to the peer group. . . . I do not question Harris's motives but I do question her judgment, which might have been better guided by the old medical oath 'first, do no harm.'

In the beginning, we don't know in detail what a boy needs beyond the basics of food, shelter, and loving holding because we haven't read his temperament very comprehensively yet. But he will quickly begin to give us messages about what he was born to be like as he came under our day-to-day care. Part of our moral attention is to act always as if we were saying to him: We are learning every day more about who you are and what you are like, and we honor you.

Talk extensively in an explanatory as well as an affectionate way to a boy from birth on, despite the fact that he understands nothing of what you're saying except the tone. It gives you practice from the outset in interposing thought and mindfulness between what he is doing and how you are responding. It will help your self-control when he is trying your patience. The more he hears from you in a calm voice, the more he will feel he is in good hands. Calm reasoning should be at the core of your method of influencing his moral development; so you're practicing even before he can get the point of it.

In the chapters that follow I will examine some of the moral issues in various age grades that lie between a newborn boy and an adolescent like Pascal Lehman who is already reasoning out for himself the application of basic moral principles to specific situations, and who is already able to advocate powerfully for the rights of others.

3

INFANTS AND TODDLERS

My first grandchild, Noah, is less than a week old, born just after I finished the preceding chapter. I sit in the living room of his parents' apartment holding him on my forearms, with his head cradled in one of my hands. I can look directly into his face. He is awake, not yet hungry again, pretty content with his situation. As for me, I am aware of my grandfatherly delight. Looking at Noah, I feel the power of a newborn to reawaken in an adult a sense of wonder. There is so much I may be able to do for him, but so much he has already done for me just by lying here in my hands, pulsing with life and promise.

Like every other grandfather, I look at him for signs of family resemblances. There's nothing scientific about this scrutiny; if someone could put Noah in a time machine and show me what he is going to look like at age twelve or eighteen, I would be surprised by what I saw. The search for family resemblances in a newborn boy is just a universally practiced way of bonding with him, of acknowledging in Noah's case that he's part of me by genetic inheritance.

But I try to avoid overinterpreting what I see. I admire his lavish display of dark hair, for example, while at the same time I wish parents of infants who are slow to grow hair didn't so often feel embarrassed by infant baldness. Maybe, I think, some of the prominent professional male athletes and musicians who have been shaving their heads without loss of perceived masculinity will give baldness itself a classy image for all ages, including both infancy and my own future old age.

Infant Senses

Hearing and Sight

I watch Noah's head turn slightly in his mother's direction when she speaks to me. Although his vision will probably not be focused enough for him to recognize Mary Helen until his second month, he already knows her by sound—and by smell; at the moment he isn't close enough to her to smell her, I believe, but he definitely identifies her voice.

The ability and desire to identify and bond with a primary voice seems innate or "hardwired," as we say. I recall my colleague, pediatrician Peter Gorski, saying that he always speaks very softly in the nursery with just-borns because he doesn't want to offer a competing voice to the mother's for an infant's attention.

Noah's hearing will require eight to ten years of development to acquire the full refinement of adult hearing. Even then, he will not hear as acutely as the average girl will, and he will probably hear better through one ear than the other. It will be fun in due time to see which of his ears he favors. I begin to talk to him lovingly, slowly but with animation, a little louder than I need to speak to Mary Helen, and his face lights up and his body tightens with attention. He is receiving me. Since he can't comprehend symbolic language yet, he is listening to me as I might listen to instrumental music. He is listening emotionally to the music in my voice, soaking up and reflecting back my happiness.

Baby talk is a universal phenomenon as caregivers compensate for the infant's underdeveloped vision, hearing, and mental development by "singing" phrases, even nonsense phrases, with exaggerated emphasis. If overly shrill or accompanied by gestures perceived as threatening, baby talk can alarm infants, but mainly it delights them even if it sounds slightly whacko to others nearby. Most infants can't get enough of it. Many infants, particularly boys, don't get enough of it. For reasons that have nothing to do with infant needs but something to do with human biology and culture, boys get talked to less than girls. They almost certainly enjoy being talked to as much as girls do. But an unnecessary and unfortunate difference in communication with children according to gender is apparent to researchers very early in infants' lives, and it is often embellished at each subsequent stage of childhood. The difference is perpetuated by mothers as much as by fathers.

Smell, Taste, and Touch

Within hours of birth, infants seem to be able to use their noses to find their mothers' nipples, identifying the mother's body and perhaps the mother's milk by smell alone. Like all babies, Noah was born with a taste for sweet. There is evidence that certain pungent odors and flavors—garlic, for example—are passed along to the fetus through the amniotic fluid, so Noah may also have been born with a disposition to like Mary Helen's favorite foods.

Noah's sensitivity to touch interests me more than his palate because of its consequences for his emotional development. As I hold him now, he has no capacity to reach out and touch me, but he has a capacity to appreciate being touched. Most newborns love to be stroked. Gentle stroking of limbs and torso before naptime or bedtime may yield benefits of better sleep, reduced irritability, and accelerated weight gains. But the greater benefit is that a boy comes to be comfortable with, and comforted by, affectionate and relaxing physical touching. Later in his life, this comfortableness becomes one of the bases of his capacity for intimacy.

Some writers assert that boys, in general, like less to be touched than girls do. But their opinion may mainly reflect a difference in how boys and girls are treated beginning in infancy. Sometimes boys are held and stroked less on the mistaken judgment that boys don't like it or, if *real boys*, shouldn't need or like it. In many families, roughhousing with boys—especially by fathers—is substituted as early as possible for gentler strokes. But a boy's ultimate character will be enhanced by loving strokes and hugs from both parents beginning soon after birth and continuing through childhood. Roughhousing is as wonderful and fun as its name implies—the kind of activity that often gets the participants invited to stop roughing up the house and move outdoors—but it is not a substitute for the direct expression of affection in words and touch.

In the daily life of many American families—especially families with two working parents, or single-parent families with minimal child-rearing assistance—the birth of a child stresses the routines of the household even while bringing satisfaction to everyone. It is easy to slip into the habit of touching an infant boy mainly when he needs to be fed, cleaned up and changed, or comforted in irritability. A "happy" baby can come to be thought of as a baby who is asleep or content enough not to require attention. Every boy needs a lot of touching given just for the pleasure it will provide; and a parent needs the heartwarming feedback of a happy boy. The emotional reservoir of goodwill and affection built up in these exchanges is a source of parental patience to cope with the times when the boy is cranky beyond easy comforting.

The Brain and Gender

It's too early to know very much about Noah's temperament, which will emerge gradually in the weeks ahead. Yet, in the first months of his life, his temperament will be as defining of him as his gender. For the first stage of his life, he will be much more like girls with temperaments similar to his than like boys of contrasting temperament. That will be true in spite of the fact that the prevailing cultural mindset into which he was born believes that he has much more in common with all other boys than he does with any girl. By the time Noah is an adult, the cultural mindset, abetted by biological development, will have made its mark: Gender will be as important as temperament in defining Noah.

In the introduction to *Sex on the Brain: The Biological Differences Between Men and Women*, Deborah Blum reports a conversation she had with an archaeologist, Donald Grayson, about adult gender-based differences. Grayson's research takes him and his teams to some quite inhospitable archaeological sites.

> What Grayson found was that come a crisis—say, a Jeep with a bad engine, stranding his group in the sandy heat—it was the men who jumped to fix it. They were efficient and cheerful as long as they could make the repair, and make it quickly. But if they couldn't, if the crisis began to drag into a lost day, then the men—himself included, Grayson acknowledges—became grouchy and irritable. . . . 'At that point, women were the glue,' Grayson said. Women comforted and teased, proposed other solutions, and kept the group from igniting in a blaze of frustration and irritation.

The origins of these differences revealed in adult crises can be traced, to a degree, to gender-based biological differences in infants, although it is always important to point out that how a child is raised has the capacity to sharpen these differences or to moderate them.

The average-sized male brain is about 15 percent larger than the average female brain. At one time, that disparity was thought to demonstrate innate male superiority; a small number of scientists still argue that brain size makes a difference in levels of intelligence, but the predominant view is that no particular benefits are traceable to brain size alone.

The bundle of nerves connecting the two hemispheres of the brain is larger in girls than in boys, and that does seem to create functional differences. Some of the nerves that might have connected the hemispheres in boys end up enriching the right hemisphere where spatial relationships are dealt with. Boys, on the whole, have a comparative advantage over girls in dealing with spatial relationships—from playing with blocks, to playing baseball, to architectural design—that is lifelong.

Boys often require more space than girls to be comfortable. They spread things out. Michael Gurian, in *The Wonder of Boys*, notes that a day-care provider complained about how "uncontrollable" three young brothers were. The space she used in her house for day-care activities was quite small, he observed, and he suggested that she let the boys play outdoors more and, if possible, provide more space for them indoors. When she did that—making an additional room available as the boys' room—her disciplinary problems lessened markedly.

Reading draws heavily upon both sides of the brain simultaneously, and girls, with the better set of connecting nerves between the brain's hemispheres, have better reading (and overall verbal) skills than boys all through life. Boys manifest reading and other learning problems at three times the frequency of girls. Since reading emotions on the faces of other people seems to require the cooperation of both sides of the brain, girls show a greater facility for this than boys.

Boys' brains appear to work differently from girls' when making sense of facial expressions. The cortex—the outer part of the brain and seat of its higher functions—is less active and sustained in males. Where girls' brains seem to tune them in continuously to information on the emotions of people in their environment, boys' brains shut on and off, focusing intensely on things that interest them. The emotional cues that arouse particular activity in boys' brains have to do with other males' expressions of anger and dominance. This may explain in part the male tendency to tune out in conversation, and the greater ease with which females simultaneously conduct a variety of tasks.

The Big "T"

In the past few years, testosterone has become to the interpretation of boys' behavior what El Niño has become to weather analysis: the quick explanation hauled in to account for any unusual activity. There is no doubt that the hormone testosterone is a powerful biological factor in the development of boys' bodies and behavior. It hardwires aggressiveness into boys' temperaments, though it must quickly be added that it doesn't mandate violence. There is an aspect of learned behavior in violence that can't be explained away as biological reflex.

Both boys and girls secrete testosterone in their bodies, but boys produce more than girls. It doesn't stay at the same level all day, but rather comes in several surges. At puberty, a boy will begin to produce ten to twenty times more testosterone than the average girl. Girls produce more serotonin than boys—serotonin being a neurotransmitter that may block aggressive behavior by countering testosterone and other hormones.

The effect of testosterone can be seen in various behavior patterns characteristic of boys: the search for activities, from sports to sex, in which the body builds up physical tension and then releases the tension climactically; relatively short attention spans as the boy moves from one activity or focus to another (for example, the male television channel-surfing that annoys many females); and the tendency to explore the problem-solving tasks in any situation—often neglecting the accompanying emotional situation—and to lose interest and patience if the problem can't be solved fairly quickly.

Aggression begins to appear in the behavior of children between the ages of six months and two years. From the beginning, it is important to distinguish between instrumental and hostile aggression. Instrumental aggression occurs when a boy is intent upon getting a toy or privilege. He doesn't have the verbal skill to negotiate a less confrontational way to get what he wants, so he pushes or shouts or attacks the person who has what he wants or is between him and what he wants. Hostile aggression adds, to whatever instrumental impulses may be involved, an intention to inflict pain on the person assaulted.

By age two, aggression begins to decline in girls but remains constant in boys. It is magnified by parents' harsher disciplining of boys. In one study, two- and three-year-old boys exposed in a laboratory setting to angry verbal exchanges between adults were more likely than girls to express their distress by becoming aggressive toward playmates in the same room.

Around age two, children begin to reflect awareness of the gender distinctions—and stereotypes!—that the culture has been signaling since they were born. Once the categories of male and female are established in their minds—not as concepts but as recognition of groupings of people and behaviors—children begin to sort out what gender signifies. The rigidity of their first grasp of this distinction is related to their immaturity as thinkers. A degree of confusion about gender follows from inevitably conflicting evidence from their environments: For example, boys grow up to be policemen, don't they, so what is that woman doing on television wearing a police uniform and packing a gun? Only at a later stage of development can boys begin to understand that their first understanding of gender was superficial, confused, and rigid.

Early Self-control

Between twelve and eighteen months of age, boys begin to manifest self-control in the form of compliance. They can obey simple requests, and show some awareness of what adults do and don't want them to do. Accepting the directives of adults means delaying other gratifications a boy has in mind; by the third birthday, there are clear differences among boys in their self-control. Compliance depends significantly on their ability to understand adults' language and to use it to guide their behavior.

Boys have a huge desire to please that the parent or caregiver can tap into, a desire that persists throughout childhood unless the child comes to distrust adults because of unkind or erratic care. To be sure, boys may also decide to do exactly the opposite of what is asked or commanded. A two-year-old will often use resistance to display his strongly felt need for autonomy, but it is here that a wise parent can be flexible, bending to the boy's need to show self-direction when time and circumstance permit.

Boys who are rewarded for good behavior and given warm and sensitive care will oppose parental directives much less often; they will generally be willing, even eager, to follow their parents' leads.

It falls to the parent or other caregiver to keep adjusting the balance of compliance and autonomy so as to minimize the degree of conflict between these two strong needs to please and to be self-directing. A parent shouldn't seek to win every little power struggle with a boy. If the parent insists upon compliance all the time, a boy's innate need to follow his desires will be frustrated; even at an early age he may lose confidence in his own ability to act on his own. On the other hand, if his demands for autonomy are usually acceded to, he may become irritable instead of pleased; every little boy needs a sense that the grown-ups are managing his world for him thoughtfully and respectfully.

What works best in such projects as toilet training is for parents to establish and explain (calmly and many times) the overall goals, but to let a boy have an autonomous voice in the details, including timing and technique. One can praise a boy for progress, but refrain from shaming him when he fails. Other areas where a rewarding degree of autonomy can be given to toddlers are some choices about diet, selection of stories to have read, clothes to wear, and choice of playmates. As they are being brought into a structure of expectations, rules, and responsibilities, one mother said to me, little boys "need to feel they're capable of sharing responsibility." This sharing may be hard for some parents to provide, because a parent has a natural temptation to believe that parent wisdom tops toddler wisdom, and because a male toddler often expresses his preferences in impulsive ways that don't yield easily to negotiation and compromise.

A sensitive parent can work out a set of mutually understood signals (tone of voice, facial expression, gesture, or, best of all, mutually understood words spoken calmly but firmly) to help a child distinguish occasions when the parent can be flexible from occasions when the directive has to be complied with.

The Emerging Self

Daniel Stern, who has written sensitively about the interior world of the preverbal child, remembers:

> When I was seven or so . . . watching an adult try to deal with an infant of one or two years. At that moment it seemed to me so obvious what the infant was all about, but the adult seemed not to understand it at all. It occurred to me that I was at a pivotal age. I knew the infant's 'language' but also knew the adult's. I was still 'bilingual' and wondered if that facility had to be lost as I grew older.

In Stern's case the facility certainly wasn't lost, but I believe many parents and caregivers don't "read" their children acutely, and miss many cues infants and toddlers put forth about their needs and perceptions. Even the newborn is a much more sophisticated organism than he is given credit for being.

Stern isolates the periods between two and three months, between nine and twelve months, and around fifteen to eighteen months as times of epochal change. In each the infant reaches a new subjective experience of the self and the other. "One is suddenly dealing with an altered person. And what is different about the infant is not simply a new batch of behaviors and abilities; the infant suddenly has an additional 'presence' and a different social 'feel' that is more than the sum of the newly acquired behaviors and capacities."

There is what Stern calls a "core self" implied in the two- or three-month-old smiling responsively, gazing into parental eyes, and making sounds that appear to be directed intentionally at the parent. Around nine months of age, an infant begins to be aware of his own interior subjective life, and that others have one, too. Even without words, he can share his pleasure about something with his caregiver. The "subjective self" of this period is enhanced by the "verbal self" beginning around fifteen months or a little later that enables the child to add symbolic language to his communication with his environment.

Other students of child development such as Bruner, Kagan, and Brazelton, have their own terminology and special emphases, and amend the developmental periods somewhat. It isn't necessary to choose one authority and reject the others. Rather one can take as authoritatively established that infants and toddlers are experiencing mental growth in quantum leaps with a rapidity they will never match the rest of their lives. The more parents read and think about child development, the more observant they will become of infant behavior and what it portends.

Many adults are just naturally intuitive about what's going on with preverbal children, but some fall into the category observed by Stern of just not understanding without some coaching. The main reason parental acuity is significant is that the infant is not developing mentally on his own. He is doing it interactively, and it helps immensely to have parents who recognize, appreciate, facilitate, and delight in what is happening.

Sociability

For a brief period of time, as a firstborn, Noah will be inhabiting a closely supportive world in which there appears to be only one child and a few adults. But it won't be long until visitors are introduced to him at home or he is carried out to social occasions where he will meet strangers, both

adults and children; and it won't be long before his mother goes back to
work at least part time, leaving his care for hours at a time to other adults,
including his father and grandparents. In our society, the bulk of child
care is performed by adults, assisted in temporary baby-sitting by older
children, mainly girls. Siblings, therefore, represent to an infant his first
contact with what will become eventually the larger world of peers: the
horizontal world of his own generation. For only children, playmates become the pathway to peer relationships.

Empathy seems to be present in the minds even of newborns when
they begin to cry upon hearing another baby cry in the nursery. By the
end of their first year of development, some children will not only respond to another infant's distress by crying themselves or seeking comfort; they will also show signs of trying to relieve the other infant's
unhappiness. At the other end of the spectrum, abused children observed
in one day-care center did not show concern for the unhappiness of another child. Their responses were fearful, angry, or even violent toward
the distressed child.

A boy's temperament plays an important role in his emerging sociability. Three of the components Chess and Thomas identified in temperament seem to reflect directly on sociability: mood (how pleasant and
friendly, or unfriendly, is he?); approach or withdrawal (how does he respond initially to new situations?); and adaptability (how does he respond
over time to new or altered situations?). These components are subject to
a degree of sensitive parental influence. One aspect of parental awareness,
therefore, is for a parent to keep asking himself or herself: How can I cultivate his sociability? At the highest level of parental awareness (Living and
Growing Together), the parent can see that drawing sociability out of an
infant boy sets off a chain reaction; it encourages the parent to be more
sociable toward him, which in turn elicits more warmth from the infant
or toddler. A boy's sociability will also affect his relationship with any siblings he may have. A study conducted by Michael Lamb, a developmental
psychologist, concluded that the sociability of the younger babies determined the amount of attention they received from their siblings rather
than older siblings aiding babies to become more sociable.

When six-month-old infants are placed near each other in the same laboratory playroom, they look at each other quite a lot, but smile or gurgle
or touch each other less often, and seldom exchange toys. During the next
six months, infants begin to gesture at each other, vocalize as best they
can, and offer toys. One sign of their increased sociability in the second
half of their first year is that infants show more animation when playing
with peers than when playing alone. They also show a preference for interacting with familiar playmates over strange children.

Conflicts over possession of toys or coveted space don't usually begin until early in the second year. How a parent deals with these incidents can have an early effect on the capacity of a male infant to share. The infant is too young to be lectured to about sharing. Many little crises of possessiveness are best handled by diverting a boy to other pursuits he enjoys. The parent can facilitate sharing by making available toys such as blocks that have many similar components, in contrast, say, to a toy truck that can't be shared in parts with playmates. Young boys will also be affected by being in the company of older children or adults who are happily sharing things.

In his third year, a boy begins to be capable of social pretend play. This represents a tremendous increase in social sophistication. The six-month-old mainly stares at a playmate while the twenty-four- to thirty-six-month-old can play games that involve shared nonliteral meanings such as roles: I'm the daddy, you're the mommy. Much of this social development is based on imitation: A boy observes what is going on around him and incorporates what he sees into his play.

Crying

At birth, there is no way to distinguish the crying of boys and girls. Some babies cry more than others, for reasons that may involve physical discomfort, emotional distress, and/or temperamental inclination, such as the "difficult child" as characterized by Chess and Thomas: infants with irregularity in biological functions, negative withdrawal reactions to many new situations and people, slow adaptability to change, and intense mood expressions that are frequently negative. But they carefully distinguish between a child who is difficult by their criteria and a child who is labeled difficult by a parent who might be bothered by the difference between the parent's temperament and the child's. If parents are patient with difficult children, they do adapt well over time even though they will never be "easy" children.

There's a "crying curve" that parents should know about that goes up and down: twenty-two minutes of crying each day for the first three weeks of life on average for infants in industrialized societies; thirty-four minutes per day from then until the beginning of the third month; and down to fourteen minutes per day by the beginning of the fourth month. It gets worse, in other words, before it gets better, but mostly it gets better. Babies also seem to cry more in the evening. A lot is accomplished by crying, for the baby and his parents. Mothers and fathers usually want to know if he's hungry, uncomfortable, or needing a diaper change, and they gradually learn to identify the different kinds of cries: the "angry" cry when a lot of air is expressed through the vocal cords, the "pain" cry that bursts out suddenly and is punctuated by periods of breath-holding, and the "frustration" cry, that builds up from a prelude of more rapid breathing, bodily agitation, and a long sucking in of air, to become a wail of dismay.

Crying is a baby's first language and deserves to be honored as such. It becomes more varied in form, month by month, sending different messages to the alert ear. The thing to remember is that the baby is communicating something, wanting to be comforted, embraced, stimulated, or engaged, or that he's uncomfortable and wants some aspect of his experience to be changed. My Children's Hospital colleagues, T. Berry Brazelton and Peter Wolff, were among the first scientists who showed the universality of crying patterns, pointing out that they are quite stable until the sixth month of age. Then, the baby begins to increase his range of verbal expressions. But crying remains a lifelong instrument of exceptional emotional release for those who avail themselves of it.

We can't—shouldn't—attend always and instantly to a baby's every cry; nor should we feel we've failed if we can't satisfy his every whim and prevent his crying at all. Some crying is inevitable. The best general response to crying is to pick the baby up and try to comfort him while analyzing as best one can what his message is. Studies show that some babies are content to lie around in soiled diapers, and some are vocally unhappy. Many babies cry when they are hungry, but some very well-fed babies cry a lot. The response that is most often effective with a crying infant boy, no matter what his discomfort, is to pick him up and comfort him with tender holding and talking.

Many parents and other caregivers find it well within their emotional capacity, if needed, to comfort a crying baby for an extended period. Others have more limited tolerance for listening to an infant or toddler wail on and on. The purpose of infant crying is to alert, or even alarm, the caregiver. It can be a very disturbing sound to some ears.

Many "shaken baby" cases have come to the attention of our clinic at Children's Hospital in Boston. The majority of these cases are provoked by crying that drove a caregiver to rage. Boys are shaken hard enough to cause grievous injury or death more often than girls. While it may not be realistic to think that every adult can be helped to be tolerant of, and respond compassionately to, sustained infant crying, most adults can be educated to be aware of their own level of tolerance. For some adults, there is a risk that understandable anger at hearing continuous crying, or frustration at not being able to alleviate it, can mushroom suddenly into rage and punitive action. In the aftermath of a violent assault on a crying, helpless infant, I'm sure that many assaulters are stupefied by the seeming suddenness with which fury overwhelmed their usual self-control.

There are physical, mental, and behavioral warning signs of incipient rage that every adult should know. Physically, the person's body gets tense, even rigid, breathing is faster, and motion more agitated. Speech gets louder and jerkier; the voice may become huskier because the throat is so tight. Mentally, the person may realize that he or she would do anything to get the baby to be quiet. A temptation to strike the infant may be perceived by the individual before the impulse boils over into action. A person's behavior may be agitated, he or she may be unable to stay calmly in one place, may be shouting to the baby to quiet down, handling the baby already more roughly than usual, perhaps squeezing the baby. Consumption of drugs or alcohol further complicates such situations, because these substances can disarm inhibitions to aggressive action.

The best way to defuse mounting rage is to put the baby down, put some space between the caregiver and the baby, and get help from a neighbor or from one of the many available stress hotlines. Toll-free telephone numbers for such agencies as ChildHelp and Parents Anonymous should be part of the emergency telephone list in every home with children, and should be known to all members of the household and to every person who comes into the household to provide child care. The subject of how to care for a very fussy baby should be discussed with every person who gives child care, even a one-time-only babysitter; the potential of prolonged crying to get under the caregiver's skin should be acknowledged, and such rules as "Never under any circumstances strike or shake a child" should be rehearsed by all adults who care for children. Perhaps by the time he is a toddler, certainly by the time he is a schoolboy, a boy will be hearing the view that boys shouldn't cry in public. Crying is discouraged in boys as a way of coping with pain, disappointment, shame, loss, or unexpected pleasure. A somewhat greater tolerance has developed for men crying in public to express grief or great happiness than existed when I was a boy, but there is, I think, still a strong general belief that it should be restrained.

We have diminished the emotional life of boys and men by defining crying so early and decisively as a shameful weakness. The cultural constraints on crying as unmasculine have obscured what crying is all about. In my work with neglected and abused children, it's when the baby *doesn't* cry that causes the greater worry: He's learned not to expect a response, or to expect an unkind one.

Tantrums

Infant crying varies all the way from restless whimpering to full-fledged outcry when the crier arches his back, clenches his fists, screws up his face, and bellows inconsolably. This most extreme variant of infant crying is a prototype of what some males will display in various ways throughout their lives: frustration and rage overwhelming self-containment. In the toddler, preschooler, and even among some schoolboys in the lower grades, the full infant cry develops into the tantrum. The type of crying remains much the same. The little boy can now move about, so the tantrum may involve flinging himself on the floor and kicking and thrashing about while he cries or screams in anger and frustration.

Eventually, the code against male crying asserts itself, so crying gets dropped from the combination of activities; from then on, the male who is boiling over with frustration will express his feelings either in violent language or in physical assault, or in both. Some tantrums by preschoolers or older boys might involve more yelling and screaming than crying.

A tantrum is a social event. A baby may work himself into a rage in isolation, and an older boy may cry by himself. But a tantrum is meant to convey a message to someone present who is frustrating the child. A parent can find it just as daunting to intervene in a tantrum as to successfully comfort an infant who is in full cry. Since toddlers and older children are often out in public more than infants, tantrums may occur more frequently in public than in the privacy of home. They may become, to a degree, manufactured outbursts a boy displays to control his parents or caregivers.

Many little boys are quick to learn that their parents react differently to a public tantrum than to a private one. Chess and Thomas recall one toddler, Lewis, who launched himself into tantrums at playgrounds and in supermarkets when one of his parents said "No." At home, they would patiently wait out Lewis's tantrum, but in the supermarket they would give in to whatever his demands were to quell their embarrassment; but they also felt victimized by his behavior, resentful of it. Once they began a strategy of removing Lewis from the scene as gently as possible and telling him they wouldn't return to the place where they had been until he quieted down, the public tantrums fell off.

Tantrums or lesser crying bouts become an early occasion for adult-child diplomacy, and the lessons a boy learns in these negotiations can influence his character step-by-step on through childhood and adolescence. Ideally, a parent will try patiently to convey empathy for whatever unhappiness has prompted the outburst while indicating that the tantrum itself is not a good way to resolve the unhappiness. It is better not to give in to the demands of the "tantrumer," but equally important not to lose sight of the boy's unhappiness just because the tantrum itself is so unnerving.

The adult needs to be aware in such a situation of the fit between the child's temperament and the adult's. Tantrums may erupt between adult and child of similar temperaments or of different temperaments. A boy who reacts intensely negatively to frustration will not be helped by a parent of equally quick temper who responds to the child with a similar outburst. Likewise, a slow-moving, low-key parent may frustrate a quick-moving, expressive boy. The issue is not whether temperaments are similar or different, but what demands are made on a particular child and what reactions the child's behavior creates in the parent.

No amount of diplomacy will do away with all parent-child frustrations. A nice item in the *New York Times* reported:

> My daughter Ellen recently attended her first evening parenting class. The following afternoon she was running errands and told her 4-year-old son, Matthew, to get in the car and put on his seat belt. He refused to put on the belt. After some failed negotiations, my daughter became frustrated and started screaming at him. Matthew looked at her and announced, 'You really didn't learn anything from your class last night.'

Superbabies, or How to Read the Charts

Parents and other child caregivers are potential beneficiaries of thousands of research projects covering every imaginable aspect of child development and family life. If we didn't have the benefits of this research, we would be limited to local customs, family traditions, personal experience, and individual impulses in electing how to raise our children.

Still, there is one downside to child research that deserves a cautionary note. Some of the research gets reduced to generalizations or statistical averages that become widely known and sometimes misapplied as yardsticks for development. On average, for example, boys begin to pull themselves to a standing position at eight months, sit (rather than simply falling) down at ten months, and walk unaided at about twelve months. But some children walk at ten months, and others don't walk until maybe eighteen months. Considered as a proportion of the child's age, this range is far more striking than the average, and individual cases fall plentifully along the range. To give one more example, some boys begin to talk intelligibly at nine months, others not until twenty-four months or later.

Child development averages may be misconstrued in two directions. Parents may become proud or boastful if their son reaches a developmental step earlier than the average. Michael Schwartzman refers to the most excessive instances as the "Superbaby Syndrome." It is, he says, "the imposition of the adult world on the developing child. Because of your insecurity over your parental judgment, you may unknowingly push your baby or child to proceed too fast, urging him on toward some elusive kind of perfection."

Parents may also become anxious, maybe even embarrassed, if their son reaches a developmental step later than the average. Neither of these responses benefit a child—the boastful because it is based on a false assumption that may shadow the child if he doesn't reach every subsequent step ahead of average, and the anxiety because it will be felt by the child and interpreted as rejection. Letting oneself be psychologically tyrannized by these statistics is one of the easiest ways to take the delight out of parenthood, and rob a boy of the natural development of self.

4

MALE CONNECTION AND EMOTION

The most troubling general criticism of men by women is that men are detached in personal relationships, uncomfortable with intimacy, lacking in a capacity to be deeply connected to others, even to their own spouses and children. No doubt these perceptions existed long before our lifetime, but criticism of men has certainly been sharpened under the influence of feminism since the early 1970s.

To the extent the criticism is true, it certainly has bearing on the subject of character. Men with close attachments to the prominent people in their lives—their families, of course, but also their neighbors, their colleagues, their clients—might be expected to feel spontaneous concern for their loved ones' welfare, and compassion for their plights; to feel protective of them in the face of dangers and threats; to feel passionate that they be treated with fairness and equity. Detached men, on the other hand, might be expected to be concerned to get their own way, to be possessive when another person served their interest, neglectful when he or she didn't, and to be selfish and manipulative in power contests. Put in its most charitable terms, this point of view sees men as incapable of enjoying the satisfaction of feeling close to and caring for the people they love. Is the criticism valid? If it's valid, could boys be raised to become more caring and connected men?

Attachment

One stream of theory and opinion, coming from psychobiology, proposes that males are fundamentally (and probably unalterably) different from females when it comes to attachment and intimacy. The difference is embedded in their respective reproductive strategies. A male has a genetic drive to spread his semen around among many receptive females. He can't have babies himself, and it is risky, therefore, for him to tie himself to the reproductive potential of a single female, who might disappoint him. Each female can only bear a limited number of children in her fertile years; she has an innate proclivity to find a potent mate and form a bond within which she can protectively raise her offspring.

The theory sounds vaguely "mathematical" and impersonal—perhaps like something concocted by a detached male? I regard the flexibility of the human mind and the power of human cultures as being too strong to leave all of us males completely at the mercy of promiscuous genes with their attendant emotional detachment. However, I don't doubt the power of genetically programmed tendencies. In other parts of the animal kingdom, it is vividly clear, as one experience my wife, Carolyn, and I had in West Africa in the late 1960s attests.

Driving home to Ouagadougou, the capitol of Burkina Faso, after visiting Peace Corps volunteers in remote villages, I was often given a couple of live chickens or a duck by the hospitable villagers. Though food was scarce in the villages, and these fowl the source of precious protein for their poor diets, one could not turn down the gifts without giving irreparable offense.

Before long, our yard in Ouagadougou was a miniature barnyard full of chickens and ducks. One day the duck eggs began to disappear, with no identifiable culprit. So we took three eggs in to incubate next to the stove. A week later, the tapping of little bills could be heard inside the shells. The moment had arrived for my first and only assisted birth.

Three ducklings were soon at Carolyn's feet, and she waddled around them, quacking and giggling. With Konrad Lorenz to thank, they imprinted to her just as ducklings do to their natural mothers. They were genetically programmed to bond to the first moving thing in their environment. After dinner we put them out on the patio. The ducklings put up such a fuss that we had to let them back in, and I caught on film their race across the room to their "mommy," Carolyn.

Konrad Lorenz's research on imprinting, featuring ducks and geese, was a principal inspiration to John Bowlby, who was a pioneer in the early 1950s in examining how human infants get attached to their environments and the principal figures in them. Bowlby concluded that "mother love in infancy and childhood is as important for mental health as are vitamins and proteins for physical health." As happens with all theories, attachment theory, too, was exaggerated by some later adherents. One study done in Colorado purported to trace the origins of child abuse to the relationships established or not established in the first twenty-four hours of the newborn's life. That's close to quackery.

Certain capacities of the newborn infant remind us of the ducklings' instinctive capacities for relating to their environment. The newborn infant can root toward his mother's nipple. Within the first ten feedings he has learned that being held in a certain position means that he is about to be fed. His newborn eyes have a fixed focus of between nine and fifteen inches—about the distance from his eyes to his mother's face and eyes when he is breast-feeding (or bottle-feeding in the same position as if he were breast-feeding). He instinctively opens his eyes and looks up when the nipple is offered.

The newborn also cries when he needs food or other assistance. Crying is a costly act in terms of the amount of energy it uses up, but it is virtually his only mode of getting attention. Fortunately, adults, too, are also programmed to react to infant crying, women with finer tuning than most men. Knowledge of the crucial nature of crying as the infant relies on it to gain attention perhaps offers some guidance on how long one should let a baby "cry it out" before trying to alleviate his distress.

Attachment for the human infant, with his very long process of maturation within the mammalian world, seems not to be so much a ducklinglike instinct as a mental construct developed over a period of time and experience. We have no way of understanding a newborn's mind; he can't report to us. So if we want to study something like attachment, we have to look for behavior from which we can infer a mental construct. So Bowlby looked for evidence that an infant not only recognized his mother but also acted in such a way as to try to maintain proximity with her.

In a family setting, Bowlby said, most infants at four months are responding differently to their mother than to other persons—measured by the amount of smiling and vocalizing when they see her, and the length of time their eyes follow her. If an infant cries when his mother leaves his eyesight, one could infer that he is trying to reestablish contact; likewise, when he is old enough to crawl and he heads in the direction he last saw her, one may infer attachment behavior. However, Bowlby reported a range of first manifestation of attachment behavior from about four months until after twelve months. He referred to other studies showing that within a month of showing attachment behavior toward the mother, an infant was exhibiting such behavior toward another person or persons as well, most often the father but also older siblings. Interestingly, this same study showed that the larger the number of persons the infant showed attachment behavior toward, the greater was his attachment to the mother likely to be. Because of the competition parents and others may wage for an infant's attachment, this observation is very significant. The infant doesn't naturally regard it as a situation in which he has to pick and choose.

Bowlby reports on two studies, one in Uganda, the other in Scotland, where a small percentage of the infants observed chose someone other than the mother as principal attachment figure. The Scottish study showed the mother beginning to share some of her principal-attachment role with the father in the child's second year of life.

Not surprisingly, attachment theorists other than Bowlby have identified instances in which they thought the attachment of infant to mother was too weak, and instances in which it was too intense. Sometimes a young boy has such an intense attachment to his mother that he has difficulty developing a social life outside the family. In the majority of such cases, the overattachment can be traced to the mother, who, having grown up anxiously attached in a difficult childhood, is now seeking to make her child her attachment figure. Far from the child being overindulged, as is sometimes asserted, he is being burdened with having to carry an overloaded relationship with his mother.

The contributions of attachment theory and research are several, not least among them the insight that threats of abandonment—"We're going to go home and leave you here if you don't start to behave"—as incentives to behavior are unwise at any age. "Not only do threats of abandonment create intense anxiety," Bowlby wrote, "they also arouse anger, often of intense degree, especially in older children and adolescents. This anger, the function of which is to dissuade the attachment figure from carrying out the threat, can easily become dysfunctional."

Our understanding of infancy and the beginnings of attachment and intimacy would be sorely diminished without the insights of attachment theory. At the same time, it should not be overemphasized. Attachment theory is great for parents when everything is going well. They will get almost all of the credit. Likewise, however, when things go awry, they will get most of the blame. I don't think that equation is in anyone's best interest. We humans have a way of taking everyday successes for granted but of being harsh and unforgiving when blame is being parceled out. Attachment theory also tempts us to attribute later developmental problems to infant attachment flaws, making us more fatalistic than we need be about our capacity to find behavioral remedies at any age.

Chess and Thomas assessed the attachment theory debate in a balanced way:

As we grow from childhood to maturity, all of us have to shed many childhood illusions. As the field of developmental studies has matured, we now have to give up the illusion that once we know the young child's psychological history, subsequent personality and functioning is ipso facto predictable. On the other hand, we now have a much more optimistic vision of human development. The emotionally traumatized child is not doomed, the parents' early mistakes are not irrevocable, and our preventive and therapeutic intervention can make a difference at all age-periods.

A Father's Attachment

My experience with the Dyson family a couple of years ago reminded me how a family can be disrupted around the birth of a child. In this case, stability was restored by the parents' reaffirming their connection to one another and to their son, and by my support for a man's candid expression of his feelings.

A colleague of mine, a pediatrician under whom I once trained, sent Mary Ann Dyson to see me when her firstborn, John, was about six months old. John wasn't sleeping through the night yet, and was fussier much of the time than Mary Ann thought he should be, despite her constant care. The pediatrician thought Mary Ann exhibited signs of stress beyond those attributable to having a fussy baby. Thinking the cause might be abuse from her husband, whom he had never met, he referred Mary Ann to me and my clinic.

After I had examined Baby John and found nothing glaringly wrong with his health, I sat down with Mary Ann and said she seemed more upset than the baby's condition warranted. Would she like to talk with one of my female associates, I asked. (Women, my associates and I have learned over the years, often discuss being abused by male partners more readily with other women than with men, even empathetic men.)

Mary Ann caught the drift of my suggestion right away. "Dr. Newberger, you don't have to worry about my husband hurting me or the baby. At least not physically. But I think John's fussiness is related to our situation at home. The tension in our house is so thick, you could cut it with a knife. That's what is interfering with John's sleep, I think."

When John was born, his father, Bruce Dyson, was caught up in the launching of an east coast documentary film business. He was working long days, arriving home late and exhausted, and wasn't much sharing in the loving care Mary Ann was showering on their first child. Since Mary Ann breast-fed her baby for several months, Bruce did not get incorporated into early feeding responsibilities.

Mary Ann saw her husband's total immersion in his business as neglect of his family at this special juncture, and complained, though her complaint didn't seem to affect Bruce's schedule very much. He didn't initiate sex with Mary Ann when she had recovered enough from childbirth to welcome it. She began to wonder if Bruce might be having an affair with a lively younger associate he took on a business trip to Los Angeles shortly before John was born.

Then, while putting away fresh laundry when John was five months old, Mary Ann saw the edge of a card sticking out from under a pile of undershirts in Bruce's dresser. It was an unsigned but sexually provocative birthday card to Bruce. (This is a fascinating human trait: our propensity to keep evidence of morally contentious or clandestine behavior right where it will probably be uncovered.)

When Mary Ann confronted Bruce with the card and her suspicions, he angrily denied having an affair. All he did, he said, was work, work, work, and if she kept up this interrogation he was going to leave. Complaining that he couldn't deal with her harping and nagging, Bruce stormed out of the house. But he came back within an hour and, avoiding Mary Ann, went directly to John's room.

Mary Ann went by the room a little later, unnoticed by Bruce, who was holding John and talking animatedly to him—about the Boston Red Sox! John was reclining against Bruce's muscular forearm, his head cradled in one of Bruce's large hands. "How 'bout those Sox?" Bruce was saying. "They just might make it to the World Series." John, to whom this vital information was so much nonsense, was pumping his arms and legs with glee, looking straight into his father's eyes, grinning with pleasure.

This episode occurred the day before Mary Ann took John to her pediatrician. It was a defining moment for her. When Bruce stormed out of the house, Mary Ann wasn't sure she cared how soon he came back, because she was certain her accusation was correct. But when she watched John in Bruce's arms, she said, "I knew I couldn't let John grow up lacking that kind of fatherly attention."

Mary Ann's determination to save her marriage opened the door to my discussing how much a husband/father may feel like an outsider to the envied intimacy of a mother and nursing baby. If she had not been intensely preoccupied with childbirth and infant care, I suggested—making sure she understood I was not implicitly justifying Bruce's alleged affair—she would doubtless have been closer to Bruce's struggle to make his new business succeed. She might have concluded that the stress it was causing for him was roughly equivalent to the stress she had experienced over childbirth and the novelty of motherhood.

I know that this kind of sharing requires a shift of perspective that is counterintuitive to many relationships. It is common to be competitive about stress—"You can't possibly be under the gun the way I am!" Or to convert it into irritation toward the partner—"If you'd get home earlier and help care for the baby, I wouldn't feel so exhausted all the time!"

Stress, in other words, invites us to concentrate on our own needs and to ignore the needs of our partners. But simple verbalizing (not to be confused with acting out) and sharing respective stresses experienced by partners usually leads to a reduction of anxiety and self-preoccupation, and to mutual confidence that the pressures can be withstood.

At the end of my first talk with Mary Ann, I said it might be helpful if I interviewed Bruce. I've become a great believer in man-to-man talks in the doctor's office. Most physicians don't initiate it nearly often enough; their reticence—usually attributed to "lack of training"—can be overcome by support from those who, like me, believe in it and have seen the results. In England, there's been a movement to facilitate this through the medium of doctors meeting in groups with a consulting psychiatrist.

Bruce was only too happy to come to see me at my clinic. All it took for him to open up was my saying at the outset, "I can imagine this must be a hard time for you." He really loved Mary Ann, Bruce said, and didn't want the marriage to end. And he wanted the very best for Baby John. "Doctor, the best thing in my life is holding that boy and seeing him light up when I talk to him. It's funny, but I think he's really talking to me when he gurgles and grins."

Somehow, Bruce went on, with the frequent nursing and interrupted sleep, his and Mary Ann's sex life went by the boards, and, yes, he did get involved with this delightful, funny, sexy associate. The affair was over, he said, even though he still felt a strong attraction to her. I believed his acknowledgment more than if he had said he no longer felt attracted to her. He was sorry, Bruce said, but these things happen.

It wasn't enough, I said to Bruce, that the affair was over. There would be a perpetual tension between him and Mary Ann until he acknowledged the affair to her, regretted it, and newly confirmed his commitment to her and John. It may be hard at first to listen to what she has to say, I warned, because women are just as furious at this kind of betrayal as men are. If you can bring yourself to do this, I added, I counsel doing it here in my presence. A third person is a kind of public witness who can take steps to ensure that each person accurately hears what the other is saying, and that fairness rules in any decisions jointly made.

So it happened that a week later Bruce and Mary Ann sat side by side in my office, and Bruce told what had happened and apologized. Tears welled in his eyes as he began to speak, and he brushed them embarrassedly away. But they welled again. This time, Mary Ann reached over and gently brushed them down his cheek, as if to say that it was just the right time for tears. I relaxed in my chair, certain that with the kind of gentle closeness they were sharing, they would get to a good resolution.

Boys and Emotions

Baby John Dyson's intense response to his father's attention reminds me of an intriguing 1984 research study. Adults were asked to rate photographs of the faces of a group of infants for emotional expressiveness; but the adults were not told the gender of the children in the photographs. They judged the infants who were boys to be more intensely expressive than the girls.

One section of the test offered the raters a sample including some girls and some boys deliberately misidentified as girls; even here, they gave a higher rating on emotional expressiveness to the misidentified boys. This is a finding that goes against conventional wisdom. To be emotionally expressive is itself usually regarded as a feminine attribute, and I'm sure most adults believe that females are inherently more "emotional" than males because they were born that way.

I can't argue the opposite case, that males are lifelong more emotionally expressive than females, because there's no such evidence. But there is strong evidence that both boys and girls begin emotional life on a level playing field. The parity shows on their faces for a few years. If you show preschoolers videotapes of various dramatic situations, photograph their expressions, and then ask adults to identify the emotions expressed in the facial expressions (happiness, sadness, fear, etc.), adults identify the emotions expressed by preschooler boys and girls equally accurately. Beginning at age five or six, boys gradually become less expressive (harder to read, more inscrutable) and girls more expressive—a disparity that will hold the rest of their lives.

What tips the level playing field? Culture, in the form of child-rearing practices and attitudes of parents and caregivers trying to shape the kinds of males and females they think they want. Not every parent feels or acts in the same way, but there is enough similarity to yield the patterns that have been observed to predominate. A blizzard of signals, many of them unconsciously sent and unconsciously received, are directed to infants and toddlers, and to children and youth throughout their development.

For example, mothers of three- to six-month-olds in one study smiled more at daughters than at sons. Mothers of eighteen- to twenty-four-month-olds in another study displayed a wider range of emotions to daughters than to sons. Mothers of thirty-two-month-olds in still another study displayed more positive emotion to daughters than to sons. Staff members at day-care centers smile more at, and are more physically affectionate toward, girls than toward boys, as observed in one study. When fathers were given textless picture books and asked to compose stories for their children, they used more emotion words in stories they created for girls than in stories they created for boys.

The urging of young boys and girls in different emotional directions continues through childhood. Parents display a wider range of emotions to their daughters than to their sons, and, except with respect to anger, discuss emotions with their daughters more than with their sons. Mothers do not neglect the more stressful emotions in conversations with their daughters; they give full exposure to sadness and fear, for example, though they do not dwell much on anger (partly because girls, more than boys, are being discouraged from expressing anger, rage, and contempt).

One study found that mothers discussed the *quality or experience* of an emotion with their daughters, whereas with sons they often tried to show them the *causes and consequences* of emotions—emphasizing, in doing so, control of emotions more than the experience of them.

Fathers, in general, have ways of interacting with children that are different from those of mothers. They use more demands, more threats, and more put-down language, especially with their sons. They also interrupt their children more than mothers do, and speak to them in terms that require more mental skill to understand than do the terms mothers use.

In these ways, males and females develop different emotional profiles. By ages three to five, children themselves are already reporting their belief that males express anger more, and females express fear, sadness, and happiness more. Eventually this duality is firmly in place: Females believe (and observers agree) that they experience emotions more intensely than males do—both positive emotions such as happiness or joy, and negative emotions such as shame or guilt or sadness, fear or nervousness. Again, the exception is anger, which males appropriate as their specialty. Women score higher on interpersonal trust than men. They exhibit more empathy toward others than men do. They regard other people more positively. They are happier than men in good times, and they are, when so inspired, sadder.

Some studies of gender differences in emotions have been able to distinguish between how intensely emotions are experienced internally and how vividly they are displayed outwardly. When this distinction is drawn, the difference between men and women narrows regarding *intensity* of experience. It is in display of emotions that they are most distinct. In other words, men and women are close to alike under the surface, but men suppress the display of much of their emotionality—except, of course for anger, and also for pride.

Why has this split between male and female emotional expressiveness been perpetuated generation after generation? One reason is that boys are being channeled toward rather stoic but self-confident participation in competitive or dangerous activities. In the past, this preparation may have made sense: toughness for a tough life. Boys were going to be, and still are intended to be, intensely occupied with winning and losing—whether in war or in sports—climbing vertical ladders of success and power, minimizing even the appearance of vulnerability. At the earliest feasible age, males are discouraged from crying because crying is a signal of a weakness that others can exploit. They are being educated to suppress their emotional expressiveness, though with less attention paid to the suppression of anger than to other emotions.

Girls, on the other hand, are encouraged to display emotions that facilitate intimate peer relationships and cooperative affiliation. Vulnerability is okay. In other words, the two sexes are being prepped for roles—or, more accurately, sets of roles—that require, or seem to require, different emotions and different levels of expressiveness. But now, in a day when women climb corporate ladders and pay mortgages, and when men are needed as nurturing fathers, teachers, and nurses, this difference in emotional expressiveness by gender may be outdated.

If the playing field is level at the beginning of life and infant boys and girls are pretty equally capable of friendliness, compassion, empathy, and the like, and if emotional expressiveness can lead to a greater capacity for closeness and intimacy, then why should it be discouraged in boys? What is gained by the suppression of their emotional life?

5

WORD MAGIC

Long before a boy begins to read letters, words, and sentences in print, and even before he has developed much of a vocabulary in his own speech, he has developed a capacity to read expressions on faces around him for the happiness or sadness or anger they portray. He has learned to read certain kinds of gestures and actions he sees others making as being comforting or threatening. He has learned what some words mean when he hears them spoken, particularly the word "no." And he has learned to identify certain words and even sounds—laughter, perhaps, or crying, or the high-pitched crooning of baby talk—for the emotions they convey. As I mentioned before, newborns in nurseries seem to cry sometimes for no discernible reason other than empathy toward the crying sounds other newborns are making within earshot.

Selma Fraiberg, a major figure in child psychology, coined the wonderful phrase "word magic" to suggest the new power a child possesses when he can himself use language instead of other kinds of action to express feelings or wishes or needs or intentions. When a boy can say, "I'm mad at you," he has added a basic way to deal with his frustrations; before, he had the options of swallowing his anger, or expressing it physically by striking out at the object of his wrath or at a scapegoat. Now, simply because he has stopped to verbalize, he has more awareness of his feeling, and more ability to control it. He has put a thought between what provoked him and how he will respond.

Words are more supple than direct action, though they too can be employed in such a way as to be extremely hurtful weapons at times. The very act of formulating words delays other forms of impulsive action. Words allow the person to whom they're addressed to acknowledge the message, to explore its meaning and accuracy, and to negotiate how the feelings lodged in the words can be safely relieved; they truly are magic.

On the whole, girls display this capacity to verbalize feelings earlier than boys and are more verbally sophisticated than boys throughout childhood and adolescence. As with other gender differences, it is hard to say how much is biologically based and how much is a consequence of the way girls and boys are taught to behave. Some commentators believe that early verbalization in girls is stimulated by the very fact that girls are discouraged more than boys from acting aggressively. I don't believe that life in general is more frustrating for boys than girls, so this explanation carries a certain plausibility with it. Whatever the origins of this gender-based difference in verbal skills, the character development of boys would be enhanced if they could narrow this gap.

When a vocabulary of feelings in young boys is missing in their upbringing, they risk growing up to become men at the mercy of their impulses. They remain unaware of their feelings and inarticulate about them. Until we can apply commonly understood words to things, we can't be fully conscious of them. Every step to a higher level of awareness in relationships requires more sophisticated command of language.

The Fischer Family

One day at a social gathering I overheard Abby Fischer, an accomplished child psychologist, talking about her fraternal twin boys, Joshua and Jeremiah. They were about to celebrate their third birthday, and some things she said indicated that she had paid attention to their having a vocabulary of feelings at an early age. I asked for an interview to get more details. This interview proved so rich in insight that I use it here to illuminate the opportunity and challenge of instilling emotional literacy in young boys.

I began my conversation with Abby by asking her if she and Ron shared the same philosophy of parenting. "We happen to have similar attitudes toward parenting. To some extent, that's not accidental. Couples are often drawn to each other because they have compatible values—more compatible than they consciously realize. But where they hold different values, and don't articulate and resolve the differences, their children are going to get conflicting messages from them.

"I think, if asked, Ron would admit that he isn't able to label his own feelings very well. Yet he's very attached to the boys. From the very beginning, he has helped with every aspect of child care—except breast-feeding, of course—with enthusiasm. He never showed any of the nervousness around newborns that many fathers confess to."

It didn't take Abby and Ron long to learn that their twins had distinctly different temperaments. "Joshua is more active and energetic. He was always more squirmy, harder to hold. He liked to stare at things or people.

I think of him as one of what the textbooks refer to as a 'slow-to-warm-up' child. But he gets very close to people he knows well. He's much more of a leader, and Jeremiah often plays his follower.

"Jeremiah is easy to get to know because he's so cuddly. He gives you a lot of feedback from one-on-one attention. Our current nanny had an easier time bonding with him than with Josh, although her relationship with Josh was complicated for a while by his crying inconsolably whenever I left and refusing to drink anything she gave him, which unnerved her—all this despite my having spent quite a lot of time with the boys and the nanny together before I left her alone with them.

"For a time I was bothered about the differences in their motor development. Joshua walked at twelve months, Jeremiah not until nineteen months. Josh started to talk earlier than Jeremiah. Even though I'm trained to be cautious about overinterpreting individual differences, I know from my own experience that it's hard not to anxiously compare your own children to each other, or other children to your own. What I saw, though, was that once Jeremiah started a phase of development where Joshua was ahead of him, he quickly caught up and often surpassed Josh.

"For example, even though Josh spoke first, Jeremiah soon showed a greater facility for language, and very keen visual and auditory memory. I told him our telephone number just once about eight months ago, and he still rattles it off. A cousin of Ron's pointed out to me—I hadn't myself noticed—that Jeremiah knew all the letters and numbers and colors when he was eighteen months old. He has a great love for books. You can ask Jeremiah if he wants to drive a car when he grows up, and he'll say, 'Yes, but first I have to learn to read.'"

Books and Feelings

One of the best methods for building a vocabulary of emotions is reading to infants and toddlers. I asked Abby when she first started reading to the twins.

"I began when they were about two months old. There are two librarians in my family, and we were showered with wonderful books from the beginning. I was so touched myself by many of the books that I couldn't wait until they were older to begin sharing them. Jeremiah was always calmed by readings even when he understood nothing of the content—something to do with the sound of my voice, I guess.

"When the boys were just over a year old, we got a book of faces showing many different expressions of feelings: happy, sad, angry, proud, shy, surprised. Right away they could label the expressions. I recommend this kind of book for every child.

"I attribute their early awareness of feelings to being read to, especially once they began to grasp storytelling. They see that the characters are revealing their feelings. Reading sessions always turn into discussions. We talk about how the characters feel, and why they do what they do. I don't have to prompt them. They have a million questions.

"The same thing happens when we watch videotapes together. They will say things like 'That's mean. I wouldn't do that,' when they see Dumbo being ridiculed for his big ears in the Disney movie. I'm grateful for every sign of empathy I see in them."

Perspective-taking

"The twins could distinguish their own feelings pretty early," Abby reported. "We were going somewhere in the car when they were just over two years old. Josh had Jeremiah's sticker. Jeremiah said, 'I'm feeling angry at Josh because he has my sticker, and I want it.' And Joshua said, 'I'm not angry. That's Jeremiah's feeling. I'm happy because I do have the sticker.' But there were also occasions when the treatment of feelings was more empathic. The vacuum cleaner always scares Jeremiah, for example, but Josh will comfort him by saying, 'Don't worry. I'm keeping you safe.' Each will usually offer the other one a treasured possession like a teddy bear when he is upset."

When the twins were about two years and nine months old, Abby and Ron left them for one evening in the care of an unfamiliar baby-sitter, a woman who had often cared for the children of close friends of Ron's, who highly recommended her. "The next morning, they told me Ricky was mean. Both of them said it. They talked about it all day. When I asked what Ricky did that was mean, they said she took their teddy bears.

"For some reason, they thought Ricky was a man—maybe because they thought Ricky had to be a man's name. They kept referring to her as 'he,' and I kept correcting them. Gradually they stopped referring to her, but about a month later—there hadn't been any other mention of her for at least a week—Josh said out of the blue, 'Ricky was mean, but she thought she was being funny.' By this time they had accepted my assurances that Ricky was a she.

"I hadn't expected Joshua to be able yet to distinguish between what a person's intentions might be and how those intentions might come across to others. It was an act of what we call 'perspective-taking,' being able to evaluate an act from your perspective and also from the perspective of the other person. Once you begin to appreciate different perspectives, then you can begin to be conscious of how the behavior of others is affecting you. Jeremiah, to give one example of this, said just recently, 'How come every time Daddy gets angry at me, I feel angry at Daddy?'"

Most treatments of cognitive development suggest that children wouldn't be capable of perspective-taking before their third birthdays, but I wonder if this capacity isn't underestimated. In my work with families where children are mistreated, I regularly encounter adults, more often men, who see everything from an egocentric point of view; they are adults, but they have no capacity to see anything from the perspective of another person. So I asked Abby how deliberately she fostered this ability in the twins.

"Yesterday was the first time Josh ever told me he was angry with me. I accidentally kicked his favorite teddy bear down the stairs. He talked about it all day. At lunch he said, 'I'm angry at you for kicking my teddy bear. I have a nice mommy, but I'm still angry.' I said, 'It's okay to be angry with me. Sometimes I'm angry with you.' I always make a point of going on to say, 'Even when I'm angry with you, I still love you. You can be angry with me and still love me.'"

"Were you deliberately helping him distinguish between his basic regard for you as a loving mommy and his distress over something you did?" I asked. "I didn't want him to be afraid of being angry with me and of expressing it," she replied. "I think it's healthy for him to be able to admit ill feelings toward me. When Josh asks me why I kicked his teddy bear down the stairs, I tell him that I didn't know it would make him so angry, and if I had known I would have tried to be more careful. Our book discussions reinforce this sense of different perspectives. Why is this character acting this way? What must he or she be feeling?"

It is the ability of Abby to function at Level Four of parental awareness (Living and Growing Together) that nurtures early perspective-taking by the twin boys. Abby knows that temporary irritation on the part of Joshua triggered by something she has done accidentally doesn't threaten his basic love for her and dependence on her. She is willing to let him express his unhappiness with the confidence that his mother won't take it too personally and get angry with him in return. He gives her an opportunity to point out that she gets irritated with him sometimes, but she doesn't let that irritation get in the way of her love. Josh can't begin to grasp conceptually all that she is doing for him, but he is benefiting from her awareness nonetheless because it promotes his emotional expressiveness and puts identifying labels on basic feelings.

Avoiding Gender Stereotypes

Like many mothers today, Abby wants to avoid gender stereotyping in her boys' toys. The twins have many traditional boys' toys, but when they were two years old, she also bought them a few dolls of both sexes, and two dollhouses. "I didn't want to pigeonhole the boys. What I found was that they've largely ignored the dolls, but they love their dollhouses. And they play a great deal with their stuffed animals as though they were people. Playing with their animals and the dollhouses, they're very nurturing. They always pretend they're the mommy, not the daddy. I think the dollhouses make Ron a little uncomfortable. He's afraid I'll go too far. Or maybe he just doesn't know what the consequences, good or bad, will be.

"Other friends and relatives have been less cautious in their criticism. 'O, come on, Abby'. . . they say with heavy sarcasm. People have intimated that I'm deliberately trying to make the boys gay. A cousin who would be a guardian for the twins if something catastrophic happened to me and Ron accused me of trying to 'feminize' them. And there have been intimations that I might make the boys crazy *because* I'm a psychologist. I work with two- and three-year-old boys all the time, though, and I know how much they love playacting.

"A few weeks ago, Ron and I took them on a weekend afternoon to the Children's Museum in Boston. One of the many attractions there is a roomful of dress-up clothes. Jeremiah got fascinated with some of the women's clothes and started putting some on. I could see that it made Ron very nervous, but I saw it as a very natural bit of exploration. Not a big deal."

Other mothers I've talked to in the course of writing this book have indicated that they know their male toddlers would be happy to have dollhouses, but they believe their husbands would be unaccepting. I haven't met any mothers who wish to exclude trucks and other "masculine" toys from their children's possessions. But they know that houses and dolls, or stuffed animals treated as humans, are the stuff of relationships. These toys generate attention to feelings, awareness of feelings, discussions of feelings. Trucks and other mechanical action toys mainly generate activity in which awareness of feelings is irrelevant, or the feelings generated focus on aggressiveness.

The origins and mechanisms of gender identity are still substantially mysterious even within the scientific community, and more widely baffling outside it. So the issue is surrounded by anxiety and ignorance. Many men regard any artifacts that seem related to femininity (dolls, even male gender dolls, are frequently regarded as feminine artifacts) as infectious, subversive of true masculinity.

We have fallen into a cultural pattern of promoting certain kinds of toys for boys and other kinds for girls. Boys' toys include many representations of human figures, but they aren't called dolls and they don't live in houses. Boys' toys rarely acquaint them with the complexity and subtlety of feelings. What Abby has shown is an entirely natural openness of boys to a vocabulary of feelings at a spectacularly early age.

Discipline

"Whenever I discipline the boys, I always explain my reasoning," Abby says. "From a very early age they have incorporated 'because' into their vocabularies. They explain themselves to me just as I explain my reasoning to them. They say, 'I did this because'. . . The only punishment I use is 'time-out,' having to stay by yourself for a while as a consequence of misbehaving. I say to them, 'I'm a good mommy and good mommies are supposed to stop their children from doing bad or dangerous things.' Recently Josh has begun to say, 'How come you put me in time-out without asking me first?' This is amusing evidence of how much the boys feel entitled to respect.

"I put them in time-out only when they've been overly aggressive. It doesn't happen often, and it's usually Josh. When he's overtired or not feeling well and gets very frustrated, he occasionally pushes or hits Jeremiah. It really bothers me, and he knows it. I do discuss the subject with them. I say, does Mommy hit Daddy? They say, no. I say, would Mommy ever hit you? They laugh at that, because they know it's so far from anything I would ever do. It would betray our relationship if I hit them. I say, you can't hit anyone; it makes people hurt.

"There was an episode a couple of months ago that shows what a sensitive issue aggression is. We were putting the boys to bed. Josh is extremely attached to his teddy bear, but that night he was slapping his teddy bear across the face. It alarmed me. I asked Josh why he was doing that to his teddy. He said a mommy in the park hit her baby. Jenny, the nanny, told me the next day that they asked her why another mommy at the park was so mean that she pulled her baby's ear. Up to this point, all their play-acting has been very protective and nurturing. I have a feeling that when they go to preschool they'll encounter a lot more aggressive behavior."

Joshua and Jeremiah haven't yet had any toy weapons at home. On a visit to another child's home, one of them picked up a toy gun and asked if it was a flashlight. But Abby knows that Ron's sister is about to give the boys a toy castle populated with guards with swords for a holiday present. "I don't think research has given us a final word on the consequences of giving little boys toy weapons to play with," Abby says. "I don't feel so strongly about it that I wouldn't let them play with the castle and armed guards. I'm curious to see what they'll make of it. But I think there could be an implied message in giving toy guns, that guns are okay. I feel very challenged right now to be able to explain meanness and aggression to them. They need to be aware of meanness because it's part of life. I just don't know how to explain to them why people are mean. Why is Mr. McGregor so mean?"

"An episode a year ago showed me how quickly very young children pick up emotional vibes around them, but sometimes at the price of misinterpreting them. For a time Josh didn't want to see the nanny we had then. Gradually I pieced together what had happened. The nanny received a telephone call one Friday in the boys' presence informing her that someone extremely close to her had died. She was very upset then and for the remainder of the day. During the day, for some reason, Josh got frustrated with her and hit her. Then he didn't want to see her again. He said he had been bad. Throughout the weekend, he refused to go downstairs because he was afraid the nanny was there. I think Josh crossed the wires from the two incidents and concluded the nanny cried throughout the day because he had hit her. It took a couple of weeks of reassurances before he got over it."

Abby finds that lunchtime is a particularly good time to discuss feelings. "This week Josh labeled jealousy for the first time. The nanny and I were both there, and we four were taking turns speaking in order to counter the boys' frequent wish to speak at the same time. It was Jeremiah's turn to hold forth. Josh couldn't bear to wait. He interrupted to say, 'I feel jealous of Jeremiah.' To me, each of these recognitions and verbalizations of feelings is a victory because it replaces the need to act out. We don't respond to such confessions by putting them down ("Ugh! You're so difficult!"). I sometimes acknowledge, 'I feel that way myself sometimes.'"

The lesson to be drawn here is that the verbalization of feelings is most critical when those feelings arise out of conflicts in boys' lives—conflicts characterized by feelings of envy, jealousy, anger, or misplaced fear that the baby-sitter cried all day because Josh hit her. The great positive emotions of love and happiness and positive excitement perhaps need verbalization a little less critically because they are well served by smiles, hugs, kisses. But conflicts need explanations, and explanations require word magic; words are the raw material of emotional literacy.

"'I have a tendency to talk a lot, and interrupt,' Abby concludes, 'but I don't think having a talkative parent is the key to having a child who expresses himself. I think the key is not what I say, but that I *listen* to them and respond to what *they* say.'"

6

DISCIPLINE AND
PUNISHMENT

Men can lead perfectly honorable lives based on observing norms of behavior they have learned from others and that are promoted by others—by their families or communities, or by their professions or the religions or philosophies they adhere to. But there is always a question of how men will behave in a situation beyond the direct influence of those institutions. Some individuals revert to behavior that is unworthy of their usual standards when they believe they can get away with it. Others, however, have deeper resources that enable them to remain consistent with their publicly scrutinized behavior. They have internalized values; their self-disciplined behavior doesn't depend on anyone's reminding them what the rules are.

Perhaps there is no more confused subject in child care than the issues that swirl around discipline and punishment. In relation to character development, the word "discipline" has acquired several different meanings. As used most broadly, it connotes training which corrects, molds, strengthens, or perfects—in other words, character formation itself, particularly as it is guided from without by a parent or mentor. ("Discipline" and "disciple" have the same root.) The word is also a synonym for punishment or chastisement—he was disciplined by being denied permission to play outside. Still another usage points to the control gained by enforcing obedience, the control implied, for example, in the phrase, "military discipline." Finally, the term can refer to rules or systems of rules that are meant to affect conduct. Except when used with the prefix "self," all of these meanings point to something that is imposed on a boy from outside and that relies heavily on rules of conduct.

Beating the Devil Out of Them

Would I be willing, an assistant attorney general in South Carolina wanted to know, to testify in behalf of a state action to close down a day-care center where children were being subjected to severe spanking? His call set off my pager a few years ago. Of course I will come, I replied, if the facts are as you allege. The facts are not in dispute, he said. It's the defense that has us perplexed. The day-care center is run by the minister of a fundamentalist church. He claims that spanking is endorsed by the Bible, and that it's essential to controlling misbehavior.

The case began in a small South Carolina town when the mother of a nine-month-old boy returned to work, entrusting him to the church day-care center several hours a day. She brought him home one afternoon during his first week at the center and found bruises on his buttocks and back when she changed his diaper. She immediately rushed the infant to the family physician, a general practitioner.

The doctor was in a quandary. The injuries were obvious, and the mother's story was credible. The law was clear. If he suspected abuse or negligent care, he was required to inform the South Carolina child protection agency. But he knew the minister personally and many of his flock. If he offended the minister, the doctor might lose some patients. The day-care center rented space in a building he owned, so the doctor could lose rental income as well. His wife, who was also his nurse, prevailed on him to report the evidence, sparking an investigation.

The nine-month-old recovered quickly from his bruises, and his mother made other arrangements for child care. State investigators were willing to allow the center to remain open if the minister and staff would agree in writing not to strike any of the children. "No deal," the minister said. "The Bible gives me the authority."

As an article in the *Houston Law Review* recently pointed out, a function of corporal punishment often stressed in evangelical Christianity is to break and conquer the will of the child. Our society as a whole, the article argued, overvalues pain as a stimulus of good character, and undervalues children.

Shortly thereafter, I flew to the state capital, conferred with child protection officials, and then rode with the attorney general for an hour and a half to the small town where the hearing was to take place. Several men in dark suits and equally dark expressions stood waiting our arrival, and followed us into the court house where I was sworn in by a rather young judge.

The judge qualified me as an expert witness, noting that he had recently read an article a colleague and I wrote for the American Bar Association, critiquing a set of proposed standards for court practice in child abuse cases. (I understood he was both complimenting me and warning me not to assume, just because I came from a Harvard-affiliated hospital, that my opinion would automatically prevail.)

Did I have an opinion on whether the admitted spanking was abusive, the attorney general asked. It was, I replied. There was no mistaking the severity of the bruises described in the medical report. A nine-month-old infant, I testified, is not certain when his mother leaves the room whether she will ever return; he hasn't achieved what pediatricians refer to as "object constancy." When a person or object disappears, an infant doesn't understand that it continues to exist and, in the case of his mother, will come back. When his mother leaves him in a strange place, he may be terrified until he comes to trust the strangers taking care of him, and also trust that his mother will return. He will almost certainly cry, maybe for extended periods of time. He was spanked because he wouldn't stop crying. The spanking could only terrify him more, and prolong his crying. It was fortunate that he didn't suffer fractures or internal organ damage.

"Doctor Newberger," the black-suited defense attorney asked loudly, drawling out each syllable to its breaking point as he approached me, book in hand, "have you ever seen this book?" I was so amused by his play to the spectators that I almost broke into a grin; he was marking me out as a carpetbagger, probably a liberal, unreligious Jew, coming down to Carolina to tell good Christian Southern folk how to raise their children.

"Yes, I have. It's the Bible." Handing his book to me after using one of its many colored ribbons to find a passage in the Book of Proverbs, he asked me to read aloud verse 24 from chapter 13: "He that spareth his rod hateth his son: but he that loveth him chasteneth him betimes." This passage isn't exactly the traditional adage of "spare the rod, spoil the child," which was enunciated in the early sixteenth century (John Skelton: "There is nothynge that more dyspleaseth God, Than from theyr children to spare the rod.") and further popularized by Samuel Butler in the mid-seventeenth century. But it's close enough not to quibble.

"What does that passage mean to you, Doctor?" I replied that the words spoke for themselves, but ought not to be taken, so to speak, as gospel truth that justifies spanking babies. There was no way, I asserted, that this baby could be regarded as disobedient. He was miserable and frightened, and completely unable to understand an order to be quiet.

The hearing was astonishingly polite for someone accustomed to the combativeness of many Northern courtrooms. The minister testified that the baby had disregarded a command to stop crying. He obligingly showed how he held the baby and brought his huge hand down on the baby's bare back and buttocks. His demonstration made me wince. The defense presented only one argument: If a child misbehaves, the Bible gives specific warrant to spank.

The judge eventually ruled in favor of the state. He gave the day-care center the choice of following written guidelines that forbade any kind of corporal punishment, or of closing down. Faced with this choice, the minister accepted the guidelines.

The historian Philip Greven has written a book, *Spare the Child*, showing the powerful connection between apocalyptic religious thought (which emphasizes a stark contrast between the forces of good and the forces of evil in the world, and anticipates a dramatic conclusion to human history in which the good will be rewarded and the evil destroyed) and the practice of corporal punishment of children. In *The Adventures of Tom Sawyer*, Tom's aunt reflects on this long and deeply embedded view in Western culture of the value of spanking in character formation:

> Hang the boy, can't I never learn anything? Ain't he played me tricks enough like that for me to be looking out for him by this time? But old fools is the biggest fools there is. Can't learn any dog new tricks, as the saying is. But, my goodness, he never plays them alike two days, and how is a body to know what's coming? He 'pears to know just how long he can torment me before I get my dander up, and he knows if he can make out to put me off for a minute or make me laugh, it's all down again, and I can't hit him a lick. I ain't doing my duty by that boy, and that's the Lord's truth, goodness knows. Spare the rod and spile the child, as the good book says. I'm a-laying up sin and suffering for us both, I know. He's full of the old scratch, but laws-a-me! he's my own dead sister's boy, poor thing, and I ain't got the heart to lash him, somehow.

One married couple I talked to have three sons, aged eleven, fifteen, and seventeen. When I asked the McCrays how they have dealt with discipline in their family, Terry spoke for herself and her husband, Tom. "We've never really agreed about it. My husband went to Catholic schools all his life. He saw lots of spanking and he believes in it. But he's six-feet-four and weighs two hundred pounds and has a temper with the boys, and even though they know he loves them, he can be frightening. Sometimes the punishments he wants are way out of whack, so I have to step in and stand up to him. We've never tried to hide our disagreements from the boys. To a degree, I've had to encourage them to stand up to him as a way of keeping him under control. With the boys, I've tried to show them when punishment is justified. 'If you feel that something's unfair,' I say to them, 'you can stand up for yourself, but when you're being justly punished, you need to recognize that.'" "Did you ever use corporal punishment with the boys?" I asked. "No," Terry said. "I wouldn't allow it. My husband didn't agree, still doesn't agree, and we've argued about it, but I've said no."

Countless adults like Tom McCray appear to believe that punishment is an indispensable ingredient in building good character, particularly for boys. Many traditions and laws, beginning, as we just saw, with the Bible, endorse physical punishment. The twenty-three states that still authorize teachers in public schools to paddle or spank children who have misbehaved are mostly in the Southern tier, the Bible Belt. (A 1994 U.S. Department of Education survey estimated that more than 478,000 students, some as young as age five, were punished by being hit at school that year.) Unless physical punishment of children at home is done so aggressively as to seriously injure the child, it is not considered child abuse in most legal jurisdictions.

How Violence Begins

Terry's worry that Tom might fly out of control is well taken, as I know from experience. I see enough instances of parents' losing control in my work on child abuse that I always take serious heed when a parent mentions it. When a mother uses the word "frightening," she often is referring to more than the kids. When hitting by adults goes on in a family, it typically spreads in many directions. Parents hit children. Children hit one another. Fathers hit mothers. Mothers hit fathers. Children hit parents.

The first experience many children have with violence is when they have annoyed or enraged an adult caring for them. A mother came to Children's Hospital in Boston in the middle of the night with her three-month-old son, Robert. She showed a nurse and doctor on duty in the emergency room a reddened patch on the baby's left cheek, and told what she thought had happened. The baby had awakened an hour earlier, she said, and it was her husband's turn to get up, go into the nursery adjacent to their bedroom, give the baby a bottle, and comfort him back to sleep. In her half-awake state, she thought she heard a slap, she said. She went into the nursery, saw the red mark on Robert's cheek, bundled him into the car, and drove to the hospital.

The emergency room staff admitted Robert for two reasons: for observation, because had the force necessary to create this bruise also been applied to other parts of his body that don't reveal bruising marks so quickly—the abdomen, for example—there could be serious underlying organ damage; and for protection, because it looked as though he might be in danger at home.

Early the next morning, my pager sounded. The pediatric resident from Robert's ward was on the line. Would I see an infant boy just admitted with a suspicious injury. An hour or so later, after reviewing the hospital records and examining Robert, I was on my way back from Robert's room to my office when I was stopped by a distinguished member of the hospital's senior pediatric staff who had just accepted Robert as a private patient.

"Eli," he said, "I knew you would be coming to consult on this case, but I have to tell you I have a problem with it." I asked him what the problem was. "Well, perhaps the problem is mostly mine, but I don't want to call this a case of child abuse. I'd rather call it an accident."

"Can you tell me about the family?" I asked. My colleague said that the father of Robert was a physician in another of Boston's teaching hospitals, a man known for his dedication to his patients, a hard-working man, a good man. The unstated but obvious implication was that public knowledge of the episode could adversely affect a colleague's career.

"Shouldn't we," I asked, "consider the downside for the doctor's career if he were to injure the baby again, with graver consequences for the baby's health? Don't we have an ethical obligation to him, as well as to his son, to protect them both against a subsequent injury? Doesn't this include putting the cards on the table, and squaring with him about what appears to have happened?"

Fortunately, my argument persuaded my colleague, and we made contact with the social worker assigned to the floor to initiate the necessary interviews. Both parents were interviewed separately during the next few days. It was evident that the doctor associated the birth of his son with a profound sense of his wife's lessening her attentions to her husband. Exhausted and overworked, he was angry at the infant's interrupting his sleep.

It all ended well. Robert did not have to be separated, for safety's sake, from his father, and he was not injured again. Individual and family therapy dealt successfully with the father's sense of pressure and loss of attention, and the family was helped to avoid a dangerous cycle of frustration and violence.

To Spank or Not to Spank

Many people still believe that under certain circumstances, inflicting pain is necessary to teach a child to avoid dangerous objects or situations. I've heard this notion expressed in several ways over the years. A former director of the national child abuse center in the Department of Health and Human Services told of a couple who worried that their eighteen-month-old child approached the hot stove too frequently, ignoring their warnings. They chose to teach her not to do this by holding her fingers against the hot stove until she cried. She never went near the stove again. The story was told with pride. The toddler was the director's own daughter!

"Caleb's Mom," an elementary school teacher, posted the following message on an Internet bulletin board devoted to child care:

> When my son was a toddler, he was very adventurous, and would often attempt to squeeze past the front door and onto our porch, where stone steps awaited his fall. Verbal reprimands and re-directing his attention elsewhere were fruitless, as he attempted time and again to get out that door when my back was turned. Rather than allow him to experience for himself the consequences of wandering too close to those steps, I swatted him smartly a couple of times on his diapered behind and placed him in his playpen for a timeout! It took two more swattings before he became convinced of the certain connection between trying to get out the front door and the painful consequences, but after that, he needed no more reminders!
>
> I have always saved physical discipline for situations similar to this—instances where his behavior is dangerous or could lead to serious injury or worse. At the age of six, Caleb was spanked soundly on the backside of his Levi's for following two older boys who led him up to the strictly forbidden train tracks behind our home. Although he well knew the train tracks were off-limits, he apparently needed a physical reminder beyond just a verbal explanation—and I complied! He knows well that these spankings are done with great concern and love and I have never detected any resentment or fear because of them. In fact, he will tell you himself that he well deserved his spanking for breaking such a critical rule!

Caleb's Mom's main concern is enforcing the rules. She sees herself as a loving parent who rarely uses spankings to enforce sticking to the rules. She resorts to spankings only when there is something risky about her son's behavior that she wants to deter him from repeating. Otherwise, she doesn't strike or cuff her son merely because she has lost her patience with him. Her concerns that Caleb not fall down the stone front steps as a toddler, or play on or near the train tracks behind the house as a six-year-old, seem at first thought to be only reasonable.

Most parents, I believe, would think her safety concerns in these instances appropriate. The very reasonableness of her approach, however, makes it a good springboard for raising the question: Is spanking, even for the sake of loving deterrence, the only or best method of nurturing a boy's character and capacity for making wise choices? Most parents of toddlers today spank or slap their boys at least occasionally when they misbehave. The amount of home spankings of school-age boys has diminished, but it certainly hasn't disappeared.

Sociologist Murray Straus has done pioneering research on corporal punishment and summarized the research of others. As he noted recently, the subject has been plagued by a central question of causality. A correlation between suffering corporal punishment and later aggression by the boys spanked has been documented for some time. The more he has received corporal punishment, for example, the more likely it is that a boy will hit his spouse when he grows up and marries. But does this connection demonstrate that corporal punishment causes a boy to become more aggressive, or is it simply that boys who are temperamentally more aggressive and challenging as children drive their parents to use corporal punishment because nothing else works?

Most American parents, Straus has found, do believe that corporal punishment works, that it produces compliant behavior and a boy of stronger character. Recent studies, however, offer strong support for the view that corporal punishment is a factor linked causally to later antisocial behavior by boys. When corporal punishment was employed at home with boys in one study, five years later they engaged in more fighting at school than boys who hadn't been spanked or slapped. Another study showed that 28 percent of 1,000 boys interviewed (average age fifteen) reported having been slapped by their parents during the preceding year, but 11 percent of these boys reported also hitting a *parent* during the same period. Slapping by parents, rather than decreasing the chances of being hit by an adolescent boy, increased the probability parents they would be assaulted by their own sons.

Other studies have shown that the more a child is hit as part of discipline, the more likely he will suffer depression in later years. Except in those unfortunately numerous cases where a boy is beaten so severely that he is injured physically, the consequences for millions of kids who are hit for punishment appears to be psychological damage and various forms of aggressive and antisocial behavior in later stages of their lives.

A study conducted by Straus himself offers an additional fascinating insight into corporal punishment. His study was prompted by the research of others showing that talking to children (including children who hadn't begun to talk themselves yet) is associated with an increase in neural connections in the brain and in cognitive performance. Talking to them, in short, fires up their brains more.

Straus theorized that when parents avoid corporal punishment, they must use verbal methods of behavior control (including the inductive techniques I shall discuss later), and the increased verbal interaction should enhance the child's cognitive ability. His research on almost 1,000 children aged one to four when he first tested them, followed by cognitive ability tests four years later, showed that the children who were not hit increased in cognitive ability and the children who were hit fell behind the cognitive development of the others in proportion to how much corporal punishment they experienced. Straus writes,

> I am convinced that if parents knew the benefits of not hitting their children and the risk they were exposing them to when they spank, millions would stop. . . . These benefits are not limited to enhanced mental ability. Studies in my book, *Beating the Devil Out of Them*, indicate that the benefits of ending corporal punishment are likely to also include less adult violence, less masochistic sex, a greater probability of completing higher education, higher income, and lower rates of depression and alcohol abuse.

Parents who hit their children are often unaware of effective alternatives. They may have uncritically accepted the advice of others that hurting is a necessary part of discipline. Spanking may be their default position, the method they unthinkingly resort to when they are aggravated by a child's behavior, and lose their self-control.

Straus mentions the 1979 law in Sweden that sets a national goal of eliminating corporal punishment. It says in part: "Children are entitled to care, security and a good upbringing. Children are to be treated with respect for their person and individuality, and may not be subjected to corporal punishment or any other humiliating treatment." The Swedes didn't stop there. They mounted a large public education campaign, emphasizing the objectives of discipline, including family harmony and a more civil society. Twenty years later, there is wide public acceptance of the policy, although at the outset there was controversy about the extent to which the government should involve itself in family life. A significant part of the law is that it is nonpunitive in its approach; no one is to be criminalized for corporal punishment that does not seriously injure a child. Instead, the methods to be used after known violations of the law are educational and therapeutic. To date, eight other countries have followed Sweden's lead. I think the United States should join them.

Straus's passing reference to sexual masochism merits brief elaboration, for many other professionals, including myself, have been aware that spanking a boy's buttocks can lead to a confusion between sexual pleasure and corporal punishment pain. There are, as we know, men whose most intense sexual pleasure as adults is evoked by being spanked. But in a more diffuse way, many men's capacity for sexual tenderness is compromised to a degree by their mental association of sexual stimulation with the pain and shame they felt when they were spanked.

Alternatives

There are several alternatives to spanking as ways of punishing boys who have misbehaved. Some, which have their drawbacks, are verbal expressions of disappointment or condemnation; loss of privileges, including "grounding"; and "time-outs" when a boy is made to spend time by himself after misbehavior. For the most part, these are better methods than spanking, but they also have their limitations.

Timing, first of all, is important. Although parents will say that they have to punish whenever they learn about certain situations—for example, that a son ran impulsively onto a busy street several hours earlier—the most effective time to deal with acts that are dangerous or misconceived is immediately prior to their occurrence or just as they begin. Punishment often has no useful lingering effect when there is a substantial time break between behavior and response.

Verbal punishment usually consists of an attempt to shame a boy. It is a method that is hard to control—to make a certain point, without causing more than the desired effect. The adult who is doing it is often too overwrought to be able to choose words carefully. Shaming done with very general language—"You're no good." "I wish you hadn't been born."—can be accepted and internalized by a boy so that it makes him feel bad about himself rather than about the misbehavior that provoked the shaming. Many times, a boy will feel that the shaming is excessive. It makes him feel mad, not sorry, especially when he reviews the experience in his mind later. Excessive shaming is associated with a propensity to violence, according to my psychiatric colleague James Gilligan, who theorizes that most violent behavior is a compensation for feelings of shame.

Time-outs—removing boys from the setting by sending them to their rooms, or to designated time-out places in the household—may be helpful when a young boy has lost self-control, and no other discipline is available. In many cases, the parent has lost patience, too. The time-out allows everyone to calm down. But when used indiscriminately, the frequency and length of the time-outs can easily become excessive. Also, time-outs may get linked to the threat of spanking: "If you don't stay in your room quietly, you're going to get a spanking!" Extended isolation of the boy may cut off opportunities to have a calm and helpful discussion with him of how the misbehavior happened and how he might avert it another time. By the time the time-out is over, life is moving on, and everyone may be hesitant to revisit the experience.

Loss of privileges, such as television, dessert, or games suffers from the same drawback as time-outs; the connection is gradually lost between the misbehavior and the punishment. I suspect that in many cases the loss of privileges isn't fully carried out; everyone decides to ignore it after a while. The method of withdrawing privileges is essentially negative: I can't communicate with you, and so I'll hurt you if you don't mind me. The positive counterpoint is: We all make mistakes, and you can trust me to help you do better in the future.

The Cycle of Hostility

Punishments achieve intended results better when they are not harsher than necessary to achieve compliance. Boys are punished more severely than are girls all through childhood. If punishments are much more severe than a boy believes is reasonable, compliance may be accompanied by fear and resentment that, in turn, might prevent a boy from adopting, for its own sake, the rule that is involved.

Children of highly punitive parents have been found to be particularly defiant and aggressive outside their homes. Harsh punishment's adverse effects include giving children adult models of aggression instead of adult models of restraint and kindness. Boys will tend to avoid, and of course to mistrust, adults who punish them severely, reducing the opportunities for friendly interaction with those adults. Harshness may work in the short term, and relieve an adult's feelings, but it often begets long-term failure.

Observations of boys who are aggressive at home have helped to identify how cycles of punishment and resistance to it grow. As a parent criticizes a boy for misbehavior and threatens punishment, the boy whines and refuses to comply. The boy's resistance is all the more predictable if his parents are unpredictable and inconsistent: Sometimes they follow through on their threats to punish, sometimes they don't. This reinforces in the boy's mind the possibility that if he keeps up his resistance long enough, his parents will give in and stop the threatening—and stop the punishing. A confrontation between them may end in a draw. Parent and child withdraw, feeling relief that the confrontation is over, but resentful that nothing has been resolved. Eventually a new misbehavior triggers a response of greater threats and greater resistance. Other members of the family may get drawn in as everyone feels forced to take sides.

Boys who experience frequent confrontations with their parents over discipline may favor friendships with peers who are similarly resentful of their treatment at home—and so the circle of hostility moves beyond the home to the surrounding community. From these cycles, boys develop outlooks toward the world as being mean and hostile. They may begin to see hostile intentions even where they do not exist—for example, when something truly accidental occurs, or when friends are trying to be helpful and their attempts are misread. These unhappy boys may fall into a pattern of provoking and attacking others, stimulating further retribution. Boys as young as four years of age have exhibited bleak outlooks; when these boys enter kindergarten, they display much higher levels of aggression than their peers.

Dangers of Shaking

To stop babies from crying, parents or other caregivers sometimes shake them, holding their torsos and making their heads whip uncontrollably back and forth. It happens more frequently than most people think. The baby's neck musculature is relatively undeveloped, and his head is disproportionately large and heavy compared to the rest of his body, so the baby has little capacity to arrest the to-and-fro motions of his head.

The effects of shaking or striking the head are both immediate and long term. But unfortunately too many adults are unaware of the risks. The baby's brain is softer, and thus more susceptible to injury. Shaking actually causes the infant brain to bounce around inside the skull. Blood leaks out of its vessels and pools around the brain tissue. The brain cells swell, also increasing the pressure inside the skull. In extreme cases, blindness and neurological damage can result. All parents should be aware of the grave dangers of shaking a baby.

What Is Discipline For?

Enforcing acceptable behavior in boys is not enough, although I think most of us would settle for that once in a while. If our objective is to foster *self*-discipline and character in boys and the men they will become, then it would be well to consider how best to help boys—and men, too, for that matter—to internalize a sense of responsibility and obligation to treat others considerately; to get them to be mindful of how their interests, desires, and impulses affect others; to guide them into being men who care and who want to do right by others. It is no small challenge, this task of promoting moral understanding.

How does the capacity for moral understanding develop in a boy? One study has shown that when parents of one- to three-year-olds applied a discipline that communicated with kindness how the parents wanted their sons to behave, and the parents bestowed abundant praise when the boys succeeded, they reinforced the boys' desire to please and faced fewer behavioral problems when the boys were five.

In another study, children close to their third birthdays were shown a picture of a child stealing a playmate's apple (a moral violation) and a picture of a child eating ice cream with his fingers (a violation of a social rule); the children were able to signal that stealing the apple was wrong in any circumstances. By forty-two months, children indicated that stealing the apple would be wrong even if the act weren't witnessed by an adult and the child hadn't been warned that stealing it could be wrong.

Studies by Turiel and others suggest that children don't depend entirely on parental instruction to derive a sense of what is right and what wrong. They have emotional reactions when they observe actions such as stealing. They somehow feel it is wrong before they have been instructed it is wrong. Parents and other caregiving adults can build on this intuitive sense.

Notions of "distributive justice"—how to divide things fairly—develop in the preschool years, with four-year-olds understanding the importance of sharing in curious, and in some respects contradictory and self-serving, ways. Asked why he shared toys with a playmate, a four-year-old boy may reply, "I shared because if I didn't, he wouldn't play with me." Fairness, at first, means the same amount for everyone. By age six or seven, fairness is seen by many boys as connected to deservings—for example, that some should get more because they've worked harder. Already boys' conceptions of what is fair are being influenced significantly by the views of their peers.

Beginning at age four, boys' instrumental aggression (trying to get something, grabbing the toys of others, for example) begins to decline, but hostile aggression (trying to injure another person or hurt his feelings) is on the upswing. When boys fight each other, they are less likely to be labeled as aggressive by their parents than girls are when they fight each other. School-aged boys expect less parental disapproval for aggression than girls, and they feel less guilty about being aggressive than girls do. Even at age two, girls' aggressiveness is beginning to decline while boys' aggressiveness is staying constant, and parents are beginning to apply harsher punishment to boys than to girls.

Inductive Discipline: The Alternative to Punishment

The attractive alternative to discipline by punishment is the employment of strategies that, as one authority on moral development put it, "lead children to focus on the actual standards that their parents are trying to communicate rather than on the disciplinary means by which the parents enforce these standards." In an influential 1994 article, Joan Grusec and Jacqueline Goodnow identified two steps in a child's processing of parental messages about the child's conduct.

The first step is understanding. If parents explain their reasons as they evaluate a child's behavior, the child will eventually comprehend the principles underpinning the messages. Such an approach is "inductive" because it begins with concrete events and moves from the concrete to the general. Events are discussed with a child as an exploration of what was wrong from the parents' point of view. The wrongness is explained in terms of the effect the misbehavior has had on others and/or on the child rather than only in terms of whether an established rule has been broken. Rules are discussed, but they aren't invoked as the beginning and the end of the discussions.

The opposite, or deductive, method is to establish a rule and then punish a child when he breaks it. In this method, it doesn't matter as much whether the child understands the reasons for the rule, while in the inductive method it is crucial. For the inductive method to work, there has to be consistent and informative communication between parent and child.

The second component of the inductive method is that the child has to *accept* the parents' views; how and whether he can accept them is affected by whether he believes that his parents' appraisal of his behavior is commensurate with his own. If a parent treats a boy's messy bedroom and a fight between siblings as being of equal gravity, a boy's agreement with that parent's judgment might justifiably be impaired.

Inductive discipline has to be centered in the basic relationship between the parent or other caregiver and the child. It doesn't begin with a problem. It begins with your love for your child, and his attachment to you and respect for you. Above all, you don't want to react to behavioral problems in a way that threatens that relationship. You want to protect the relationship steadfastly, even fiercely. You want your son to see that you are above all protective of him, and happy with him. From that central conviction, you praise his every achievement and reward his good behavior with approbation.

Even when the parent-child relationship is deeply rooted and loving, there will be episodes—perhaps even repetitive types of episodes—when your son's behavior is a problem. He may become oppositional as he tests his own wish for autonomy. He may play too aggressively with other children. He may disregard your suggestions in a way that embarrasses you publicly. The problems may be very trying (to him as well as you) at times.

Practicing the inductive method involves distinguishing feelings from behavior, beginning very early in a boy's life. Children's feelings are always recognized and responded to empathically in this method. "I know it's hard to share Mommy's attention with your baby brother." "I know you are angry when Ben refuses to share his toys." The behavior, the acting out of feelings, is what is subject to the setting of limits and to guidance in behavior. "But you may not hit the baby because it hurts him and it hurts me, too." "But you can't take away his truck just because you want to play with it. Would you like to build a tower of blocks with me?"

Sensitive adults will remove their children from situations where other children have lost control, when that seems the best way to calm the situation. A mother of four-year-old twin boys who share their toys with each other so equally that they have a sense of fierce possessiveness only toward their special blankets and teddy bears, took them for a play date where the host child went into meltdown, crawled into his bed, and sucked his thumb for solace when the visiting children casually commandeered some of his favorite toys. She calmly put the twins' jackets on them and took them out for an ice cream treat and then home.

Employing the inductive method doesn't mean that you have to be passive or spineless. It is inevitable that you will have to set reasonable limits and to make a certain number of rules. But you will take care to acknowledge and deal respectfully with feelings when abiding by the rules is frustrating. One of the fathers I've talked to in the past year recalled his own boyhood in South Africa. "I was out with a bunch of kids during a holiday night," Nicholas Kriek said, "and we were running around the neighborhood doing crazy things. I must have been around twelve years old. We were throwing stones onto roofs, and when they bounced down we would run away.

"One of the other boys misjudged a throw, and his stone went through the front window of a house. Naturally, that wasn't funny. The family called the police. We boys all scattered in different directions. I managed to get home, but my father was there and had heard by telephone that the police were trying to find out who was in the group. He sat me down and said to me, 'I'm going to make something very clear to you. If you ever do something you shouldn't, and get in trouble, I'm not going to rescue you. You have to pay the price for your own behavior.'

"I don't remember exactly what my response was," Nick continued, "but I think I was taken aback. Usually, boys think that their parents are going to rescue them no matter what. In some respects I've tried to be that kind of parent with my own boys. I show them that I love them unconditionally, and I try to provide every opportunity for them that I can, but I also tell them: If you misbehave and get in trouble with others, you have to deal with the consequences yourself."

I'll tell more later in the book about how this father's philosophy worked out with his boys, but here I just want to emphasize that the father's love for his son didn't prevent him from refusing to cover up any of his son's public misbehavior; their relationship of mutual love and respect was not damaged by this stand. Nick grasped the reasons for his father's position, and internalized them as his own: He, and eventually his own

sons, must accept responsibility and the consequences for public misbehavior.

When actions, not just words, provide inspiration, one might call this
inductive by example. One father put it this way: "When I was growing up,
my mother stressed to me the importance of learning how to cook, wash,
iron, sew. I became very self-sufficient. Now I do most of the cooking. I
look after the children. I take care of my family, and I'm teaching Andrew
all these things. He sees it. It might be annoying for him at times, but it's
important that he make his bed every day and learn how to do the laundry. If I model it for him, eventually it will become natural for him. Later
on, he will appreciate it." Andrew's dad reminds us here that discipline
doesn't have to be limited to a set of mostly negative rules. Discipline is
just as much a positive way of life.

The mother of eleven-year-old Brad Jefferson voiced to me another important aspect of inductive parenting. In deductive methods of parenting,
there is enormous emphasis on keeping to the rules, whatever they are.
The parent is supposed to win all the time. But in inductive parenting,
where the preservation of love and respect is at the heart of the parent-
child relationship, it doesn't seem so important for the parent to win every
disagreement over behavior. "Brad is involved in student government, and
one of their issues this fall was that the principal said no one could wear a
hat in school. You know, no baseball caps worn backward, that sort of
thing. The kids talked it over among themselves, and decided they would
make a pitch for a change in the rule. Brad asked me my opinion. I said,
'You already know what I think. I wouldn't vote for it.' In the end the student council won one day when anyone could wear a hat. So I said to Brad,
'You'd better be careful that this doesn't go too much further, or I might
have to go down to the school and ask why the standards have loosened
up.' Really, this is just an example of where he clearly knows our opinion,
and he thinks something different. We've all talked about it a lot, and
we've agreed to disagree. For me, that's been a nice experience."

Restitution

One of the readers of this book in its early stages was a school principal
who said she was troubled by the very first story I told. You may recall that
I recounted how my cousin, Sam, decided to sabotage the new housing development that was destroying a lovely forest next to his parents' thereto-
fore pleasantly secluded home.

Who paid for the damage, the principal wanted to know. Did I really
want to begin my book with a story in which there was no restitution?
Well, I did. One of the things I wanted to convey at the outset is that char-

acter isn't about perfection. We all do things we later regret, and that we believe were not typical of the choices we usually make. Sam was the acknowledged star of our extended family in my generation, the envy of everyone. And he went on to a distinguished career in public service that could only have been achieved by a person who had adopted very sound moral principles during his childhood and adolescence.

But the principal has a point. At the time, Sam and his family were preoccupied with the event as something that might lead to punishment and a damaged reputation. Where punishment orientations prevail, restitution is sometimes required, but as part of the punishment.

When people switch from a punishment philosophy of discipline to inductive discipline, restitution becomes a much more prominent aspect of the situation. Now the emphasis is: whom and what have I harmed, and how may I make amends? This outward capacity to make amends requires an inner development of self-discipline—the capacity to ask: What are my responsibilities to others?

The goal of inductive discipline is to bring everyone involved back to a good relationship, having learned something about responsibility; that will be all the harder if the person who has caused harm isn't interested in restitution. Restitution of damage to property is important, but the restoration of relationships—often left in tatters when punishment has been administered—is even more critical.

I wish I had a better term for inductive discipline. The phrase sounds too cold or abstract for the humane purpose the phrase is meant to convey. But I hope I've shown what I mean by it. It involves both parent and child. The parent establishes a foundation for communication and trust. He, she, or they love, guide, teach, remind, set limits for behavior—and make mistakes; every parent-child relationship is strengthened when a parent acknowledges mistakes to his child, and makes amends. The boy learns the parents' values, takes them in, makes them his own, makes mistakes, begins to make amends for his mistakes, begins to take responsibility for his own behavior. Eventually the boy's discipline will come as much from within as without.

7

Preschoolers

Unlike any other time in childhood, preschool is a period when boys are not systematically in contact with any social institutions, for example, the health-care system or schools. Many still get occasional physical checkups, but not with the frequency or thoroughness of infants and toddlers. Much of their medical care is on an as-needed basis. Many are enrolled in day-care centers and kindergartens, but they are not required by law to go to school yet. Parents, thus, are very much on their own during this time.

Also during this time three-, four-, or five-year-old boys are experiencing a lively transition from home to a wider world, whether or not they leave home for a portion of each day. In these years, a boy will come to see himself more vividly as separate and different from others around him, especially from females. He will pick up some of the most important tools—language and other symbols—for managing relationships. He will experience changes in his family if a new sibling is introduced or when his mother goes back to work. Inevitably, he will begin to figure out where he stands in a whole community of people around him.

Physical and Intellectual Development

Right in the middle of the preschool period, a boy will probably experience a spurt in height, with three or more of them to follow at intervals before he completes elementary school. By age five, boys can throw a ball five feet farther than girls can, on average, despite having about the same muscle mass as girls. They can also run a little faster and jump a little farther than girls. Girls have better balance and fine motor skills, but boys' athleticism is superior, not because of physical superiority so much as because they have been encouraged to practice athletic skills.

A three-year-old preschooler is just beginning to store some of his experience as long-term, recoverable memory. Two-year-olds can remember events for quite long periods of time after they occur, but eventually the memories disappear in what is called infantile amnesia, and become irretrievable. Some researchers attribute this amnesia to lack of brain development. Others say that a child can't develop long-term memory until he has a reasonably well developed image of himself—that is, not before age three.

Children between the ages of three and six become increasingly able to describe past experiences with detail, organization, background information, and personal interpretation. There's an important connection between the development of this capacity and the amount the child converses with adults. As I've already noted, parents and other caregivers talk more to girls than to boys about the past as well as other matters. Girls, therefore, remember sequences of events sooner than boys, report earlier first memories than boys, and report more vivid details of those memories. Youngsters growing up in impoverished conditions suffer in their intellectual development, and these early deficits become harder to overcome as children grow older. Thus the rock solid case for programs such as Project Headstart.

Enhanced memory enables a boy to function better in the present as well as to recall the past. For example, at about age four, boys can search systematically for a lost object, first looking where they last saw the object or where they were when they discovered it was missing.

Mathematical reasoning begins in toddlerhood. Sixteen-month-olds already have a sense of ordinality, or the order relationship among quantities—three is more than two, for example. By age three, they are attaching verbal labels such as "big" or "small" to different sizes and amounts. Most boys begin to "recite their numbers," usually from one to as high as ten, as two-year-olds. By age three or four, boys can supply the accurate number of a small group of items; and by age five, most boys can deal with small numbers without having to count up from one. There's actually a nice leap in reasoning from the boy who shows you his age by counting up on his fingers, and the boy who can simply finger-flash the right number.

Not until age five does testing of IQ begin to be a dependable measure, and even then test results need to be qualified by many factors: among them, the child's nutrition and its effect on brain function; the amount of enriching life experience, or lack thereof, the child has benefited from; and the level of encouragement the child has received to be curious and expressive.

My own passion for music prompts me to report that, on average, children who receive keyboard instruction beginning no later than age four show increased spatial reasoning as a bonus. Kids who receive early music instruction display, as a group, higher than average intelligence later. Is there a causal factor here? The coordination of hands doing independent things, plus feet on pedals doing something else at the same time, plus reading music and giving instruction to hands and feet exercises many parts of the brain. This concerted activity of the brain has a long-lasting effect. Intelligence is affected by how much—and how elaborately—the brain practices.

Preschoolers tend to be learning optimists. That is, they rate their abilities very high, underestimate the difficulties of completing tasks, and are generally positive about succeeding at them. They are, of course, at an age when the number of things expected of them is increasing dramatically. Mostly, they believe that a person who has failed at a task can succeed if he keeps trying. They tolerate frustration and failure pretty well. Because they cannot distinguish cleanly between effort and ability in relation to success, they retain a natural optimism. They already see that some failures lead eventually to successes.

Yet some boys, by age four, give up easily when confronted with hard tasks. Even if the tasks are age-appropriate, like building a tower of blocks, their assessment of their efforts is negative. If asked to act out with dolls what adults would do or say in response to such failures, they frequently respond with statements such as "Daddy's gonna be very mad and spank him." Nonpersisting four-year-olds are likely to see themselves as bad. They expect that even minor mistakes will lead to berating criticism. At this period a boy's sense of self-worth, whether he is confident or pessimistic, is very much oriented toward the judgments of others, as opposed to having an internal standard.

Emotional Development

Most four-year-olds can identify basic emotions and behavior associated with the emotions. But they emphasize external factors rather than internal feelings when telling you why a fellow preschooler is sad or happy or angry. There is evidence that children who grow up in families where feelings are talked about openly will develop a greater facility for assessing others' emotions accurately. That's certainly not a surprising finding. But I suspect that many parents don't think of four-year-olds as developing this capacity quite so early.

If adults in a family disagree with each other on their interpretations of feelings and discuss their differing opinions in their children's presence, their children become even more skilled in such activity. Several studies conclude that, as early as ages three to five, the capacity to recognize emotions is associated with acceptance by peers, the ability to apologize and repair rifts generated by conflict, and the capacity to manifest considerate and friendly behavior.

Self-esteem originates early. How three-year-olds see themselves is directly connected to their experiences of pride and shame. To no one's surprise, warm, responsive parents who set reasonable expectations for behavior have children who feel especially good about themselves. Coercive parenting makes children feel inadequate, and overly indulgent child care creates a shaky sense of self-esteem.

By the third birthday, there are clear differences among children in their self-control. The best predictor of this is advanced language development. If preschoolers are taught to de-emphasize the arousing qualities of a specific stimulus—for example, to think of marshmallows as "white and puffy clouds"—they are able to wait longer to eat the reward than if they think of them as sweet and chewy. Adults can encourage the development of preschoolers' self-control by such simple techniques as having rules about waiting to be called on during group discussions.

One study of four-year-olds showed that those who were better able to delay gratification were more advanced when they became adolescents in thinking through the implications of behavior and regulating it; they were more often seen by their parents as responsive to reason, verbally fluent, able to concentrate and plan ahead, and able to cope maturely with stress. These enduring individual differences probably have to do both with temperament and with child-rearing practices. Temperamental mismatches between children and parents—for example, temperamentally vulnerable children exposed to power-assertive or inconsistent disciplinarians—often lead to serious conduct disorders, particularly among boys.

Over the preschool years, physical aggression is gradually replaced by verbal aggression. The better the boy's verbal development, the sooner he will make this transition and become able to substitute verbal expression of feelings and negotiation for physical aggression.

How can we make this happen without pressuring him? By lots of talking. By giving priority to *inductive* discipline. By reading, and using stories to help label his feelings as he thinks about the characters. By having family meetings where all members solve problems together. It is also important to control toxic exposures: to television violence and to physical and verbal aggression by other people. Aggressive children see hostile intentions in others, whether or not they exist; this misperception has been seen as early as age four in boys who have suffered physical abuse.

Gender Consciousness

Around two years of age, children begin to label their gender and that of others. Once the categories are established, they start to sort out what gender signifies in activities and behaviors. Preschoolers connect numerous things to gender: clothing, household items, occupations, even colors.

Their gender stereotypes act less as guidelines than as blanket rules, and in experiments where boys were told of the characteristics of a particular child that stretched the boundaries—for example, a boy who enjoyed playing house—most responded by insisting that they preferred to play with cars and trucks.

One mother, writing in to an Internet bulletin board, described how much her four-year-old son's gender identifications bothered her, and how resistant to amendment they seemed:

> I actually had a conversation tonight regarding the merits of SailorMoon versus Batman. I lost. Apparently SailorMoon, although VERY cool, could not possibly hope to surpass Batman because (cough, choke, splutter!) she is a WOMAN.
>
> Where is he getting this stuff? I have always been very conscious about raising my son to believe that women can do anything men can do, and suddenly I am faced with this four-year-old chauvinistic terror. Women cannot drive big trucks, fly heavy airplanes, carry heavy objects, mow the lawn, or shovel snow. Not only that, but men are smarter as well. If I casually point out that women CAN drive big trucks, he will just as casually insist, "No, Mommy, you're wrong." Although I hate to admit it, I have started stooping to arguments about it.
>
> By the way, this is a boy that lives with his Mom and his Grandma and both of us work, take out our own garbage, shovel our own driveway, and mow the lawn.

This mother may be misreading her son's behavior as an expression of knowing chauvinism when it is actually a reflection of his level of development. The rigidity of preschoolers' gender stereotypes appear to derive from the boys' intellectual immaturity, particularly as they try to process conflicting information or as they respond to the evidence in their own environment—"Girls don't drive fire engines." "Boys can't be the teacher." Most of them don't realize that the occupations they've associated with gender are not restricted to that gender.

If four- and five-year-olds are shown gender-neutral toys, they will make predictions of whether other children will like them based on gender. If a boy likes a toy, he will predict that other boys will like it, too. If the same toy is labeled as being a toy for girls, it will not be appealing to a boy even if it is highly attractive. If boys are shown a picture of a boy cooking at a stove, many will remember it as a picture of a girl. If shown a film with a male nurse, they may recall that he was a doctor.

A study done in 1989 showed that children as young as age three who learn to distinguish males and females by genital characteristics most frequently answer gender identification questions correctly. Because many children in Western cultures do not often see members of the other sex naked, giving them additional information and vocabulary equips them to make more accurate identifications, and therefore not to derive gender from hairstyles, clothes, or conventional activities. Sandra Bem, who conducted research on this issue, suggests that if children know that their genders are going to remain the same regardless of role and other factors, they may be more comfortable with unconventional behavior. I recommend using anatomical names rather than humorous or slangy substitutes. The real words, when used, take some of the discomfort away and make it easier for all of us to acknowledge what the differences are, and aren't.

Adults' feelings of awkwardness about sex, whether shown in choosing the right words to describe sex differences or in their concerns about boys' sexuality, is also reflected in rigid notions about how boys should behave. Consider, for example, the following story, again from the Internet, where a boy's gender-bending play caused his parents considerable anxiety.

My son will be 4 in a few months. He is a very intelligent, sweet, and caring child. I also have a 2.5-year-old daughter who is just as sweet and loving but a bit feistier. I have always encouraged them both to play with all types of toys and set no gender barriers. When my daughter was born, my mother bought my son a baby doll to care for just like Mommy was caring for the new baby. He was only 15 months old at the time, and I felt (and still do) that this was a great way to help him feel not left out when Mom was busy with the baby. My husband thought we were nuts . . . What, buy a doll for a boy?!?! My son would at times carry around his baby just like Mommy. No big deal. He could take it or leave it.

For about the past 6 months, he has become obsessed with Barbie dolls. I have two friends that both have daughters and buckets full of Barbies. My son is obsessed with visiting their homes and spending endless hours dressing and undressing Barbie. He is also possessive of my daughter's play jewelry and make-up. He pretends to polish his nails, puts curlers in his hair, and wears the jewelry. My husband is not happy.

I hate to admit this, but I am starting to question my own feelings and become a bit concerned. I even bought him a soldier doll (a G.I. Joe, the same size as Barbie), something I never wanted to do. He rarely plays with it. He is not into guns, weapons, Power Rangers or any other type of action/violence toys, and I have not exposed him to any of that. (Now my husband is telling me that I should have.) He does at times play with his cars and trains, but Barbie is clearly his first choice. What is his obsession with this unrealistic, misproportionate doll?

My advice to this mother is: Relax! Give him a range of toys and let him play with whatever he wants. That's what play is: experimentation, exploration, and, hopefully, fun.

What are we afraid of? Is it fear of homosexuality? It's not likely a boy is going to sense his sexuality is different from other boys' so young, but many gay teenagers and adults recall that they sensed certain differences, some very subtle, between themselves and other boys when they were in their early school years. Some of those differences were in the kinds of play that they most enjoyed. Whatever a boy's sexuality is going to be, he doesn't understand anything about it at this age and a parent isn't going to be able to impose a sexual orientation by controlling his play. It's important not to burden him early with a sense of stigma and shame that will make his life more difficult later on. Let him play as he wishes. Encourage him to define himself positively in relation to others. Don't insist that his play conform to stereotyped expectations of what boys are supposed to be. Don't make him feel bad about his preferences. With his parents' support, he'll find himself. Other children will also help.

Play

Look at any playground, and watch who's playing with whom. Toddlers seem to have little gender preference in their playmates, but by age four children spend three times as much time with same-gender playmates as with other-gender. By age six, the ratio will reach eleven to one.

Prior to the age of five, boys and girls spend equal amounts of time talking to or playing with babies. Subsequently, boys' interest in communicating with infants and toddlers declines. However, they retain their interest in pets and elderly friends and relatives.

The quality of a boy's play increases in complexity in the preschool period. It's always more rough-and-tumble than girls', as it's been observed in virtually every society, and, for that matter, in youngsters in every primate species, not to say in *girls* who exhibit certain masculinizing hormonal conditions. This tendency appears mainly to be driven by our genes and our wiring. But the content of complex play derives from the world and relationships that children see. By age four, story lines in dramatic play are getting quite detailed, and players can have multiple roles. Boys from three and a half to four years of age can deal with their own and others' imagined roles—for example, putting out a fire or herding toy animals.

Preschoolers are starting to make sense of what is on other people's minds. The more time preschoolers spend with other kids in sociodramatic play, the better—the first of the reasons not to keep your son exclusively at home. Preschoolers who engage in a lot of dramatized play are seen by teachers as having better social skills and more advanced intellectual development. The more adults get incorporated into this play, the better; the story lines get more elaborate and prolonged. But it's important to remember, too, that a boy needs a balance of quiet time, time with family, time to feel that it's OK just to be alone for a while. I worry, along with David Elkind, author of *The Hurried Child*, that we push kids too hard to engage and to accomplish, and we push boys too hard to achieve over others, starting in earliest childhood.

By age four, boys are showing how they relate behavior to gender and social roles. In play with hand puppets, they will issue more commands when playing teacher or doctor, or adult male roles such as father; but if they are asked to play student, patient, or mother, they will be more polite and indirect.

In the final preschool year, five-year-olds exhibit a change in their preferences at play. Their interest in representational or pretend play declines sharply. Their interest in playing games with rules increases. This is a time when boys can use board and card games to exercise their ability to follow rules and sharpen their concentration skills. Five-year-olds also enjoy the challenges of construction sets and puzzles that imitate the world of adults.

In a recently published list of recommended toys I was delighted to find in the preschool bracket my favorite from those years, Lincoln Logs. How many forts I made—and destroyed—with my brother, Henry! We were master architects and master demolition experts, never running out of enthusiasm for the red-stained wood sticks with the notched ends. I didn't know, and wouldn't have cared, in those years that John Lloyd Wright, son of Frank Lloyd Wright, invented Lincoln Logs in the 1920s. Another chip off the old block.

Guns

As a former dedicated childhood cowboy, I'm not worried about most boys playing with toy "Western" guns or the space age intergalactic equivalents. My experience and lots of research indicates, however, that they can be overstimulating and support the development of aggression in the hands of *some* boys. I've already noted that aggression is about as stable a developmental attribute as intelligence. Habitual aggression can get turned on as early as age two by a boy's exposure to violence. Toys that invite destructive or hurtful pretend play should be kept as much as is feasible out of the play of boys who in other ways exhibit unusual aggressiveness. However, it is unclear whether their absence has any real role in diminishing aggressive behavior. Rather, for these children, attention should be paid not only to the child's exposure to violence through the media, the family and toys, but also to providing experiences and play opportunities that promote *nonviolent* mastery.

If you're going to buy toy guns for your boy, or accept them as gifts for him, be careful that they really look like toys. Some of the more elaborate toy guns, such as the popular large water guns, have prompted people seeing them from a distance to call the police. There have been several tragic preemptive police shootings of boys wielding toy guns.

If you have a real firearm in your house and a preschool male, now is the time to assure that it is locked up and the ammunition stored in a separate locked container—all of it well out of the reach of children. Several hundred children, including some preschoolers, are injured or killed each year in the U.S. in incidents involving firearms stored at home that boys take without permission. Better yet, get rid of firearms at home. We have far too many of them, and their very presence can stimulate curiosity and motivate a boy and his pals to make clever efforts to get at them.

Books

One of my fondest memories from preschool years is of twice-weekly trips to the public library for the children's hour. The pleasures of being read to were evident to me long before I could make sense of any of the words myself.

Sometimes, but not always, pictures were held up to illustrate the stories. You had to listen with concentration to get the drift of the story. The preschool years are the time to get boys to fall in love with being read to, as a stimulus to learning soon to read for themselves. It's one way to head off boys' greater deficiencies, compared to girls', in reading skills, that in a few years will be manifest in remedial reading classes, where boys far outnumber girls.

Jim Trelease, author of *The Read-Aloud Handbook,* encourages mixing in some books that are a little advanced in subject matter and vocabulary for the boy. "Hearing stories that are more complicated than they can handle on their own makes children want to take on more, because they've tasted how good the stuff is."

A "Miniadolescence"

A colleague of mine who has a four-year-old son named Zeke says that he is experiencing and exhibiting a "miniadolescence." That's a fascinating metaphor for the preschooler. Everyone recognizes that boys undergo a variety of changes in their teen years, even a little earlier depending on when puberty occurs, and that one of the crucial changes is growing further away from closeness to parents and parental guidance toward self-reliance and close relations to peers. Something similar happens when a boy becomes a schoolboy. A set of teachers and fellow students become a major factor in his experience, collaborating with, but also to a degree competing with, parents for influence in his life.

Zeke's mother says that something similar to adolescent change is going on with Zeke, though it is easier to see it at home than at the day-care center he attends (where she occasionally goes and quietly watches him to see how he is adapting). She has noticed that Zeke is newly aware of the range of feelings he has for his mother. "What days do I go to preschool?" he asks. "Monday, Wednesday, and Friday, Zeke." "Well, I love you on Tuesday, Thursday, and Saturday, but I don't love you on Monday, Wednesday, and Friday." Toward his younger brother, Zeke is more affectionate than he was as a toddler, but also more competitive ("I can drink my milk faster than you can drink yours!"), and more aggressive—he likes to wrestle amiably with his brother, but sometimes when he is tired or particularly frustrated, he hits his brother.

Zeke has begun to question his parents' guidance more often: "Why do I have to do that?" "What'll you do to me if I don't do it?" He has begun to weigh the consequences of his actions and to imagine alternative solutions. When he broke a plate one night while in the care of a sitter, he thought aloud about burying the shards in the garbage and covering them with mustard so his parents wouldn't see them, perhaps wouldn't even miss the plate. But when he awoke the next morning, the first thing he told his mother was that he had broken a plate. She was relieved, because she had learned from the sitter what happened, and is most concerned that her boys trust her, and not lie to her.

Other parents say of their sons what Zeke's mother reports of him— that his almost adolescent-like volatility is more evident at home than at day care. Here is the predicament as seen by one of those parents, who posted this message on the Internet:

> We have the most adorable 3-year-old son in the world. Just one problem. He is SO aggressive. When he is at nursery school, for the most part, he is well-behaved, but get him home and around other kids, his age or older, and he turns into a hitting machine. He seems to know the kids he can get away with it with. We've tried whatever popular child-rearing/discipline suggestions I've come across (just short of giving him his own back), and nothing seems to get through to him. I've heard the theory that they hit when they don't know the words to express themselves, but my son spoke very early and very clearly.

People are astonished to find out how young he is when they hear him speak. He just seems to have absolutely No impulse control, and often he throws things or hits for no apparent reason. We're at our wit's end. HELP!!!

A friend said to me that parenthood is like walking a tightrope. As the rope moves, or your weight shifts the wrong way, you go slightly out of balance, so you have to make swift little adjustments with your out-stretched arms to bring your body back into balance over the rope, lest you stray too far from your center of gravity and fall. Walking the rope requires constant vigilance, the flexibility to make unending adjustments—and more than a little nerve.

The mother calling for help on the Internet doesn't have a choice when her three-year-old behaves destructively. There's an *im*balance here, and the boy, I think, is confused about his autonomy and her limit-setting. If she doesn't do something effective, and fast, he's going to suffer, not least because other kids will not want to play with him, now and in the future.

To get things in balance in such a situation requires several steps, and some consistency, not just an experimental sampling of disciplinary bromides. First off, a message has got to be clearly telegraphed: *Hitting and throwing things are not allowed in our house, or anywhere. Period.* Just like they're not allowed in nursery school. The parents must also consider—and change—any exposures to aggressive models of behavior he's experiencing at home. They should also keep in mind the principle of *inductive* discipline as they talk with him about how his hurtful actions affect others.

Parents should also make use of any opportunity to talk with the head of the nursery school or day-care center. Most people in these positions have, in addition to education about children's development and behavior, a lot of experience with boys' aggressive behavior. They also really want to help parents. Try to *listen* to how she or he describes your child's behavior; it is hard for many parents to hear about trouble their boys cause. Listen also to her and her colleagues' suggestions: talk about them with people you trust. Don't feel you have to go it alone. If you're tempted to "give him his own back," as this mother put it, definitely call a parenting hotline. Don't hit him, ever! If the aggression persists, ask your doctor for a referral to a professional. It's never too soon, I believe, to act to prevent violence from becoming ingrained in a boy's behavior.

Changes at Home

By the time a boy reaches his preschool years, he stands a good chance of having a younger sibling, toward whom he feels jealousy, among other feelings; or he has formed a more complex relationship to an older sibling, who may feel jealousy toward the preschooler as the (pampered) "baby" of the family. Sibling relationships deserve attentive guidance. Toddlers, males as much as females, may be able to control their jealousy more easily if they are given a doll when a new baby arrives, to be *their* baby. Older siblings, even preschoolers, can be enlisted as special helpers to assist parents in care of the newborn infant, and be much praised for their efforts. Sibling jealousy is also reduced by tending to the parent–older sibling relationship. I know parents who keep a stock of treats handy, so that when friends and relatives visit with a gift for one child in the family, there is something to get out as a happy surprise for the sibling; and I know people who never take a gift for a newborn without taking gifts for the siblings.

Home for the preschooler is not quite like it was when he was infant and toddler. His mother may have gone back to work, leaving his daytime care to one or a patchwork of caretakers: sitters, grandparents or other relatives, or day-care staff. Many boys have a shifting schedule of care they must adjust to.

In the face of parental separation and divorce, boys are often more aggressive, competitive, and quarrelsome with their siblings—just when, I realize, parents are hoping that other family relationships might be as stable and benign as possible. Prior to the breakup, boys' behavior, particularly in situations where they are exposed to serious conflict over child-rearing or to domestic violence, is more impulsive and their self-control more unreliable than that of girls the same age.

The World on Screen

One companion often found in the preschooler's life is the television set, which is arguably the bearer of many of the worst messages about masculinity. The degree of incursion of television into the lives of preschoolers (and even of toddlers) is powerful and troubling. Social critics talk about it and write about it all the time, but I think household by household it's hard to grasp the power of the screen for shaping early values. There is scarcely a parent who doesn't worry about how peer pressure is going to pull children away from family standards in preadolescence and adolescence. Yet many of these parents have already lost their children to a comparable extent in preschool to the influence of television.

Nearly 25 percent of children in the United States, ages two to five, one study concluded, have *their own* television sets. Boys watch even more television than girls. One analyst of television and computers sees them as characteristic inventions of the male mind: quick-moving images, small bites, short on thoughtful commentary and explanation. Youngsters ages two to eleven watch an average of three to fours hour a day of television. Some of this is children's programming, but we know that they are watching, and deeply influenced by, much adult programming as well. One father mentioned to me that his eighteen-month-old son stays up very late; sometimes, to get some sleep themselves, he and his wife simply give him the remote control after midnight so he can watch whatever he chooses until he falls asleep.

The amount of realistic or cartoonish violence that most youngsters see on television is mind-boggling. Equally striking is the depiction of discipline in the guise of punishment: characters err and either get caught and punished (most of the time) or get away with it. Moral understanding is limited in these programs to the attempt to teach deterrence based on showing what the punishment will be if you're caught. It is unusual to find a dramatization produced for children in which perspectives are explored, feelings shared empathically, and rules carefully reasoned.

Television isn't going to go away. The task for parents is to think through how best to edit its content for their children and how to control its place in their lives. I have a few guidelines to suggest for preschoolers:

1. Use videocassettes as much as possible rather than regular programming. Most public libraries have cassettes to borrow. You can get descriptions and critics' appraisals and ratings reasonably easily. Cassettes do not usually contain consumer ads to appeal to your boys' desires. Most preschoolers are content to watch favorite cassettes many times, just as they are happy to hear the same bedtime stories read again and again. Preview the cassettes. Rent them from the video store before buying them. Some material intended for children contains powerful and objectionable messages that you'll want to see before they do, even stuff produced by such "family" icons as Disney!

2. Make it a practice to join your boy regularly for some of his television viewing. You can observe his reactions, and he can observe yours. You can discuss his opinions about the dramatizations, see what he understands and what he doesn't understand. Some of his observations will surely surprise you.

3. Minimize using television viewing as a reward for something else. ("If you put your toys away, you can watch television for a half-hour.") Television is attention-grabbing enough without treating it as though it were a treat even the parent considers something extra special.

4. Likewise, use it as a distracter of a fussy or bored preschooler as rarely as you can. The temptations are many, from the beginning

of the day when you might love to doze for a while but he is raring to go, until the end of his day when he is tired and irritable but there are still many things the adults of the household have to do before his bedtime.

5. Remind yourself regularly that television, more effectively than most other things a boy can occupy himself with, is produced with the intention of grabbing and holding his attention. It's easy to get hooked on it. It is your responsibility as a parent to work out a good balance between television and time for other activities.

Finding balance is a perfect metaphor for what this time in a boy's life is all about, both for him and for those around him. It's a time for both holding on and letting go; for strict supervision and free play; to run and tussle, and to be quiet; to know that home is safe and loving, but that the world around is a feast to enjoy; to learn that while the game has rules, the imagination has no limits.

8

SHARING

A clergyman friend of mine took over spiritual leadership of a congregation that had a longstanding custom for its children. All children younger than school age were asked to bring to church, on the Sunday before Christmas, already gift-wrapped, a favorite toy they had received the previous Christmas. These toys were presented by the children as an offering, piled up before the altar, and later distributed to needy children outside the congregation.

To my friend, there was something baffling about this custom. What was the point of taking a familiar, much-loved toy from one child and giving it to another child to whom it would seem used and secondhand, and with whose need the giver had no immediate contact? Any real generosity of it would escape both the giver and the receiver. (It was, however, one of those customs that develops a crust of sentimentality around it, so he had to bide his time before gradually shifting the annual offering to new presents, and beginning to arrange some direct contact between families who could afford generous Christmas presents and families who couldn't.)

What he noticed was that toddlers weren't much bothered by the little ceremony, but preschoolers, especially preschool boys, were frequently unhappy with it, participating obviously under a certain amount of duress. Occasionally one of them balked at the last minute, and having carried his favorite toy up to the altar, also carried it away in his tight little grip.

Preschoolers may not be ready to comprehend generosity as an abstract concept, or the meaning of a ritual of giving, but they do have experiences with *sharing*—or, as the case may be, refusing to share—especially toys or playthings: objects they have in their possession and someone else wants to play with. The toy that two playmates want at the same time may be one a preschooler owns, is particularly attached to, and would never share except reluctantly; but it might also be a toy from a day-care center playroom that two preschool boys want to enjoy at the same time. The great increase in the number of preschool boys spending their days in day-care centers means that all those boys are confronting sharing situations in groups outside the home as well as sharing with siblings and playmates at home.

Even for boys older than preschoolers, sharing may be better than generosity as a word for the aspect of character that concerns dividing up resources in some relation to need. Generosity is mostly about giving, and having the giving acknowledged; the benefit to the giver is the feeling of having done a good thing. Sharing is about giving *and* receiving, or dividing things up, in ways that are beneficial to everyone, and suited to the needs of the situation: Sometimes one is in the condition of being able to give, and sometimes one is in the condition of needing to receive, and often one is in a situation where one has something to give and needs something in return if an exchange is feasible.

Sharing and Parental Awareness

If his caregivers are selfish and egocentric, it's unlikely that a boy is going to share anything easily. A parent operating at Me First (Level One) doesn't provide a powerful model for sharing or considering the needs of others. A preschool boy functioning at Level One won't want to share a toy until he is tired of playing with it, and the very fact that a playmate wants to use it may be all it takes to reawaken his interest in the toy.

Follow the Rules (Level Two) can be a powerful spur to sharing, depending on the effectiveness of the rules on sharing honored in the household. In ancient Israel, for example, there were stringent rules for giving a portion of household income (the tithe) each year for such purposes as the relief of widows and orphans; and there were rules for the occasional forgiving of debts. We don't know how widely the rules were followed. But I think we can predict that such rules would be more widely honored in tight-knit families and communities where a failure to adhere to rules of sharing or generosity might subject a person to shame or dishonor, than in circumstances where a failure to share would at worst cause personal discomfort.

A secular equivalent today to the tithe in ancient Israel is the personal income tax in the United States. It is a rule that citizens must share some of their income each year for the good of all. But the rules are subject to loopholes, frequent underreporting of income or overreporting of exemptions, and much griping. Many adults, if they believe they can get away with it, falsify their tax reports because they don't want to share.

It was in the context of ancient Israel's rules that one visionary Jew, Jesus of Nazareth, told a story that has inspired many moral philosophers, and also artists such as Rembrandt, Prokoviev, and Balanchine. The younger of two brothers asks for his inheritance early (before his father dies), gets it, and travels to a foreign country where he lives very licentiously until the country falls into a recession and his money runs out. His plight becomes truly desperate. He decides to return to his old home and ask his father to hire him as a servant. His father is so happy the son has come back that he immediately throws a party and dresses the son in a fine suit.

The story of "The Prodigal Son" is so familiar in Western culture that no one is surprised by it. But Israelites hearing the story for the first time were surprised. As they heard the story unfold, they expected the father to say to his son, "You've been very foolish. You already got your share. There's no more I can do for you. Go away." The rules of the society would have endorsed the father's being very rejecting of his penitent son. That is precisely what the Prodigal Son's older brother would have liked the father to do. He comes in from his day's work to find a party in full swing and his wasteful brother the guest of honor. He immediately begins to whine to his father that he has always been a faithful son, but that the father has never thrown such a party for him and his friends.

"All that I have is yours," the father tells the older brother. It is true. The older brother will inherit all that the father still owns, and it is the lion's share, since at that time the oldest son always inherited by far the most at that time. In this and other stories and sayings, Jesus made it clear that he wasn't discarding the rules of ancient Israel, but that the rules weren't enough. If there were nothing besides rules operative in the situation from the standpoint of character, it was too easy to drift into the posture of the older brother: follow the rules, but otherwise me first.

Preschool boys can understand and follow rules of sharing, though probably not perfectly. I believe it's reasonable to select with them some things precious to them that they need never share unless they are inclined to, and parents and others caring for them at home will protect whatever possessiveness they display toward those items—negotiating with them over the rough patches when they first choose to share a prized toy with another child, and then impulsively want it back again. Other things can be designated as subject to agreed-upon rules of sharing with siblings or visiting playmates. One mother I know keeps a sharing box where the family, including her preschool boys, regularly put money and other gifts to be given to others.

Rules may be very helpful in causing a certain amount of sharing by the preschooler, but I don't think they will inspire sharing behavior as much as will his seeing the older members of the household be very sharing with each other, with others outside the household, and with him. Sharing is contagious behavior.

During my childhood, my father, even with two jobs, made barely enough income to pay for the essentials. By the time I was a preschooler, my parents were quarreling regularly about money; that is, my father frequently complained about what my mother spent. My mother had an old piano, on which she occasionally played Beethoven's "Für Elise." When I begged for piano lessons at age five, and a teacher told my mother I had enough talent to justify having a good instrument at home, she, without consulting my father, upgraded the old piano to a Steinway, signing a contract to pay for it in installments. My father was predictably furious, but after his outbursts he would eventually subside.

Looking back, I realize that my parents were playing out the normal middle-class division of labor of that time; a wife stayed home, took charge of the household, and raised the children while her husband earned a living for the household. When such a conventional marriage was not a true partnership—as was the case with my parents—it was easy for the breadwinner to slip into the resentment of thinking his wife was merely a consumer devouring his earnings, and an insatiable one at that. To me, as a preschooler and schoolboy, it often looked as though my mother was caring and giving, to the extent of her ability, and that my father was ungenerous toward her and his children.

In my high school years, when I was earning money playing gigs as a jazz pianist and giving it to my father to save for my college expenses, but also making the tuba my principal instrument, my renowned tuba teacher, William Bell of the New York Philharmonic, offered to sell me one of his favorite horns that he had already loaned me for three years—a Conn pitched in the key of C—for the giveaway price of two hundred dollars. My father refused to release any of my savings to buy the tuba; he said it was a foolish idea. I went off to college without my own instrument. Though I now have four tubas at home and have given several others from my collection to museums over the years, I yearn to this day for the one that belonged to a teacher with faith in me.

From our household's struggle over finances, I grew up determined to be generous toward others. Yet the legacy of my childhood experience is that I do sometimes find myself calculating the cost of being generous: What is it going to take out of me? When I'm really tired or upset or under pressure, one of the things I do is get very uptight about money. My childhood comes back to haunt me, to remind me of the tremendous long-term power, for better or for worse, in the parent-child relationship.

The character strengths we treasure and foster in ourselves are in dynamic tension inside us with their very opposites—generosity and stinginess, courage and timidity. Under stress we risk becoming the very opposite of what we most aspire to. In the first century, Paul of Asia Minor described this struggle: "The good which I want to do, I fail to do; but what I do is the wrong which is against my will." The qualities that we try to cultivate within ourselves do not come from a textbook or from "character education." Each one reflects a problem or challenge in our lives, against which we try to construct an inner strength to cope with it.

Sharing in a Competitive Society

The message many boys hear is: If you cannot compete for the symbols of success you are a failure. The material emblems of male accomplishment, from shiny cars to cool clothes to sexy women, rain from television screens and billboards. They are inescapable. Personal failure is equated with the possessions boys and their families *don't* have.

American children get on one of two trains when they are born, Cornell psychologist Urie Bronfenbrenner once argued. One train goes straight to heaven, and one goes straight to hell. A boy's family doesn't get to choose the train; their wealth, or poverty, makes the choice for them. Their means, or "social position," define where a son ends up, notwithstanding the libertarian ideal proclaimed in the Declaration of Independence. Only the rich, his analysis asserted, have a fair shot at life, liberty, and the pursuit of happiness.

There are precious few switching stations, Bronfenbrenner continued, like Project Headstart, or, later in life, college scholarships for disadvantaged minorities, that transfer kids from the train to hell to the train to heaven. The train windows are open; the kids on the poor train see what they're missing, all through childhood and later life.

His metaphor is pungent and memorable, if slightly overstated. American society actually has somewhat greater social mobility and opportunity for youngsters with pluck and brains than many other countries, although the Horatio Alger myth comes true all too seldom. A boy learns early that he lives in a world where competitiveness and acquisitiveness rule. As the saying that circulated a few years ago puts it: "Whoever has the most toys when he dies, wins." In this mindset, there is never enough. Someone else always has more, and therefore the chase goes on. The more successful one is, the more one is motivated to chase more. So there is often an inverse relationship between wealth and generosity or the inclination to share. Generosity, as those who have worked in the nonindustrial world tell us, is often easier to find among the less well off than among the well-to-do.

The great European social welfare experiments—in Sweden, Britain, and the Netherlands, among other countries—are declining in political favor just as the safety net constructed in the U.S. beginning in the 1930s has been substantially dismantled. Modern politicians assert, and the electorates appear to believe, that generous social policies sap a nation's vitality of commerce and the value of its currency. Dependency is demeaned; every penny of tax money committed to education, child care, or low-income housing must be justified six ways to Sunday.

For boys, the puzzle is: Why should I share if everyone else is so competitive and self-absorbed? For the preschooler in the church Christmas ritual, who is probably not familiar with the needs of the poor, a parent might decide that this boy, at this time, shouldn't be forced to part with a particularly precious plaything. The point of his participation in the ritual is to expose him to the concern felt by his community of faith for children who are less well off. To the extent that he understands that this is part of his family's spiritual or religious observance, the custom is meaningful. But he shouldn't have to participate until he gets, and accepts, the point of it; he can give when he's ready, and he probably will.

At the highest level of parental awareness—the perspective that identifies an unfolding, reciprocal parent-child relationship—parent and child can grow in social concern. Awareness of poverty, and of what one family can do to relieve it, can be woven into discussion and action. Parent and child can decide on joint ways of sharing that are different in quantity but proportional to what each has to give. The child sees that his willingness to share is commensurate with his parents' generosity. From this viewpoint, a boy can learn to give without feeling depleted within; he can grow into a man who, even as he succeeds, can feel compassion and responsibility for those whom the system deprives. Sharing at this level goes beyond ritualized observance to a more transcendent sense of shared humanity, the spiritual connection that religious ritual can but doesn't always promote.

The whole of Chapter 21 is devoted to *giving back:* ways to channel the energy and idealism of adolescent boys. But here I would like to underline the connection between generosity and parental care with one quote. Marion Pritchard, one of the Europeans who risked their very lives rescuing Jews from the Holocaust, said of her wartime activity:

> I think it was my parents' unusual way of child-rearing that provided the motivation for me to behave the way I did during the war. I was never punished and always encouraged to express my feelings, both the negative and the positive ones, in words. And when I asked questions I got answers. I was never told I was too young or anything like that. I was treated with respect and consideration from the time I was born.

Sharing Oneself

As much as we might want to inspire boys and the men they will become to share material possessions more freely, sharing the self in friendliness and acceptance of others is far more important. By the end of their preschool years, boys are already familiar with patterns of social inclusion and exclusion. These patterns are persistent and hard to change.

Vivian Paley, a teacher and author at the University of Chicago Laboratory Schools, is known for inventive storytelling in her classrooms. She felt inspired one year to try to do something about the harsh ways many of her kindergartners excluded others from play.

> By kindergarten, however, a structure begins to be revealed and will soon be carved in stone. Certain children will have the right to limit the social experience of their classmates. Henceforth a ruling class will notify others of their acceptability, and the outsiders learn to anticipate the sting of rejection. Long after hitting and name-calling have been outlawed by the teachers, a more damaging phenomenon is allowed to take root, spreading like a weed from grade to grade.

Paley posted a sign for her kindergarten class at the beginning of that year: You Can't Say You Can't Play. Only four—two boys and two girls—of the twenty-five classmates liked the idea; they were the four most often excluded from play by other children. Those who complained the loudest about the new rule were the kids who most often excluded others from their play activities. "But then what's the whole point of playing [if you can't decide who's in and who's out]?" one student asked. There was rather widespread agreement that the new rule was fair but unworkable. At a much later age they might have said it was contrary to human nature.

Not long after she posted You Can't Say You Can't Play and explained what it meant, Paley discovered a very shy girl, Clara, crying by the building blocks. Cynthia and Lisa had told her she couldn't help them build a block house for their puppies and that Clara wasn't their friend. The incident was discussed at the next regular discussion where the children and teacher sit together on a rug.

Angelo and Nelson quickly reported, after hearing Clara's story, that Ben wouldn't let them join a boys' game, and Ben tried to lay the responsibility off on Charlie, saying Charlie was the "boss" of the game.

Being told you can't play, Paley believes, is the most painful thing that happens to a child at school. Already in kindergarten the rejected children know who they are, often more accurately than their teachers know. Children frequently say rejecting things to each other that would be considered deeply offensive if said by an adult in a faculty meeting; but in the classroom many teachers are uncertain how to handle these exclusions between children.

When Paley found Clara crying, she took her over to Lisa and Cynthia. Cynthia said she was willing to let Clara into the game, but Lisa was adamant that they didn't need another person. Now Lisa was tearful herself during the discussion on the rug as she said, "But it was my game! . . . It's up to me! . . . Okay, I won't play then, ever!"

The impasse allowed Paley to raise the moral question whether it's fair in school, which is not a private place like a home, to keep another child out of play. Ben suggested that anyone who felt strongly enough to cry about it should be let into the game. Paley asked whether simply feeling sad couldn't be important enough. She also asked the children whether the teacher should make a group let an unwelcome child into a game. The majority cried, no, no.

Angelo pointed out that Lisa and Cynthia were inconsistent; sometimes they let Clara play, sometimes they didn't, which was unsettling. Charlie said if it was up to him, he'd let Clara play, but when Paley asked him whether he and his pal Ben always let others into their games, Charlie admitted, "Not if it's too special I might not." Ben complained that Nelson *always* wanted to join their games—in other words, a pest.

When Angelo proposed instituting the new rule—let anybody who asks play—Lisa retorted, "But then what's the whole point of playing? . . . I could play alone. Why can't Clara play alone?" And Angelo observed, "I think that's pretty sad. People that is alone they has water in their eyes."

When Paley later read to some fifth graders a transcript of the kindergartners' audiotaped discussion of Clara's rejection, they agreed philosophically with Angelo's proposal but admitted that in practice they were all more like Lisa. One boy reminded her that no one gets through life never being excluded. Better to learn it early, he suggested. Paley replied that the classroom might aspire to be nicer than the outside world. And she confessed to the fifth graders that what bothered her most was that the same few children are rejected year after year. "They are made to feel like strangers."

Changing the Mindset

Paley told the kindergartners that her next step would be to discuss the You Can't Say You Can't Play rule with the other teachers and then with the children in the higher grades, one through five. To the curious and receptive teachers, Paley said that dealing with rejection in the past had mostly taken the course of trying to make the excluded students feel better episode by episode; but she was proposing to change the mindset of the whole class so as to prevent the occurrence of so many exclusions in the first place.

In her discussions with the higher grades, Paley found different emphases year by year, but intensely emotional responses everywhere. The first graders, whom she had shepherded the previous year, remembered every kindergarten exclusion as though it had happened yesterday. She learned of painful episodes she was unaware of at the time they occurred. "That's like these guys, a lot of time they said I couldn't play," one first grade boy told her, "but then someone came they like better than me and they let him play." From the first graders, Paley brought back a number of questions: Can the person running the game assign undesirable roles to someone who wants to play even if the newcomer hates those roles? If the owner (initiator or leader) of the game says no to one person, can he say yes to another? If the owner says no, can another player in the game say yes? Can boys keep girls out of their games, and vice versa? Only this latter gender-based concern had not been touched on in the kindergartners' own discussions.

The second graders dove with familiarity into the topic when Paley gathered them on their rug. "'That's like my big brother,' a boy says. 'I ask can I play and he always says no and my mom tells us work it out.'" The role of the boss of the game—usually the person who initiates it, sometimes a person who later takes charge of it—dominates the second graders' discussion. There is a hint that the boss can take responsibility for exclusions that others agree with but for which they don't want to be identified as responsible. They agree that open voting on admitting another person to the game works generally in favor of the asker, but they prefer the boss system. The verdict of the second grade is that You Can't Say You Can't Play should be applied to kindergartners but not to second graders. "Let's not have bosses until we're in second grade," suggests one of them.

When Paley gathered the third graders, they immediately and openly identified an overweight girl in their midst as someone almost everyone excluded from playground games; soon a boy identified himself as the male who was most frequently excluded. The frankness of their reporting took Paley aback. But the candor was short-lived. Fourth and fifth graders talked about the way "people" acted or "boys" acted instead of identifying the classmates who were most often excluded.

One third-grade girl was praised as someone who was nice to everyone, so Paley asked her if the rule You Can't Say You Can't Play would work in the school. "'Maybe,' she answers slowly. 'Only maybe. If they get to know each other better.'" The boy who had been most excluded added that the rule would work "if we could get along." The third graders were of the opinion that forcing the issue of inclusion would be counterproductive, which led Paley to ponder: "But why, I wonder. A no-hitting rule doesn't produce more hitting. The children themselves enforce the rule. Even popular children can't get away with hitting."

One thing I noticed in Paley's reports of her visits to the classes was that girls set much of the tone of the discussion. Boys seemed more to react to points girls had put into play. It was an example of a gender difference I mentioned earlier, that mothers foster relational interest and skills in daughters more than in sons. (These relational skills, of course, can be put in the service of exclusion as well as of inclusion.)

When Paley proposed her new rule to the fourth graders, the girls were certain that they were the transgressors who inspired the plan; they said they were meaner to each other than boys were to other boys, that girls were meaner even to their friends than boys were to classmates who weren't their friends. The most excluded boys didn't agree with the girls' assessment; boys, they said, can be every bit as mean as girls.

The fourth graders said it was too late to reform them. "'They (the kindergartners) trust you. They'll do what you say. It's too late to give *us* a new rule.' 'She's right,' a boy says. 'If you want a rule like that to work, start at a very early age. Even nursery school. My little sister could do it.'"

The fifth graders saw more hope for the success of the new rule than any of the other grades. For one student it was as simple as taking on a new habit. "Like buckling your seat belt . . . My parents never made a big thing of that when my big brother was little so he argues about it, but me and my little brother do it before we think about it." When the fifth graders recollect their play experiences all the way back to kindergarten, none of them mentions an incident in which he was the excluder; all that is re- called are the times of being excluded.

A curly-haired fifth-grade boy asks Paley if she invented the new rule herself.

> Well, no, I didn't make it up, only the words themselves. The idea is very old, as old as the civilized world. You'll find it in the Bible: 'The stranger that so- journeth with you shall be unto you as the homeborn among you.' . . . You see, lately, I've come to understand that although we all begin school as strangers, some children never learn to feel at home, to feel they really be- long. They are not made welcome enough.

The rule of hospitality Paley was quoting comes from the book of Leviti- cus in the Torah or Old Testament.

Mutuality

The open and democratic method Paley has used to implement her rule is as important as the rule itself. You Can't Say You Can't Play was under discussion for weeks before Paley announced that it was in effect. When she did make her announcement, she said that she realized she had to change *her own* behavior to conform to the rule. The kindergartners were startled to hear this. What, Paley asked her class, do I do when Karl won't put his blocks neatly away? You tell him he can't play with them again until he does, they respond. "Right . . . However, if you can't say you can't play, then even I mustn't tell Karl not to play." The five-year-olds are curious to see what other method their teacher will use to persuade Karl to put the blocks away.

Acceptance of the new rule was astonishingly quick among kindergartners. There were only minor exclusionary mishaps during the first week, each resolved quickly by a student's reminder or by asking a teacher for assistance. One of the four children who had suffered frequent exclusion in the past and now enjoyed open inclusion couldn't resist the temptation to hand out a few exclusions himself.

The mishaps raised the question of what penalty should follow an act of exclusion. Paley told them all that You Can't Say You Can't Play is not the kind of rule for which there is any penalty. What happens is that a violation of the rule creates a situation that has to be remedied by discussion and reacceptance of the rule before life can go on as usual. This approach makes use of what teachers call a "teachable moment."

Paley writes that acceptance of the new rule gave her the same sense of relief she felt in a previous year when she gave up the time-out chair. "It [consignment to the chair] made children sad and lonely to be removed from the group, which in turn made me feel inadequate and mean and— I am convinced—made everyone feel tentative and unsafe." She sees the rule of inclusive play as a "ladder out of a trap." Thinking about the children who long for the previous status quo, Paley sees that what they most covet and have lost is being the "owner" of the game who can include or exclude at will. It is possessiveness that is the greatest enemy of inclusion.

At the end of the year, Paley thought to herself that she would miss the excitement of working through the new rule when the children returned for a new year with the rule already in place. "However, the concept of open access, I suspect, can never be taken for granted, but must in fact be rediscovered each year by each new group. 'You can't say you can't play' is apparently not as natural a law as, for example, 'I say you can't play.'"

Rules and Fairness

An elementary school principal from the Boston area talked to me about how to establish and administer rules in general. "I think," Carol Schraft said, "it needs to be very clear in advance what the rules are, and what the consequences of breaking the rules are. Then you are set to deal with problems as they arise, and everything is not a crisis. Everyone needs to know the rules and consequences: teachers, students, parents. Then you have to enforce the consequences in an even-handed way.

"Of course, fairness is in the eye of the beholder. The child's version of the event is usually not exactly the same as an adult's, and Child A may have quite a different view from Child B. Where kids run into difficulty in developing a sense of values is that parents frequently align themselves with their child's point of view; they come to school simply to be a more articulate version of the child. They think that's what support is. Frequently parents come in and say that their child does not do such things at home. I take such assertions at face value. But I do reply that children act differently in different places; they may not have done this kind of misdeed at home, but they have undeniably done it at school.

"An example that comes to mind is a boy who was suspended from school for erasing another student's computer files. In general we're having a difficult time with computer ethics. Kids have a hard time understanding that messing around with stored files in a computer is the same thing as going into a kid's locker and burning his notebooks. We have e-mail accounts for each of the kids, and we store their material on a server, not on disks. Some kids casually give their access codes to others, and then they're vulnerable to having their files invaded without specific permission. But there are hackers who try to penetrate the code without anyone's permission or cooperation. Once or twice a year we have an incident.

"When this boy's parents came back with him, as is required, before readmittance, they proudly said that during the day of the suspension he refused to do any homework because he was making a moral stand. I said, 'I don't really understand. How does this line up with Martin Luther King or Gandhi? What is the moral stand here?' He was being stubborn, and they were allowing him. They completely bought into his way of thinking. On the other side of the equation, it is very difficult for many kids to understand what the bystander role is. They get very conflicted about standing up for the rules of adults against their peers, because many of the kids who get into trouble are pretty powerful kids within the peer group.

"Often, students are great when it comes to abstract principles of behavior, but they can't make the connection between the principles and their behavior. The application is a huge leap for kids. That's why I'm not big on these prepackaged moral development kits. You have to use a 'teachable moment' strategy. When we have a case of computer hacking, we stop the classes and have discussion in all the classrooms based on a specific incident and a kid they all know."

Take-home Lessons

How do parents treat reluctance to share things or to include others in group play at home? It is more common, I think, for parents to decide what is best in the situation and to tell the children to abide by their decisions than it is for teachers to make such decisions, especially in play situations. Otherwise, parents often use the same methods relied on by teachers. They try to persuade the excluder to change his mind. They try to distract the excluded child with other playmates and activities. They negotiate time-sharing arrangements for sought-after toys. Sometimes they say that the children will just have to work it out—which is often a way of saying don't bother *me* with it. And sometimes they criticize the excluded child—"Don't be a crybaby"—for expressing his hurt.

Several studies of parental methods have demonstrated that when sharing is the issue, the way the parent deals with the child is critically important. Physical punishment, withdrawal of privileges, or threats have the wrong effect on a boy; they lead to lack of consideration for others, stinginess, and self-centered values.

Refusal to share is often assumed to be a problem mainly for toddlers and preschoolers as they warm up to their first experiences playing with other children. But I know a ten-year-old boy, an only child, who won't share his computer games when his friends come over to play—he'll let them *watch* him but won't let them take over the controls. And I know an eleven-year-old girl who likes to play with dolls, but friends coming to play have to bring their own dolls with them: She won't share hers.

In many homes and in every school there are children who are very secure, friendly to everybody, and everybody is friendly to them. They aren't excluded by other children, and they do not practice exclusion of others. It's not as though living models don't exist. But even their peers seem often to view these children as models beyond emulation. Too good to be true.

The nurturing of generosity has to take temperament into account. A naturally shy and cautious boy, for example, has to exert more effort to reach out generously to others than another boy who is temperamentally outgoing.

Families can do things together that change a boy's perspective without making a lecture out of it. An eleven-year-old boy I met recalled the difference in perspective he acquired when his parents took a year off to work for Habitat for Humanity in Georgia. From classrooms where he was accustomed to having one or two black kids in the mix, Brady spent a year in a classroom where he was the only white kid. "I think my parents brought me there for two reasons," he said to me. "They wanted to work for Habitat for Humanity and they thought the move would affect me and my younger brother and give us a different view of the world. I personally would go back there. I think I am a totally different person after going." "Do you look back on the experience?" I asked. "Yeah, I look through the photo album. I think your brain grows in different ways. Going on that trip made my brain take a U-turn."

9

CURIOSITY

A four-year-old boy I know woke his mother up at five o'clock in the morning to ask her why airplanes have wings. Maybe at breakfast she would have been able to say something about aerodynamics that satisfied Adam, but shortly before dawn it was out of the question. Many four-year-olds ask several questions a day that merit a call to the reference department at the nearest university library. Their curiosity can be as staggering in its directness as it is difficult to satisfy: Where did Grandpa go when he died? Where do babies come from? What is behind the mirror? Why do airplanes have wings? Their curiosity extends to time as well as space, and will surely include that most predictable of all childhood questions: When are we going to get there?

We speak of "natural curiosity" because most children exhibit it in the first few weeks of life. Within months it is insatiable. Perhaps it can be seen as a kind of hunger. It is unimaginable to think of someone as having a love of life who is without lively curiosity.

Boys' curiosity begins with experience of their own bodies, and then stretches out to whatever they encounter—at first a mother, then the household and the many objects in each home with which they come in contact. Eventually curiosity reaches to the world outside their homes. T. Berry Brazelton and Marshall Klaus are among those who have studied the extensive built-in capabilities that infants possess at birth. As they root about toward the nipple, or quickly learn to identify their mother's voice, or lightly grip a finger pressed against their tiny palms, newborns show that their senses are already alert. All of their senses, linked to a developing mind, constitute the machinery of curiosity.

Curiosity and Play in the Animal Kingdom

The literature on child development is surprisingly light on discussions of curiosity—why we have it, how we develop it, when we might lose it. Most of the general reviews of the stages of childhood I consulted didn't refer to curiosity in their indexes. But I did find that ethologists—scientists who study animal behavior—treat curiosity as a subject of lively interest. They have watched many species to evaluate their levels of curiosity and their modes of expressing it.

When a new object is placed in a room inhabited by rats, one ethologist found, all the rats will explore it in short order. They approach the object cautiously but repeatedly. As they overcome their hesitation, they sniff and lick the object, maybe bite or scratch it, and often climb on it and urinate on it to mark it as part of their territory. If the object is portable, they may move it.

Primates and carnivores exhibit more curiosity than rodents, and among the rodents, porcupines are more curious than mice, with squirrels falling somewhere between the two. Some fish and birds also exhibit curiosity. There appears to be a biological drive to learn, that some ethologists refer to as a "curiosity drive." Sometimes the drive seems to operate independently of any other practical motivation. For example, rhesus monkeys in one study learned a puzzle game without being offered any other reward such as food.

This drive, or innate appetite, to learn seems to underlie the animal activity we call "play" as well as activity related to the satisfaction of basic needs. Play is not the easiest thing to define, as can be shown by asking whether a professional football player taking part in a game on Sunday afternoon is more playing a game or just doing his job.

Animal play, notably fake fights and chases, is often a burlesque of more serious activity. In their play, young mammals are practicing patterns of behavior they later will pursue seriously. Role reversals occur with lightning speed. One squirrel may chase another for several seconds; then, without any signal that a human can catch, the chaser becomes the chased.

Ethologists report with glee watching an animal experience something accidentally, and then playfully practice it again and again both for the pleasure of it and to get better at it. Eibl-Eibesfeldt described a young badger that discovered by happenstance how to turn a forward somersault, then practiced the technique until he was able to roll down a long hill in one continuous series. On another occasion, the badger slipped and slid on an icy road, after which he tirelessly practiced sliding until he perfected his technique. His curiosity led to new learning that stimulated practice until he had mastered the new movement.

Human Curiosity

When I began writing Chapter 3, my grandson Noah had just been born. He has been growing as I've continued writing. At his first birthday party recently, I watched his ebullient display of curiosity. He put his hands onto or into everything he could reach, exploring shapes and textures—into every glass, every bowl, every open mouth of a person holding him. If an object he grabbed was not too large, he tried to put it into his mouth, because he uses his tongue to taste but also to explore textures the way his fingers do. As a year-old toddler, he has a more curious mouth than most adults.

Noah showed the same way of approaching new things Eibl-Eibesfeldt observed in other mammals; approach, make connection, withdraw, approach again, perhaps from a new perspective. Noah would put his hand into something, feel around, take his hand out, put his hand in again. He put objects into his mouth, tasted them, took them out, looked at them, put them in his mouth again or switched them to his other hand.

I watched Noah interact with his mother, Mary Helen, as he pursued his new career as toddler. He would venture out by himself to investigate something, toddle back for a reassuring hug, then launch out again in a rhythm of exploration, withdrawal, re-exploration. She says he is on a quest to explore new things from the time he awakes in the morning. There appears to be a degree of randomness about the direction in which he explores, but he clearly makes choices as he goes along about what interests him; sometimes he takes a fancy to an object his parents don't want him to play with, and it can be difficult to distract him with an alternative. His curiosity is already affected by his relationship with his parents and other caregivers, by what kinds of curious explorations they encourage and what they discourage.

Some toddlers Noah's age are more placid than he, more content to let things come to them than to go out searching for them. But their curiosity may be no less active than his. I remember another infant in our extended family who was often content to sit in her infant seat and watch. Her eyes took in everything. She didn't need to go and touch in order to learn a great deal about her environment.

When Carolyn, Noah's grandmother, held him on her lap at a piano and played four notes in a scale, Noah pulled her hand away from the keys and tried to sing the scale. He is as curious with his ears as with his eyes. He is only just beginning to say a few intelligible one-syllable words, but I noticed that when someone spoke very exaggerated baby talk to him, he intuitively understood the humor of it, and laughed delightedly at the nonsense sounds. These details from his birthday party reminded me how important it is not to ignore any of the senses when considering how a boy exercises curiosity.

Many aspects of human curiosity distinguish us from other mammals. One is that we have the capacity, if we cherish it and if the practicalities of life do not overburden us, to remain curious and playful throughout our lifetimes. I can, at a grandfatherly age, enjoy playing with Noah as much as he enjoys playing with me.

A second difference is that we can pursue our curiosity with a degree of indirection that is beyond the capacity of other mammals. This book is an example. I am writing about raising boys because the subject interests me. I am curious about it, and curious readers will take up the book. We don't have to meet in a public square to share our thoughts. I can write mine in a book and others can read and reflect, agree and disagree. But other mammals have to express their curiosity in direct physical engagement with whatever in their environments fires their curiosity.

Yet another difference is the range of our curiosity. Other mammals display a degree of curiosity about both their own and the different species they encounter, but their curiosity is weak compared to human curiosity.

Still another difference lies in the profound significance of mood and outlook in human behavior. There is a rather large industry devoted to techniques for keeping people's spirits up, their hopes alive. Nurturing curiosity can in itself contribute to the strength of hopefulness. So long as we feel impelled to learn more, to experience more, we cannot be without hope. The kind of curiosity Noah exhibits is the kind we need to treasure as much and as long as we can. Noah seeks out the excitement of the new as well as the humorous absurdity of the present; keeping both these urges alive is an antidote to cynicism and despair.

Scientists and philosophers are driven by curiosity about the phenomena they are trying to understand. Artists of many kinds assert that curiosity about their environment motivates their creativity. As Jonathan Lear, a philosopher interested in curiosity—he calls it being open-minded—puts it, we do designate certain occupations for which curiosity is less important than it is in philosophy: "We do not want our dentists, for example, to be too creative in their activity. We want there to be a relatively fixed set of norms of dental hygiene, and we want our dentists to adhere to those norms rigidly, over and over again." Well, yes, except that each mouth is different and presents its own challenges. A dentist's curiosity might lead to the invention of a technique that is less painful than the existing state-of-the-art technology.

Protecting Curiosity

Selma Fraiberg wrote about one boy who made his sense of curiosity work for him in spite of his many fears about his environment; E. J. Anthony paraphrased her analysis as follows:

> Tony was a small boy with generalized fears of the strange, the unfamiliar, and the unknown. His approach to dealing with this was mainly an inves-

tigative one. 'If he could find out how something worked, if he could locate the causes for events, he felt himself in control and lost his fear.' His favorite toy at the age of 2 was a pocket-sized screwdriver that he carried with him everywhere and with which he managed to unhinge doors, tables, and chairs. Since he was afraid, like many small children, of the vacuum cleaner, he took it to pieces to find where the frightening noise came from. With his handy instrument, he imperiled himself by removing plates from wall outlets, and when his parents put a stop to this research, he was furious. Warnings only served to increase his need to locate the source of danger and to find out 'why.' As he grew older, he not only wanted to take dangerous things to pieces, but also to reassemble them and make them work again. At the age of 4, he had an emergency appendectomy, which was a frightening experience. Relatives brought him toys, but what he wanted and asked for was 'an old alarm clock that doesn't work,' and he occupied himself during his convalescence repairing it. In working through the psychologically traumatic experience of the surgical operation for which he was unprepared, he took apart the alarm clock and made it work again, just as the doctor took him apart and made him work again. 'In this way he employed a well-established sublimation, mechanical investigation and construction, to overcome a frightening experience.' Yet the anxiety provided a powerful motive 'to fix something' so that the little boy could go beyond his age-appropriate capacities and accomplish something that had not been possible before. During latency, he continued his scientific interests in the basement, inventing new projects. Small explosions unsettled the family from time to time. There was never any question, at this point, that he would grow up to become a scientist, and eventually he became a physicist.

Between the natural curiosity of the infant and the more practiced curiosity of the adult, there are many years in which a boy's curiosity is going to be greatly affected by the adults responsible for his care. If he is shy or temperamentally inclined to reject new experiences and ideas, will those adults patiently draw out his curiosity and reassure him of his capacity to approach new things? If a boy is naturally and zestfully curious, will the adults around him encourage or squelch his interests? Will they find that essential balance between encouraging curiosity and maintaining safety and necessary order? (Will they, to make a metaphor of Tony's childhood, keep the small explosions in the basement reasonably safe?)

Growing up can be seen, in one of its many aspects, as a process of squelching curiosity. The two-year-old boy whom I mentioned in Chapter 6 on discipline, eager to get out on the front porch where the dangerous stone steps lurked, was spanked on his diapered behind and told not to be curious about what was outside the front door. The four-year-old who asked about airplanes at five o'clock in the morning wasn't told to "stop bothering me" because he has a sensitive mother eager to cultivate his curiosity, but many mothers and fathers might have said that; his mother promised to discuss his question a little later in the morning.

When a toddler gets to school age, he will find that his teachers want him to learn some things he isn't personally curious about at all, and they will be comparatively uninterested in some things that he is immensely curious about. A considerable degree of free curiosity has to be reined in to accommodate programmed learning that may often seem frustrating or boring rather than wonderful.

A mother recently told me about an experience her three-year-old son had at a preschool she chose partly for its diverse group of kids. Her son was playing with another boy on a rug, building towers with blocks. At the end of the play period, the boys were to put the blocks away and roll up the rug. The boys did that. Instead of rolling the rug together in one direction, they rolled it from two opposite sides until they met in the center. With a sense of discovery, they carried the rug to the teacher to tell her that what they had done looked like two rugs but was in fact just one rug. The teacher looked at the rug, frowned, and told them they'd done it wrong, to go back and "do it right." One of the pleasures of curiosity is to diverge from the usual path, use toys in "wrong ways," make up new uses. Curiosity here is very much like what we mean when we speak of imagination.

Curiosity, I believe, is discouraged far more often in a series of little incidents like the rug-rolling than in dramatic episodes that might be long remembered by a boy. The squelching of curiosity is far more common for the schoolboy than for the toddler, perhaps, but the reason I choose to discuss it in relation to a very young age group is so that parents and other adults can become aware of the potential of diminishing this wonderful attribute of a boy's life—and then, ideally, resist squelching it throughout a boy's path to adulthood.

Encouraging Curiosity

In many instances, encouraging curiosity requires nothing more than providing opportunities to explore. A boy's appetite to learn will do the rest. Some games or activities may exist in boy's minds as innate dispositions. For example, boys during their school years like to build tree houses or other structures of their own in secluded places where they may playfully invent their own secret societies. When they have an opportunity to go to the country for vacations, city boys who have never seen other people doing this sometimes begin to build tree houses or other shelters for play.

But sometimes curiosity needs a little guidance lest a boy become discouraged and abandon an activity before he has persevered enough to have his curiosity rewarded. The mother of a three-year-old told me he refused to do puzzles for a period of time. They were more frustrating than fun for him. Charles Snow gives this example, which he adapted from the research of Laura Berk, of how a mother helps her two-and-a-half-year-old child put a puzzle together:

Child: *Oh, now where's this one go?* (Picks up a blue piece and looks at the form board.)
Mother: *Which piece might go here?* (Points to the bottom of the puzzle.)
Child: *His hat?* (Picks up another piece, but tries the wrong one.)
Mother: *See if you can find a piece that looks like this shape.* (Points to the bottom of the puzzle again.)
Child: *The red one!* (Tries it, but can't quite get it to fit.)
Mother: *Try turning it just a little more this way.* (Gestures to show her.)
Child: *There, it fits!* (Picks up another piece and says:) *Now this green one should fit. Oh, I need to turn it just a little! Look, Mom, this fits, too!*

Educators speak of this kind of adult assistance as "scaffolding." The adult is trying to provide just enough assistance to keep the child from getting discouraged, but leaving as much responsibility as possible in the hands of the child. The key to good scaffolding is to wait until the child is about to give up, then help just enough to keep the exploration going. The Russian theorist, L. S. Vygotsky, a contemporary of Piaget, was the pioneer of the concept that adults can encourage children's learning by presenting them with materials that are a little beyond their easy mastery—for example, stories with more advanced vocabulary than the listeners have mastered yet. He called it the "zone of proximal development."

I've talked with parents who incorporate this principle into selections of books and toys and outings for their children, but they are aware that there is a balance to be struck. If the level of knowledge assumed by the experience is too high, the child will withdraw. What sparks a child's curiosity one day may seem too daunting the next. No parent is going to find the best—that is, acceptably challenging—level for a child all the time.

Maria Montessori once wrote that children themselves give clues about what is the right amount of help to offer. "They do not help one another as we do. If a child is carrying something heavy, none of the others runs to his aid. They respect one another's efforts, and give help only when it is necessary. This is very illuminating, because it means they respect intuitively the essential need of childhood, which is not to be helped unnecessarily."

Restraining Curiosity

I'm not advocating the encouragement of unfettered boyish curiosity. Boys may be curious about a huge number of things from which they need to be protected: untended swimming pools, violent or sexually explicit programs on television, railroad tracks, and electrical plugs, to name a few. The adults in their lives have to set certain limits for them, thus helping them strike a balance between curiosity and prudence or responsibility.

"Morality," Adam Phillips wrote in *The Beast in the Nursery*, "is the way we set limits to wanting; the way we redescribe wanting so that it seems to work for us." Put this way, morality stresses the negative—setting limits to curiosity as well as desire. But Phillips also quotes a phrase from Henry Sidgwick, a well-known writer on ethics, about "the moral ideal being presented as attractive rather than imperative." This phrase appeals greatly to me. The more adults can express morality as something attractive one might be drawn to, and avoid the imperative, which is bound to be couched as a "no" at least as often as it is a "yes," the more often a boy is going to say "yes" freely and willingly.

One area of children's curiosity that often perplexes adults as to what is appropriate concerns boys' interest in bodies, bodily functions, and gender differences. Enlightened adults today know what *not* to do about a child's masturbation or sex play—not to act in such a way as to threaten or shame the child. But where is the balance to be struck between overreacting and inappropriately ignoring behavior?

Selma Fraiberg offers a story from her experience counseling parents. The mother of a six-year-old boy overheard her son invite a girl he often played with to go up to his room. The invitation made the mother uncomfortable because she knew that her son had recently been sent home with a stern warning after the girl's mother found the two children playing toilet games in the backyard. After a brief interval, the boy's mother went upstairs and approached the closed bedroom door. She wasn't quite sure whether it was her right to intrude. Summoning her courage, she knocked on the door and asked permission to enter. The reply was inaudible to her, but she went in. The two children exhibited remarkable poise in view of the fact that they both were partly undressed. The mother fumbled for something to say—something clearly not an overreaction. "Don't you children feel chilly?" she asked. Still unflustered, "No," they replied. The mother later learned from her son that he was relieved that she knew about his interest in female bodies and that she wasn't condemning his interest as shameful or bad. But, as Fraiberg commented, it should have been possible for the mother to quietly suggest that they get dressed and play another game. Later she could let her son know that his curiosity about how differently boys and girls were made was natural, but that a better way to understand the differences was to ask his parents questions.

Deciding whether a specific instance of sexual curiosity is appropriate or inappropriate, Fraiberg commented, requires knowing what is typical of the stage of development the child is in.

> If a three-year-old boy in nursery school finds it fascinating to observe how little girls urinate, we would consider this a normal expression of interest in sexual differences; that is, *normal for his age.*. . . Normally, this type of interest subsides so that in school-age youngsters it will take the form of some giggling and joking about toilet functions, but a diminished interest in direct observation. But suppose our three year old cannot give up his fascination with looking and at the age of eight creates a problem in his summer camp by his insistent and repetitious peeking into the girls' lavatories. We would no longer consider this activity appropriate for his age. . . . The camp staff would be correct in not allowing this behavior, in placing realistic limits as kindly and firmly as possible.

Similar questions arise with respect to the wisdom of letting young children see their parents or other adults nude. Boys are quite open in their curiosity about how grown-ups are made. Girls, too. Fraiberg writes of one father who said his four-year-old daughter repeatedly asked to visit her father in the bathroom, and asked to touch his penis. His wife thought it best to let the little girl satisfy her curiosity. But the father said he found it embarrassing. He was both surprised and relieved when Fraiberg said she didn't think it was necessary to satisfy his daughter's curiosity as she requested. Direct observations, she suggested, do not really satisfy the child's curiosity because the curiosity is about how such a body feels and works, not just how it looks. Looking without understanding may secretly excite the child in a way the child doesn't understand and make him feel secretly ashamed.

Elsewhere, Fraiberg reminds us that young children out of curiosity often develop their own theories about something before they ask questions or ask to see something. The wise parent tries to ascertain, through gentle and friendly questioning, what the child understands—or, often, misunderstands—before venturing an explanation. And the wise parent answers only what the child is asking, confident that when the child has digested that much he will return to ask more about the same subject.

Writing about forty years ago, Fraiberg exhibited a sensitively balanced viewpoint of her time. Today, we would perhaps approach a boy's curiosity about bodies slightly differently. His curiosity, we might find, is no more than a wish to see in general what bodies of different genders and ages look like. To satisfy such curiosity, we have available a variety of books, videos, and museum exhibits that didn't exist in the 1950s.

Must Curiosity Wane?

Robert Sapolsky, a neurobiologist, once wrote a fascinating piece in the *New Yorker* prompted by the behavior of a lab administrative assistant he had hired straight out of college. To Sapolsky's irritation, the assistant played different music every day as he worked. He would go from folk music to classical to jazz to rock to swing. He appeared to be spending his income from his first post-college job giving himself a crash course in music history. He didn't like all of what he listened to—some of the music he confessed to hating. But he loved the exploration. His reading list went from Melville to Chaucer to contemporary realists. When he first took the job, the assistant had long hair and a beard, but one day he appeared with a shaven head; he said he wanted to see if people would interact differently with him if he were bald. His open-mindedness was unsettling to his new boss.

What the lab assistant did was make Sapolsky aware how much he himself had settled into narrow interests, favoring the familiar. Why does that happen, he wondered. Not finding anything helpful in the literature, he decided to do some quick research to see whether our mental windows close at certain ages. "As a CD of Wagner highlights played on ukulele boomed outside my office, I decided to try to figure out when we form our musical tastes, and when we stop being open to most new music."

Sapolsky and his research assistants canvassed radio stations that specialize in broadcasting popular music from different decades, and related the age of the musical style to the average age of listeners. He concluded that most people select the style of popular music they will prefer for the rest of their lives before their twenty-first birthdays; and if a person is older than thirty-five when a new form of popular music is introduced, there is a greater than 95 percent chance the person will never choose to listen to it.

Next, Sapolsky looked into curiosity about new kinds of food, taking as his index the introduction of Japanese sushi to some Midwestern cities. The typical Midwestern patron of sushi was younger than twenty-eight when the first sushi bar arrived in town; and if a resident of any of those cities was thirty-nine or older when sushi arrived, there was a greater than 95 percent chance the resident would never try it.

Even great minds slow in their creativity as they age, Sapolsky notes, and they resist new ideas or even the further application of their own; he cites

Einstein's resistance to quantum mechanics and recalls the physicist Max Planck's observation that established generations of scientists don't accept new theories: they die first. "There's a consistent trend emerging here. As we age, all of us—the senior scientist flailing against his errant disciples, the commuter twiddling with the radio dial for a familiar tune—become less open to someone else's novelty."

Does it really matter whether we lose our curiosity, Sapolsky asks. And he answers: "When I see the finest of my students ready to run off to the Peace Corps and minister to lepers in the Congo—or teach some kid in the barrio just outside the university how to read—I remember that, once, it was easier to be that way. An open mind is a prerequisite to an open heart." Exactly!

The waning of curiosity doesn't seem fated to me. In fact, it is the kind of phenomenon that should respond positively to heightened awareness of its threat to our enjoyment of life and our creativity.

Toddlers have enormous fun with their newly mobile curiosity. I believe they feel something of the tingling sensation of risk-taking when they set off to explore space and people new to them; and I believe they feel the thrill of new knowledge. Their exuberance when their curiosity is in high gear is completely infectious to anyone open to enjoying their mood. They are delighted with every novelty or absurdity they encounter.

Nothing about parenting is more fun than joining boys in their explorations. A parent doesn't always have to be the guide. Youngsters are happy to have coexplorers as the curiosity of the child and of the parent feed off each other.

We know that we aren't fated—as badgers may be fated—to have curiosity evaporate in the face of adult responsibility. We can recommend curiosity as a lifetime guide. C. P. Cavafy's poem "Ithaka," inspired by Homer's characterization of Odysseus, suggests that curiosity above all can lead us past fears and real threats to a life that one could look back on, at the end, without regret. It is the journey, not the destination, that we should pay most attention to:

> As you set out for Ithaka
> hope the voyage is a long one,
> full of adventure, full of discovery.
> Laistrygonians and Cyclops,
> angry Poseidon—don't be afraid of them:
> you'll never find things like that on your way
> as long as you keep your thoughts raised high,
> as long as a rare excitement
> stirs your spirit and your body.

10

SCHOOLBOYS

A large majority of schoolboys look up at a number of taller kids in their classes—who happen to be girls. Physical growth is less rapid during the elementary school years than it was from infancy through preschool years, and than it will be during puberty. Both boys and girls grow in spurts, but the girls' spurts on average precede the boys' by about six months.

Boys, from ages six to twelve, have on average only a small amount more muscle mass than girls of the same ages; and girls have better balance and precision in movement. Why, then, do most schoolboys kick and throw footballs, dribble basketballs, and bat baseballs more expertly than girls? Because boys are given the equipment and encouraged to master these sports as part of being boys, while girls are given the jump ropes and jacks that promote balance and finely tuned motor skills. As overdue attention has been paid in the 1990s to schoolgirl sports that match boys' sports, girls have begun to close the average performance gap with boys in one sport after another.

Height and Weight

Both heredity and environment affect the height and other physical attributes of a boy. The height attained by a boy is the result of interplay between growth hormones secreted by his pituitary gland, and the receptivity of the growth plates in the long bones of his legs and arms. The growth plates eventually close, so it is important that hormones are released to stimulate growth at the opportune period. Boys lacking natural growth hormones and not administered synthetic hormones at the appropriate time would reach a height of only about four feet four inches.

Diet certainly plays a part in the physical development of a boy's body. Where food is abundant, and illness relatively controlled, as in industrial countries, boys grow bigger; where hunger and illness are prevalent, boys are smaller. On average, shorter children are found in Asia, South America, and parts of Africa. Taller boys are found in Australia, northern and central Europe, and the United States.

Boys can grow wider and heavier as well as taller. In our society, being overweight may consign a boy to stigmatized isolation. Obesity in the school years is associated with low self-esteem, depression, and behavioral problems. Many boys come to feel personally responsible, guilty and ashamed, for the physical build dealt them in part by a genetic hand. Their families may reinforce this shame through demeaning comments or punishment. Overeating and sadness can compound each other. An overweight boy may be mercilessly teased or ostracized. Unhappy, he consoles himself by eating more than he needs. An obese boy is more likely to drop out of school early. Less educated, he earns lower average income as an adult. With excess weight, moreover, comes vulnerability to chronic health problems.

Childhood obesity is often part of a larger family disturbance. The most effective interventions focus on changing family patterns of eating, exercise, and parent-child interactions. When overweight boys do lose pounds, they tend to avoid regaining them more effectively than do adults who have deliberately lost weight. Therefore, the earlier obesity is treated, the better the prognosis.

I have personal familiarity with this subject. My genes dealt me a stocky frame. As a child, I learned that one of the surest ways to make my mother happy was to eat lots of what she cooked. One of my earliest memories of my maternal grandmother is of her urging me to eat everything down to the glazed flower decorating the bottom of the cereal bowl. There was cheering when I finished an especially prodigious bit of eating.

When I was in ninth grade, the gym teacher took me aside one day. I was then an overweight kid not greatly interested in athletics. Mr. Saldano told me I was going to have trouble socially in high school unless I lost some weight. He said he didn't mean to be critical, and he didn't care whether I liked athletics or not, but I would not be attractive to other kids if I stayed fat. I committed the summer between ninth and tenth grades to losing weight. As my family switched from overfeeding me to supporting my new goal, my father offered to pay me one dollar for every pound I lost. He also bought me a book entitled *The Fat Boy's Book*. It was full of inane bromides, but I learned from one chapter how to count calories. I used the book to establish both a diet and a behavioral regimen for myself. Net loss: twenty pounds. Net gain: twenty dollars.

In hindsight, what made the difference was the kindliness of Mr. Saldano's intervention. He didn't—as many parents and teachers do with overweight kids—express disgust with my weight. He didn't try to humiliate me. He approached me as mentor and friend to let me know what I might suffer if I stayed fat. I doubt that my father's financial incentive would have worked by itself; and I'm sure I would have reacted badly to being sent to a fat boys' summer camp.

The Next Most Important Day

When they enroll at an elementary school, boys enter a public arena for almost half of their weekday waking hours. They cannot be insulated by their families from a combination of fulfilling and painful experiences there. Perhaps nothing since the day of his birth rivals in importance the first day a boy goes to school.

My parents moved from Brooklyn to Mount Vernon, New York, less than a month before I was to enter public school. When my mother escorted me to school the first day, it wasn't clear whether, as a December-born, I would spend the year in kindergarten or be advanced to first grade. Nor was it clear which of two elementary schools was the right one for a boy living at our address. We went to the wrong one. I didn't know anyone, the teacher wasn't very welcoming, and my mother was told to take me to the other school the next morning. I responded to the situation by dissolving in tears, aware the moment I did so that something fundamental had shifted in my life; while tears might still be tolerated at home, crying was not the recommended behavior for boys at school. Happily, my first day at the second school was crisis-free and pleasant.

One of the things boys do when faced with new and fluid social situations is to develop dominance hierarchies. These hierarchies may even be seen among preschoolers in kindergartens and day-care centers. Each dominance hierarchy is an ordering of individuals that predicts who will prevail when conflict breaks out among members of the group. It may take a while, through the medium of arguments, threats, and perhaps even fights, for the ranking to be established in a group of boys. Once established, the function of the hierarchy is to reduce aggression. Hostility within the group may thereafter be dealt with mainly by playful verbal insults that can be accepted by their targets fairly cheerfully.

The school playground at recess time is perhaps the single most important location of this group formation, just as it is one of the less closely monitored places and times of the school day. School hallways and boys' locker rooms are other locations where dominance hierarchies hold sway. The structure is usually not entirely rigid. A growth spurt, the successful cultivation of a sport, or even a new social prominence for his family may allow a boy to bid successfully for a higher place. By junior and senior high school years, dominance hierarchies are less malleable.

School is a social challenge even for those boys who have had a relatively tranquil and happy childhood. But most boys enter school bearing the scar tissue of unresolved challenges from earlier childhood: sibling rivalry, teasing by relatives and neighbors, the divorce of parents, or even parental neglect or abuse, to name just a few aspects of childhood that can cause pain. School thus becomes a second front where a boy may find social acceptance and respect, but where he may instead experience both repetition of some childhood conflicts and imposition of new stresses indigenous to schools.

One of the options for boys who diverge from the most esteemed peer attributes is the role of clown. The fat boy, the short boy, the unathletic boy, or the nerdy boy may be tolerated if he plays the comic, particularly if his humor is self-directed and self-deprecating. In effect, the clown articulates what the listener is already thinking and makes it socially acceptable to laugh at him. The routines and the life stories of many successful stand-up comedians show that they got their start playing the clown at school. It is a very hard role to shake, once established, and the self-deprecating aspect deepens over time.

Another compensatory role for a boy who otherwise might be a social pariah is the cutup. Boys can win acceptance by displaying just the right amount—in their peers' eyes—of breaking rules and resisting authority. Not enough to get them in serious trouble, but enough to win the admiration of their classmates. As with the role of the clown, the cutup role can have long-lasting consequences. It is hard to avoid having to keep raising the level of mischief in order to keep the social admiration intact.

Cognitive Leaps

When I was a youngster, kids who were bright enough to skip grades were generally envied, with little attention paid to the consequences of their relative social immaturity at their new grade levels. In the 1990s, parents ambitious for their children are likely to be pleased if their sons are among the *oldest* rather than the youngest in their classes. They may even deliberately hold their children back at times in order to give them the benefit of increased maturation and the social leverage it may provide at school.

Whether a boy begins first grade as a five-, six-, or seven-year-old, the establishment of this age span as the right time to begin formal education is not all happenstance. Important cognitive shifts take place in the brains of five- to seven-year-olds. They can think in more logical and organized ways; they can give and take clear directions; and they have become interested in the classification of things.

A preschooler who loses an object will generally look only where he remembers last seeing it, but a schoolboy will utilize a more thoughtful strategy of reconstructing events to determine where the object might have been lost. If a five-year-old boy and a nine-year-old boy are given lists of items to obtain from a play supermarket, the older boy will take time to organize his list to enable him to proceed in a methodical way through the aisles, but the younger boy will shuttle about, acquiring one object after another from the list without advance organizing and planning.

If you ask a five-year-old—or even many six-year-olds—who is standing facing you to indicate whether an object is to your left or right, he probably won't be able to do it accurately; he is still applying the perspective of his own right and left to others. But around age seven or eight he will grasp how to perform mental rotations, and how to imagine himself seeing things from another person's perspective. Seven- or eight-year-old boys can give street directions by imagining the route in their minds and thinking how to get efficiently from one place to another, but most six-year-olds can perform the task only after following the route themselves and remembering how they did it.

Just as girls have a physical advantage over boys because their childhood growth spurts occur before the equivalent ones for boys, so they also have an edge over boys in academic performance through the elementary school years. During this time, their average language development is faster, and their reading and writing achievements are superior to boys'.

There isn't as much difference at this age between boys' and girls' performance in mathematics as in verbal disciplines. In early adolescence, boys will pull ahead of girls in mathematics and establish an average superiority that is lifelong. The difference is most striking at the highest levels of mathematics; many more boys than girls have exceptional mathematical talent. Researchers have noted that these academic differences are reinforced by gender-based expectations. Already in elementary school boys perceive themselves as more apt to succeed in mathematics, mechanical subjects, and sports, while girls foresee success in languages and art.

Only in spatial perception and reasoning do boys show a superiority over girls in the elementary years. The lifelong persistence of this difference suggests there is some biological underpinning to it. Environmental factors probably contribute to whatever is biologically established. Toys and sporting equipment favored for and by boys require more spatial perception and manipulation than some of the toys and sporting equipment favored for and by girls.

Multiple Intelligences

When a boy is ready for school, his parents are interested in finding out how he stacks up against other boys and girls, and schools comply with that interest by grading intellectual performance in academic subjects.

Howard Gardner has been a leader in a movement to rescue the definition of intelligence from the domination of a small number of variables (verbal and mathematical, or general IQ) and from the desire to measure these few variables and then put children into learning tracks depending on how they score. He has identified seven kinds of intelligence discernible at all ages including early childhood:

Linguistic intelligence: sensitivity to the functions of language and the meaning of words;

Logical/mathematical intelligence: sensitivity to numerical patterns, and the ability to master chains of logical reasoning;

Musical intelligence: an appreciation of melodies and rhythms, and an understanding of the several modes of musical expression;

Spatial intelligence: comprehension of the visual world, and the ability to connect the dimensions of visual experience;

Bodily intelligence: the capacity to use one's body to manipulate objects and achieve goals;

Interpersonal intelligence: the ability to discern the moods and intentions of others, and to respond appropriately;

Intra-personal intelligence: the sensitivity to discern one's own feelings and to guide and regulate one's behavior accordingly, as well as the comprehension of one's own strengths, weaknesses and wishes.

Through the lens of Gardner's definitions, we gain a much greater understanding of the intellectual gifts of a boy, as well as those talents not yet developed. To a degree, the several intelligences are independent of each other. Mozart, to use an example from the field of music, was composing at age five, but he showed no comparably prodigious talent among Gardner's other intelligences; above all, he lacked interpersonal intelligence.

Why do some intelligent boys not do well in academic subjects? Differences in motivation account for some of the variance. Even in infancy one can detect a drive toward mastery, and it is believed that some part of achievement motivation is established then. By age two, boys are responding to parental expressions of approval and disapproval with matching expressions of pride or shame; they understand that praise, or lack thereof, is related to competency.

Boys have begun to calculate what it takes to succeed or fail in their parents' eyes by age three; the mental scripts they create influence how hard they will try in the future to win approval. Four- to six-year-old boys who fail to persist until tasks are completed are likely to see themselves as bad—deserving of criticism. These boys frequently report that they are harshly berated for what they regard as minor errors.

In the interval between ages six and eight, boys begin to see how another person is viewing something; they see differences of perspective. They learn to think about another person's way of thinking. It is a vital development, because it helps people sort out misunderstandings based mainly on points of view. Boys skillful at understanding perspectives are often well accepted by their peers because they can recognize and acknowledge others' viewpoints rather than insisting on the primacy of their own; and they can think their way through complicated social situations.

A boy with poor social skills, especially a boy with an angry, aggressive style, nearly always has difficulty imagining how others think. Such a boy may then mistreat others without triggering the remorse or guilt he might experience if he could read how others are thinking or feeling about his behavior. Sometimes, therefore, antisocial behavior can be corrected simply by interventions that promote perspective-taking in the mind of the offender.

One ramification of a boy's developing skill in grasping another person's perspective is that boys may now see more clearly what other persons think of them. There has been a foretaste of this capacity in the way a preschool boy assesses whether his parents or caregivers approve or disapprove specific kinds of activities. But schoolboys become aware that they are constantly being evaluated by a number of adults at school. Some psychologists believe this awareness of how other people are evaluating them contributes to a decline of self-esteem in the early school years.

Empathy

In the schoolboy years, a boy's mind is developing a capacity to discern psychological nuances. Schoolboys can assess the nature of relationships and draw inferences from what they observe. This enhanced capacity seems to be a combination of growing powers of perception and growing powers of expression.

A six-year-old boy, noticing how upset his mother was becoming as she failed to find a motel vacancy after driving all day, said, "You're pretty sad, aren't you, Mom? Well, I think it's going to be all right. I think we'll find a nice place, and it'll be all right." An observation of this sort requires the boy's ability to see the situation from his mother's perspective, to take their relationship into account, and to express his sentiments simply but eloquently—far easier for most six- or seven-year-old boys than for most five-year-olds, who would be more apt to pick up on their mothers' infectious anxiety and frustration, and themselves begin to fuss.

Empathy involves comprehending the perspectives of other people, and acknowledging their emotional needs. Boys who are able to display empathy generally have parents who are nurturing and encouraging, though they do not hesitate to correct their sons when they fail to fulfill the parents' sense of appropriate behavior. When parents are harsh and punitive toward their sons, the boys' empathy develops more slowly, if at all. Abused children display little concern for other distressed children; in fact, they may display hostility toward them.

Empathic behavior takes practice, so one should expect the frequency and depth of its expression to increase during the elementary school years. The more mature forms of empathy involve the capacity of children of dominant social classes or races or ethnic groups to relate sensitively to the poor or those in crisis. Through schools or scouts or religious groups, all boys would benefit from providing direct assistance to the needy during the second half of elementary school—helping with food pantries or other charitable services.

Friendship

Harry Stack Sullivan, an influential psychiatrist and personality theorist, wrote in 1953:

> If you look very closely at one of your children when he finally finds a chum—somewhere between eight-and-a-half and ten—you'll discover something very different in the relationship, namely, that your child begins to develop a real sensitivity to what matters to another person. And this is not in the sense of 'what should I do to get what I want,' but instead 'what should I do to contribute to the happiness or to support the prestige and feeling of worthwhileness of my chum.' So far as I've been able to discover, nothing remotely like this appears before. . . . Thus the developmental epoch of preadolescence is marked by the coming of integrative tendencies which, when they are completely developed, we call love.

This is an immensely helpful insight. Boys and girls aged eight and older differ considerably in describing their closest friends. Girls refer to emotional closeness and trust as the basis of their friendships with other girls. Boys' descriptions of their friendships are more varied, focused more on shared activities and interests. Boys, however, do develop a capacity for close friendship late in childhood when there is still much social separation of the sexes. Girls have had greater capacity for friendship, mostly with other girls, since early childhood because they are tutored in the establishment of such relationships by their mothers and other female role models.

At puberty, both biology and culture are signaling to males that they should now shift the focus of their peer relationships, such as they are, from other boys to girls. The earliest maturing males feel the brunt of this signaling. Inevitably, they gain less practice in the art of friendship between males if their interest has been diverted early to highly sexualized relations with girls. Late maturing males have a longer opportunity to cultivate friendships with other males, and to a degree with females who appreciate that the boys' interest isn't predominantly sexual. But our culture admires the early maturing male's sexual prowess more than it honors the late maturer's superior capacity for friendship.

Throughout adolescence and adulthood, the capacity to form and maintain friendships can make an enormous difference in the quality of a male's life. So it is unfortunate if the friendship impulse detected by Sullivan in the eight-and-a-half- to ten-year-old male is too quickly diverted.

There are two ways parents and other caregivers can help boys develop friendships. The first is to explain what friendship is when one sees that they are baffled, that they don't get it. The shift of perspective from egocentric to concern for the welfare of the other that is at the heart of friendship is explainable. An adult can relate his or her own experiences making first friends, and discuss what binds his or her adult friendships. If an older male can nurture the art of friendship in a boy, so much the better; a woman may assume that a boy has the perspectives and impulses common to females, who have generally practiced the art of relationships more than boys or men.

The second contribution is to make your home a happy gathering place for children, a place where friendships have an opportunity to grow. When I arrived at the home of a single mother and her sixth-grade son to talk with them about some of the topics in this book, the yard was full of children playing, and there was a ball game in progress on the street. There were rules for what her son and other children could and couldn't do on the premises; everyone understood them. There was also a very welcoming spirit. For the neighborhood, it was obviously a favorite place to hang out.

Self-esteem

Cross-cultural research shows that self-esteem is not emphasized equally from country to country. It is a highly valued trait in North American and Northern European societies, but is less significant in most Asian and Mediterranean societies. In the latter societies, the collective takes precedence over the individual; a Japanese or a Sicilian boy would likely be more finely tuned to the station or honor of his family than to his individual esteem.

Where self-esteem is highly valued, it has to be cultivated. By age two, boys have begun to see themselves in a basically positive or negative light.

By age three, there are signs that self-perceived failure has an effect on how hard a boy will attempt the same task again. Boys are certainly not capable of detached self-evaluation at age two or three. Their self-regard is a reading of how they have been treated. Smiles and praise weigh on the positive side, frowns and scolding on the negative. To no one's surprise, warm and responsive parents raise boys who feel good about themselves.

Individual temperament affects how a boy tallies up the arithmetic of smiles and frowns. An easygoing boy may reflect the balance of pluses and minuses over a period of time, but a shy or overreactive youngster may allow one severe scolding to wipe away the effects of many moderate smiles. Boys need signals from an early age—are they pleasing or disappointing their caregivers. Being studiously noncommittal will be viewed by them as being negative.

Over the course of childhood, self-esteem ebbs and flows, to some extent predictably. It's high in the preschool years, then falls in the first two school years as boys begin to compare themselves to classmates, levels off in third grade, and begins to rise again in fourth grade. By the age of seven or eight, boys are developing separate feelings of self-esteem related to physical prowess and appearance, social acceptance (separately, by parents and peers), and academic performance (increasingly separately by subject). Somewhere in a boy's mind he is both monitoring the individual components and giving himself a general rating of self-esteem.

As childhood gives way to puberty, sometimes in the final elementary school years, the transition affects boys and girls differently. Early maturing girls sometimes suffer loss of self-esteem as they feel inadequate to deal socially with the attention their physical maturity has brought them. Among boys, early sexual maturation tends to promote self-esteem, while late maturation provokes self-doubt.

Early Tests of Character

Home Alone

Approximately 2.4 million children aged five to thirteen are in charge of themselves at home after school until an adult arrives from his or her workday. Many of these children are sitters for younger siblings at the same time. Most observers agree that children younger than eight or nine should not be left unsupervised, if only because they lack the capacity to respond to emergencies. However, there are not enough after-school programs to serve the population of these children, who are referred to as "latchkey children." As I describe later in the book, I began as a schoolboy to have responsibility for the care of my younger brother and sister because of my mother's illness. Caring for younger siblings can stimulate an early sense of responsibility, or "parentification," but it can also generate feelings in a boy that he has been burdened with more obligations than he can comfortably handle, and that his own needs are being ignored.

If children are unattended because their single mothers are at work, boys may be affected more adversely than girls. The determination of the single mother to keep her family intact, even if she is not usually at home to welcome the children back from school, may be an inspiration to her daughters. But in many single-mother households, the father of the children has failed as a provider and is not a positive role model for sons. The opportunity of a father to be a positive role model for a son is linked to social class. Boys in poor families admire their fathers less on average than do boys in higher social classes; they often have little, or unsatisfactory, interaction with their fathers.

Divorce

Studies in both Great Britain and the United States show that most divorces terminate an extended period of spousal conflict and family turmoil. The effects of the situation on children begin when their parents first enter the period of turbulence. Everyone in the family may show a loss, gradual or precipitous, of capacity to cope with conflict. Impulse control declines. A cloud of argument and resentment falls over the household. Parents may be less attentive to their children, and less patient with their trying moments. Siblings may take out their anxiety on one another. As distressing as this situation may be, the developmental consequences for boys are generally worse when the conflict-ridden family stays together than when parents separate and begin lives apart.

Boys, however, do often experience serious adjustment problems when their parents separate. Their academic performance is apt to slip more than the performance of girls in similar situations. The more aggressive the temperament of the boy, the worse he responds to the uprooting. When parents separate and divorce, sons generally receive less emotional support than daughters receive. Because they may act out their confusion and unhappiness, boys are frequently viewed more negatively by their mothers and their teachers. Even their friends view them less positively. It is as though whatever blame attaches to the family breakup rubs off especially heavily on boys.

Several studies suggest that boys do as well or better after divorce in the custody of their fathers than with their mothers. Obviously, this depends on the level of attention and care given by a father, but in any case it helps boys' development to have regular contact with their fathers after divorce;

their fathers are more likely to praise sons' good behavior, less likely to ignore bad behavior.

When their divorced mothers remarry, schoolboys usually adjust well to
it. If the new stepfather displays concern and affection for a stepson but does
not try to exert parental authority too quickly or strongly, he will be welcomed by his stepson. One study suggests that conflict between mothers
and sons tends to decline after the mother remarries—testimony in part,
perhaps, to the enhanced financial security of the family and to the mother's
reduced loneliness and sense of vulnerability. Within two years after their
mothers' remarriage, the schoolboys in one study were doing almost as well
academically and socially as boys of the same age in intact families. But this
outcome is less common for adolescent boys who often find adjustment to
blended families very trying. When fathers have custody and remarry, their
school-age sons often respond negatively to the remarriage.

The divorce rate for second marriages is even higher than for first marriages, so there is no guarantee that a schoolboy who has worked his way
through one of these great transitions will not have to endure another.
One study of fourth-grade boys showed that their reaction to the conflict
that led to a second divorce for their custodial parents was deeper and
lasted longer than anything observed in the first family divorce experienced by them.

Every character issue confronted by a boy growing up will be complicated by his having to adjust to basic rearrangements in his family. His
anxiety and resentment about the change in his family configuration will
seem, if only unconsciously, to be a justification for acting out his unhappiness or failing to address his developmental tasks with enthusiasm. He
will certainly wonder why fate dealt him such a difficult hand. He will not
fail to notice when his caregivers are paying him less attention because
they are preoccupied with their own adjustments to changing households.
It is a particularly opportune time for other adult relatives and friends of
the divorcing couple to offer to spend more time with the children involved.

Prejudice

The essence of prejudice is to take characteristics that differentiate people
and apply to them attitudes of superiority and inferiority. Even as
preschoolers, boys are deeply influenced by prevailing attitudes in their
homes and neighborhoods about race, ethnicity, social class, religious affiliation, gender, sexual orientation and other characteristics that have become the subjects of prejudice. The younger a boy adopts a prejudicial
attitude, the more rigid it is apt to be. Already among schoolboys, observers have noted a divergence between professed attitudes and actual be-

havior in some boys who describe themselves as tolerant but behave as though prejudiced; in such situations, one may assume that the prejudice was learned or absorbed earlier, and the overlay of tolerance taught later hasn't been able to transform the underlying attitudes. Some expressions of prejudice have a free-floating usage as early as grade school; a boy who doesn't like another boy may call him a "fag" not because sexual orientation is in question but because it is a commonly accepted way to insult anyone one doesn't like.

Parents and other caregivers have a double agenda on the issue of prejudice. They will help their boys' character development insofar as they can influence them not to develop attitudes of superiority about those characteristics the boys have that are culturally dominant in their environments. Likewise, they will help them when they influence them to have a positive view of their characteristics that are not dominant—not, in other words, to accept images and stereotypes that are intended to convey inferiority. Many boys have some characteristics that are dominant and others that aren't. Thus they need sensitive guidance in dealing simultaneously with both sides of the issue of prejudice.

What parents and teachers need to be aware of is that the earliest foundation a boy has about prejudice is not something he has thought through for himself, but what he has absorbed consciously and unconsciously from the most influential people in his environment. As a schoolboy, and even more as a teenager, he will begin to think about his own views. It is common for a boy who is among a minority in terms of race or ethnicity or religion and has been taught to be accepting or proud of it, to go through a period in which he wishes that he belonged to a more dominant group.

Gradual Change

Stand a sixth-grade boy next to a first-grade boy of similar temperament and intelligence, and the differences are likely to seem striking. Size, articulateness, poise, and knowledge have all increased, but nothing more than the older boy's knowledge. The first grader is a beginning reader; the sixth grader is a veteran of independent research projects, perhaps already able to read and speak the fundamentals of a second language. Yet they are very much the same, too. Most of this development, for the majority of boys, has taken place under the calm blanket of sexual latency. The changes have taken place in quiet, almost imperceptible increments. Quantitatively, they are impressive. Qualitatively, they don't seem as far-reaching as the shift from preschool development to schoolboy development, or from boyhood to adolescence. Puberty, in contrast, brings dramatic, unmistakable change.

11

Honesty

The father of a nine-year-old boy told me that he returned from an overseas business trip this year carrying a joint of marijuana in his luggage. One of his business hosts abroad, wanting to show the utmost hospitality—drug consumption is widespread in their industry—had put the joint in his houseguest's bedroom as an amenity, much as hotel staff might leave a chocolate treat on a pillow. Back home, the father put the joint in the top drawer of his bureau at home, and forgot about it. A week later, the drawer was open one morning as he dressed for work while his son was in the room. His son saw the joint, picked it up, and asked, "What's this, Dad?"

"It caught me off guard. I've thought a lot about drugs, and what I'll say to him when he's thirteen or fourteen. Basically, I plan to tell him honestly about my experience with drugs as a teenager, but I'm going to tell him that times have changed a lot since then, and what was okay for me at fourteen *isn't* okay for him at fourteen."

"What did you say to your son about the joint?" I asked. "Oh, I said it was a hand-rolled cigarette that I had been offered at a business dinner and kept as a curiosity." He went on to tell me about other male friends of his who consumed drugs extensively as adolescents, and who intend to lie if their own children ever ask them whether they consumed drugs when they were boys.

This man obviously wanted to preserve a certain moral clout with his son when they inevitably will have to address the subject of drugs in a few years. (One could argue that the subject is timely even for nine-year-olds these days.) He said he wanted to be able to say, "I did it then, but I don't do it now, and I don't want you to do it because drugs are so much more dangerous now. They were dangerous even when I was a kid, but I was lucky. Now I know more about drugs. I want you to know what I know, because you might do what I did and not be as lucky as I was."

Perhaps if the father hadn't been caught by surprise and wasn't in a hurry to get to work, he could have handled his son's discovery and question more truthfully, using it as an opening to the subject of drugs that all parents should begin to discuss with schoolboys. Impulsively, he evaded the subject with a partial truth. He misled his son in the service of what he saw as his responsibility to protect his son from harmful exposure to drugs. He didn't want his son to be able to justify his own possible consumption of drugs by saying: My dad does it, why shouldn't I?

Varieties of Dishonesty

Honesty, which at first glance looks like one of the simpler topics to be dealt with in character-building, is actually one of the most complex—as even this mundane father-son incident shows. Ethicists often assume that honesty is the obvious policy of choice except for extreme cases in which lying, or one of its related avoidances of the truth, might be morally justifiable—for example, should a soldier captured in battle tell his captors false information about the deployment and strategies of his own army, or should a physician tell a terminally ill and deeply depressed patient what he knows and estimates to be the patient's condition and life expectancy if the patient asks. Extreme examples, however, don't necessarily help us make wise choices in commonplace situations.

The ambiguity of dishonesty is that much of it is habitual and scarcely recognized. You could ask a copywriter for an advertising agency if he is aware that much of what he writes is, at best, distortion, and he will probably resist the characterization; he is just doing "marketing." You can ask the preacher or speechwriter if he realizes that many of his generalizations wouldn't stand up to close factual scrutiny—though they sound appealing—and he will say that he is just conveying political or philosophical truth. So a boy grows up in a culture where there is pervasive dishonesty but yet occasions when truth-telling is, perhaps without warning, regarded as terribly important.

The corrosive effects of lies between adults are frequently celebrated in contemporary literature. A review of a recent novel says of one of the characters: "Klima (the novelist) reminds us that Hana, too, is to be considered. She has found out, by chance, that her husband has a lover, and in the goodness of her heart she truly forgives him. But she weeps because he has deceived her, and she doesn't know whether she'll ever believe him again."

Everyday life is seldom quite as clear as fictional life, but adults in real life do generally know that exposed lies between partners are going to have lasting effects. This knowledge doesn't always inhibit adults from lying to their intimates, but they rarely defend the lying itself. They will rationalize it away if they can, but they rarely say that it's really OK to lie to an intimate.

In my talks with parents, however, I've met quite a few who have no reservations about lying to their children. What about? Most often, about their own pasts, and about subjects that intrinsically make them uncomfortable. I've learned of children who do not know that one of their parents was married—and, in some cases, had children—before entering the marriage to which these children were born.

The tree of dishonesty has a number of separate branches. There is the branch of *equivocation*—deliberately using ambiguous or unclear expressions, intending to mislead. This is what the aforementioned father was doing. It was true that the object in the bureau was a hand-rolled cigarette; what he was falsely implying was that it contained ordinary tobacco. There is a branch called *duplicity*—speaking in two different and mutually contradictory ways about the same subject to different parties, intending to deceive one or both. Another branch is called *distortion*—willfully twisting something out of its true meaning. And there is *lying*—knowingly telling something one believes is false with the intent that the hearer will believe it is true. Boys are capable of doing all of these, if they choose, at quite young ages. None of these branches of dishonesty is to be confused with innocent errors. All of us say things that we believe to be true only to discover later that we were wrong. A large place has to be reserved in everyday life for unintentional errors—for misconceptions and misperceptions.

Just as dishonesty has many branches, so honesty has many limitations or qualifications that keep the subject from being one of those "night and day" simplicities. Let me mention a few.

Conflicting Perspectives

What is true—and therefore what one might try to communicate honestly or obscure dishonestly—is influenced by one's perspective. One of the most fascinating studies of perspective was done by Swiss psychologist Jean Piaget. None other than Albert Einstein requested the study. Einstein's theory of relativity, unlike the reigning Newtonian physics, in which velocity was defined as distance divided by time, posited that time and velocity are defined in terms of each other. Einstein wanted to know if children are born with innate notions of time and velocity, and how their first notions of one affect their learning of the other.

Piaget had four- and five-year-olds observe two toy trains running on parallel tracks. Which train, he asked each young observer, traveled faster? Which ran the longer time? Which went the longer distance? Most of the children said that the train that stopped ahead of the other train was the faster, took longer, and went the greater distance (the trains did not necessarily begin at the same point). Focusing on the stopping points, they ignored all other evidence. They could deal with only one dimension. From the perspective of children, the relations between two or more variables such as time, speed, and distance are more difficult to perceive than they are for adults.

In another experiment, Piaget seated four-year-olds around a play table on which sat a model of three mountains. The children were shown photographs of how the model looked from the perspectives of the other children ranged around the table. Could the children see differences between the photographs and what they saw from their chairs? No. For most four-year-olds, it was impossible. Preschoolers can't see the world from the perspective of others; they think theirs is the only possible viewpoint.

The answer to Einstein, delivered in five hundred pages of text, was that these concepts aren't inborn; distance, time, and velocity aren't comprehended in relation to each other until the school years, generally after the age of six.

Preschoolers are already capable of saying what they think will please the listener, whether or not what they say is true. When David Parker was five years old, and his brother, Jason, was four, their mother found a nearly empty bottle of children's liquid aspirin on the bathroom floor one Saturday morning about a year ago. She knew that both boys liked the cherry flavoring when they had tasted it in past doses to quell fevers; and she knew that the bottle had been more than three-quarters full when she last used it.

Panicked, Angela Parker confronted her sons with the empty bottle and asked who had drunk the aspirin. She had good cause to be alarmed. Overdoses of aspirin can cause major damage to the liver or heart or brain. In sufficient quantity, an overdose can be lethal.

"I didn't do it," David said. "I didn't do it," Jason said. "One of you had to have done it," Angela shouted. "The bottle was almost full. Now it's empty. Taking too much aspirin could make you very, very sick. Now, which one of you drank it?" The combination of her anxiety and scare tactics had no useful effect. Both boys reiterated their claims of innocence; they both began to accuse the other of having done it!

Knowing that she needed to treat promptly whichever son had drunk the aspirin, Angela made both David and Jason swallow a dose of Ipecac syrup to induce vomiting. The pink coloration from the aspirin showed up only in the contents of Jason's stomach.

The limitations that we see in preschoolers' capacity to deal with perspective and with truth is even more evident in toddlers. Stanley Cath has written up a study of how one intelligent mother, who kept a journal, dealt over a period of years with her son's absent father. The woman and her husband divorced before Jeff was born, and while the father paid a few visits to his son in his first months of life, those visits had ceased entirely before Jeff was two years old; by that age, Jeff was able to articulate his awareness that he didn't have what most of his playmates had: a daddy.

Jeff: Where is my daddy? Why doesn't he stay here the way the other daddies do?

Mother: Because we are divorced, and he lives somewhere else.

Jeff: What does 'divorced' mean?

Mother: Sometimes when two people get married, they find out that they didn't love each other and would be happier living apart or being married to someone else. The divorce was between your father and myself, and you had nothing to do with it. Your father wants you to be very happy, just as I do.

Jeff: Does he live far away from here?

Mother: Not very far away, but he lives away from here.

Jeff: Where?

Mother: In an apartment.

Jeff: Will he come to see us?

Mother: No, we both thought that since we would be happier living apart, it would be better to start again. That is why I date, so we can find a man we will love, and who will love us. You can kind of pick your own daddy, won't that be fun?

Jeff: Did Karen (his cousin) and Janie (a neighbor's child) pick out their daddies?

Mother: No, but your other friend, Louise, can pick out her daddy because her parents are divorced, too.

Jeff raised the subject endlessly in what his mother referred to as the "father question hour." His mother is, to a degree, cloaking the indifference of Jeff's biological father to his son, and slightly exaggerating the significance of Jeff's role in her choosing a new partner, though she is clear in her mind that a new partner would have to win Jeff's confidence (she relates with humor how Jeff drove one suitor away). With his two-year-old sense of concreteness, Jeff decided his father was living on the train tracks.

Eventually Jeff asked about living with his father: Why didn't he live with him? His mother answered: "Aren't you happy living with me?" She writes:

Then, pulling my emotions together for the time being, I added to that overly sensitive, guilt-ridden question of mine, 'Also, Jeff, your father works all day and mothers usually take care of the children.' Jeff said, 'I want to live with you, all of us together, I mean.' I would venture to say this conversation was not exactly my finest hour! Inside I was screaming (to myself). Here I was, left alone with the child, to explain why he can't see his father; left to make excuses. I knew I wouldn't hurt Jeff that badly to tell him that his father just couldn't care. And yet, I couldn't be a martyr, and take all the blame my son would most understandably place on me. I had to learn that nothing I could say would be the right thing, because Jeff was not in a right or normal situation. But I could say the wrong thing! Somehow, I had to find a middle ground where I could be honest with Jeff, without deliberately hurting him or his opinion of himself. I would try to have us live together with as little resentment as possible.

Honesty here has to take account of a dilemma: If Jeff knows fully of his father's indifference to him, he will be wounded. But if he doesn't know of it, he will blame his mother for his father's absence because she is present and available to play his feelings against. She is subordinating what she decides to say about Jeff's father to the greater value of minimizing resentment between herself and her son. I like her statement that she is searching for a middle ground that contains honesty but other considerations as well.

Honesty among older children and adults is deeply influenced by their various motives in the same way that the toddler or preschooler is motivated to say what he thinks will please or to avoid saying what he thinks will displease. To avoid shame, for example, adolescents or adults addicted to alcohol or drugs may resolutely deny their problems in the face even of overwhelming evidence.

Slanted Truth

The older we get, the more opportunity we have to see the subtleties of honesty and dishonesty. We come to see the difference between literal and figurative truth—to see that a phrase like "I'll do it in a minute" is probably literally untruthful but what we really meant was a metaphorical "I'll do it in a short while." Youngsters of literal mind who are impatient with our "in a minute" promises sometimes begin to count the seconds aloud.

We also come to see that many things are open to interpretation, depending on needs, interests, and perspectives. The cynical word these days is "spin" for the activity of putting forth an interpretation as much in one's self interest as possible; some people are acknowledged to be spin-masters. But cynicism aside, it's hard to deny the frequency with which we appeal for readings of events sympathetic to our own situation. An aware adult will be compelled to acknowledge the legitimacy of others' doing the same.

We all construct our own versions of reality and try to get others to adopt them or at least accommodate them. So one person's truth differs inevitably from another's. Some distortion of truth, or of what we best believe to be true, helps most of us manage to cope in the world. In her book, *Lying*, Sissela Bok—who makes a strong case for eliminating as much burdensome dishonesty and deception from our lives as we can—nevertheless quotes Emily Dickinson on the subject of honesty:

> *Tell all the truth but tell it slant—*
> *Success in Circuit lies*
> *Too bright for our infirm Delight*
> *The Truth's superb surprise*
> *As Lightning to our Children eased*
> *With explanation kind*
> *The Truth must dazzle gradually*
> *Or every man be blind—*

Unless the truth comes to us gently or obliquely, and in moderate doses, we can't always tolerate it. It blinds us like lightning. We need truth to be circuitous, on the slant.

Lessons from the Law

If truth is open to conflicting perspectives and claims, then what is left of the character trait of honesty? Has our subject dissolved in a sea of relativism?

I don't think so. For a moment, I'd like to look at the way honesty is dealt with in one of our central institutions, judicial courts. Truthfulness is so important to the courtroom that testimony is usually given after the taking of a solemn oath to be truthful; demonstrated dishonesty under oath, or perjury, is itself subject to penalties. Our judicial systems are far from up to date on their understandings of how truth is subject to perspectives and other qualifications. Cases are still put to juries to decide adversarial proceedings one way or the other "beyond a reasonable doubt." Many of us can scarcely imagine a situation that didn't contain at least one reasonable doubt. Courts also overestimate the reliability of human memory. Yet in spite of these faults, courts have a very sophisticated way of dealing with honesty.

Five separate safeguards to truth-telling in court have tremendous relevance, I believe, for other situations such as family life or school affairs. They all have as their purpose maintaining respect for every person, no matter what that person has done.

First, the law gives a person the right to remain silent rather than to testify truthfully to what might be detrimental to the person's perceived self-interest. Lots of people, including lots of children, lie or equivocate or distort because they can't bring themselves to tell the truth, and they haven't been given the option to remain silent; they have been pressured to speak up, maybe threatened with punishment for silence alone. What a difference it would make in family life if a boy could elect silence as an honorable choice rather than as an act of stubborn resistance.

Second, the burden of proof in court usually falls to the party doing the complaining—to the plaintiff in a civil action or the prosecutor in a criminal procedure. All the party in the defensive position has to do is raise a substantial enough measure of doubt about the validity of the complaint. The method in court is to look into the complaint at a rather plodding pace, sorting out the conflicting testimony and evidence in search of a verdict.

Many episodes in domestic life have the opposite dynamic: The person accused is expected to defend his complete innocence; the presumption in many family "hearings" is that the accused child or partner is guilty unless he can demonstrate otherwise. An angry child who is skilled in histrionics can often get a sibling summarily convicted and punished by unthinking adults.

Third, the law goes to considerable lengths to inform a person of what the potential consequences might be of telling the truth, especially of admitting to wrongdoing or negligence. The defendant thus knows what the potential range of punishments or sanctions is before deciding whether or not to be truthful. (Often this safeguard is realized by providing counsel, someone who can inform the defendant of the best way to defend himself. Competent counsel educates the client about the law.)

Again, this element is missing in countless domestic situations in which an annoyed or impatient or enraged caregiver is demanding that a child tell the truth without giving any indication of what the consequences of truth-telling might be if the accuser's suspicions are confirmed. This is another of the safeguards in public litigation that I would like to have applied to other social situations at home, at school, at work.

Fourth, courtroom procedures mandate careful distinction between what a witness knows from direct experience and what he knows only indirectly—from hearsay, for example. The law values fact above mere opinion. It is a distinction often missing in everyday life. All of us, I venture, occasionally confuse our meritorious opinions with the actual facts, which, often, we don't really know. In the absence of fact, opinion is often sent in to substitute.

Rewarding Honesty

The final safeguard of honesty in the law is the most profound. It is that honesty is in some way *rewarded*. I wish I could help every parent and teacher grasp and accept this rule, which is so often neglected. Honesty isn't its own reward. The reward has to be added. In the main, all that is needed is that honesty be praised. Toddlers should always be thanked for telling the truth, as should schoolboys and adolescents.

When honesty involves the acknowledgment of a regrettable act, the reward may be mainly in the form of a reduction of punishment for having owned up to the act. Every act of truth-telling, even if what is confessed reflects badly on the speaker, should be acknowledged as an instance of moral courage. In other words, we should distinguish between the careful establishment by others' testimony of a truth that the doer denies to the bitter end, and the honest admission of a truth that the speaker rues.

I'm not, of course, advocating that every home and school be turned into a part-time courthouse. What courts do with great formality—and great expense—can be done informally but carefully in any other venue. If the safeguards of honesty common to the courts could be more deeply incorporated into domestic or school situations, everyone would be better off. A sense of orderliness would replace what is now often impulsive and hot-tempered accusation and judgment. Relatively minor incidents would not be blown out of proportion. What I'm advocating, as I shall discuss in more detail later, is a higher level of parental consciousness about honesty in situations where honesty is undeniably an issue.

Entrapment

Before we leave analogies between honesty in the courtroom and in everyday life, let me note that the judicial system leans—though with some exceptions—toward sympathy for people who have been deliberately tempted by government officials to participate in unlawful activities. The process is called entrapment. Life, the courts seem to say, offers more than enough temptations without having to produce more culprits by using enticing governmental snares.

This concept of entrapment has some application to child-rearing and honesty, even at a very early age. When I asked Shannon, the mother of two toddlers, how she dealt with honesty, she said that she is careful not to provide temptations for her young sons to lie. For example, if she notices that one of the boys has a soiled diaper but is fully engaged in play, she doesn't ask him if he needs a diaper change.

"I try to make the question perfectly clear. If I ask him whether his diaper needs changing, we might have a difference of opinion rather than fact. If he says 'no,' he might be telling me that he knows his diaper is dirty, but he doesn't care because his play is too much fun to be interrupted. I also don't ask him—which *is* a clear question—whether he has a soiled diaper. If he's fully engaged in play, he'll then be tempted to lie.

"I say, 'L.J., I can smell your dirty diaper. Do you want me to change it now or in five minutes?' I've given him a bit of choice, I've acknowledged how important his play is to him at that moment, but I haven't surrendered my nose indefinitely to his whims, either. I find that with this kind of approach we avoid many little power struggles, and I don't encourage him to lie."

This is a very important principle. Honesty is a demanding virtue to practice. It will not be inspired in a young boy—or a boy of any age—by setting up little entrapments followed by little lectures when the test is failed. This kind of tactic can hardly help yielding a mindset in which a boy is calculating the odds each time of being caught in a lie.

I know of a father who irreparably damaged his relationship with his son by inquiring of his son every day, when he came home from work, whether the boy had been sucking his thumb. The boy always said he hadn't; but he usually had been, and his thumb had the telltale wrinkled skin to prove it. The father then examined the thumb and delivered a reproachful look or lecture. The thumb-sucking continued until the boy was at least ten years old because the thumb was one of his main consolations for his unhappiness.

In a society like ours, boys even in childhood are regularly in situations of being alone or anonymous, with the odds of a lie being detected not transparently high—unlike those of our thumb-sucker. Detection calculations, if that is the way a boy deals with a situation, are often going to yield a decision to lie. A more effective path is to reward every instance of honesty that takes special courage or other virtue, establishing honesty as an aspect of character that every person should honor and cultivate.

When Not to Tell the Truth

Preschoolers, with their somewhat inflexible sense of rules and their developmental inability to see things from the perspectives of others, are apt to say truthful but embarrassing things in public. You may recall the preschooler I mentioned earlier who informed the police officer, over his father's protestations, that the father had been trying to steal a car.

Schoolboys, however, have begun to appreciate that the advantages of telling the truth vary from one person's perspective to another's. Parents can begin to discuss with schoolboys the kinds of situations when dishonesty in the form of what we call "white lies" is appropriate. A schoolboy asks a friend whether the schoolboy played soccer well that afternoon. The friend doesn't really think the boy did play well, but doesn't see any way to evade the question. If he tells the truth, he's going to hurt his teammate's self-confidence. Is it better to be truthful or to be reassuring? While an exaggerated compliment may backfire, no harm is done by being reassuring. The boy who reassures his pal with a white lie doesn't gain anything except the satisfaction of making his teammate feel better.

Only detailed discussion of possible situations can enable a parent and a son to refine an understanding of when and why a white lie is appropriate and when it is inappropriate or can be avoided by an effective and yet truthful strategy. These discussions will be all the more compelling to a boy if they are reciprocal—parents relating some of the situations they have confronted when white lies seemed to them the responsible thing to say.

From such discussions a boy might learn to say, "I think you're a good soccer player," which might be true but not as true of today's game; or he might say, "I think you're a good player. You didn't have your best game today, but I'm sure you will next time," which could be both truthful and reassuring.

I had an early experience of a protective lie. Shortly after my sister was born, my mother's mother died. As if traumatized by this gain of a third child and loss of a parent, my mother fell into the first of several episodes of mental illness. Mental illness was more stigmatized then than now, and I never confided my mother's illness even to my closest friends. It's possible that some of them knew of it from other sources, but they didn't embarrass me by mentioning it. Until my junior year in high school, my mother suffered through, and recovered from, recurrent stretches of depression and other symptoms at home. Then she was hospitalized for the first time. My father instructed us children to say, if asked, that she was spending time at a dairy farm. Since mental illness was seen as shameful, a case could be made for protecting my mother—and us—from public gossip.

While my siblings were perhaps not old enough to understand, my father could have explained to me why it made sense to protect my mother's situation. Instead, his way of handling the situation within the family implied that he was ashamed of my mother's condition, and, by implication, we children should be ashamed of her, too. The lies we were instructed to tell might be regarded by some people as inconsequential white lies, but their effect on our family was significant: We lived as though we had something major to hide; we lived without the solace and perhaps the help that others might have offered us. When I think back to the nature of the community we lived in, I think that our situation would, if widely known, have generated sympathy and comfort.

Alcohol or drug abuse within a family often generates a household conspiracy to lie to cover up the situation. Sometimes the conspiracy doesn't even have to be articulated. Everyone besides the addict notices that everyone else is ashamed; tacitly, everyone agrees to be silent, or untruthful. Children of separated or divorced parents frequently get drawn into the conspiracies of one parent to hide facts known to the children from the other parent—"I'm dating Linda now, but I don't want you to tell Mommy."

Honesty and discretion get confusingly intertwined in family life at times. Parents obscure or deny certain facts about themselves or others in the family to their children; sometimes these are facts that, if known, would damage their children's idealized images of family members. At other times, information is withheld because parents don't trust the children to handle it discreetly outside the home. Their concern isn't unrealistic. Boys may be moved to brag or confess to their peers family information that their parents have very good reason to want to keep private.

The adults of each household have certain rights of privacy. One of their responsibilities is to determine what to divulge within the family about topics such as mental and physical health, family finances, marital conflict, job security or loss. In my clinical practice I have encountered situations in which parents shared more discretionary information with their children than the children could bear, creating levels of anxiety—because there was nothing the children could do to alter the situation—that impeded the children's development for years, even into adulthood. But many boys are capable, even in their school years, of handling some sensitive information if it is explained to them why it would be important not to broadcast the information outside the family.

Children also have significant rights of privacy, I believe, that bear on issues of honesty. When the appropriate privacy rights of everyone in the family are outlined and protected, incentives to dishonesty within the family cannot but decline. I still wince when I think of the story of a mother who came upon her adolescent daughter's private journal. Indefensibly heedless of her daughter's privacy, she read through the journal, finding there expressions of the sexual feelings and fantasies the daughter had experienced for her boyfriend. The mother confronted her daughter with the journal and forbade her ever to date the boy again; and I daresay the daughter learned never to trust her mother again.

"Abuse of truth ought to be as much punishment as the introduction of falsehood," said Pascal. The moral issue isn't, as one might suppose, between the always honorable truth and the always dishonorable false-hood. Truth can be used in a way that is profoundly inhumane. False-hoods can be gently and lovingly protective without any adverse side effects.

When boys reach school age, they begin to have more complex peer re-lations in which many of the incentives to dishonesty already experienced at home are confronted but without as much adult guidance. Then, as we see, boys and girls begin constructing separate and intertwined social structures that by the adolescent years will be hiding as much from their parents as their parents ever hid from them.

Honesty and Parental Awareness

The four levels of parental awareness that we have seen earlier have bear-ing on the subject of honesty. At the first level—Me First—we see my fa-ther exhorting his children to lie if necessary to hide the fact of my mother's illness. He might have made the same suggestion based on a higher level of awareness—and therefore for different reasons—but I be-lieve he acted most of all on the basis of his own needs. What he did, and why he did it, is more common than unusual.

The safeguards to honesty from courtroom procedures can also be re-lated to levels of awareness. Courts handle conflicts between parties con-ducted on an adversarial basis. People who come to court are usually preoccupied with their own interests; they are in a Me First frame of mind. Courts work at the second level: Follow the Rules. These rules about honesty, contain sophisticated safeguards, but they are only rules, and rules can't distinguish between modest dishonesty of little consequence and lying with major consequence except by variations in punishment once people are found guilty. In other words, courts are basically con-cerned about whether you lied, not why you lied.

At the third and fourth levels of parental consciousness, a parent be-comes aware of the needs of others and tries to act responsibly and re-spectfully in relation to those needs. If my father had considered our situation at Level Three, he would have been able to recognize his chil-dren's need to express our fears and fantasies about our mother's illness, our need to feel we were good children even though our mother was sick. His strategy meant that he didn't reassure us himself even as he cut us off from the possibility that others would reassure us.

Only at Levels Three and Four does a parent move past concern with whether a child lied and ask *why* he lied. Addressing the why usually gets to more important issues than whether. If the why can be clarified and re-solved, the offending dishonesty will often cease. As I've indicated before, we all carry the lower levels of awareness with us when we act in accordance with the higher levels; we continue to feel the press of our own needs, and we continue to acknowledge the rules that we believe in; but we relate those factors to the needs of others and to the relationships we have with others.

Robert Coles, in *The Moral Intelligence of Children*, tells about one classroom situation in which it was hard to find a solution because there was no common agreement about application of the rules and the why question was raised in a way more to try to exonerate the alleged offender than to understand her motive. The central character of the story was a fourth-grade girl, Elaine, who excelled in the classroom and in athletics, was popular and attractive, and lived in solid upper-middle class comfort. She was especially admired by her teacher, who had written a published article about Elaine's accomplishments in math and science, subjects that boys usually dominated in the teacher's classroom.

One day, a boy sitting beside her reported to the teacher that Elaine was using a crib sheet on a math test, and not for the first time. The boy had talked with his parents about Elaine's regular cheating, and they had suggested he discuss the matter with Elaine herself, but when he did so on two occasions she angrily denied cheating, accused him of jealousy, and called *him* a liar. The teacher acted surprised and irritated by the boy's accusation, despite the fact that he was delivering Elaine's crib sheet to her. She sent him back to his seat, gave him a look he regarded as reproving; he became upset over the rebuff and couldn't finish the test.

The boy's parents counseled him to let the matter drop, but Elaine began boastfully to tease him about the impossibility of his making his accusation stick. He felt the teacher was less friendly. He became more timid, apprehensive about the teacher's view of him. And he saw Elaine continue to cheat in other subjects.

Eventually the whole matter landed in the principal's lap because the boy's parents wisely felt they had to do something to protect his feelings and situation at school. His mother went to see the teacher, who rebuffed her for intruding on a situation the teacher felt she should handle in her own way without parental interference. When the teacher was unhelpful, both parents went to the principal. Though, as we shall see, the situation was really never resolved, the boy must have felt that his parents gave him and his honesty invaluable support at a time of confusion and self-doubt.

At least two other students in the class corroborated the boy's story that Elaine had been cheating. Before the principal, Elaine denied cheating, and suggested the boy must have a problem of his own. The teacher was angry that others were intruding on her classroom; she said Elaine was going through a stressful time—a beloved grandfather was ill, and her mother, a lawyer, had just lost a big case—and she would not acknowledge that Elaine had cheated in class, though she eventually said she had seen Elaine "fudge" a little in sports.

Coles, who was doing research at the school, was pulled into the situation as it became quasi-judicial. Gradually he felt that a problem essentially moral in nature was being psychologized away. If Elaine had cheated and lied about it—no one except a few of her classmates and the parents of one of them and Coles were willing to say that the evidence was convincing—then it must be a "psychiatric" problem rather than a moral problem.

As happens in many such situations, this one drifted out of focus rather than moved to resolution. Elaine and her parents had some family counseling on subjects other than cheating and lying. School went on. Elaine continued to excel, but she had her doubters among her peers. She had grounds for believing that she could continue to cheat, to lie about it if accused, with impunity.

This story is of particular interest because our gender stereotypes suggest it might have been the other way around: the star male student-athlete, the timid female who catches him cheating. Coles doesn't say what became of the boy who cried "Cheat." Yet in many schools today, where most of the teachers are female, boys believe that their eagerness, their competitiveness, and their sense of fair play are put down in favor of a superior feminine standard. Also, the unnamed boy in this story has done something impeccably honest yet often stigmatized because there is an informal social contract against it. The contract is to the effect that it's one thing to be caught cheating by the teacher—she has the rule on her side—but quite another to be nailed by a fellow student who is violating the understanding that it's us (students) against them (teachers).

I share Coles's judgment that it is best for everyone to confront situations such as these promptly, to prevent them from festering until they become public with attendant shame for the accused. While it may overstate the case to say that the integrity of the entire class is at stake, many students could well have taken away the wrong lesson about cheating.

The situation in Elaine's classroom does have a moral center to it, but it also has interpersonal dimensions that can't be ignored, and they have their moral implications, too. The teacher had made a star out of Elaine, and both the teacher and Elaine were living within that exaggerated expectation. The teacher exhibited some of the same impulse to protect Elaine from damaging exposure (and to stonewall or even punish someone who punctured Elaine's public reputation) that her parents did; any public shame Elaine suffered was, they appeared to fear, going to rub off on both the teacher and Elaine's family. The longer the situation played out, the more lies several people told until breaking the circle of dishonesty promised enough shame that no one had the nerve to bring it to resolution.

Coles's story raises the question of whether one aspect of the situation was that Elaine was trying to handle more than even a very bright fourth grader could. She had been built up as a star student, she was active in school sports, she was active in peer group leadership, she took riding lessons, and had extensive chores to do at home. Perhaps cheating began as a mechanism to help her cope with a too-full plate of activities. Many schoolboys and adolescents are under the same pressures: Their academics and sports and maybe a part-time job and peer group relations add up to a set of responsibilities they can't cope with. They begin to look for shortcuts.

Honesty, Trust, Intimacy

As I've tried to show in a variety of ways, honesty is a complex and subtle subject, not so much an end in itself as a means of being responsible and respectful to the needs of others and of oneself. When honesty is at issue, there is usually something about the situation that makes being honest an act of courage. It isn't easy to be honest. Often the easy way is some version of dishonesty, which is why the dishonest way is so frequently taken.

Honesty is a principal ingredient in any establishment of trust. One person can't trust another deeply without believing that the interaction between them will be carried on at a high level of honesty. Trustful relations can bear the occasional white lie to be sensitive to the feelings of others, but not habitual dishonesty. Beyond the damage it does in specific situations, the reason we all are anxious about dishonesty is that it erodes trust. What misrepresentation of the truth will the person who is known to have been dishonest next put forth? When? For what motive?

One of many places where the fragility of trust can be observed is in the scientific community. When a research scientist is accused of falsely manipulating experimental evidence, a ripple of shock runs through that branch of science. Because scientists are always building upon the work of others, it is extremely worrisome to think that some of that work might be unreliable or deliberately falsified.

In personal relationships, however, trust involves not just truth as accuracy but truth as vulnerability. And that is where many men, whatever their strengths, are apt to stumble. The exaggeration of the self, or misrepresentation of the self can be second nature to a man.

In his school years, when he begins to compare himself regularly to others, a boy's sense of himself, in some measure, exaggerates his best qualities and masks some of his deficiencies or limitations. As Robert Coles's story of Elaine showed, a teacher can contribute mightily to a student's idealized image and then conspire to protect the student from realities that might diminish that image. Parents likewise want to believe that their sons match the idealized images the parents have of them. Several teachers have told me of parents who simply couldn't accept that their sons might have done what their schools report they have done. The ideal sons in their heads couldn't be reconciled with the boys in real life.

These ideal images get intertwined with the understanding of what it is to love and to be loved. Boys may believe that they will be loved only to the extent that they live up to their idealized images, and that they can love others only to the extent that the objects of their affection, too, fulfill their idealized images. So they are tempted to lie about truths that might adversely affect the esteem in which they are held.

When a parent and son build a relationship characterized by deep and dependable love, and that acknowledges the frailties as well as the strengths of each other, a boy will learn that some others can be trusted with the truth about him and that he can handle the truth about them.

12

SELF-CONTROL

John Henry Faulk told this boyhood story to television journalist Bill Moyers: "Boots Cooper and I used to pretend we were law-and-order men. I was a Texas Ranger and he was a United States marshal. We were both twelve years old and we rode the frontier between Momma's back door and her henhouse. One day Momma told us there was a chicken snake in one of the hen's nests out there, and she asked us mighty lawmen to go and execute it. We laid aside our stick horses, got a hoe, and went in. The hens were in a state of acute agitation. We had to stand on tiptoe to look in the top nests, and about the third top nest we looked in, a chicken snake looked out. I don't know, Bill, whether you've ever viewed a chicken snake from a distance of six inches from the end of your nose—the damn thing looks like a boa constrictor from that distance, although it's about the size of your finger. All of our frontier courage drained out our heels—actually, it trickled down our overall legs—and Boots and I made a new door through the henhouse wall.

"Momma came out and said, 'Well, you've lulled me into a false sense of security. I thought I was safe from all hurt and harm and here you've let a chicken snake run you out of the henhouse, and a little chicken snake at that. Don't you know chicken snakes are harmless? They can't hurt you.' Boots said, 'Yes, Mrs. Faulk, I know that,' and he's rubbing his forehead and behind at the same time, 'but they can scare you so bad it'll cause you to hurt yourself.'"

One of the most enduring stereotypes of males is that they should be able to control any demonstration of fear. Perhaps fearful inside, but never on the outside. Stereotypes may be distortions, more false than true, but they are powerful, nonetheless. So it isn't surprising that some of our early memories have to do with being scared out of control. When I read Faulk's reminiscence, it put me in mind of the time, at about age seven, I attached a generator light to my Schwinn bicycle and set out for my first ride in the dark to visit a friend. The streets that were familiar in daylight had turned very spooky, and I was more than once close to turning around and pedaling furiously back home. A frisson still tingles up my spine when I recall how scared I was.

What makes Boots Cooper's insight all the more winsome is that he has just been at play impersonating characters renowned for their courage, or ability to contain fear—rangers and marshals. But that is one thing boys do at play: rehearse, by means of repetition and trial solutions, how to master problems that are beyond their capacity in real life. One of the most pressing of these problems is how to confront danger with poise. In reality, Faulk and Cooper would have been even more terrified if a real robber had appeared at the kitchen door than they were of the chicken snake.

Three Dimensions of Control

From the moment of his birth until the moment of his death, a male is caught up in three different dimensions of control. First, he wants to control his environment so that it meets his desires adequately and promptly, from his perspective. Second, he wishes to contain to a degree tolerable to him the environment's efforts to control *him*. Third, he develops internal self-control with the encouragement of the environment and for his own purposes. By "environment," I mean not only the natural world, but also his family, his community, his school, his friends, his country, his material surroundings, his whole world.

Controlling the Environment

A boy is born without a distinct sense of separateness between himself and his immediate environment, especially his mother, but he is born with a set of lungs and vocal cords to sound the alarm when he is frustrated or uncomfortable, and he uses his instrument of complaint naturally.

His awareness of separateness begins in the first year of his life, and as it develops, so does his will to control his environment as effectively as he can—both the things and the people in it. He uses every method at his command—from smiles and requests to whines, tears, and tantrums; when what he wants is within reach, he grabs it. His wishes, in the beginning, are totalistic; that is, he cannot weigh their importance against the wishes and needs of others in his environment. If his needs and wishes are not met to some minimum degree of satisfaction, he can lapse into a kind of despair at a very early age. The infant's moods are mercurial; he may switch very quickly from one mood to another—from intently building a block tower one moment to stormy tears the next when he or someone else knocks it over, to building it again and laughing when it falls, and then fretting for food a moment later.

The script of a male's efforts to establish a measure of control over his environment can reflect many plots and subplots. Regarding just one goal, the desire to control women, Neil Jacobson and John Gottman have described two very different patterns among the most predatory of men. They refer to these two types as the pit bulls and the cobras. "Pit bulls are great guys," Jacobson told Jane Brody of the *New York Times*, "until they get into intimate relationships. O. J. Simpson is a classic pit bull. Pit bulls confine their monstrous behavior to the women they love, acting out of emotional dependence and a fear of abandonment. Pit bulls are the stalkers, the jealous husbands and boyfriends who are charming to everyone except their wives and girlfriends." Pit bulls, he added, are quick to see betrayal and it infuriates them. When their fury explodes into violence, they appear to lose control. Because their violence grows out of a dependency they feel has been betrayed, pit bulls often portray themselves as the ones who have been victimized in the violent relationship. "O. J. Simpson said he felt like a battered husband."

Cobras are relatively free of webs of emotional dependence, and their intended spheres of influence are not compartmentalized like the pit bulls'. They have a powerful need to be the boss, and to make sure that everyone—but particularly their wives and girlfriends—submits. They are not motivated by jealous love and dependence, but by unsentimental, antisocial attitudes. They are likely to be aggressive toward strangers and pets, as well as friends, relatives, and coworkers. When they think their dominance has been challenged, cobras strike swiftly and ferociously. In a cold-blooded way, cobras may use violence to establish complete control in a relationship and then back off and maintain the dominance with verbal threats.

Pit bulls get very physiologically aroused as their fury rises, but cobras calm down internally as they become more physically or verbally assaultive. When the police are called to intervene in a marital situation provoked by a cobra, they often find a hysterical woman and a very calm man who explains that it was all the woman's doing; sometimes the police accept the cobra's story and arrest the wrong person—the woman who has been assaulted.

While the pit bull/cobra metaphor depicts a particularly extreme behavior, it does serve to demonstrate how different the psychological motivations to control may be, varying in scope from quite generalized to very narrow and compartmentalized. A little boy may be indulged and seem to himself to be getting his way much of the time, yet he may moderate his control needs as he matures. Another little boy may experience frequent failure to control his environment to his satisfaction, but his failure, rather than making him resigned or stoic, may only intensify his need and efforts to control others as he matures. One boy may appear to be flexible in his control efforts, achieving control when he can, accepting lack of control resiliently when he can't; another little boy may be on a path to extreme rigidity on control issues, pursuing each one as though it were a life and death struggle. Every male will sometimes use control for altruistic purposes, and sometimes for selfish purposes. Temperament obviously has a large role in this, but so does the accretion of life experience interacting with temperament.

Resisting Control

Almost as soon as he is born, a boy will feel a countervailing force to his own desires. Those who are taking care of him will, in the process, inevitably try to control him in specific ways. His parents and other caregivers are going to feel happier if they can regularize his feeding schedule, get him to sleep through the night, persuade him to accept baths with relative equanimity, and eventually get him to accept toilet training as an alternative to their having to change his diapers. Others are going to regard him more positively if it appears that his daily life exhibits regularity. Much of this process, therefore, is wholly positive, and much of it is welcomed as reassuring by the infant and toddler; he flourishes knowing what to expect and how to behave. A give and take is established; he will find comfort in a structure of care.

There is, however, going to be a degree of frustration for the young male in this process as well. Caregivers are sometimes going to put tending to their own needs ahead of dealing with his. They are sometimes going to express frustration or irritation over the way he is behaving—chastising him, maybe punishing him. Siblings or playmates are going to deny him what he wants, and perhaps be aggressive toward him. Many children have to contend with caregivers who resent their responsibilities and take out their resentment on the children in their charge.

From the beginning there are some intrusions by his environment that a boy doesn't welcome, and would fend off if he could—even things in his best interest such as immunization shots at the pediatrician's office. So begins a lifelong dialectic between the need to be taken care of and the desire to be in charge, between dependence and autonomy. At each stage of development, the young boy will be more able to know what he wants and doesn't want, what he likes and doesn't like, and he can apply this knowledge to the various efforts to care for him; and at each stage it will be more apparent to him that his environment wants him to be obedient about some things.

The stage appears to be set for a long conflict of wills between a boy and his environment over the issue of control—and conflict does occur, particularly if parents and other caregivers don't comprehend this struggle and are rigid in their attempts to take charge. But the power struggle is also moderated by the third dimension of control: self-control.

Self-control

The prefacing of the word "control" with the word "self" changes its meaning entirely. Gaining self-control is a long process of learning to moderate and modulate one's desires and goals in a way that is appropriate to one's age and circumstances.

Both caregivers and a boy himself have much to gain by his development of self-control—caregivers because every enhancement of appropriate self-control diminishes the amount of oversight and influence they need to exert, and the boy because self-control gets others off his case and also reassures him that he won't spin impulsively out of control, at least not easily.

When this three-part process is successful, a grown man will find a reasonable balance of the three modes of control: he will have enough influence within his environment to pursue a satisfying life, but won't exploit opportunities to dominate others in ways hurtful to them; he will have enough power to keep his environment from exploiting him in hurtful ways; and he will have enough self-control to be able to handle challenging situations thoughtfully and creatively rather than impulsively and unreflectively.

The impressive scope of this process is dramatized if we remember the situation of the newborn. He has no power, is at the mercy of his caregivers to meet every one of his needs, and has virtually no self-control. By his preschool years, however, a boy begins to assume some responsibility for the control of himself. The development of language plays a large role in this shift of responsibility. As early as age two, boys begin to use "private speech" to monitor or control their own behavior. Playing by themselves, two- or three-year-olds can be overheard giving themselves instructions, or describing or commenting on what they are doing: "I put that there," "No, not there," etc. Some persons continue to talk to themselves in this way in much later stages of their lives, especially if they are working on a demanding task that requires a high level of concentration.

As with the first two aspects of control I've discussed, the term self-control is neutral, in that a male may achieve self-control in creative ways and for good purposes, or he may use his self-control for selfish or antisocial purposes. He may exhibit the rigid self-control of the zealot, or he may exhibit the resilient self-control of the compassionate person.

Temperament and Self-control

Self-control involves more than an exercise of willpower. It is not a constant from one person to another. To one boy it comes fairly easily, to another only as a struggle, all within the bounds of normal variation. Every boy's temperament needs to be read sensitively by those responsible for his care. There are many possible combinations of temperament and frustration tolerance. Stella Chess and Alexander Thomas describe a boy who had a high level of persistence, but if his concentration was interrupted in the wrong way he would immediately lose self-control.

> One day in the first grade he insisted on continuing his complicated block building when it was time to move to another activity. He could not be budged, and the exasperated teacher finally swept away his carefully constructed edifice. Richard responded with loud, prolonged crying and kicking. Immediately he became the class scapegoat, the 'cry baby' and the butt of teasing. The situation went from bad to worse until he was finally transferred to another school. Here Richard made a fresh start, and his persistent efforts in the school activities brought him the approval of teachers and the friendship of his classmates. . . .
>
> Another disruptive incident occurred several years later. For Brotherhood Week, a poster contest was arranged, and three students from his class, not including Richard, were chosen for the contest. Richard, however, was fired with the idea and labored long and hard to make his own poster, which he proudly brought to school. His teacher construed this behavior as gross disobedience, scolded him, and tore up his poster. Predictably, Richard had a massive blowup that included throwing a book at the teacher. He was now labeled not only a disobedient child but a violent one. Again he became the school scapegoat. His self-esteem hit bottom, and he told us, 'I just have a monster inside of me, and every once in a while it gets out.'

In both of these situations, an insensitive teacher is being challenged by a student she doesn't understand very well, a student who works with fierce concentration that looks like self-control but is actually precarious. Neither of these teachers appears to have been briefed about Richard's temperament before he arrived at their classrooms. Faced with a challenge to their authority, both teachers reacted in a provocative way guaranteed to set Richard off; they destroyed his creations in which he had invested immense care.

The second teacher had perhaps the easier challenge. He or she could have explained to Richard that since there was a contest that others won to design the school poster, it would be unfair to display his poster exactly as the winning poster was to be displayed, but the teacher could have evaluated his poster, and praised his initiative, and discussed with him some mutually satisfactory way to display his poster; the theme, brotherhood, would seem to suggest no less. If he had shown extra initiative in an academic subject, the teacher probably would have praised his effort. By turning the incident into a power struggle, and disrespecting his efforts so heartlessly, the teacher lost an opportunity to forge an alliance with the student, and turned Richard into a pariah once again.

Eliciting cooperation by every child with the routines of the class is one of the goals of a first-grade teacher, and some children inevitably resist more than others. In the earlier incident, the teacher turned Richard's stubborn persistence into a power struggle with the kind of gesture that would make boys even less persistent than Richard angry. If she had been flexible for the moment and found a quiet moment later to talk with Richard, the incident and its very unhappy aftermath might have been averted.

A more vigorous male response against female aggression was found in one of the few large studies of boys' and girls' temperaments in relation to the parenting styles of their mothers and fathers. Sophia Bezirganian and Patricia Cohen noted that sons with difficult temperaments were particularly resistant to controlling strategies by their mothers. If the mothers were rigid in their expectations and punitive in their responses to misbehavior, the boys' temperaments actually worsened. Daughters didn't experience such deteriorations in response either to their mothers or their fathers, and neither did boys' temperaments become more difficult in response to their fathers.

The Components of Self-control

One component of self-control is the neurological capacity to delay responses to stimuli. This "hardwiring" varies considerably from child to child. In some children, the capacity is very compromised. They simply cannot delay their reactions, and punishing them for not having the capacity of a child with a different neurological inheritance is doubly cruel. Observation of a boy in the first months of his life will give a parent some clues as to the intensity of his reactions, the swiftness of his reactions, and the amount of stimulation it takes to evoke a response. Even a hardwired capacity such as this can be affected to a degree by the environment—for better or worse. In cases of post-traumatic stress disorder, for example, the capacity to delay response can be markedly reduced. Signals that ordinarily would be sent in a split second to areas in the brain that allow a person to reflect on their experience and make plans to cope with it are interrupted by hyperreactive responses.

In her clinical practice as a psychologist, my wife, Carolyn, once worked with a little boy who was overwhelmed by his impulses. When he felt he needed something, he wanted it without any delay. She remembers a day when he felt such a strong desire for a doughnut that he couldn't concentrate on anything else until the desire was satisfied. Carolyn wanted to help him buy some time between his feeling a need and his satisfying the need.

So Carolyn made up a pretend game with him. To get the doughnut, they would have to drive to a store that sold doughnuts. Together, in fantasized play, they drove street by street to the store, parked the car, went into the store, found some doughnuts, carried them to the checkout counter, and took the doughnuts back by car to her office. Then they fantasized eating a doughnut. The little boy was fully aware that a pretend doughnut was much less satisfying than a real one. But he participated gleefully in the game and learned to use fantasy and planning as a strategy for tolerating the frustration of not getting what he wanted when he wanted it. This is an example of how one can work patiently and imaginatively with a boy to insinuate a bit of time and reflection between a stimulus and the response to it.

Daniel Goleman, in *Emotional Intelligence*, recounted an experiment conducted at Stanford University in the 1960s. Four-year-olds were called individually into a room where a kindly man gave each a marshmallow and said the child could choose either to eat the marshmallow at once or wait for him to return from doing an errand. If the child waited, he would get an additional marshmallow when the man returned. Then the kindly man left the room, leaving the child by himself.

The children who elected to wait until the man returned—and thus earn an additional marshmallow—did all sorts of things to control their desire. Some of them covered their eyes or rested their heads on their arms so they couldn't see the tempting marshmallow in front of them. Others sang or played games by themselves. About a third of the children grabbed the marshmallow and ate it as soon as the man left the room.

A dozen years later, the very same children, now adolescents, were tested again with more elaborate techniques. The ones who had delayed eating the marshmallow in order to get a reward were still capable of self-control. "They were less likely to go to pieces, freeze or regress under stress, or become rattled and disorganized when pressured; they embraced challenges and pursued them instead of giving up even in the face of difficulties; they were self-reliant and confident, trustworthy and dependable."

The youngsters who had immediately eaten their marshmallows were "more likely to be seen as shying away from social contacts, to be stubborn and indecisive, to be easily upset by frustrations, to think of themselves as unworthy, to become immobilized by stress, to be mistrustful or prone to jealousy, to overreact with a sharp temper." What this study doesn't show us is whether in those intervening twelve years anyone made a sensitive and concerted effort to help any of the impulsive marshmallow-eaters to develop self-control; the implication is that no one did.

Carolyn once worked with a twelve-year-old boy who was extremely impulsive. His reactions to any provocations were explosive. If someone "pulled his chain," as we say, he punched first and thought about it later. What he needed, she knew, was some mechanism that would help him stop to think before he acted.

With this particular boy, she believed a visual image might be useful. So she concocted the image/metaphor of the "thought sandwich." A sandwich was an image that the boy could, and did, draw in cross-section. The bottom layer of bread in the sandwich, as Carolyn and he defined it, was usually an enraging provocation by another child; the top layer was his response to the provocation, usually a punch in the face or an insulting taunt. The filling in the sandwich was the thought—the heart of the sandwich, actually—that he could put between the two pieces of bread. Without any filling he didn't have much of a sandwich. The filling consisted of identifying what was provoking him to react, then weighing his choices and their probable consequences before coming to a decision about how to react. He sometimes activated this method of self-control by actually visualizing a sandwich in his mind.

There are many potential techniques and metaphors for helping a boy gain a measure of control over impulsivity, and maybe the best ones are invented in the concrete interactions between two people who are trying to find a way to deal with everyday life.

Awareness of Standards

If the first element of self-control is neurological capacity, then the second element is knowledge and awareness of standards of behavior expected by people that a boy should respect. A boy is now reading his environment for clues as to how he should behave—the *script*, as it were, of his self-control. This is not a simple task. By the time he reaches school age, a boy has encountered several systems of rules and expectations every day. None of those systems is entirely consistent from day to day or even hour to hour. Few of those systems spend much time explaining and justifying the expected standards of behavior. Boys, moreover, are less consistently monitored in terms of hewing to expected standards of behavior than girls are, so boys are understandably uncertain, at times, how strictly standards are being upheld.

From the Internet, however, I offer an example of the level of self-control that can be obtained in a boy who has control problems when the expectations are clearly stated just before an event. A father writes about his school-age son, Larry, who carries the diagnosis of ADHD (attention deficit hyperactive disorder):

> Last night we took Larry to his soccer team awards dinner. My wife and I were not looking forward to having Larry in this exciting situation, and he was already 'bouncing off the wall' before we left. While I was parking the car, we had a very serious talk about how we expected him to act, and what the consequences would be if he didn't comply.
>
> The soccer team consisted of eleven 8 to 10-year-old boys. They all sat at one big table while all of the family members and friends sat at other tables. We sat next to Larry's table. It was noisy and crowded. The boys were hungry and restless. Lots of loud talking and banging of silverware on the table. Several boys were shooting spitballs with straws at others. Three boys were putting pieces of paper napkins in the lit candles until someone took the candles away. Some boys were cutting in line at the buffet table. One chair fell over with a boy in it. Lots of parents were calling out to their sons to 'knock it off.'
>
> My wife and I were ready for Larry to add to this big storm. But, HE DIDN'T! He just sat calmly and smiled at the other boys. He played with his water and straw but didn't do anything inappropriate. We couldn't believe how well he acted. We praised him dearly after the dinner, and of course he was hyped up all the way home (he must have saved it up). My wife and I laughed and sighed, wondering if Larry would ever behave this well again.

Motivation and Self-control

As a boy moves from control by others to internalized self-control, he has to develop more than knowledge of what others expect of him; he has to develop motivation to meet those expectations. There is an emotional component to self-control. A person must *want* to maintain self-control.

Louis Armstrong grew up in a tough New Orleans neighborhood called "The Battlefield" because of its reputation for drunken street fights involving knives and guns. On New Year's Eve of 1912 or 1913, Louis took his grandmother's boyfriend's pistol from its hiding place and went out with friends to fire it during the celebration. They were walking along South Rampart Street when a boy fired a blank in Armstrong's direction. Louis impulsively fired back a real bullet, and a policeman arrested him. The next day, after a short hearing, he was sent to the Colored Waifs' Home to begin an indeterminate sentence.

The home was one of many established as part of the American child welfare movement, but was unusual in that it was started by an African-American, a former soldier named Joseph Jones and his wife, Manuella. One observer recalled: "The boys were taught reading, writing and arithmetic, with garden work as a sideline. Twice weekly, the boys marched around the yard outside, with wooden guns and wooden drums."

Peter Davis was the leader of the Colored Waifs' Home Band that performed around town to raise money for the home. The band consisted of a bass drum and about fifteen brass instruments, "perhaps three or four cornets and a roughly equal assortment of alto and baritone horns, trombones and perhaps a tuba. The boys wore long white pants turned up to look like knickers, blue gabardine coats, black stockings, sneakers, and caps." Davis didn't take to Louis at the outset. Day after day, Louis sat quietly in the band room, listening and watching. Finally he was offered a tambourine to play, then the bass drum, and still later an alto horn, on which Armstrong shone. The rest is history. After his release years later, Louis rented a cornet for gigs on the street and in dance halls. Once he found a musical sponsor in Joseph "King" Oliver, with whom he made an influential set of recordings on second cornet, he was on his way.

I cite this story as a stirring example of how the three aspects of control can come to an harmonious intersection. Louis Armstrong's love and fabulous talent for music gave him the motive to master his instrument, the mastery itself a paradigm of self-control and self-discipline. The mastery also gave him tremendous influence in the musical world and the culture at large. But first of all, he gained the motivation to control the impulsivity that had led him into trouble and into the Waifs' Home.

Music gave Louis the means to avoid being exploited by the environment. His particular kind of music, jazz, exemplifies freedom within limits. It's a form of music that demands respect for the rules of a particular style—traditional, blues, swing, bebop, for example—but then the performer is free to improvise. Within those bounds, the best players, like Louis Armstrong, constantly invent new melodies, harmonies, and rhythms, salting them with deep and honest feeling. Jazz is a nice metaphor for the combination of self-control and creative action that constitute character.

Louis Armstrong's story contains something to be hoped for in every boy's life: that he will find a thing or things he is passionate about, and his passion will enable him to tolerate the long hours of practice to master the discipline. For many boys, the passion is sports of one type or another, but for others it is music—as it was for me—or other arts, or rebuilding cars, or collecting things, or mastering the technology of computers and other electronic instruments. Whatever the discipline, one hopes that a boy has a substantial amount of autonomy in its selection. History offers many examples of a parent's passion contagiously becoming the passion of a son, who may even surpass the parent in accomplishment. There are far too many boys, however, playing a sport because it's Dad's idea or unhappily practicing the piano because it's Mom's idea. Then a boy's continuation in the activity tends to become a power struggle between him and his parent. The parent may win such a struggle, at least temporarily, but often at the cost of losing any possibility that the activity will ever be an enthusiastic passion for the boy.

My own experience convinces me of the enormous value of such a strong individual passion. During my year in sixth grade, the band director looked over the available boys interested in musical performance, noted my stocky build, and asked if I'd like to try the tuba. It was a match made in heaven. I liked the instrument immediately—its size, its range of tone from the throatiest growls through the mellow middle range to squeals at the top.

In seventh grade, the school orchestra director announced tryouts, and I went, intending to try out for the piano position, since piano was still my principal instrument. The tryout was a sight-reading test. I played fairly well, but when I heard my classmate Paul Hersh play I was flabbergasted. He tore into difficult music and played it as though he had been practicing for weeks. It was a revelatory moment for me. The thought flashed through my mind: No matter how long I practice, I'll never be able to play like that. This was followed immediately by a second thought: But I have a fallback position; I can be as good on the tuba as Paul on the piano. In a nanosecond my musical career tacked in a new direction. It was my first important experience in evaluating my own talents and taking the prudent (and equally fulfilling) path.

A few months ago I talked with the parents of three boys aged eleven, fifteen, and seventeen. We talked most about the fifteen-year-old, Toby, because I had heard from a mutual friend that he was already a good musician. In the fourth grade, Toby had a music teacher who introduced him to the trumpet; it was love at first sound. Soon he was in a little school jazz band, and in his second year got to accompany the school chorus in "White Christmas" and play another solo.

Toby's mother said he is "borderline" ADD (attention deficit disorder) but doesn't take medication for it. He had recently been ejected from an academic class, and when the teacher was asked why, he said that there was one too many students assigned to the room and Toby was the most disruptive one. He scores very well in intelligence tests, but his academic record is very mixed because he can't apply himself consistently to his schoolwork.

But music is a very different story because his passion for it overrides his fidgetiness. Even there, his path is not entirely smooth. He was expelled from the school jazz band in eighth grade because he wasn't doing well enough in academic subjects to qualify for extracurricular activities—a disciplinary move, to my mind, of dubious wisdom. He had also gotten tossed out of a concert orchestra by inserting some bars of "Take Me Out to the Ball Game" in the middle of Brahms's Symphony No. 1 during a performance at a museum! But music is the great stabilizer in his life. Without it, he would be an adolescent defined mainly by his problems; because of music, he manages to get by in school, and he has a ground for self-confidence and a future. One of his teachers, who found Toby disruptive in the classroom, said to Toby's mother after attending a performance in which Toby shone on the trumpet, "If I hadn't seen him here I wouldn't have known how great a kid he is."

Stages of Self-control

The process by which a boy acquires self-control mirrors in many ways the process by which an adult may develop different levels of parental awareness. Each begins at a self-centered stage. The infant's first focus is on his own needs for survival: food, comfort, loving attention. Every adult has equivalent needs. It is important not to equate this early stage with selfishness. Since the newborn is both helpless to care for himself, and entirely unable to contribute care to anyone else, it is beside the point to refer to his behavior as selfish. Selfishness comes into the picture only when he has developed the capacity to help himself and others and has the mental acuity to weigh his own needs against the needs of others.

A boy's first step in self-control comes when he begins to absorb the network of rules and values by which he is being raised. Through a series of daily rewards and reprimands or punishments, a boy learns what adults expect of him. He begins to internalize these benchmarks of good behavior and to fulfill them of his own accord without having to be reminded or constrained every time. His parents and other caregivers have reached the Level Two of playing by the rules long before he has, and for both parent and child observing rules of good behavior will continue to be a major component of exerting control over others and exerting self-control for the remainder of their lives.

As a boy matures in self-control, he begins to see the effect of his actions on particular others. He may at first see this impact in stereotypical ways, but further experience can pave the way to more sensitive evaluations of what he has done. Now he can begin to tailor his subsequent actions to what he believes their effects will probably be. Without this capacity, a boy invited to a birthday party might decide to take a model airplane as a present because he himself loves model airplanes. A moment's reflection might have told him that the birthday boy collects baseball cards and has never shown the slightest bit of interest in the gift-giver's model airplane collection; the model airplane kit will never be built.

This development corresponds to a parent's understanding a son in his individuality—operating at We are Both Individuals—Level Three—awareness. I see this as a critical development in dealing with issues of control. Until the parent begins to operate at this level, the principal resource the parent has available is rules. But rules are frequently believed to apply equally to all children.

At Level Three, a parent comprehends what a mystery each child is, and how unique. With respect to control and self-control, for example, each child is affected by his particular biological-neurological inheritance and development, which has something in common with that of other children but is also different from every other temperament. As a parent respectfully interacts with a son, the son will reveal what his temperament allows as a base for self-control, but his behavior as a reflection of his temperament will vary some from situation to situation, and will change as the child matures.

Likewise, a son will give clues to the inquiring parent of his emotional-motivational basis for self-control—or for impulsive loss of control. When a boy exhibits problematical behavior—let's say he teases others at school or even shows some bullying behavior—a parent operating at Level Three will want to get a sense of what this behavior means to the son; what needs or fears are provoking the boy to poor behavior? How may those needs and fears be treated in order to remove the incentive for the boy to take out his frustration on others? Addressing these reasons for his behavior will help such a boy far more than merely reasserting rules and promising to punish him if he repeats the behavior (a typical Level Two response) or chastising him on the grounds that his behavior is an embarrassment to his parents (a Level One response)

Not only are boys a mystery to their parents and other caregivers; they are a mystery in many respects to themselves. They are very much in the process of exploring themselves, discovering themselves, even as their selves change before their own eyes. As a parent takes an inquiring posture toward a son, so the son is encouraged to take an inquiring posture toward himself.

At the highest level of self-control, some boys begin to be aware both of their effects on others, and of others' effects on them—and even aware of others being aware of them. In other words, social interactions have become the subject of awareness. Interactions become available for discussion when they are accompanied by awareness.

Parents can discuss with a son why another boy gets under his skin, challenges his self-control. Role-playing by family members can give a boy practice in thinking before he acts, and in imagining the motives and consequences of a particular strategy: Why do you think he does that? What are *your* thoughts about how to make the situation better? What if he doesn't do what you expect him to do? What if your first response makes the situation worse? Have you considered all of the available strategies—staying cool, buying time or delaying, defusing the conflict, even backing off?

ADD/ADHD

By age six, girls, on average, have an advantage over boys with respect to self-control. Girls can sit longer without feeling frustrated by inactivity. They pay attention with less apparent effort. Boys innately desire a more vigorous level of physical activity than girls. Boys fidget. This quickly becomes an issue because boys' rambunctiousness gets labeled as character deficiency. Girls get praised for their self-regulation; boys get criticized for their lack of it.

A diagnostic category has been developed in the past few decades to identify impulsivity, inattentiveness, and hyperactivity in children that is outside normal temperamental variation, and also certain cognitive problems. The current terms of this diagnostic category, known as attention deficit disorder (ADD) and attention deficit hyperactive disorder (ADHD), state that the symptoms must have been present before the child's seventh birthday, must have been present for at least six months, must have been observed in at least two settings—home and school, for example—must have caused significant social problems, and must not be traceable to some other known primary factor.

When the problems are principally related to inattention, the child might be observed especially frequently to: make careless mistakes; have difficulty sustaining attention; seem not to listen even when spoken to directly; fail to pursue instructions and finish assignments.

When the symptoms are predominantly hyperactive-impulsive, the child often fidgets and squirms; leaves his seat in school without permission; talks excessively and blurts out answers before questions have been completed; has difficulty waiting his turn; runs about excessively when it is inappropriate; interrupts others; has difficulty playing quietly; sometimes distracts others with repetitive actions such as drumming with a pencil or tapping with a foot.

When the symptoms are cognitive, the child may have difficulty understanding and following a set of directions, or organizing material according to its central theme, or even identifying the central theme; may find it unusually difficult to retain memorized data such as multiplication tables; may appear to avoid tasks that require sustained mental effort; may frequently lose or misplace things necessary for tasks; may find it difficult to follow routines for such tasks as getting ready for school; may have difficulty relating work assignment to the passage of time. This complex phenomenon of absorbing information, processing it, remembering it, and applying it to specific tasks as needed is often referred to as "the executive function."

The labels ADD and ADHD, especially the latter hyperactive variety, are considered by many pediatricians and child development specialists to be a diagnostic wastebasket. A neurological disorder is implied in the diagnostics, but how does one distinguish between instances of neurological impairment and normal temperamental variation shown by children— factoring in, as one must, the level of activity most boys desire? As William Carey of Children's Hospital of Philadelphia has written, "It seems highly likely that most of the children being given the diagnosis of ADHD today are completely intact neurologically and merely have temperaments that are poorly understood, tolerated, or managed by their caregivers."

Parents, Carey notes, often complain about their children's temperaments even in the absence of behavioral problems because there is an uncomfortable temperamental fit between parent and child.

> The pediatrician who does not understand these important variations is likely to ignore, belittle, or pathologize them. When there is dysfunctional behavior (aggression, school underachievement, poor self-regulation, etc.), a knowledge of the child's temperament is essential for two reasons. It often helps to explain why this particular child happened to develop the disorder, that is, how the risk factor predisposed this child to develop the behavior problem while an equally stressed sibling or peer did not. It also helps to distinguish the part of the behavior that is the largely inborn temperament and not easily altered from the part that is a reaction to the situation and therefore more changeable by an intervention. For example, is the child's oppositional behavior problem entirely a reflection of unfavorable experiences, or did it come at least in part from an inflexible temperament and the caregiver's mishandling of it due to lack of understanding, tolerance, or skill?

Mark Vonnegut, a pediatrician, recently wrote a column commenting on his experience as a member of a National Institutes of Health panel assembled to review the state of current knowledge of ADHD, listen to testimony by thirty experts, and make a consensus statement.

> I know there is a real disease hiding under the confusion. I have patients who have it, and I have seen its effects. But the disease itself is hard to measure. There's no clear cause, and nothing unequivocal—like a blood test or CAT scan finding—to determine when someone has it. So we are left with a disease that is defined only by behavior. And the qualities that define it by inattention, hyperactivity, and poor impulse control—are present to some degree in virtually all children. Indeed, those qualities are also a common reaction to many different kinds of stress.

This debate within pediatrics and child development would be more of an academic exercise if it weren't for pharmacology. Approximately a million schoolchildren—the large majority of them boys—are currently taking either psychostimulants such as Ritalin or, when these are not effective, tricyclic antidepressants such as Impramine to increase attention span, improve concentration, and decrease motor activity. In many of these cases, medication has been prescribed without anyone conducting the extensive physical and psychological tests that might adequately support a diagnosis of ADD or ADHD. I disagree with Dr. Vonnegut's assertion that we are limited to behavioral symptoms. Extensive—but expensive—psychological testing can establish with a high degree of probability whether a child has ADD or ADHD impairment.

However, I haven't any doubts about his assertion that even the behavioral symptoms are often glossed over in practice. The problem, as Vonnegut sees it, is that the medications work too well. "If you take a child who doesn't have ADHD but acts out in class, and treat him with Ritalin, he will stop acting out in class. If you take someone who doesn't have ADHD but has trouble settling down to his homework and give him a little Ritalin, he will settle down and do his homework. If a child is having trouble concentrating because he was drunk the night before, Ritalin will help him focus." So, he concludes, it takes more and more conscious exercise of responsibility for a caregiver or physician to look for the real cause of problematic behavior without turning to the quick fix of an ADHD diagnosis and a bottle of Ritalin.

One should also bear in mind that many families would be hard pressed to afford the expensive tests involved in clinically diagnosing ADD or ADHD. Faced with either inattention or hyperactivity-impulsivity behavior, a prescription of Ritalin on a trial basis, though not inexpensive, is far

less expensive than a battery of tests and perhaps a course of counseling
or therapy to treat problematic behavior.

The misapplication of ADHD diagnoses and medication to behavioral
disorders best understood and treated by other means obscures the fact
that there is such a thing as ADD and ADHD, and that, in the view of one
recent theorist, it centrally involves "delays in the development of inhibition and self-regulation," or, in simpler terms, that this is a disorder of
self-control.

Neuropsychologist Russell Barkley asserts that his is the first formulation of ADHD

> to predict that the disorder (1) disrupts the capacity for working or represen-
> tational memory and the power of covertly sensing, or, more accurately, re-
> sensing, information to oneself; (2) creates a delay in the internalization of
> speech during development and the self-control dependent upon this rather
> miraculous developmental process; (3) impairs the development of the psy-
> chological sense of time, hindsight, and forethought and, particularly, the em-
> ployment of those senses in the regulation of one's own behavior relative to
> time and the future; (4) disrupts not only the power to internally represent in-
> formation but also the capacity to reconstitute that information in the service
> of goal-directed behavioral creativity and the temporal organization of be-
> havior; (5) diminishes the capacity for private, covert emoting and motivating
> oneself that is critical to objectivity, perspicacity, intentionality, and the moti-
> vational support of behavior as it is driven toward the future; (6) impairs the
> capacity to imitate or replicate the complex behavioral sequences of others; (7)
> results in more externalized or public than internalized or covert 'thinking' be-
> havior than is typical of normal individuals; and (8) interferes with the goal-
> directed persistence, volition, and free-will of the individual.

Barkley centers ADHD in a flawed interior process of self-regulation, emphasizing the deficiencies of executive function that are often not as obvious as hyperactive behavior or inattentiveness.

We have already seen how fundamentally early self-control depends on
the ability of the toddler and preschooler to use language to create an internal dialogue with himself (that he sometimes articulates aloud when he
is working or playing by himself). In this interior process, the child stores
information, retrieving it as needed, organizes the performance of tasks,
watches others do things and imagines how he could replicate their activity, reenacts emotional conflicts prior to dealing with them externally, relates his activities to the passage of time, and makes plans and anticipates
the future.

All of these functions may be impaired in the mind of a child with true
ADD or ADHD. He impulsively acts out because he can't stop to consider

his response the way other children can. Without a strong sense of time past and time future, he lives in a dominant present time; as soon as his attention wanes, he skips on to something else. He has an impaired capacity to select out of all the activity and other stimuli around him—other children moving slightly, an airplane visible out the window or heard passing overhead, the second hand moving on the wall clock—the thing he most needs to pay attention to: the teacher explaining an arithmetic problem. (I once accompanied the mother of a boy clinically diagnosed with ADHD on a visit to a classroom where every bit of wall space was covered with maps and charts and art. "My son would find this room a nightmare of distraction," she said.) Ill-equipped to "read" other children who are operating mentally in a very different mode, the child with ADD or ADHD may have a difficult time making and maintaining friendships. His disorder often disguises his real intelligence, and he may be teased as being "stupid" or "dumb."

An appreciation of the dimensions of accurately diagnosed ADD or ADHD implies the importance of distinguishing it from normal-range temperamental hyperactivity or inattentiveness. Both need the assistance of an empathic environment. In the case of normal temperamental variation, there are many small adjustments a school or family can make to adapt to a boy's temperament without resorting to drugs. When the behavior is excessive and problematic, the search for environmental explanations and resolutions should always precede the use of medications to dampen the symptoms.

When ADD or ADHD exists, the challenge is greater. A boy with a disturbance of executive function needs disciplined help with storing information so he can find it and review it when, as often, memory fails him; help with understanding directions and organizing his schoolwork and other projects; help with tracking time; help to get himself back under control when he impulsively vents frustration without stopping to think what effect he's having on others. Psychostimulants or tricyclic antidepressants may benefit a boy with ADD or ADHD, though not all boys respond well and some are too bothered by side effects on appetite and sleep; but they would rarely, if ever, be all that such a boy would need to regain and maintain all the dimensions of self-control in a normal range. But then neither are they all that the hundreds of thousands of boys need who have exhibited temperamental lack of self-control, and then have been swiftly misdiagnosed as having ADD or ADHD and medicated.

Self-control and Character

To exhibit sterling character, a boy growing up has to pay attention to all three dimensions of control: control of his environment, control by his environment, and self-control. If any of the three gets seriously out of balance, his life is going to be destructive or unhappy. By balance, I mean that life involves a series of quests for power and influence that are positive and necessary, but that, overdone, become destructive, even evil. The balance of each quest has to be reevaluated day by day, year by year: has the line been crossed between justifiable goals and unjustifiable dominance, or not? Has the line been crossed between others' appropriate assertion of influence toward a boy, and unjustifiable subordination?

The male's wish to control his environment is affected deeply by his hardwired drive to construct hierarchies of power and influence and acquire as much dominance in those hierarchies as he can. It's in his genes. This drive has so many unconscious elements that males often pursue control without awareness of what they are doing. They pursue it individually in personal relationships, particularly intimate and marital relationships, and they pursue it collectively in groups and teams.

Power is, as the cliché has it, the ultimate aphrodisiac. Males pursue it with enormous ardor, and there is no one institution in their lives that reliably educates them about this disposition and its potential for hurting others. So males are often out of control in their quest for control.

Power out of control has to be countered by conscious resistance. Others have to push back in an effective way. The principal historical examples in our society of pushing back against domination are the antislavery movement that eventually led to the civil rights movement; the women's movement against male dominance in many institutions; the union movement in behalf of laborers against management and ownership; several ethnic solidarity movements in behalf of ethnic minorities against dominant ethnic groups; the environmental movement against the destruction of the natural world; peace movements protesting war as an instrument of national policy against weaker nations; and an emerging concern for children's rights to education, health, and protection from harm and exploitation, manifested in the recent United Nations Convention on the Rights of the Child. Every male growing up has to determine how he will align himself against dominating powers in his personal life and in his social life. His character will be tested time and time again as he is challenged to defend his own rights and to align himself with others struggling collectively.

Self-control plays a critical role in all of this. As I've suggested, a flexible and resilient self-control is a goal in itself. A male who has himself under control is a happier man than a male teetering at the edge. Self-control also plays a part in decisions to pull back from opportunities to dominate others or to stand up effectively to oppressors.

13

TEASING AND BULLYING

In January of 1998, in the middle of his fifth-grade year, Charlie Green—known to everyone as "Chip"—moved from one town to another in suburban Boston. His family, including his younger sister, Alice, moved in two installments because his mother and father had been separated for a few years. Both parents agreed to relocate to a more highly regarded public school system.

In his old school, Chip had breezed along at the top of the class. He had a couple of close buddies to whom he was fiercely loyal, which was what he wanted. With his slow-to-warm-up temperament, he would not necessarily find one or two new buddies in six months to replace the ones he cultivated in five years at his old school. In his new school, moreover, Chip found himself in a class where several others were as bright as he. He lost his academic buoyancy at the same time that he was finding himself challenged socially. Though he was in fact doing well academically, he actually was fearful that he might fail and be held back; this tendency to overreact to being suddenly immersed in a larger pool of talent is something one sees in boys all the way from preschool to graduate school—and throughout adult life as well.

Chip's new teacher, Mrs. Lewis, was absent recovering from surgery the first several weeks of Chip's experience in his new school, but everything seemed satisfactory so far as his mother, Elaine, could tell, though Chip rarely said anything to her about his classmates. "The great truths with Chip," she says, "are likely to come out when I snuggle with him in that somnolent state as he goes to sleep. I don't know how I'll stay close to him when he is too old to want that."

One bedtime in late January, Chip confessed that "I don't like my school." His chin quivered a little as he said it. "The kids don't like me. They call me names. They push me out." When Elaine asked him how bothered he was by the situation, Chip said he was okay, and seemed to mean it. "I'm the new kid," he said, by way of explanation.

Another month passed and Mrs. Lewis was back with her class. The night before Chip's parents were to attend the first parent-teacher conference of the year, Chip made another bedtime confession. "I don't like the school, Mom. The other kids are mean to me. They don't like me, and I don't like them."

The first thing Mrs. Lewis said to Elaine and Tony Green at the conference was that there had been an incident on the playground the day before. Chip's new school, unlike his old, employed aides to monitor the playground. The aides reported that two boys in his class were teasing Chip, tripping him as they all played a game they called "Virus," taunting him as clumsy, and urging other classmates to gang up on Chip to force him out of the game.

The school had a clearly stated ethic of student conduct, so Mrs. Lewis was not addressing a vacuum when, as she reported, she pulled the two teasers aside and dressed them down. She said she had lost a great deal of respect for them. This episode would be dealt with just between the teacher and students, but if there were repetition of the teasing she would immediately call their parents. She told the boys she expected everyone in the class to be an *advocate* for anyone subjected to teasing at the school.

For another several weeks, all seemed to be well. Then, in late April, Chip made another bedtime confession. "The kids will never like me. And I will never like them. This is not the school for me. I can't take it anymore." Each of the three times Chip had mentioned this subject, he had said about the same thing, but the message had gotten progressively more urgent. Neither then, nor earlier, would Chip actually describe any teasing episodes to his parents. But Elaine assumed there had been another incident. Mrs. Lewis confirmed it when Elaine dropped by the school a couple of days later. She said that the school counselor had been called in to devise a plan to deal with the situation.

The counselor and teacher mailed a letter to the parents of over a dozen classmates who had led, cooperated with, or gone along with the teasing— mostly boys, but a few girls as well:

Dear Parents,
　　It has come to my attention through my observations and through a parent's concern for her child that a majority of the students in this room are less than tolerant of one of their classmates.
　　Teasing and excluding a classmate, snickering at responses and making someone feel uncomfortable and unwelcome are behaviors that have caused a great deal of pain. I will not tolerate this from

anyone in my class.

I have had private discussions with a few of the children in the past and have said nothing to you because "we had a deal"—their behavior would change and I wouldn't say anything.

But when a parent writes that her child can't take it anymore, doesn't want to come to school and doesn't feel that s/he belongs, it is time that I mention it to all of you.

I had the new counselor in the class today while she and I talked with the boys. Tomorrow, I will talk with the girls, but I need your help. Ostracizing anyone is not acceptable.

Please help your child understand this.   Thank you

Then the two women talked with Chip and told him they planned to have a session with the classmates who had been teasing him, first with the boys, and then with the girls. He was invited to attend if he chose, but he elected not to. Choosing a time when many students were in transition from one activity to another, school staff quietly summoned the offending students to the two sessions. Chip's family knows little of what happened at the sessions except that the school ethic was discussed and students were asked to describe any experiences they might have had of being excluded and teased. This was to reinforce the sympathetic argument: How would you feel if someone did this to you?

The day after the session with the boys, Elaine was driving Chip to an appointment when he said, "You know, Mom, they had a meeting." "Who?" "Mrs. Lewis and all the boys." "Did you go?" "No, I decided not to." "What do you think about it?" "I think," said Chip, who is nothing if not verbal, "grown-ups can be quite useful. And guess what?" "What?" "I have a secret code. If something happens and I say the code word to Mrs. Lewis, I can go right away and see the counselor about it." "I don't know whether he will or not—or need to," Elaine said to me, "but I think it must be a very big comfort to him."

Teasing

Pascal Lehman, whom I introduced in the first chapter, remembered a teasing episode when he was seven years old. His step-father, who participated in this conversation, brought it up: "Who was that young man, I can't remember his name, oh yes, Joshua, that everyone was teasing in Mrs. Stone's class. Everyone was hammering him, right? And you told us about it and we said, 'Look, we don't want you teasing this boy.' And you said, 'My friends are doing it, and if I don't go along they're going to give me a hard time.' And we said, 'Well, then, I guess they're not your friends if they do that. If you treat that kid with respect and show him some decency, you'll have a friend for life.' If his friends didn't like it, then that was that. He had to do the mature thing, and he did."

"What was it about this kid that made other kids tease him?" I asked.

"Well, he wore pretty much the same clothes every day, and he smelled pretty bad, and he wasn't making friends, and he stuttered pretty bad. He wasn't really athletic, and, ah, he was overweight, and he was just picked on because he wanted to make friends, but he wanted to make friends so badly that he'd follow boys around, and they didn't like that. So they started calling him names and beating him up, but he still followed them."

"Did you feel when you were that age that you didn't have any choice but to participate?"

"You gotta know the environment," said Pascal. "If it was in the classroom, I wouldn't participate in it. If it was outside on the playground, and my friends started calling him names, then I would call him names, too."

"What caused you to mention it to your parents?" I asked.

"I told them because it started getting really bad. They started throwing rocks at him. I didn't like that at all. I didn't say anything, but I didn't do it. So I told my mom and dad, and asked what I should do. They told me that I shouldn't go along with other kids—I should look at what the right thing to do is. And they said that if you go against your friends for the right thing, and they make fun of you, too, then they're not really your friends. So I went back to school, and kids started calling him names, and I stood up against these kids, and they respected me, so they didn't push me around. They walked away, and called me 'Joshua lover' or something like that. Joshua never really talked to me after that point, but none of the kids made fun of him anymore. I don't know what happened. I guess he was so shocked that someone stood up for him that he actually found another friend."

Speaking to Pascal's step-father, I said, "Was there anything else you did other than talk to Pascal about the situation?"

"No, my feeling was: here's what we believe. Whether it's hard or not, it's the right thing, and you have to do it. This is what we think will be the result, but whether we get the result we want or not, this is the right thing to do. I trusted Pascal a lot. I think that is part of it, too, that we showed him that trust. Of course, he didn't accept it right away. There was a little bit of 'But Dad, gee I don't know, the other guys'. . . You know, there were a lot of 'yeah, but's.'"

Teasing manifests a lack of respect. Or, to put it a little more forcefully: Teasing is an active display of disrespect. What Pascal did was pull an ostracized boy within his own aura of respect, and Pascal's reputation was such that if he signaled becoming a protector of the ostracized boy, no other boys were going to challenge him very much. Teasing shows an unwillingness to empathize with whatever it is about a person that subjects him to teasing—in Chip's case, his newcomer status, and in Pascal's classmate's case, the stuttering and obesity and deficient personal hygiene. It's quite possible that the boy Pascal defended understood what he had and hadn't received: He had received a classmate's intervention that won him relief from teasing and taunting, but he hadn't received the empathic recognition from Pascal that might have become the basis of friendship.

On the Web page managed by the department of neurology at Massachusetts General Hospital to provide a support network for people with neurological disturbances, I found a mother's posting:

> I have a nine-year-old son who is autistic. He is very high functioning, but still experiences most of the social problems normally associated with autism. He attends a regular fourth grade class in public school with no extra assistance (despite my endless lobbying for teaching assistant support). Children remind me of chickens, seeking out the weak and wounded and pecking them to death. They have discovered that my son is bothered by loud noises, and scream and whistle in his ear until he is crying. I've tried discussing this problem with the parents of the children involved, as well as the school principal, but the situation has not improved. My husband's idea is to teach him to fight, but I believe that violence is not the answer, and our son is a very passive little boy.

Another mother responded to her.

> I have a son with high functioning autism. We moved to a new state last school year. I was scared to death for him. I was so fortunate for him to have the teacher that he had. I gave her and his special ed teacher permission to talk to the class on a day he was at a doctor's appointment. They talked about the different behaviors they would see and hear, how we all are here to help each other. That he also would have wonderful things to add to his class. A lot of his classmates became his advocates. He has gross and fine motor difficulties, and children cheer him on when he has trouble. I find the adults set the pace. Your son needs a mentor like mine had. She made it 'cool' for him to be him.

The first autistic boy enjoyed neither respect nor empathy from classmates or school personnel, and one's heart goes out to him and his distressed mother. The second little boy got far more than two teacher-mentors. He entered a situation where adults knew how to evoke empathy from classmates. They explained unusual behavior so it wouldn't seem threatening. They conveyed how classmates could be of assistance. They turned a profound limitation into something "cool."

We can see a vital lesson in teasing stories, namely, that empathy isn't just an occasional blessing. It is a universal necessity, and where it is lacking, there is often meanness or worse. The two teachers who explained autism to classmates and evoked empathy did more than Chip Green's school did; his school taught respect and enforced rules, but that falls short of leading Chip's classmates to be empathic toward a newcomer. Respect may be difficult to enforce where it is not accompanied by empathy.

Shaming

Teasing—sometimes mild, sometimes sporadic, sometimes incessant, sometimes unspeakably inhumane—occurs everywhere. At school, teasing is observable in almost every classroom, on every playground, in every school hallway, in every lavatory. Certain attributes are frequently the theme of teasing: physical characteristics such as weight, behavioral characteristics such as stuttering, appearance characteristics such as dress or haircuts, social characteristics such as poverty, and of course the specifics of racial, ethnic, religious, and gender identity. Yet to understand teasing one has to see that it doesn't always represent an automatic, unthinking expression of prejudicial opinion; often it represents human meanness deliberately looking for an available target.

Teasing is also observable in most homes, and on most streets. There is a very good chance that your son has been teased somewhere along the line, and an equally good chance that he has done some teasing. The parent or other caregiver concerned about character formation can't limit attention to how not to be a victim of teasing, but needs to pay equal attention to teaching boys not to tease others.

Teasing is a major schoolboy issue. Most boys bring to first grade the baggage of having been teased in earlier childhood and having already teased siblings or playmates or strangers. They already know how to tease, and virtually all have been on the receiving end enough to know the sting. But a lack of capacity for empathy keeps them from translating their own experience of being shamed into a determination not to inflict shame on others. Quite the opposite: The effect of the experience on a boy often drives him to take out his resentment on someone else.

The goal of the teaser is to make the teased feel ashamed. Depending on the content of the tease, the teased person may feel unworthy or inadequate or unattractive. If the teaser then drops the tease and reestablishes a positive relationship, the teased person feels great relief, his gratitude perhaps outweighing any resentment for being teased in the first place. But if, as often happens, the teasing is persistent and without restoration of relationships, the teased person remains in a state of shame, feeling rejected, insulted, injured.

Teasing is an extremely prevalent form of shaming. Since there often isn't any remedy for its accusations—how can I change my skin color or ethnic origin or level of intelligence or height or newcomer status?—the emotion the teased person feels, besides shame, is resentment. Resentment implies anger, but anger frosted with a belief that one has received unfair or unjust treatment. Chip Green shows signs of resentment when he goes from saying, "They don't like me, and I don't like them," to saying, "They'll *never* like me, and I'll *never* like them."

Teasing doesn't have to "work," of course. The person being teased can sometimes turn the tables, either neutralizing the situation or even turning it to his advantage by refusing to acquiesce into shame. Robert Kayton, a psychologist, has worked on strategies for boys to refute and defuse teasing challenges. When we feel shame, he says, our faces turn red, our head and eyes turn away and are lowered, our bodies droop. One can resist shame in part through physical posture alone. Standing erect, looking upward and forward, tightening biceps and jaws—it is more difficult for a person to feel shame when this posture has been deliberately adopted.

Breathing plays a part in the physical response to teasing. While physical tension is a good response to teasing, emotional tension isn't. If a person feels under attack, breathing gets more rapid. One way to calm emotions is to breathe more deeply and slowly. Once a boy gets his body and breathing under control, he can begin to devise a strategy of countering the tease; lacking emotional self-control, he might act impulsively.

With time and patience, teasing can be defused and even turned into friendship. Chip's younger sister, Alice, went through an extended period of teasing by a boy in her preschool group. Alice was one of the smallest in her group, as was another little boy, Ben. Frequently Alice would come home in tears because of taunting by Ben, who may have enjoyed the expressions of unhappiness he could reliably provoke from her. But time passed, the preschool staff worked patiently on Ben's behavior, and Alice grew enough that she was bigger than Ben. One day she came home and asked if Ben could come over to play. They had become friends.

Much teasing is purely mean-spirited. But some teasing is a roundabout and insecure way of expressing interest and attraction. It features prominently in pre- and early adolescent exchanges between boys and girls. The boys who have previously used teasing of all girls as a way to maintain gender boundaries now use it selectively as a safe way of expressing interest. Not ready to venture direct expressions of interest and risk the humiliation of rebuff, boys will gently tease girls, hoping that the girls will read the tease accurately as a way of making safe contact. And vice versa.

Family Teasing

There's a lot of teasing in family life, not just between siblings but between parents and children and between children and other relatives—grandparents, cousins, uncles, and aunts. Why do parents tease their own children? They may consider it a means of being critical while taking the edge off their criticism with humor, forgetting, perhaps, that the humorous aspect of teasing is at the expense of the teased. At other times, they may feel that direct advice and criticism are not being taken seriously by a child, so the parents choose to add the shaming aspect of teasing to their criticism. In still other cases, they are somewhat indirectly venting disappointment that their children aren't quite what they hoped they would be. The ability to read teasing for what it implies develops very early. In all teasing there is an element of hostility, larger, frequently, than the teaser realizes.

Parents use shaming techniques on preschool children far more frequently than they are aware, and often acquiesce when their boys are teased or otherwise shamed by siblings, or other relatives or caregivers. The consequence is that boys learn these techniques and use them with varying degrees of consciousness and unconsciousness the rest of their lives, or until someone teaches them otherwise. One of the most significant contributions a parent can make to the character development of a boy is to refrain from shaming him, and to be his active and public ally when others try to use shaming techniques toward him.

The Outsider

Some authorities say that boys and girls tease differently, boys teasing on themes of strength and weakness, girls on themes of inclusion and exclusion. But this distinction isn't very useful in the case of Chip Green, who was teased and intimidated physically on the playground and snickered at in the classroom, and correctly interpreted it all as exclusion. Beginning in the third grade, other researchers say, teasing between classmates escalates in meanness, and is sometimes difficult to distinguish from bullying, which I shall discuss later in the chapter.

Dorothea Ross, describing her research in a pediatric hospital, helps to put the pain of teasing in perspective: "In the early 1980s, as part of a major study of childhood pain, we asked children with leukemia what their worst pain experience had been. We expected the answers to be some of the often-excruciating treatment-related pains that these children must endure. To our amazement many children said that their worst pain was to be teased about their appearance (for example, baldness, extreme pallor) when they returned to school."

I read about a family in the Midwest that fell upon hard times when the father lost his job. To keep their family intact, the parents of Russell and Amanda, both in elementary school, had to move into a homeless shelter. Russell made friends with a boy who lived across the street from the shelter, but when the boy's other friends asked him why he was playing with someone who was homeless, he broke off the friendship. Russell and his sister were subjected to relentless teasing at school over their homelessness. "The neighbors know this is a shelter for homeless families," said Russell's mother. "I guess they don't want anything to do with people like that. It's really hard on the kids. They go through enough without being teased. They're teased because they cannot afford 'good' clothes. They're told that the reason they're homeless is because their parents are bums."

Alex Gordon is a boy who has experienced being an outsider. He had just turned thirteen when I talked with him and his mother about his boyhood. At Passover he had celebrated his bar mitzvah or coming of age ceremony, one part of which was to read and comment on an assigned passage from the Hebrew Scriptures. The passage from the Torah assigned to Alex for commentary read in English translation: "And the stranger you do not humiliate and do not oppress, for you were a stranger in the land of Egypt." I read Alex's commentary, which persuaded me that he was surely mature enough to join the company of men. He said in part:

> I believe this law of non-oppression is a very important law for the world to follow, not just the Jewish nation. And I think it might be good law to remind some of Israel's leaders of. . . . I believe that the verse has a different meaning each time it is used. Its first appearance is in a paragraph that includes similar protection to widows and orphans: "You shall not cause pain to any widow or orphan." These three, the widow, the stranger, and the orphan all had virtually no power in a patriarchal society, so we should be especially careful not to hurt them. . . . These laws set our standards, they remind us. If we do something unjust or unfair or cruel, our consciences kick us mentally. We feel bad if we commit one of these acts. They set guidelines for life, not just for criminal behavior.

Alex might well have added, if he had delved into the sociology of its time, that ancient Israel had very strong conventions of hospitality. An itinerant stranger was accorded the status of an honored guest; he received the best meals and accommodations the host could offer. In our society, older people remember the hospitable invoking of FHB—family hold back—as family members, including young children, deliberately took sparing portions of a meal until it was certain that guests at the table had eaten their fill.

Boys grow up today with less experience in the practice of hospitality to the stranger. Most of us regard strangers with caution at best, or even habitual suspicion. The newcomer to the class, as Chip Green and every other new kid learns, is dealt with on an ad hoc basis. If he's big and strong and self-confident, he will ordinarily be accorded insider status quickly. But if he's vulnerable to teasing for any number of possible reasons and isn't self-confident enough to assert himself into the insider group, he'll probably be dealt with as an outsider and forced to work his way in.

Alex is the only child of a lesbian mother who was in a committed relationship with her companion before conceiving by artificial insemination; he is an easy target for teasing in conventional settings. Fortunately, Alex attends an alternative public school where atypical lifestyles are as much the norm as the exception. His longer than shoulder length hair and earrings, however, do make him prone to street teasing. Helen Gordon recalled a recent social gathering after which Alex and two other boys he knew wanted to walk home rather than ride with her. "They happened to run into a bunch of local guys. Alex and this other kid have really long hair. Somebody called them faggots, but everyone laughed rather than challenged, and they went away."

Despite his insight and confidence, Alex, when I talked with him by himself, was completely fatalistic about teasing. Yes, he got teased a lot— more in public than at school. Yes, he sometimes joined in teasing others at school, or at least went along with it. When I asked him if he didn't think there was some remedy for teasing, he said simply that one would have to start educating kids a lot younger than he was if one wished to make a difference. He did not expect adults to be able to intervene effectively in the culture of teasing.

Brian

In Chapter 6, I described a mother's attempts to avoid gender stereotyping in the toys and play of her twin three-year-olds, Joshua and Jeremiah. In later stages of childhood and adolescence, it gets harder and harder to find examples of boys who avoid such stereotypes because they are teased so relentlessly if they do not abide by the stereotypes. In *Gender Play: Girls and Boys in School*, Barrie Thorne observed a fourth-grade boy on a school playground who had carved just such a path for himself. Thorne watched Brian, wearing cowboy boots, jeans, and T-shirt, join a game of jump rope played by bigger girls. (She wrote in her notebook: "I almost gasped when I saw Brian join the row of girls; I've never seen a boy do that.") Brian knew the chants and the rules, he was as skillful as the girls, and they let him play.

Another time, after he had been playing kickball with the boys, Brian walked over to the jungle gym and joined a line of girls waiting to do tricks on the uneven parallel bars. He ignored the attempt of one girl to exclude him from the line. When one of the girls lost her momentum while she was swinging, Brian walked over and gently pushed her heel to get her going again. Given his turn, he swung in unison with another girl, doing named maneuvers that require considerable physical skill. He was self-confident enough to call out, "Watch me," the way the most skilled girls did.

Thorne began to think of Brian as a "Waldo" figure. Where might he turn up next? She once found him pitching in a mixed-gender ball game of older kids, all of whom were larger than he. He was usually able to traverse both gender and age boundaries, but not always. Sometimes the girls would shoo him away. Once Thorne watched a group of boys pick sides for kickball in a procedure laced with teasing, leaving out Brian and three other boys. As Brian walked away in his unfashionable one-piece snowsuit, another boy "yelled at Brian, 'Why are you wearing that sissy snowsuit?' Brian angrily exploded, 'Cause my mom wants me to, I told you a million times.'" There doesn't seem to be any problem of gender identification with Brian. He doesn't have any doubts or unhappiness about being a boy. He just doesn't confine his activities to fit gender stereotypes and boundaries. The price of this chosen path is that he has to be something of a loner. He hasn't settled on trying to bond with one group and its activities. When he crosses the boundary to girls' activities, he does so with sincere intent, not teasing intent. He isn't there to disrupt, he's there to play. His path requires a considerable amount of self-possession for his age, but it is a satisfying path for a boy who has the nerve to follow it.

Codes

Students develop codes about when it is cool and when it is not cool (most of the time) to complain to adults about the behavior of other kids. Boys emphasize these codes more than girls do, and boys accept fewer limitations on the imposition of the codes than girls do. Barrie Thorne describes the code that lies at the heart of Alex's fatalism.

> The boys' code is illustrated by a brewing conflict on the Ashton playground. A third-grade boy wearing a dark-green shirt angrily leaned toward a girl who was holding the arm of a boy in a blue jacket and said, 'He hit me in the gut; he's dead.' The girl let go of the second boy's arm and said, 'He's yours.' The boy in the green shirt continued, 'I already beat his butt,' as he and the other boy, both with hostile facial expressions, squared off to fight. As they

pushed toward each other, a much taller boy came up behind and said calmly, 'Break it up.' The two pushed some more as the tall boy inserted himself between them. The boy in the blue jacket stomped away, calling over his shoulder, 'I'm tellin'.' 'Only tattletales tell,' the boy in the green shirt taunted after him. The boy who had threatened to tattle continued to walk off the playing field but didn't approach an adult.

As Thorne shows, a complaining student can't automatically count on support from a nearby teacher or playground aide. If one student has provoked another, and has been challenged in a way he can't handle, the adult present may refuse to intervene on the basis that the complainer has "brought it on himself." If there is adult intervention, it is apt to be episodic, that is, dealing only with the specific behavior involved rather than making the episode an opportunity for a broader discussion of malicious teasing or fighting by the offender(s). This kind of intervention probably has little carryover effect when the same children are at play and there are no adults present.

The code has its origins in experience dating back to early childhood, when toddlers, either siblings or playmates, say to one another, "I'm gonna tell on you." Toddlers begin to learn over time how their appeals for intervention and assistance will be met. When, as is often the case, the adult appealed to has not witnessed the act generating the complaint, and there are no other witnesses, the adult is left with all the problems of a court of law when the case comes down to one person's word against another's. Such complaints bother many parents, especially if lodged by boys, because their conception of a "real boy" is of one who can deal with such matters without having to depend on outside assistance. Other parents react immediately and emotionally to all such complaints, assuming their validity, encouraging children to complain when there is no real provocation, when they're simply annoyed with, but not really threatened or teased by, another child.

Another observation by Barrie Thorne shows how well developed this aspect of behavior is when boys leave home to enter kindergarten:

As Mrs. Smith's kindergarten students entered the culture of schooling, they continually assessed the reach of adult authority, including whether and when to 'tell' on one another. Boys and girls peppered their daily talk with threats like 'I'm gonna tell the teacher' and 'I'm tellin'.' Mrs. Smith tried to set limits by simply ignoring the requests for intervention and by repeatedly telling the students that she wanted 'none of that tattling stuff.' The amount diminished over time, but 'tattling' continued even when the teacher refused to intervene.

By the time boys reach the higher elementary grades, the code is often so well entrenched that they are extremely reluctant to offer their parents the opportunity to intervene in school situations. I watched half a dozen sixth-grade boys being interviewed recently on television. They were all articulate and personable. One of them admitted that he had been struck on the shin playing ball in the schoolyard at mid year, and it hurt so much he broke into tears. He said he expected to be teased about crying for the rest of the school year, but he hoped it would be forgotten over the summer break. He and his classmates on the show agreed solemnly that it would be useless, counterproductive even, if his mom or dad tried to intervene at school to put a stop to the teasing.

The code against complaining to a higher authority gives an immense advantage to the strongest, who already have a decisive advantage to begin with. To the extent that it has been maintained by boys themselves, it has been promoted by the strong to heighten their power. To the extent that it has been reinforced by parents or teachers, it has been reinforced to try to motivate all boys to be among the strong. But what recourse do the teased and taunted or physically threatened have when they are beset by the strong, except to appeal for assistance?

If adults are physically assaulted or slandered—garden variety "crimes" on the playground—they have recourse to both criminal and civil remedies at law. But they may not lawfully take matters into their own hands and slander or assault back, except in self-defense in physically threatening situations. Why do we not matter-of-factly provide comparable protection for boys and girls? Because we do not regard them as enjoying full legal standing as persons, children must make do with "the code."

Dominance Hierarchies

Aggression between members of a group, as I've earlier noted, is controlled in many animal species by the establishment of dominance hierarchies. Endless scuffling for privilege and position between group members who really need to cooperate with each other for survival is avoided by a process by which each member finds his rank relative to all the others. Then a slight signal from a member of superior rank to an inferior is enough to get the latter to back off; they don't have to fight it out every time. Where dominance hierarchies are most firmly established, aggressiveness by the whole group toward a stranger increases.

Human animals share this tendency to form dominance hierarchies. Dominance hierarchies are often discussed in relation to males, perhaps because they are more liable than females to establish and maintain hierarchies by the use or threat of physical force, but females also form these hierarchies. Humans often fail to exercise the same restraint other animals do in their hierarchies; humans often go far beyond mere dominance to severely injure or kill others in their group.

So it is important not to make too simple a jump from the behavior of other animals to the human situation. Human hierarchies often are related to purposes other than survival. And a single human being may be related to a bewildering variety of dominance hierarchies, each with its own dynamics. A schoolboy, for example, might be related to siblings, to nuclear family, to extended family, to neighborhood playmates, to classmates at school, to the school as a whole, to various organized sports teams, to a scouting organization, to a religious youth group; in each of them he has to find and maintain his place, and the degree of competition may cause some variation in his ranking from one group to another.

Teasing, as a symbolic and verbal substitute for physical aggression, plays an important role in the dynamics of dominance hierarchies. If a tease will do to put an inferior in his place, why bother to fight? Yet the matter is more complex than that. Verbal skills tied to social skills may enable a boy to dominate another boy of equal or even slightly greater physical strength. And shifting alliances among inferiors made possible by language mean that it is more difficult for humans to establish a dominance hierarchy and have it hold stably for an extended period of time.

The novelist Jacquelyn Mitchard recently described a suburban neighborhood group composed of her two younger sons and two brothers of ages comparable to her sons' who live down the block. The four boys have formed the Dog Club. Each of the four has a dog name. Mad Dog, from down the block, is the president of the club even though Mitchard's older son is the largest and oldest of the four. Mad has the most friends outside the club, and is athletic and smart. He also knows how to work daily alliances with the others to his advantage. An established hierarchy breaks down into a Dog fight about every other day, she says.

Every day the Dogs have to make up rules for the day. There is so much arguing and threatening that sometimes Mitchard has to lean out the window and yell, "Don't you guys dare talk to each other that way! Be civil—or don't play!" They don't actually play games that much because so much time is taken up with making the rules and fighting about them. Mitchard writes:

> What's most peculiar about many children's games, particularly these social-creative types, is how the fun seems to go out of them when there's no one left to devil. The same thing happens when Watch Dog (an occasional fifth member) comes over. Dangerous to everyone, Watch is capable of forming

coalitions with any of the others, and a coalition can mean a mutiny. Also, since Watch lives in another neighborhood, he is, to use the technical term, 'funner,' simply by his novelty. After a few minutes, Dog meetings with Watch usually break down into a sort of group consensus to play baseball.

Richard Hawley, the headmaster of a private boys' school in Cleveland, Ohio, and a writer, has described a number of the boys who have gone through his school. One of them, named Colin, was masterful at cruel teasing, but he did it more as a loner than to maintain his place in a tight-knit hierarchy. An accomplished athlete, he would furtively insult opponents until they were enraged and lost control, drawing penalties on their teams. His classmates and teammates feared him and felt powerless to control him. Colin was even adept at playing off faculty members against each other with cleverly engineered lies and misquotes.

About once a term, Colin would choose a new boy at school, a boy who for one or another reason was going to have a hard time being popular, and establish a mock friendship. The new boy would have no idea why this blessing had fallen out of the sky upon him, but was too hungry for recognition to ask why he had been favored. If he was shy, Colin would find him dates. If he was not a driver, Colin would give him rides. He took his credulous and fully dependent new cohorts to unchaperoned parties and got them drunk. Seasoned classmates learned to identify quickly what was going on. Some watched it from a distance, but others took the opportunity to collaborate in the game of setting up the new boy for a fall. Eventually, when he tired of the masquerade, Colin would let loose his contempt for the gullible boy, distance himself, spurn the boy entirely.

Hawley referred to Colin as being evil. That is an extreme term to use. If I have a reservation about it, it is because I have frequently seen boys subjected to simplistic classification in the work and proceedings of juvenile courts and departments of social services: "He's just a bad kid!" "He's really a good kid despite what he's done." These evaluations may be associated with the decision whether and how severely to charge a boy with a criminal offense.

But perhaps the term is not too extreme. We do not hesitate to use it with respect to some adult criminal acts. Yet we brush off juvenile assaults on playgrounds and streets, and petty theft, as though they were failures we have to tolerate while boys grow up. Colin, in an affluent private school, may be perceived by his headmaster as "evil," but he's not likely to find himself before a judge unless one of the kids he importunes gets seriously hurt.

Bullying

Chip Green's teasing problem in fifth grade took a new turn in sixth grade. The classmate who had led the attempt to marginalize Chip from his classmates tried again a year later. He had only a few allies, but his methods were even more confrontational. He would shove and trip Chip during organized sports with apparent intent to injure him, and he repeatedly challenged Chip to fight, boasting of how badly he would beat him. Chip's father is accomplished in martial arts, and Chip has had some instruction in them as well, but with the philosophy of avoiding fights whenever possible and being mainly defensive if forced to fight.

By sixth grade, however, Chip had his own friends and allies. They were both boys and girls, they were among the "brains" of the class, and their way of standing up to the attempt to intimidate Chip was verbal. The ringleader soon discovered that verbal taunts were ineffective because Chip and his allies gave back more biting remarks than they got. Chip's father was reluctant to intervene and was hoping that a little coaching of Chip would enable him to deal with the situation effectively himself. Disappointingly, the school seemed not to have tracked what was an obvious problem from the previous year.

The fifth grader's attempts to tease and marginalize Chip crossed the border in sixth grade into attempts to bully. The line between harsh or relentless episodes of teasing and episodes of bullying may not be apparent to the casual observer. Both aim to demean the victim, but the two activities are also different in one fundamental respect: Teasing is done to provoke shame, to make the victim feel bad and, if anything, go away or stay away. Bullying is done to inspire fear, to intimidate the victim; it is an act of terrorism. A bully usually wishes the opposite of driving the victim away; he often wishes the victim to be available within his domain of influence to reinforce the bully's sense of power.

When a boy is an excessive teaser or a bully, it is usually a symptom of something wrong in that boy's life. Likewise, if a boy is an habitual victim, the problem isn't always the victimizer, but the climate or culture, where boys are routinely sorted into bullies, victims, or bystanders, and where every boy comes to see the victimization of some boys as inevitable because everyone subscribes to or acknowledges the victimizer/victim/bystander culture. Alex Gordon, whose eloquent bar mitzvah speech I cited above, told me that if you were an adult visitor to his school, you probably wouldn't recognize for a number of days the dominance hierarchies in which, he believed, all the children had their roles to play—some as bullies and teasers, some as victims, some as passive bystanders lucky not to be victims. And worse, he said, if you saw it, you couldn't do anything about it, because it was so deeply ingrained. You had to start younger than thirteen, he insisted, if you wanted to make a difference with kids.

All children whose bullying behavior suggests serious trouble should promptly get the help they need: a careful and competent diagnostic workup and the development of an intervention plan involving home, therapist, and school, tailored to their needs and considerate of their social responsibilities. If adults show they will not turn a blind eye to the "code," or cede to a bully's culture, then kids will quickly hear the counterpart message to "You can't say you can't play": no teasing or bullying here.

Richard Hawley writes about another of his students, Tyler, who was a classic bully. "No one, least of all his parents, could recall a time when he was not, literally, dreadful." As a preschooler, Tyler already showed a preoccupation with spiders and reptiles that most people are repelled by. During his school years, he kept poisonous spiders and boa constrictors that he liked to exhibit unexpectedly to people he wanted to terrify. "'How big are your snakes?' I asked him once, when I learned he kept boa constrictors. 'They're getting big enough to kill you,' he said, smiling but not joking."

Tyler took special pleasure in threatening younger boys. By the end of junior high school, his bullying had become generalized into antisocial behavior. He voiced the slogans and wore the symbols of Nazis and of the Ku Klux Klan. A succession of child therapists didn't lessen his troublesome behavior, and he was eventually expelled for repeated racial harassment of two black classmates.

Maybe therapists weren't the answer, or not the only answer. Whenever racism is part of the script, I always worry about what the child is exposed to at home. Too often, the problem is seen as the child, when in fact the child is expressing a family pathology.

And what is the school's role? Much more than girls, boys are likely to express psychological distress with overt aggression. Not to intervene telegraphs to all boys and girls that adults can't and won't respond to serious—and dangerous—symptoms.

This is one lesson, I think, to be gleaned from several recent tragedies where boys have brought guns to school and killed or wounded schoolmates and teachers. Nearly all of the boys signaled their distress in advance in some way, and some even telegraphed their intentions, mainly to peers. But in all the stories where threats were made, no one really believed they would be carried out.

The merciless teasing and bullying of boys by other boys of higher status that is permitted to go on in many schools, especially those dominated by athletes, appears to have played a part in some of these murders; in some instances, boys have brought guns to school to act out their resentment over such treatment.

The "victim to victimizer transition" is a familiar notion to people who work in battered women's shelters, child abuse treatment programs, and adult prisons. Stated simply, the offending persons have themselves previously suffered serious abuse, often in childhood, and have stored up horrible feelings of not being able to stop the unacceptable from happening to them and their dearest intimates. The transition from passivity to action is made as boys channel their bottled rage and shame into dominating and controlling the lives of other innocents, abusing and sometimes killing the very people they should protect and love. Along the way, they learn to justify their behavior to themselves. This is the most corrosive character-forming experience I know.

Stopping the cycle of violence will require a sustained effort to ensure the physical and psychological safety of both homes and schools. Far too few political leaders take this task seriously, although the murders at Columbine High School in Littleton, Colorado, have sounded a wake-up call. Good mental health services for all abuse victims are necessary, but I should also express my dismay at the shortage of capable psychological assessment and appropriate treatment. Neither the will nor the money is there, and we continue to reap a whirlwind of suffering for our inaction.

Bullying and Self-regard

The *Harvard Mental Health Letter* recently described a study touching on the self-image of aggressive children. Second- and third-grade teachers in some Texas schools were asked to identify two or three children in their classrooms with habits of teasing, intimidating other children, and starting fights. Forty-six of the sample of sixty-two students were boys. These students were compared with fifty-three "average" (nonaggressive) children from the same classrooms matched for age and sex.

> Teachers, parents, and other children showed the expected responses to the bullies, but the bullies apparently had no idea what others thought of them. They tended to deny any conflict with other children or with their mothers (they considered it acceptable to admit more than average trouble with teachers).... Above all, they were likely to think that others saw them as they saw themselves. They believed they were held in high esteem by their mothers and by other children; many gave themselves the highest possible ratings on these scales. Nonaggressive children almost never did; they were more likely to underestimate how well others thought of them.... The authors

suspect that the apparent self-satisfaction is a pose that disguises hidden in-security and emotional conflict, but they admit that helping these children is difficult as long as they see no need to change.

Some bullies have suffered bullying at home or witnessed domestic vi-olence against their mothers and felt inadequate to deal with it. Others have been sexually abused. Still others have overdosed on media scripts that sensationalize and glorify violence as well as masculine and feminine stereotypes. In general, I believe, a bully needs professional help beyond the competence of the typical parent or teacher, while interrupting, ex-plaining, and reducing teasing that isn't an expression of bullying is within the competence of the ordinary adult motivated to study its dy-namics.

Bullying and teasing also differ with respect to their prevalence. Teasing of one degree or another, as I've said, is ubiquitous. Almost every class-room and playground is the site of some of it. Bullying is much rarer, yet prevalent enough to merit everyone's concern. A 1995 survey of junior and senior high school students in the United States showed 5 percent of the boys (one out of every twenty, or about one boy in every classroom) acknowledging being the victim of at least one violent episode (not a mu-tually inspired fight) initiated by another boy.

Many observers have noted that the victims of teasing and even of bul-lying are sometimes complicit in the event. They don't necessarily want it, but they don't know how to escape it. Victims, victimizers, and bystanders are not separate actors. They are linked, as much as they may despise one another, by a culture in which violence is accepted as inevitable. The chal-lenge is to break through this entire culture, in school and in the family, to say "No, this is not acceptable." As the following example from a superb violence prevention program shows, boys can embrace an alternative view, one that demonstrates that children can care, and can effectively teach other children kindly alternatives to violence in the face of conflict.

Monica and Kiesha were yelling at each other. Jose, a student mediator, heard the commotion and put his skills to work. He approached the girls and got them to stop yelling. He asked each of them if they would agree to a mediation. They agreed. He set out the ground rules he learned in his train-ing. No name calling. Each side would listen respectfully to the other. They would work together to find a solution. Each girl told her side of the argu-ment. Careful not to take sides, Jose listened to each side, repeating each girl's story and clarifying points as necessary. After each was done, Jose re-stated each girl's position. He helped them talk out problems and reach an understanding. Peer mediator coordinators report not only that schools become friendlier and fights become fewer, but the young mediators report improved academic performance, better home lives, and boosted self-confidence.

Intervening

Most parents have to deal with teasing and bullying. Their children are either suffering it, or committing it, or both.

If a parent is predominantly egocentric in his approach to the problem he will read the situation through his own experiences and needs. If the parent has suffered teasing on the same theme in his own past and still feels resentful about it, he may want to get very involved in the situation—"overidentified" is the clinical term for it—and fight his son's battles for him. But if the son is being teased for something the father has never had experience with, he may not be touched by his son's experience.

What an egocentric parent may fail to take into consideration is his son's needs and preferences, and the rules and resources available in his son's situation. In some cases, "he's got to work it out for himself" may be a very wise strategy because the parent realizes that his son wants to do that and can handle it, and the place where he is facing the teasing will help him. But in other cases, parental detachment may leave a boy feeling as though he has no allies.

If a parent's inclination is to resolve such situations through the application of rules, again there may be very different outcomes depending on the rules and their effectiveness. Many venues, including many schools, are so tolerant of teasing, and even of bullying, that stated rules are of little import. There are, moreover, informal rules such as "boys don't cry" and "boys don't tattle" that perversely reinforce teasing and bullying practices.

It should be pointed out that adults are erecting ever stronger safeguards for themselves in public places and private workplaces under the umbrella of preventing "harassment" of colleagues, subordinates, and strangers. Many of the practices now being outlawed are analogous to teasing and bullying, but we are slow to apply these safeguards to children except in dramatically abusive instances.

There are some excellent rules that parents might consider putting into effect with their children, and in their households, and even in public. A "respect policy" might be instituted for everyone in the household; if a whole school can do it, a household can do it. The sanctions needn't be any more elaborate than a sincere apology.

Though much teasing and bullying is out of sight and earshot of adults, much isn't. So one might politely but firmly—and unvaryingly—defend one's boys from teasing by others in one's presence, and equally firmly and kindly correct them when they tease others. Label what is going on as teasing. State what is exaggerated and untrue about it. Emphasize that it is unkind and mean-spirited, and that it is trying to build up the teaser merely by diminishing someone else. Skillful teasers can do it in such a way as to say hurtful things but smoothly deny their intent—"I was just kidding!"—if challenged. It's important not to be diverted by such tactics, and to suggest that since it is sometimes difficult to distinguish a certain kind of joking from teasing, it would be better not to joke that way. Always invite the boys involved to talk about the incident—it is, to recall Carol Schraft's comments from Chapter 8, a "teachable moment"—and invite them to advocate for others they see being teased or bullied.

Parents and teachers have to deal with many complaints about teasing that they have not witnessed. Calm and patient discussion really pays dividends here. Share your thinking with the children; don't just hand down a decision, which may seem arbitrary. Let them know that there are difficulties involved in sorting out situations where it's just one person's word against another's, yet judgments have to be made. When the adult is patient and under control, the truth is more apt to emerge from discussion. Everyone deserves a complete hearing. If a boy who has been teased whines about it, find an opportunity later to show him that whining creates its own syndrome of unsympathetic reaction—better to report the offense as calmly as possible under the circumstances.

Boys aren't teased only about themselves. They may be teased about their families. This creates additional pressure for the boy who is teased. Now he has to champion his family as well as himself, or implicitly accept shame in behalf of his family. It helps, of course, for parents to signal to their boy that the family doesn't feel shamed by it, and that they wish he didn't have to face teasing about his family. But a situation has been created in which the family has a more complex role than if a boy has been teased only about himself. In such situations, family meetings about teasing seem essential to me. A family could decide whether and how they might want to air this matter with the school staff. The message is: We're all in this together, son; we can't be there on the playground every day, but we can investigate the willingness of the school to step in; you shouldn't have to bear the burden of protecting all of us.

Of the several techniques that have been advanced for helping boys cope with teasing, I have already mentioned the suggestion of maintaining erect posture rather than hanging one's head and slumping to show shame. Another technique is to ignore the teaser, neither looking at him nor fronting him.

Another set of responses to teasing involves repartee. The teased person diverts or deflects the tease with humor or sarcasm or distraction, or even with what Robert Kayton calls "fogging"—defusing the tease by passively agreeing with its message so that the teaser doesn't derive the pleasure of having the teased boy rise to the bait. Another psychologist, Fred Frankel, emphasizes the use of humor to undermine the teaser—"I heard that one in kindergarten." "That's so old it's got dust on it." Frankel asserts that these responses do work. He suggests that boys below third grade level should be coached in specific responses, the simpler the better. Boys from third grade on can be coached in the tactic, taught a number of possible responses, and encouraged to use their repertory or invent new responses to fit the situation.

Most of the suggested responses are themselves put-downs, though of less demeaning quality, probably, than the content of the tease that initiated the event. So they do nothing to deal with the general situation. When the defensive tactic is successful, presumably, the teaser goes off in search of more vulnerable prey. The slightly hostile content of many recommended responses does, however, usefully remind us that boys who are teased often feel angry as well as shamed. The repartee gives them an opportunity to work off some of the anger. Boys who have been teased and have not asserted themselves in response need encouragement to express their anger in some form rather than nursing it below the surface.

Parents and other caregivers should avail themselves of every opportunity to break "the code" against reporting teasing and bullying to adults. Boys can be taught at home and in school that the code only makes it easier for aggressive and angry boys to make others miserable. Reporting misconduct should never be disparaged as "tattling," but again boys should be taught that if the report or complaint can be made evenhandedly (and in behalf of others rather than oneself, which is why teaching boys advocacy for others who are mistreated, creating a system of mutual solidarity, is so important) rather than emotionally, it may be responded to more vigorously by adults.

Teasing and bullying are subjects that lend themselves well to understanding the limited way rules are often applied, and the more constructive ways they might be construed. The limited way is to view rules rather rigidly as principles or policies that, if violated, lead to punishments. Rules may be viewed this way both at home and at school. At school, the punishments for some violations may be stated in writing for parents and students to learn as the student enters the school. But the weakness of this approach is the same as for the rules for observing speed limits on the highway. You may speed without being caught, and feel little compunction about it; if caught and fined, you are still free to speed again.

The rules that might be applied to teasing and bullying, however, might better be seen as ideals that the community (family or school or play-ground) aspires to realize for the good of its members. When the ideal of respect for everyone is articulated, then teasing and bullying become injuries to the community. The way to heal such an injury is to heal the offender as well as his target, and to reinforce the values of the community. Punishment doesn't necessarily accomplish that. Rather, one has to ask the offender: Why are you doing that? What makes you need to build yourself up by tearing others down?

I believe that in teasing and bullying the most healing things happen when one stops judging and punishing and begins to investigate and treat the why of the behavior. This perspective automatically elevates the consideration of teasing or bullying above the level of rigid rules and penalties to an examination of everyone's needs and injuries. Then one often sees that the schoolyard bully, for example, has helplessly witnessed or suffered bullying at home. The bully needs as much help as his victims, and treating his behavior thoughtfully and compassionately, but firmly, is the surest way to stop his predations.

When the subject of teasing is moved to the higher levels of awareness, parents and teachers see that children themselves have much to contribute to the elimination of the problem. The thesis behind many programs to "bully-proof" schools—that all the kids can be classified as bullies, victims, or bystanders—may need revision to incorporate the proactive potential many kids exhibit. Barrie Thorne has set forth ideas for promoting cooperative relations between boys and girls at school. Perhaps the most important of these ideas is to *intervene actively* to challenge the dynamics of stereotyping and power.

> Drawing boys and girls together is only one step; the dynamics of stereotyping and power may have to be explicitly confronted. Barbara Porro and Kevin Karkau engaged their classes in discussions about gender stereotyping, persistent separation between girls and boys, and the teasing ('sissies,' 'tomboys,' 'you're in love') that kept them apart. Porro explained sexism to her students by finding terms that six-year-olds could understand. . . . Raphaella Best, a reading teacher . . . encouraged (students) to challenge stereotypes, especially the one boys had of themselves as superior and girls as inferior, and she tried to help boys and girls relate to one another as friends rather than potential romantic partners.

When adults have forcefully and consistently taught the inappropriateness of teasing and bullying, and have shown boys how and why these behaviors occur, boys are ready to grasp the potential of collective action in teasing and other problem situations. It may not be as romantic as the old Western plots—the lone hero standing up all by himself to the bad gang—but it's definitely more effective. Here's an example from my conversation with Brady, an eleven-year-old: "One time a kid kept throwing erasers across the room and hitting kids, and the kids were saying 'ouch' and they would end up getting in trouble. So one day me and a bunch of other kids went up to him and said, 'It's starting to get annoying that we end up getting in trouble all the time when *you* are the one starting the trouble.' After that he sort of went off by himself, and I think that's what had an impact on him. Everyone realized that if we wanted to make a difference we could." I said to Brady, "Were you the leader of the group challenging your classmate to behave differently?" He replied, "It was sort of all of us together. It seemed like it had gone too far, so we decided to do something about it." Stories like Brady's give me optimism that a less fatalistic view may prevail.

14

EARLY ADOLESCENCE

Thirteen is a hard age, very hard. A lot of people say you have it easy, you're a kid, but there's a lot of pressure being thirteen—to be respected by people in your school, to be liked, always feeling like you have to be good. There's pressure to do drugs, too, so you try not to succumb to that. But you don't want to be made fun of, so you have to look cool. You gotta wear the right shoes, the right clothes—if you have Jordans, then it's all right. From, like, twelve to seventeen, there are a lot of transitions going on, a lot of moving around. It's not like you know what's going to happen tomorrow. Life gets different when you get older—there's more work. And when you go to college it's hard because you're alone for the first time. But when you get out of college you start to establish yourself and who you think you are and what you're about. That's a good time.'

— Carlos Quintana, New York City, 1998

'Thirteen is an all-right age, but I'd much rather be fourteen or fifteen. I hate the people in our grade—they're all so boring! People usually think we're older, and we hang out with fifteen-year-olds. They're just so much fun. But thirteen is better than twelve; I hated being twelve, it's too young. At least thirteen has "teen" on the end.'

— Andrea Minissale, Ringwood, N.J., 1998

'Everyone in our grade is so immature. Not really the girls, but all of the guys are. All of them are really short, and they act retarded. At dances they won't dance; they think they're too cool to do that. But it is annoying how everyone thinks we're so much older. . . . I wish we looked our age.'

— Deirdre Minissale (Andrea's twin sister), 1998

The poignance of early adolescence is crystallized in these fragments from an article in the *New York Times*. The girls, feeling with some justification more socially poised than their male classmates but not aware how unsophisticated and vulnerable they really are, look to older males for companionship (though not without a degree of apprehension over being taken for older than they are); and they often find older males, sometimes significantly older, looking for them. Their male age-mates, largely unwilling to risk inviting a relationship with a girl and being rejected, hold back, refuse to dance, tease anyone who breaks gender ranks. In their own eyes they're being "cool," but from the girl's point of view, they "act retarded." Both genders are quick to label anything or anyone that frustrates them as "boring."

Resetting the Thermostat

The mechanisms that set off the physical changes of puberty are not entirely understood. It may be more accurate to say that the brain *inhibits* puberty all during childhood than that the brain *triggers* puberty at a particular point as a totally new development. In infancy, a low-level set point is established for the body's sex hormones. The thermostat is set on cool. Shortly before pubertal changes make their appearance, the hormonal feedback systems change the thermostat from, say, sixty degrees to eighty degrees. Now a much higher level of sex hormones is allowed to function in the body before the hypothalamus at the center of the brain tells the pituitary gland to cool the endocrine system down enough to keep the sex hormone level from going any higher.

The pituitary gland, on command from the hypothalamus, also releases growth hormones, although the release may be delayed by factors such as stress, nutritional deficiency, illness, excessive athletic training, or diet-induced thinness. The rapidity of adolescent growth is astonishing. For boys the peak velocity averages about 4.1 inches of height per year. Not all parts of the body grow at the same time. The hands, head, and feet are the first to accelerate, followed by the arms and legs, and finally the torso and shoulders. As Tanner put it, "a boy stops growing out of his trousers (at least in length) a year before he stops growing out of his jackets."

At the peak of the growth surge, the larynx having grown prominently, a boy's voice begins to deepen gradually. For a while, the voice breaks unexpectedly between its higher childhood range and its lower adolescent range until the level of the mature voice is established late in adolescence. Since girls as a group begin their growth spurts a couple of years before boys, they are on average taller than boys from age eleven to thirteen. From age fourteen on, males have gained a height advantage that they never lose. They also develop a marked superiority in strength and muscular development. Body fat increases for both genders at puberty, but the gains are greater for girls. In late adolescence boys have average muscle to fat ratio of three to one, while girls' comparable ratio is five to four. This ratio alone accounts for much of the difference in adolescents' physical performance. At the end of adolescence, boys are stronger; they have "larger hearts and lungs relative to their size, a higher systolic blood pressure, a lower resting heart rate, a greater capacity for carrying oxygen to the blood, a greater power for neutralizing the chemical products of muscular exercise, such as lactic acid," higher blood hemoglobin, and more red blood cells.

What Is Puberty?

Symmetry would be nicely served if all five of the male developmental periods in this book could be firmly age-related. The nature of adolescence, however, necessitates a relaxation of age-relatedness in the last two periods. I've designated the fourth stage (early adolescence) as ages thirteen to fifteen, and the final stage (late adolescence) as ages sixteen to eighteen, but where a boy stands in his adolescent maturation matters more than his age. The arrival of puberty, which starts the engine of adolescence, occurs over a surprising range of time. Some boys' testes begin to enlarge as early as age nine, some as late as age thirteen. Very fine pubic hair makes a first appearance over the same range of age, changing in color (darker) and texture (coarser) a year or so after first appearance. The penis exhibits a growth spurt as early as age ten, as late as age fourteen.

Facial hair appears only after genital development is well underway, about two years after the first appearance of pubic hair—first at the corners of the upper lip, then across the upper lip, still later across the upper cheeks and in the midline below the lips, and lastly along the sides of the face and lower border of the chin. Underarm hair begins to grow about the same time as facial hair, and body hair increases in density on legs, arms, and chests.

Puberty brings changes in skin quality. The skin becomes rougher, especially around the upper arms and thighs, concurrent with the enlargement of sweat glands. These skin changes often give rise to enhanced oiliness, and to acne and other skin eruptions that can plague the self-confidence of the male adolescent as painfully as that of the female adolescent.

Pubertal changes occur in the male breast, stimulated by the body's production of estrogens. Both estrogen and androgens (male hormones) are manufactured by glands in both sexes, but in different amounts on average.

In the male teenager, the area around the nipple, the areola, increases in circumference; the nipples also become more prominent. Some boys develop gynecomastia, a breast enlargement that includes the growth of subcutaneous breast tissue. The tissue on one side of the chest may grow larger than on the other. The condition usually goes away with continued growth of the torso, but it can be observed in males of all ages, particularly among overweight males. The condition is widespread enough to provoke advertisements in many publications for surgical treatment of gynecomastia—essentially the same kind of breast reduction that some heavily breasted females elect.

While a boy's body is changing on the outside, it is also changing on the inside. As the penis grows in length and thickness, the internal sexual organs enlarge. The seminal vesicles that carry sperm from the testicles to the opening of the penis develop, and the prostate and bilbo-urethral glands begin to generate seminal fluid.

A year or so after the acceleration of growth of the penis, the first ejaculation of seminal fluid occurs. It might take the form of a spontaneous nocturnal emission, but probably more often it is the result of masturbation provoked by spontaneous erection and other genital sensations, or by the conversations of cohorts describing their own introductions to masturbation. Boys are not apt to report their very first ejaculations as much as girls report their first menstrual periods to each other, but most boys remember the occurrence. Given the extent to which the adolescent and adult male seek orgasmic pleasure through masturbation or interpersonal sexual contact, and the extent to which their sexuality is reinforced by an active fantasy life, one is tempted to say that the day of first ejaculation is the third keystone day in a male's life after his day of birth and his first day of school.

A shift in sleep and alertness patterns also occurs near this time. Some educators have been lobbying for a later beginning to the school day for adolescents. If allowed to regulate their own sleep schedules, most teenagers stay up to about 1:00 AM and sleep until 10:00 AM or later. Studies of their alertness patterns show that they are least alert between 8:00 AM and 9:00 AM, when classes begin in most schools, and most alert after 3:00 PM, when the school day concludes. It seems likely that this shift in sleep and alertness patterns, combined with the demands of the classroom, would affect their moods significantly.

A number of researchers believe that adolescents are not inherently moodier than younger children, notwithstanding widely held opinions to the contrary. Stressful circumstances—such as academic problems, family conflict, or strained friendships—appear to play more substantial roles in the development of mood disturbances and depression in adolescence than do hormones. To the extent that a connection has been established between hormonal changes and behavior, the effects seem to be strongest early in puberty when the system is being "turned on." The culprit is not the absolute increases in hormonal levels but the rapid fluctuations. Once the levels stabilize, later in puberty, problematic effects decrease. Through it all, boys show fewer adverse psychological effects from going through puberty than do girls.

What Is Adolescence?

Lawrence Steinberg has identified as many ways of defining adolescence as Howard Gardner has found varieties of intelligence. Biologically, he writes, adolescence begins with the onset of puberty and ends when a person feels ready for sexual reproduction. Emotionally, adolescence marks the beginning of self-conscious detachment from parents and ends with the attainment of a separate sense of identity. Cognitively, adolescence begins with the emergence of more advanced reasoning abilities, and ends with their consolidation in the ability to entertain hypotheses, weigh contingent possibilities, see situations from the perspectives of others, and draw inferences from available evidence. Interpersonally, to continue Steinberg's catalog, adolescence deepens a shift in interest from family relations to peer relations, culminating in a capacity for deeper intimacy with peers and commitment to a loved one. Socially, adolescence begins with training for adult work and citizen roles, and ends with full attainment of adult status and privileges. Educationally, adolescence begins with entry into junior high school and ends with a completion of formal schooling. Legally, adolescence begins with the attainment of juvenile status and ends with the attainment of majority status. Culturally, adolescence begins in some societies with training for a ceremonial rite of passage and ends with admission to adulthood upon completion of the rite.

There is pertinent information in each of these definitions, but none is sufficient by itself to define adolescence. Biologically, for example, a boy is capable of performing his role in reproduction long before we are ready to say that he has completed his adolescent tasks. Again, a boy may have quite fully shifted his frame of reference from family relations to peer intimacy as a teenager, but we might still judge him to have left other tasks of adolescence incomplete. As we know, many boys reach the age of legal majority without fulfilling all of the tasks of adolescence.

Perhaps we could define adolescence as an interrelated and overlapping set of processes. They don't begin at exactly the same age for every boy, and they certainly don't end at the same age. One can say of many boys in the midstream of adolescence: "He's fifteen years old—going on sixteen most days, on twenty some days, on ten other days." Since there is so much individual variation in the onset and resolution of the several processes that constitute adolescence, neat formulas tied to age can't be offered for parental guidance and reassurance. What can be done is to describe the signs of each process; then each boy has to be read by his parents, teachers, and other caregivers to see where he stands day by day, month by month, year by year.

If a thirteen-year-old boy falls ill and misses school for two or three months, he is not doomed to stay behind his class for the remainder of his academic career. When they set their minds to it, boys can catch up with breathtaking speed. Their minds are prone to bursts of activity just as their bodies grow in spurts separated by periods of leveling off. On the question of overall maturation, however, the principle of quick catch-up doesn't apply. The later a boy enters puberty, the longer his adolescent maturation usually takes. This may appear to be a rather cruel caprice of nature, compounded by cultural attitudes. Early maturing boys steal the show. Their increased strength and sexuality are rewarded with approbation. Some of them become the star athletes. Everyone treats them as more grown-up.

Meanwhile, the parents of the late maturer may be worrying as much as the late maturer himself. There is often more stress attendant upon delay of male maturation than upon maturation itself. Every step is more trying for the late maturer because he knows that many of his peers have gotten there before him. The social roles available to the late maturer—the clown or the cut-up, for example—may themselves hinder more than assist maturation. In fact, studies show that late maturers are seen both by other adolescents and by adults as overly anxious and as seeking attention through immature behavior. From a cross-gender perspective, then, the *late* maturing male is subject to the kind of unease and self-doubt that often marks the *early* maturing female, who may not feel ready for the social and sexual attention early puberty has brought her.

Cliques

In the *New York Times*, an anonymous mother described the teenage social order in a suburb of Minneapolis as a three-tier system. She didn't say so, but I infer that the system is pyramidal: far fewer kids at the top than at the bottom. Tier one consists of the trend setters. They are "the kids who stand out, are a little noisier, more noticed, have a group of kids following them. They're probably a little more risk-taking. They set the pace." Below them on tier two are the aspiring "wannabes." "Everyone else" is on tier three. Most of these cliques in early adolescence are limited to members of the same sex, just as they were in elementary school. Ways of speaking, dressing, and behaving are developed by a trendsetting clique to distinguish themselves from lesser-status peers and from adults. It takes a considerable amount of energy and drive—and financial investment— to be a trendsetter. But teenagers have the financial resources to support their social order. They spend $122 billion a year, including 10 percent of all supermarket sales.

Later in adolescence, same-sex cliques will partially give way to mixed-sex cliques in which boys and girls can interact without having to have intimate relations. By late adolescence, most boys and girls feel comfortable establishing relations as couples. They no longer need the mixed-sex clique, which may then dissolve.

It is important, especially with respect to issues of character development, not to fall into the trap of imagining the early adolescent boy as pulling away from the domination of his stuffy hierarchical family in order to enjoy the simple pleasures of democratic life with peer groups. Adolescent cliques often exhibit hierarchical strategies of inclusion and exclusion that are more ruthless and mean-spirited than anything an adolescent boy has experienced before.

Conflict between adolescent males is often expressed physically, and for that reason studies of adolescent aggression have frequently focused on the behavior of boys. But girls use rumor-mongering, exclusion, withdrawal of friendship, and other forms of "relational aggression" to equally painful—if not quite so dramatic—effect. One study refers tellingly to blows to the heart rather than blows to the body.

As boys move from same-sex cliques early in adolescence to mixed-sex cliques, they learn more of the techniques of relational aggression by seeing and imitating them, or suffering them. Being on the receiving end of both physical and relational aggression leads in one direction to submissive, depressive behavior, and in another direction to hostile, bitter behavior. Boys, as well as girls, can follow either path; indeed, girls today may be more prone to respond with hostility, even physical aggression, than they were, say, twenty years ago. Parents and teachers should take account of the fact that relational aggression often leaves the victim with a simmering anger that can break out with slight provocation, and that may be a roadblock to future relationships. The key to dealing with both kinds of aggression is to teach the adolescent negotiating skills so that he can assert his interests effectively without resorting to physical aggression or barely suppressed anger.

A boy is well served by parents and teachers who discuss the advantages and disadvantages of joining cliques: pointing out the temptations to trendsetters to be arrogant and condescending; raising the question of whether the energy and anxiety devoted to becoming a trendsetter is worth it to a wannabe; pointing out alternative paths of opportunity and enjoyment to boys who are members of "everyone else."

Fathers and Sons

In nonindustrial societies, boys in the first surge of puberty are often subjected to an intense rite of passage. The purpose of the rite is to wrest a boy from the social context of women and children where he has been living, and to initiate him into the life and company of manhood. The more anxious the society is about getting boys to make the leap, the more rigorous the preparation and ceremonies. Elders teach boys the ways of men. Feats of strength and endurance may be required. Fasting may be imposed. The boy's penis may be cut or marked to signal his change of status. Upon the conclusion of the ceremonies, the male, who was just a boy only a few weeks earlier, is regarded as a man—ready to work as an adult once he sleeps off his exhaustion, ready to marry within a few years.

Industrial societies need a much longer period to educate a boy for the various occupations of manhood. Rigorous rites of passage don't make much sense when adolescence is expected to last close to a decade for most boys, even longer for those who elect careers requiring extensive postgraduate education. The few remnants we have from such rites—notably religious "confirmations" or bar mitzvahs—have become pleasant celebrations of adolescence; no one pretends that the male recipients have really become adults, or that their social status has changed in any significant way. To a degree these early adolescent ceremonies symbolize separation from parents toward deeper association with peers rather than cohortship with adults. What happens in industrial societies is that a male adolescent goes through an extended period in which he is regarded partly as an adult, partly as a youth, and maybe still partly as a child. It can be quite confusing to him to sort out. In mid-adolescence he is given adult status as a driver. He can at the same stage acquire a paying job in which the expectations are the same for him as for adults: He is expected to arrive for work on time, perform his prescribed responsibilities satisfactorily, and, if he earns enough, pay taxes. But at school he is still confronted with a framework that hasn't changed all that much since grade school. While he may be old enough to be drafted into military service, at home he may be treated as a child or as a teenager.

Kathleen Norris, in a wise and humorous essay on "Infallibility," caught the irony of the situation:

The mother of a fifteen-year-old boy who had recently obtained a learner's permit for driving . . . accompanied him while he drove to a shopping mall, but as it had begun to rain heavily while they were indoors, she suggested that she drive home. Her son had never driven in the rain, which gave her pause. He insisted that he needed the experience. She acquiesced, but reluctantly, and as he drove out of the parking lot, she began to offer a steady stream of advice. The boy snapped at her to cut it out. She snapped back, 'I don't know what you know, and what you don't know—I'm only trying to help!' 'Mom,' he said, 'just assume that I know everything.'

The onset of puberty provokes a revision of a boy's relation to his parents—to his mother, as we've just seen, but particularly to his father. The very nature of sexual maturation promotes a boy's deeper identification with his father. There is an opportunity for a father to get closer to his son, yet there are provocations that can lead fathers and sons to be more estranged than ever. It is important to keep in mind that as their sons are approaching or traversing adolescence, many fathers are experiencing what is called "midlife crisis," an awareness of their mortality and limitations, a questioning of their life goals.

The relationships between fathers and adolescent sons have been studied frequently without yielding a consistent profile, partly because the samples studied aren't the same, partly because there are many aspects to the relationship and some of them appear to be at cross-purposes. Here is a catalog of some of the findings:

- The stereotype of the father as playmate for his children when he is around is borne out by research. Adolescents help their fathers less around the house than they help their mothers. Watching television together is the most common father-son activity.
- Fathers typically do not talk to their adolescent sons about emotional problems and relationships; they talk about academic performance, future education, occupational plans, etc., and sports. Boys—girls, too–see their fathers as more enabling, less constraining than their mothers, but that may be because the mother is often chief administrator of home life.
- Fathers are, on the whole, more likely to try to exert control over adolescent boys, and mothers to relinquish control. As still another study put it, fathers have greater needs for dominance, are less likely to be permissive than mothers. Sons in one study said their fathers knew them better than they knew their sisters, but they also felt their relationships with their fathers were less affec-

tionate than their mothers' relationships with their sisters. Popular conceptions have adolescent boys in rebellion from their parents over broad issues such as religion and politics, but several studies indicate the major conflicts are over house rules such as curfews and how messy a boy's bedroom is.

- For fathers, there's an increase of negative feelings toward their sons as they mature sexually. Teenagers do not report negative emotion toward their fathers in relation to sexual maturation. The fathers' level of moral maturity and emotional warmth during early adolescence is more predictive of their sons' behavior during adolescence than it was during childhood. Looking back from later adulthood, adults who enjoy happy marriages and plentiful friendships overwhelmingly report having had warm and loving fathers.
- A high level of supportive fatherly involvement in an adolescent boy's life is positively correlated with good school adjustment.
- When boys regard themselves as understood sympathetically by their fathers, they rate time spent with the fathers as pleasurable; conversely, when they feel misunderstood, they see time spent with fathers as forced or unwanted and conflictual. If fathers are controlling and rigid toward adolescent sons, their sons have less masculine self-images and more passive personalities. Positive gender identity and social development are encouraged when a father allows his son to be reasonably self-assertive.
- Adolescents whose fathers disappeared from their lives in early childhood have lower self-esteem than adolescents whose fathers were present throughout childhood.
- As teenagers renegotiate their roles to gain more autonomy, power becomes an important issue. Younger adolescent males regard their fathers as being more powerful than older adolescent males regard them. But as adolescent boys mature physically, their fathers often counter by being more assertive toward them, and the boys tend to back off rather than challenge their fathers too openly.
- The largest study of sexual orientation among the offspring of gay fathers showed that only 9 percent were gay or bisexual—a little, but not dramatically, larger segment than one would expect in a random sample of adult males. The sons' sexual orientation was unrelated to frequency of contact with their fathers or the quality of the relationship. Another study established that gay fathers are no more likely than heterosexual fathers to offend sexually against their own or other children. The findings suggest

that the parental contribution to sexual orientation must be small.

Mothers and Sons

From the very beginning of puberty, there is some lessening of emotional closeness and attachment to both parents by boys, although boys still describe themselves as enjoying more self-disclosure (but selectively as to subject) and affection with mothers than with fathers. The frequency of arguments between mothers and sons increases. This pulling away may contribute to the "gnawing loneliness" Harry Stack Sullivan attributes to boys at the onset of puberty. But the separation probably saddens mothers more than fathers because mothers have usually enjoyed the closer preadolescent bonds. Sixth-grade boys describe themselves as feeling closer to their mothers than to their fathers, but by ninth grade boys see their fathers as being as close to them as their mothers.

There are, to be sure, variations in adolescent development attributable to ethnic diversity. Chinese-American parents, for example, describe themselves as more demanding of obedience and respect from their sons than Caucasian-American parents. In Hispanic and Asian Pacific Island families, strong paternal authority is paired with unusually high maternal warmth; this combination causes most of their children to be compliant to family values and deeply loyal to immediate and extended family members.

Spouses do not operate in vacuums as parents. When there is serious conflict between them, they may try to undermine each other's parental roles. Or they may develop uncoordinated but subtly competing relationships to their adolescent son, as we shall see in more detail in the next chapter. When Mark gets into trouble as a computer hacker at school, he and his dad, Harvey, will conspire to keep his mother, Nina, in the dark for a couple of weeks—"She's too emotional about such things"—until they have thought through a strategy for dealing with the crisis.

Mothers' attitudes toward the fathering role of their spouses reflects their experiences with their own fathers. If mothers see their own fathers as having been nurturing, their husbands are more likely to be strongly involved in the children's lives. When fathers restrict themselves—or are restricted—to roles as disciplinarians, playmates, and economic providers, their participation in family life is seen more as "mother's helper" rather than as co-responsible parent. The man who sees his role principally as the breadwinner, as opposed to being an emotionally supportive caregiver, is almost certain to have a rather distant relationship with his son.

The big picture is that despite what the typical mother of an adolescent boy has lost in closeness with him as he matures physically and socially, she continues to be regarded as the superior caregiver. One piece of research that disputes conventional wisdom shows just how influential the mother remains in most families. The conventional wisdom is that sons undoubtedly learn their aggressive behaviors from their fathers, while daughters learn such behaviors from their mothers. It is true that men rank higher than women in degrees of assertiveness, argumentativeness, and verbal aggressiveness. The surprise is that mothers serve as the main model for these traits in both daughters and sons. They model assertiveness and verbal aggressiveness for all their children—perhaps simply because they spend more time with their children. Despite the rich opportunity the adolescence of a son offers the father to forge a deeper and closer relationship, the evidence suggests that many fathers do not take advantage of the opportunity.

Safe Passage versus High Risk

Joy Dryfoos formulated the notion of "safe passage" to represent what we all wish for adolescent boys: that they will not be too severely affected by the risk factors lodged in all of the opportunities they will encounter passing from childhood to adulthood. A 1995 national survey of fourteen-year-olds indicated the extent of new experience already accumulated.

Sexual Activity.   Forty-one percent of fourteen-year-old boys acknowledged being sexually active, that is already introduced to sexual intercourse. Among the 41 percent, two-thirds said they used condoms to prevent pregnancy and transmission of disease. By twelfth grade, two-thirds of boys will be sexually active. African-American males have their first sexual intercourse earlier on average (41 percent before age thirteen) than white adolescent males, but by age fourteen white males have caught up.

Drugs.   Thirty-two percent of fourteen-year-old boys have smoked a cigarette within the past month. Many smoked their first cigarette before age thirteen. (I am treating cigarettes here as an addictive substance with serious demonstrated health implications.) Approximately 25 percent of boys said that they had smoked marijuana at least once in the past month. As the popularity of smoking has increased, and notwithstanding demonstrations of adverse effects, peer disapproval of smoking marijuana has dropped dramatically. Five percent claim that they have used heavy drugs such as cocaine.

Alcohol.   Twenty-eight percent of boys have already done some heavy drinking by age fourteen. Broken down ethnically and racially, the data indicate that Hispanic males are the heaviest drinkers, whites come next, and African-Americans trail behind. Six percent say they have drunk alcohol and 9 percent have smoked marijuana on school premises.

Academic Problems.   Twenty-six percent of boys in the 1995 survey were already a year behind in school; 5 percent were two years behind. Boys are much more likely than girls to be kept back. Not a few researchers of adolescence believe that the transition into ninth grade is a "make or break" time for teenagers. If intimidated by the challenge, they may take up with peers who are experimenting with high-risk activities.

Violence.   Almost half of adolescent males acknowledge they've been in a fight during the previous year. Approximately 16 percent have fought on school grounds. Thirty-one percent of adolescent males report carrying weapons of one kind or another; 12 percent say they have carried a gun within the past month. There is certainly accuracy in the claim of boys that schools—to say nothing of streets and popular hangouts—are dangerous places, even if there isn't justification for their claim that the most reasonable response to the danger is to carry a weapon.

Crime.   From 1988 to 1993 the number of juvenile arrests almost doubled to about 2 million—five times as many males as females and twice as many whites as African-Americans, although, because of the ratio in the population, the rate is higher for African-Americans. One in five arrested teenagers is held in secure detention. In one decade, from the mid-1980s to the mid-1990s, the homicide rate among teens from fourteen to seventeen years old almost tripled. The increasing availability of handguns is undoubtedly a factor. Professor James Fox of Northeastern University, a specialist on youth crime, writes:

> The problem of kids with guns cannot be overstated. The fourteen year old armed with a gun is far more menacing than a forty-four year old with a gun. While the negative socializing forces of drugs, youth gangs and the

media have become more threatening, the positive socializing forces of family, school, religion, and neighborhood have grown relatively weak and ineffective.

Risk Clusters.   Many adolescent boys are trustworthily low-risk for experimenting with dangerous behaviors. Search Institute analyzed several large-scale studies to see how risk factors attract each other in predictable clusters. Unfortunately, these statistics are not broken down by gender, but we can safely assume that boys outnumber girls in all categories except eating disorders. In a national sample of ninth graders (the upper end of early adolescence), about 22 percent reported no history of substance abuse, excessive drinking, unsafe sexual activity, depression or suicide attempts, antisocial behavior or crime, unsafe driving, or eating disorders. An additional 29 percent acknowledged only one type of risk-taking. Eighteen percent acknowledged two types, 31 percent three or more. In one Michigan survey, about 40 percent of the ninth graders who acknowledged school problems also reported excessive alcohol use; this compared to 17 percent acknowledgment of school problems among those who did not report excessive drinking. About 60 percent of the adolescents with school problems testified to having had unprotected sex, compared to 30 percent of those who did not acknowledge academic failures.

Ten percent of fourteen-year-olds (again, a higher percentage of boys) could be characterized as living at very high risk. Eighty percent of this segment drank, 40 percent used illegal drugs, 90 percent were sexually active without using protection, and more than half had been arrested at least once during the year preceding the survey. Approximately 40 percent reported episodes of depression. Though only a few had dropped out of school, about 40 percent were two or more classes behind their age-mates.

Not surprisingly, the earlier any type of risk-taking begins, the greater the chance that it will increase in severity and cluster with other risky behaviors. The boy who begins to consume alcohol at age ten, for example, may start sexual intercourse at age twelve. If a boy has been aggressive in preschool, the likelihood of his exhibiting worrisome aggressiveness in later childhood and adolescence is substantial.

About 40 percent of American children appear to be on an "achievement track." They live in safe neighborhoods with supportive families, attending schools that are relatively responsive to their needs. Yet every family is vulnerable to parents' unemployment, separation or divorce, and the like. There is no way to construct an impenetrable safety net around adolescent boys. Each family with boys, therefore, has to consider how to prepare them for inevitable temptations and crises.

The risk factors confronting male adolescents in the United States are found in other societies as well. But there are differences in how societies deal with these factors. The United States, for example, is distinctive in the access to firearms it grants to youth and even younger children. Although levels of adolescent sexual activity do not differ much between the United States and the societies of Western Europe, much lower rates of contraception prevail in the United States, reflecting both lack of access to contraceptives and ambivalent attitudes on the part of adolescents, their parents, and the society.

Professor Michael Rutter, a child psychiatrist in London, has studied the differences in social policy toward adolescents in the industrialized societies. It would be "unthinkable," he noted, for a teenage schoolgirl in the Netherlands to bear a child because all social institutions—family, schools, churches, media, and government—are united in the objective to provide adolescent birth control information and services to insure that adolescents' sexual activity is safe, pregnancy rare, and abortion available for the small number of unintended pregnancies. Social institutions in the United States lack this unified approach. In the absence of such consensus, each individual floats on his own. Adolescents are often blamed for their lapses and risk-taking more than they are helped to take reponsibility for them, pick up the pieces, and go on with their lives.

Depression

Eighteen percent of fourteen-year-old boys say they have had suicidal thoughts. Seven percent say they have attempted to commit suicide. The percentages are lower than for girls the same age, but boys are more effective in completing the act, killing themselves four to six times more often than girls.

William Pollack's writing on depression among young males has been especially cogent in my view. After suggesting that our culture gives many signals to boys not to exhibit sadness, and that some of the methods of diagnosis of depression were originally designed to ascertain depression in adult women and are inappropriate for young males, he argues for a broad definition of depression in boys:

> If we dwell merely on the most extreme—and obvious—instances of full-blown, or 'clinical,' depression, we risk failing to help boys cope with emotional states that, though less intense on the surface, are actually very painful for them, emotional states that without appropriate intervention may very

well evolve into a major depression or provoke suicidal feelings. There's also a risk that by ignoring certain related behaviors, most notably irritable conduct and the abuse of substances, we may also fail to recognize the onset of serious depression.

Pollack gives some useful suggestions for distinguishing sadness from depression (without downplaying either one). "For instance, a boy who occasionally shuts himself into his room when he's feeling down is probably just momentarily feeling sad. By contrast, a boy who frequently comes home from school, goes into his room, shuts the door, and refuses to talk to anyone is obviously exhibiting behaviors that fall squarely within the continuum of depression. Likewise, a boy who has had a bad day and doesn't feel like coming to the dinner table is clearly quite different from one who consistently refuses to eat or dine with his family." Pollack also notes that depression may be expressed as anger or irritation rather than through the clearer signals of sadness, withdrawal, or apparent hopelessness; parents and other caregivers therefore need to be alert to signs of anger or irritation to see whether they ascertain depression behind or beneath the surface. "Being sad is the same as being mad for me," said one boy quoted by Pollack.

Depression manifests itself differently in boys and girls, according to a study by Per Gjerde, and Jack and Jeanne Block. Fourteen-year-old girls who developed symptoms of depression were found to be anxious, low in self-esteem, very concerned about their bodies, and, mostly, quite intelligent. Boys who exhibited high levels of symptoms of depression, also at age fourteen, showed lack of concern for interpersonal relationships, displayed hostile and antisocial attitudes, and were below average in intellectual prowess.

Pollack gives some specific pointers for handling signs of sadness or depression in a boy:

1. Create a private place to talk with him, so he won't feel ashamed if he loses his composure.
2. Be available to talk with full attention, but don't press him to open up until he is comfortable. Invite but don't force.
3. Be careful not to shame him when you respond to his disclosure of sadness or depression. Don't tease, or joke, or paper over his feelings with assertions that everything will be fine. Acknowledge that you see his discomfort and are lovingly concerned. Avoid facile advice.
4. The signs a parent might be alert to include: intense or prolonged social withdrawal from family and friends; prolonged depletion

or fatigue; increase in impulsive outbursts of anger or aggressiveness; denial of pain; sleeping and eating disorders; increasingly rigid acting out; failure to exhibit appropriate emotion; harsh self-criticism; falling below usual academic level; increased risk-taking; evidence of exposure to alcohol and drugs; change in sexual behavior; and, obviously, unusual mention of suicide, death, or dying.

A parent or other caregiver who notes unusual signs of sadness or symptoms that might be related to depression would be wise to consult a professional, both for the boy himself and to foster the adult's capacity to cope sensitively and effectively with the situation.

Attention Deficit Hyperactivity Disorder

Somewhere between 30 and 70 percent of children, by one estimate, who were diagnosed as having attention deficit disorder (ADD) or attention deficit hyperactivity disorder (ADHD)as children still have the disorder when they reach adolescence and adulthood. I suspect the wide range of the estimate is related both to the variations in diagnostic criteria and to the occasional misdiagnosis of normal-range temperamental variation as ADHD among children, especially boys.

Treating adolescent ADD/ADHD may be more complex than treating childhood ADD/ADHD. Adolescents may deny having the disorder, may fake taking prescribed medication, may give their medication to friends who don't have the disorder but want a chemical boost to study for an examination. Medication needs regular evaluation, including off-periods when the effect of the medication can be compared to behavior during a period of abstinence. Since metabolism is changing during adolescence, teenagers may need higher dosages. ADD/ADHD may reduce an adolescent's prudent appraisal of risk-taking, so teenagers with ADD/ADHD need special training in how they cope with driving or handling machinery. Most adolescents with ADD/ADHD benefit from a continuing relationship with a counselor whom they come to trust.

How to Get Boys to Talk

When I was in pediatric training, only a few of my class were interested in child psychiatry. A wise older psychiatrist at the Judge Baker Guidance Center across the street from Children's Hospital in Boston, Donald Russell, offered an elective on psychiatric diagnosis. He put us immediately to work on the evaluation of boys who were referred by the Massachusetts

division of youth services. Most of these kids had committed pretty serious crimes.

Not a few of these kids were, as the term is used, "hardened." That's to
say that they were familiar with therapists and jaded with people who professed interest in helping them. Getting them to talk was no small task.

Dr. Russell had a technique that he repeated often on the subject. The
best way to get a teenager to talk is to take him for a ride in a car. That way,
you're not looking face-to-face, there's time to pass as you proceed to a
destination, and there's always something to comment on along the way.

It became clear that boys, particularly boys in trouble, want to tell their
stories to a sympathetic listener. Avoiding a posture of making judgments
about them, their behavior, their backgrounds, their experiences with the
juvenile justice system—and especially avoiding characterizing them as
"bad kids"—was important. Being oneself, without airs, expressing interest and concern, also went a long way. But perhaps most importantly, one
had honestly to play one's role, not to pretend that one wasn't a doctor in
an institution assigned to evaluate them.

Any conversation of any weight with a teenager should take place in a
private setting. Therapists also learn the importance of timing. One does-
n't jump in on the most sensitive material; if the child is embarrassed or
ashamed, it's much better to approach the subject indirectly. If possible,
wait until he introduces it.

One of the time-honored techniques of interviewing on sensitive issues
is to use the word "sometimes": "Sometimes kids . . ." That takes the emphasis away from the particular situation, allows a boy to maintain some
distance, and enables one to avoid embarrassing him.

An activity may help a boy to relax and confide his problems. Shooting
baskets or playing catch can make a neutral, enjoyable setting for a talk.

Lastly, it's important that we not fill up all the time with words. Silence
is helpful, because it lets a boy take the lead and bring up what's on *his*
mind.

15

IDENTITY AND FRIENDSHIP

In *Childhood and Society*, first published in 1950, Erik Erikson reworked Freud's stages of psychosocial development in the young child, and extended the stages to eight, encompassing the whole human life span. On college campuses, where Erikson's theory first became popular, most attention was paid to the stage of adolescence because students were working through it themselves. The critical task of adolescence, Erikson wrote, is to form a personal identity amid such a storm of biological and social maturation and psychic turbulence that he spoke of the stage as a *crisis*. He elaborated these views in *Identity and the Life Cycle: Psychological Issues* published in 1959, and in other subsequent books.

Where did I come from? Who am I? What do I want to become? These are the three great questions of identity. The formation of a personal identity, or a reasonably coherent sense of self, is a lifelong process. The specifics change over time; but adolescence is the stage of life in which a person first confronts (at first in a dramatic and even exaggerated way, gradually in a more nuanced way) all of the elements of his later adult identity: sexual maturity and experimentation with romantic relationships; the friendships and peer group attachments that give the person a social base outside the family; the first employment and first steps toward an appraisal of the person's talent and career interests; awareness of participating in a youth culture, with its own media, arts, language, and style. All of these elements are fraught with opportunity and promise, and all of them are about equally laden with frustration and disappointment.

The glory of adolescence is its opening this window of possibility to a world of feeling, of deep connection to others, of meaningful contribution. Its peril is closing the window, thus constricting a boy's emotional, personal, aesthetic, and intellectual range. Decades before Erikson's theory was published, the writer Anais Nin captured the downside with humor and sympathy:

How heavy this life, the life of men. Is it true they cannot raise one eyebrow without the other? So weighted with their work, eagerly curving their shoulders to the contours of the yoke. A world dry to tears and bleached of colour. One never hears the wind chimes or the music of jewelry. In the mornings they brush away their dreams like flies. There is no carpet and no grass over the rough brown boards of their existence. Perhaps, never owning more than two pairs of shoes, the richness of life has escaped them.

Adolescence is not an easy stage of life; many adults, if asked whether they would like to relive adolescence, would say "No, thank you" very firmly.

Part of an identity consists of emulating people the adolescent admires, trying to be like them or like what he thinks they are; an adolescent may be trying to be like several people simultaneously. Internally—and largely unconsciously—he is synthesizing as best he can these fragments of identification. Another aspect of identity consists of the adolescent's continuing appraisal and reappraisal of what he has achieved and what he can do. This appraisal concerns academic work, extracurricular pursuits such as sports and the arts, perhaps part-time employment, social and romantic status, and finding a new place in the family. Yet another aspect of identity has to do with the adolescent's self-image. It is a combination of self-appraisal of his achievements and attributes, including physical attractiveness and talent, and his perception of how others regard him.

All this striving takes place while the adolescent is buffeted by physiological maturation. Sexual and aggressive drives, which had been relatively dormant through school years, now surface from within with tremendous energy and threaten to overwhelm the conscious self and its ability to cope with challenges coming from a world without. It isn't an exaggeration to say that adolescents sometimes feel as though their impulses have wills of their own. Perhaps in no other life stage is there as pervasive confusion as there is in adolescence.

Generalizations never quite convey the intricacy of the challenges each adolescent boy faces as he works on identity issues, as I hope to show by telling Mark's story.

A Hacker

Mark is fourteen, about to graduate from eighth grade and go to boarding school. He is tall and muscular, and could easily pass for a ninth or tenth grader. One might assume that a boy as physically imposing as he is would always be able to assert himself quickly into the center of any new situation with peers, but Mark's path hasn't been easy, even though he has always been one of the biggest kids in his class.

"When he was younger," his mother, Nina, says, "he had a lot more friends than he has now. I pulled him out of a very progressive, 'touchy-feely' school and put him in a K–8 prep school in second grade. He was the center of everything in his old school, and then when he moved to this new school it was very hard for him. The other boys in his class had been together since kindergarten and they weren't open or friendly. There are a lot of rich kids in the school. Some other new boys who joined the class when Mark did, or later, found it too unfriendly and left. But Mark has stuck it out. It was horrible for him in second grade. But he made another friend or two every year, and I thought things were getting better.

"In fourth grade, another new boy, whom Mark liked, joined the class. This particular kid was very observant, very bright. One day the class was discussing a book titled *There's a Boy in the Girls' Bathroom*. Something led the teacher to ask, 'How would it feel if no one came and sat next to you in class?' The new kid said, 'Oh, you mean the way Mark feels all the time?' He said this in class. It must have made Mark feel terrible. The teacher—she's a wonderful reading teacher—called me. I took Mark to his pediatrician, who happened to be the father of one of his classmates at school, and his attitude was, well, we all need character built in us, and Mark is just learning to deal with these situations a little earlier than most of the kids. Mark came home one day toward the end of that year and said to me, 'Why do they all want to be like each other?'"

Since he never went to school in his hometown, Mark doesn't have a set of neighborhood friends to offset his aloof classmates. His private school is about ten miles from his home, which itself inhibits socializing after school hours. "When he was very little," Nina recalls, "the kids in the neighborhood would throw rocks at each other. There was no way I was sending him to public school."

When I first talked with Mark, he was just coming out of a school crisis linked to the school computer files that had embroiled and shaken the whole family. Both his parents have worked in computer companies. His dad, Harvey, is self-taught—never went to college—and has built two companies in the fields of computer systems design and Internet access. Mark's school is one of his clients.

Mark and his dad have built their close relationship around being computer buffs. Already Mark has graduated from playing videogames to basic programming. "Before this problem," Harvey told me, "Mark and I had been having discussions about computers and the different people that use them: consumers are one group, and the people called crackers, who are malicious, are another. Crackers are the skinheads of the computer world. And then there is a third group called hackers; I count myself proudly among them. Hackers learn everything there is to know about a computer or a system, but never have malicious intent. But if a hacker ever discovers holes in a security system or flaws in a piece of software, he feels a personal duty to inform the owner of the machine that there's a problem.

"A short time before this problem came to a head, Mark told me he'd found a serious problem with the school's security system. He had been writing some software programs at school, and he said he needed to disable the security system to finish what he was doing. The year before he'd found out the system's password, and now he discovered it hadn't ever been changed. 'You know what to do about it,' I said. And he said, 'Well, yeah, I gotta tell them.' So what he did, after discussing it with me, was go to a classroom computer, turn off the security system using the password, and write an anonymous e-mail message to the school's technology director briefly outlining the security problem. He used a method that was completely untraceable because hackers often find themselves dealing with people who can't tell the difference between hackers and crackers; if you ask anyone on the street, they think hackers are bad people."

Nina was a bit more explicit about the origins of the problem. In seventh grade, Mark installed a program of his own devising on a computer in the school library that, unbeknownst to any of the faculty, recorded all of the keystrokes of everyone who used the computer after him. From the recorded data he learned passwords that gave him access to all of the faculty's and administration's confidential computerized files. When Mark revisited the passwords midway through eighth grade, he found that none of them had been changed. They were all operational; the security system was eminently breachable.

Upon receipt of the anonymous memo from Mark, the school staff alerted his dad, their outside expert. The school staff also called in another expert to check all of the school's computers. There was evidence that a file containing a teacher's personal material had been entered by someone else, and quite a lot of other evidence of outside intrusion. Harvey knew all along that his son had sent the anonymous message. News of the additional evidence of computer security breaches sent him hurrying home to meet with Mark.

Mark didn't know that there were a couple of other hackers or crackers among the student body. According to him, a teacher heard one of the others talking about what he was doing. The teachers assumed it was a co-operative venture of any boys involved, but Mark didn't know anything of the others' activities. As one of the most computer-literate boys in the school, he was an immediate suspect. He and two other boys were approached separately and asked if they had sent the message about the vulnerability of the system. Mark acknowledged that he had sent it, and gave a dean additional details of the system's vulnerability to intrusion.

After the school had conducted a thorough search for evidence of unauthorized access to its files, all the students of the upper school were called to an assembly. The dean, by Harvey's account, "made it clear that the problem was taking up a lot of time and money, and there was now a trust issue. It was strongly implied that if any perpetrator came forward and was candid about his involvement nothing would happen, but if the school had to figure everything out by evidence and inference, there'd be serious hell to pay." Suspension was among the punishments threatened for those who were guilty but did not voluntarily come forward. Students were given twenty-four hours to comply with the request. What could have been a valuable "teachable moment" was handled by the school in a rather limited way as a disciplinary moment: Find the culprit and punish him.

"Mark had already told them about the password thing," Nina recounted, "enough for them to know that he had exercised poor judgment. Without consulting us, he made a decision on his own. An hour after the assembly, he slipped away from class, went to an assistant principal—not a computer expert, but someone I have a good relationship with—and said, 'Excuse me, we need to talk.' He was asked to make a list of things he had done."

A disciplinary meeting was convened the same day to deal with what Mark had acknowledged doing, and the next day Mark was called in and told his punishment for all of his past breaches of the security system: a three-day suspension, a ban on using school computers for the rest of the year, three days of "community service" doing work in the school technology lab, and reimbursement to the school of the thirteen hundred dollars it had cost to have the school's computers evaluated for signs of intrusion.

The school staff, in Mark's view, never abandoned their theory that the cracking had been a cooperative activity, and that Mark was the leader. He somewhat relished his new reputation as a computer data bandit, but he was chagrined by the severity of the punishment, especially in view of his contention that he was not himself guilty of the acts that had most disturbed the disciplinary committee. Mark was the only student to receive such painful sanctions. One other student came forward, a fellow eighth grader—and friend of Mark's—who admitted to a few minor infractions and was not disciplined. The school did not aggressively pursue identification of any other crackers, apparently intending to use the severity of sanctions in Mark's case as deterrent to anyone tempted to breach computer security in the future.

The situation had to be handled diplomatically. His school knew where he had been accepted for ninth grade and planned to attend. Almost certainly, a report to the boarding school about his computer cracking would undo the admission. Nevertheless, Nina and Harvey were not disposed to accept the sanctions without an appeal. They felt strongly about two matters. The first was that school officials had strongly implied that any student who stepped forward and admitted breaking into the school's computerized files would not be suspended. The second factor was that Mark was scheduled to play a major role in the eighth grade play. His suspension would prevent his taking part in the final days of rehearsal, and might jeopardize his being able to appear in the play at all.

"Within hours of the announcement of Mark's punishment," said Nina, "Harvey was on the phone to the head of the upper school, the dean of students, and the assistant principal to whom Mark reported what he had done. We didn't want Mark to be let off the hook. We wanted him to learn from his experience. It's much better that it happened now before he goes off to boarding school. I mean, he could get in trouble with the feds if he does any more cracking. This was a wonderful opportunity for him to learn an important lesson: You don't mess with computer security, period, end of discussion.

"Before we knew that they might not suspend Mark, I asked him, 'What have you learned?' He said, 'I learned never to 'fess up. I learned to never come clean. 'Cause I came clean and I'm getting hung.' That was the very reason my husband and I thought it was important to persuade these people that they were doing the wrong thing. After consulting the three people my husband talked to, the head of the school invited us to a conference. Mark had to sit in the library—he was very pale and very quiet—while we found out if he was suspended or not."

The suspension was voided, but the other sanctions remained in place. Nina thinks the amended disciplinary action was fair. Harvey believes Mark was overpunished: "The fine was to pay for sweeping through all the machines and identifying all the problems he had nothing to do with." Still, Harvey acknowledges, "Mark really did use a password that he shouldn't have. So in the most basic sense, he did violate by trespassing. Initially, our reaction was one of betrayal and intense rage at the school. We thought about it, though, and cooled our tempers. Mark knows the difference between right and wrong clearly, or else he wouldn't be where he is now. He came to me voluntarily, out of the blue, and asked for help. He did the right thing, and that's the man-on-the-white-horse way. If he'd taken the other path, he wouldn't have said boo to me; I would've had no idea what he'd done, and he would have gone his merry way."

Identity Formation

Erik Erikson suggested four different ways of characterizing the many individual ways boys confront the tasks of adolescence. These four statuses are more distinct in theory than they may be in actual life. In Mark's case, one might find signs of all four, which shouldn't be surprising in an eighth grader.

Some boys, Erikson said, exhibit *identity diffusion*. A boy in this position is adrift. He may have explored alternatives but found the task too threatening or overwhelming. He may reflect an "I don't care" attitude. He may unthinkingly go along with whatever his crowd is doing. Boys in this status are most likely to use and abuse alcohol and drugs. Many are vulnerable to depression. In relation to this status and its accompanying sense of isolation and ineffectualness, Erikson quoted the adolescent son, Biff, in Arthur Miller's play, *Death of a Salesman:* "I just can't take hold, Mom, I can't take hold of some kind of life." It's easy to distinguish Mark from Biff, but there are hints of "I don't care" in Mark's story. He has pretty much given up on making a satisfying connection to more than a few of his peers at school.

Adolescent boys can also exhibit *identity foreclosure*. A boy in this position has prematurely cut off exploration by accepting a ready-made identity urged upon him by one of—or a coalition of—the social forces that impinge on him: his parents, his teachers, religious leaders, his romantic partner, or a gang or other group of cohorts. Foreclosed adolescent boys tend to be inflexible and intolerant, to use their commitments in a defensive way, and to see contrary expressions of opinion as threats. Some foreclosed boys, alienated from their families, are vulnerable to the invitations of cults as they adopt lives unequivocally different from their pasts. Fathers with particularly powerful urges to define their sons' lives for them are prone to drive their sons into foreclosure—sometimes by an adoption of the fathers' wishes, sometimes by a blind rebellion against them.

While I would not say that Mark has foreclosed his identity formation, he lacks strong peer relationships to counterbalance the loving but powerful influence of his parents on the direction of his life. He may very well find those connections at boarding school, perhaps developing friendships slowly but cumulatively, one or two a year, as he has done in his school years.

Erikson's third category is *identity moratorium*. This might be called a holding pattern before a boy makes basic identity commitments. He is exploring, gathering information, maybe experimentally trying on different roles and activities. He may be driving his parents crazy, but the process is healthy—essential, really, to a well-fashioned identity. Mark is definitely exploring different ways of being an adolescent.

Some adolescent boys reach what Erikson called *identity achievement*. At this stage a boy knows where he's going, and has a sense of psychological well-being. He has explored enough alternatives to make informed choices for himself. He is, among his peers, most apt to be comfortable with critical and abstract thought, and also to exhibit advanced moral reasoning. On the surface, he may look very much like his age-mate in identity foreclosure, who has adopted for himself the style and dreams of his parents or other authority figures; closer scrutiny will reveal, however, that the adolescent who has enjoyed the freedom to select his own identity is very different from the adolescent who has acceded to someone else's dream.

Thinking of Mark's story, I see aspects of identity achievement, especially in his comfort with abstract thought and in the moral maturity he showed in owning up to his computer cracking. The intellectual aptitude tests he has taken predict that his eventual S.A.T. scores will qualify him for any college in the country. The boarding school he has been admitted to has very high academic standards and routinely has its graduates admitted to the most prestigious colleges. Mark's parents haven't hesitated to let him know their high view of his talent, and the prospects it offers him. But he hasn't explored enough alternatives different from the courses of his parents' lives, or found enough sense of psychological well-being, to say that he has a fully formed identity.

Cliques and Crowds

Teenage boys spend more than half of their waking hours with other teenagers, less than 5 percent of their time with either parent. That fact alone establishes the power of peer relations in adolescence even if there weren't sometimes the further motivation of detachment and conflict between parents and sons.

The classic study of how adolescents form groups was done by Dunphy forty years ago in Australia. He noted that in early adolescence boys and girls formed same-sex *cliques* of four to six members in which all the members were strongly attached to one another. The same-sex pattern was a holdover from patterns of gender separation in previous school years. Gradually the cliques combined into larger heterosexual *crowds*. Later in adolescence, the crowds broke down into heterosexual cliques, and finally, as males and females became more comfortable with their sexuality, the cliques were abandoned by some of them in favor of loose associations of dating couples.

Subsequent studies in the United States have pointed out how often these *early* adolescent cliques and crowds—reputation-based groupings—are defined and named by stereotypical labels, even caricatures: jocks, brains, nerds, dweebs, druggies, toughs, normals, preppies, etc. Stereotypical thinking cuts across many aspects of adolescent activity. A boy's conception of the career ahead of him may, for example, feature fantasies of being a rock musician or race car driver—something more dramatic than the jobs his parents go to every day, and perhaps beyond his talent.

Yet despite the simplistic thought, which is very much a side effect of inexperience, these groupings give adolescents the feedback they covet. Rolf Muuss, discussing Erikson's concepts, puts it thus:

> The peer group, the clique, and the gang, even the lover, aid the individual in the search for a personal identity since they provide both a role model and very personal social feedback. The seemingly endless telephone conversations during adolescence and later, the bull session in college, can serve genuine psychological purposes by providing this kind of personal information. As long as the adolescent depends on role models and feedback, the in-group feeling that the peer group provides will remain quite strong. Also, behaviors of conformity to the expectations of the peer group reflect the learned skill of not making oneself an easy target of 'catty remarks' or to avoid being 'mocked out.' . . . Particularly during the time when the body image changes so rapidly, when genital maturation stimulates sexual fantasies, and when intimacy with the opposite sex appears as a possibility with simultaneously positive and negative valences, the adolescent relies on peers for advice, comfort, companionship, and uses peers as a personal sounding board.

Friendship and Peer Acceptance

The numerous crushes and infatuations that mark adolescence were interpreted by Erikson primarily as a means of evaluating the self through the eyes of a girlfriend or boyfriend, not as attempts to form long-lasting partnerships. The latter require a capacity for intimacy that Erikson believed was normally achieved only in the next life stage, early adulthood.

In adolescence, however, boys have the opportunity to develop friendships of a more enduring nature than those typical of their earlier childhood: with other boys, with girls either within romance or when romance is not at issue, and with adults. Robert and Beverly Cairns did one longitudinal study that showed only 20 percent of friendships between fourth graders lasting as long as a year, but 40 percent of friendships formed by the same students in tenth grade proving to be enduring. The depth and enduring nature of adolescent friendships reflects how friendship has come to involve more than shared play; the full panoply of identity formation has been drawn into the dynamics of friendship.

In one of his later works, Erikson noted that fidelity is a special strength of early adolescents. He traced its potential back to the development of trust in early childhood. What gives fidelity relevance in the early adolescent stage is that a person is in effect asking himself: To whom can I be true outside my family? Family ties have an obvious inevitability about them. They may be predominantly positive or negative in a boy's evaluation, but they can't be expunged just because they are negative; they can only be buffered by detachment and distance.

Friendships are voluntary, not inevitable, and sooner or later each one hits a snag that could end it unless some accommodation is made. Then a person has to decide whether or not to sustain the commitment despite the contradictions in values between himself and his friend. Again, one hopes to see in a boy's passage through adolescence a development from applying brittle standards of perfection toward tolerating differences and imperfections within friendships, and a perception that he himself is far from perfect.

How does one know when friendship obtains between two people, and how can one evaluate its quality? Jeffrey Parker and Steven Asher defined six aspects for a study of children's friendships:

1. How much do the friends appear to care for and support each other?
2. How much do the friends argue with each other, disagree, or annoy each other?
3. How much enjoyable time do the friends spend together in and outside school?
4. How much do the friends assist each other with tasks such as homework?
5. How much do the friends disclose personal information and feelings to each other?
6. How efficiently and fairly do the friends resolve disagreements?

Parker and Asher were conducting a study of about eight hundred third, fourth, and fifth graders, but I suspect some of their findings would still hold up fairly accurately for early adolescents. They made a very useful distinction between peer acceptance—measured by having every subject rate his/her interest in playing with every other classmate—and friendship—measured by having each subject submit a list of best and very best friends, and then comparing the lists to see if alleged friendships matched up. Peer acceptance relates to the probability that a student would be invited into cliques and crowds, and friendship relates to the establishment of close relationships with other individuals.

What they found was that many students who were not well accepted by their peers generally nevertheless had friends, though less frequently *best* friends; this distinction between acceptance and friendship is useful in Mark's case because he is not well accepted by his schoolmates as a whole, but is not without friendships that he values. Parker and Asher found that children without best friends were lonelier than children with best friends, no matter how well they were accepted; and that low friendship quality and low level of acceptance contributed separately and about equally to feelings of loneliness. (Parker and Asher also found some students with high acceptance levels who did not have best friends; they were popular, but had not felt the need to establish close friendships with a few cohorts.)

"I came to this school in the second grade," said Mark, "and I didn't know anyone, so I've always been kind of an outcast. I'm not popular or anything." "Did all that teasing make you feel like you had to look out for yourself?" I asked. "Well, I do, because there is no one else."

"Have you ever teased other kids?" I asked. "Yeah, probably, yeah. It's natural. I don't tease anyone now. I used to, when I was younger, because I thought people would like me more if I teased someone else, but that doesn't happen. There is no friendship involved in being popular; there's just acknowledgment that you're popular. When you're an outcast, you're out in your own little groups. You actually become friends with other outcasts because you join together. My best friend, he was one of the most popular kids in the class. But he doesn't want to hang out with them because they're not real friends—they're only looking out for themselves. But when you're real friends, it's not passive, it's more outgoing. I think the reason my friend and I are together now is because we like the same thing—computers—and he doesn't want to be friends with boys if it means he has to wash their backs."

These comments by Mark are perceptive about popularity and friendship, but they also show how much he has felt himself to be an outsider through most of his childhood and early adolescence. That's why his computer offense at school is so poignant: It perfectly symbolized his position and his plight—the outsider eavesdropping. It wouldn't have been nearly as revelatory if Mark had gotten caught doing something commonplace such as spraying graffiti or drinking alcohol on school property. His first incursions into the school computer files used a method that could be traced. Then he figured out how to use "hot keys" to disable the security system and peruse the files without changing any settings; no one could tell he was intruding. The consummate outsider was penetrating to the very core of the school's inner secrets—and no one knew. Mark had become an insider at last—until he told the truth about it. Then he became even more of an outsider again.

One part of my conversation with Mark reflected some of the resentment he must harbor. "The faculty thought they were secure in their secure world. I knew what was going on. I knew their information. So they weren't really secure when they thought they were." "Does that give you a sense of power?" "Yes." "What are your goals?" I asked. "To be the highest on the totem pole of the security field—not in a corporation, but in the world—as someone who can write security codes and break into things."

Patterns of Friendship

When they compared the quality of boys' and girls' friendships, Parker and Asher found little difference in how much they argued and disagreed with their friends, or with how much time they spent companionably in and out of school. The latter finding is consistent with William Pollack's assertion that boys who are friends are more often to be found doing the same activity side by side than expressing closeness face-to-face. However, Parker and Asher found that girls give their friends more validation and support, help each other more with tasks, and resolve their differences more efficiently and fairly.

Kathryn Urberg and three colleagues at Wayne State University studied peer networks in sixth, eighth, tenth, and twelfth grades in one Midwestern city. Their clearest finding was that girls have stronger connections to their schools' social networks than boys do. Girls were more likely than boys to have a best friend, and a larger portion of their friendship lists belonged to their same social crowd than was true of boys. Boys showed more diversity of friendship; a larger portion of their friends did not belong to the same social crowd as the boy himself. The researchers speculate that since girls value and exhibit more closeness in their friendships than boys do, girls may therefore prefer to relate to other girls most like themselves. Urberg found that with each rise in grade from sixth to eighth to tenth to twelfth, adolescents appeared to become more selective in identifying friends. They made fewer overtures to others to become friends and received fewer invitations in return.

Not surprisingly, the peer networks seemed a little more complex and fluid than the pattern Dunphy described several decades ago. One of the most interesting findings of Urberg was that many adolescents have strong enough ties to more than one peer group that moving from one group to another may not be difficult if an adolescent loses favor within a group, becomes unhappy with a group and decides to abandon it, or opts for a new group because it better represents his interests and style.

One father recalled to me the abrupt switch of social crowds his son made in tenth grade. "I believe it happened incredibly swiftly, though Pete's mother and I didn't recognize it right away. The precipitating factor was his falling in love for the first time—or at least the first time he had the nerve to approach the girl he admired. She fully reciprocated his crush. Until then, Pete had a set of friends that everyone in the family enjoyed, especially his buddy Jim; the two boys were inseparable.

"But the girlfriend belonged to a different crowd. Her crowd was a lot faster than the old crowd. The first glimpse I got of Pete's new social life was when I went to pick him up after what was billed as a casual Friday night get together. Pete wasn't at the house whose address I had. There was a lot of delaying, and finally I was told he was at another house up the street. So far as I could tell, there weren't any adults present at either house. At the second house I was asked to wait in the car, that Pete would be out 'in a minute.' I waited at least fifteen minutes. Then two other kids walked Pete down the driveway. He was so glassy-eyed from alcohol or drugs, or both, that he couldn't walk unassisted. They helped Pete into the backseat of my car, and as I pulled away he threw up all over the backseat.

"In middle school and earlier, Pete was an excellent student and a great kid. Teachers would write on his report cards that if they had a son, they hoped he would be as fine a kid as Pete. But in about thirty seconds that Friday night, I saw what the downside of being the father of an adolescent could be. It was quite a long time before it got any better. The break from Pete's old crowd to the new one was so complete that we never saw his former buddy Jim at our house again. Academic achievement wasn't prized by the new crowd, and soon we had to begin dealing with evidence that Pete was cutting most of his classes, dropping out."

Pete's dad could hardly wait until the end of the year to get Pete transferred to another school. He did this by moving to another school district, even though the school Pete was attending had a national reputation for academic achievement. In a new town, Pete made friends who were also pretty familiar with alcohol and drugs but hadn't abandoned academic achievement; friendships he made there have endured into his adult life.

Friendship and Homosexuality

Growing up gay complicates the issue of friendship because the social networks adolescents construct at school usually presume heterosexuality. When homosexual adolescents tell their stories, many of them testify to thinking or feeling themselves to be different well before puberty. So they come to adolescence with an awareness of being drawn to others of the same sex. As Michael, now twenty-two, recalls, "As I entered adolescence I started to notice the other boys in my class. In history I would find myself fantasizing about the boy sitting in front of me. During the whole week of sex education when we learned about the male anatomy, I was barely able to control my excitement. By now I felt sure that I was attracted to boys and not girls."

One issue for the gay adolescent is whether he can form friendships with heterosexual males. If he keeps his sexual orientation hidden, he feels that he is hiding something essential to his identity; yet he fears that if he comes out, heterosexual males will shun him. As Craig, now sixteen, recalls, "In fourth grade I secretly fell in love with my best friend. My love lasted six years. He and I never actually had a relationship but our friendship was more than anybody could ever fathom. Imagine loving somebody so close to you, so much, and you could never touch that person, kiss him, or hold him with the intimacy you need when you're in love. Imagine never being able to say I love you."

Craig doesn't say so, but a possible inference that can be drawn from his story is that this friendship did not survive Craig's coming out. Adolescent homosexuals are fully aware of the amount of social prejudice toward their sexual preference. Each of them has to wrestle with the question of self-disclosure and its potential consequences. As Don, now a college student, recalls: "When I was sixteen years old, I began to seriously question my sexuality. I really wanted to tell people about the feelings I was having but was afraid of getting hurt physically, emotionally, and mentally. I didn't feel like losing my friends or being called names. I decided to talk to a very close friend. Luckily, he was accepting and said it didn't change anything. I didn't tell anyone else for a while. Eventually I told this girl in my class who I thought I could trust. She acted very accepting and swore that she wouldn't tell anyone. A few weeks later, I found out that she told several other people because 'she didn't know how to handle it.' . . . I decided (then) to be honest with everyone, so I told my friends, or people I thought were my friends, that I was gay. They acted very accepting at first, but they gradually stopped calling me to hang out with them. I felt ignored and betrayed. My junior and senior years of high school, which are supposed to be fun, were simply hell. I couldn't wait to get out of there."

One lesson Don learned that parents and others might well teach boys growing up is that confidences are often broken. While sometimes it is because the gossiper wants to spread information to be hurtful or to cultivate social power by trading in confidences, it can also be because the information is more than the confidee can handle. Spreading the confidence becomes a way of trying to make others responsible for it, thus removing the burden of anxiety from the person who received it. But the larger lesson is that friendship with heterosexuals is going to be a very difficult issue for uncloseted gay adolescents until there is a broader tolerance for homosexuality in the society at large.

Parents and Identity

Adolescent identity formation, in general, and adolescent friendships, in particular, put a lot of issues on parents' plates. There are so many opportunities for friction between parents and adolescents that some parents wonder whether there is any room left for common cause. It would be a grave mistake to read adolescence as the withering of need for strong relationships with the family. To the contrary, a strong family relationship can give an adolescent the self-assurance he needs to cope with all of the challenges of identity formation, including the welding of important peer friendships and winning acceptance in cliques and crowds.

In the period of early adolescence, it is a temptation to parents to overreact to matters of style. Perhaps it isn't too exaggerated to say that the perfect early adolescent fad in hair style or dress or body ornamentation is something that will turn on peers and turn off elders to an equal degree. It's sporting to offer them some of the criticism they are courting, but not to make these fads the center of an overheated culture clash. With regard to style and other identity issues as well, a parent should count on, and find comfort in, the general trend of adolescence to move slowly from stereotypical thought and action to more refined and nuanced behavior and thought; from eccentric fads to slightly less eccentric fads; from larger, less sophisticated crowds to smaller, more like-minded groupings.

Adolescence and identity formation cannot be pegged to specific years in school. There is an overlap between adolescence and a boy's middle and high school years, but the various parts of identity formation—especially to the extent they are intertwined with sexual maturation—begin at different ages from boy to boy and proceed at different paces, often extending into a male's twenties. As a boy makes his way through high school, however, his whole environment begins to coach him that he has to prepare himself for greater independence—he can't stay a kid forever. Parents don't have to carry the whole burden of this coaching; others make their contributions, and together the voices urge a boy toward more thoughtful consideration of his prospects.

An adolescent boy's friends and crowd are almost inevitably going to invite him to do things sometimes that would make his parents apprehensive about the risk involved, or disapproving about the moral values implicit in the activity. At those moments, a boy who has been raised with unexamined rules is vulnerable to withering ridicule if all he can say is "I'm not allowed to." Parental values can certainly be voiced at such a time, but more effectively if the rationale for those values as applied to the situation can be articulated as well. Many of these temptations are entirely foreseeable and can be discussed in family meetings. There a boy can be educated, for example, about the dynamics of clique or crowd behavior and how to avoid being swept up in them to later chagrin or sorrow.

Many factors can contribute to a boy's entering adolescence with few or no friends. Boys who are temperamentally "slow to warm up" may have gotten stuck on the outskirts of a class—as Mark was marooned in second grade—and not have many later opportunities to win acceptance, no matter how talented they are. Many parents feel concerned but helpless if their boys appear to be outsiders. They feel guilty, too, even though they don't quite know how they "caused" the situation, and they are baffled what to do about it. One can't just throw a couple of boys in early adolescence into a room and tell them not to come out until they're friends. But ours is a flexible and mobile society. Not every parent has every option, by a long shot, but many parents have the opportunity to offer alternative school and extracurricular environments to their sons if they are foundering socially among their classmates.

Very few boys are indifferent to the issue of whether they have friends and a crowd of their own. A parent should be alert to any signs that a boy wants to talk about his relative friendlessness. Sometimes a boy may be more comfortable talking about his social situation with a counselor than with his parents, and parents needn't be disappointed if that is the case.

Parents whose adolescent sons have what the parents consider "the wrong friends" face as perplexing a situation as the parents of the relatively friendless. Again, it's important to distinguish between friends a parent objects to on grounds of style, friends a parent dislikes because the parent's and the friend's temperaments clash, and friends who seriously are the wrong friends because they may lead a son in harmful directions. Time and patience may allow the first two scenarios to recede, but a parent who believes a son has taken up with the wrong friends or crowd bears a responsibility to state his concern and invite the boy to discuss the matter.

A thoughtful dicussion may not be easy when both parties are deeply emotionally involved. A mediator can be very helpful in keeping the discussion coherent and balanced. An adolescent may feel at a deep disadvantage in disagreeing with parents; his apprehension may cause him to overstate his opinions or take refuge in obstinacy. Parents likewise may err by implying that only their opinions carry legitimacy. Thoughtful parents see that family tensions need to be resolved in relation to the deeper issue:

a boy's interaction with his whole environment. Is he being supported enough to make his way, or will he be mistrustful because the world has hurt him too much?

Judging from what he and his parents report, Mark did not emerge from his computer-cracking incident with more self-knowledge, or with trust in the capacity of his school and classmates to recognize his talent and forgive his mistakes; but the jury is still out. His parents and he faced the crisis with honesty intact. In a new school, he can make a fresh start. His parents are unambiguously passionate about him. All he needs is a friend or two, and a welcoming clique or crowd, to give him an anchor in the pursuit of identity: peers as supportive of him as his parents are.

16

ALCOHOL AND DRUGS

During the past year, I've asked a number of adolescent boys, Daniel among them, about their first exposure to alcohol and the pattern of drinking that developed in their lives. After returning from a seventh-grade class trip, Daniel got his older brother to drive him and six of his friends—four boys and two girls—from the school in suburban Boston to the family's vacation home on Cape Cod. Everyone settled into the guest house. One of the boys suggested they all try drinking. The others all said it wasn't a "cool" thing to do, but soon they were bored and started to express curiosity about what drinking was like. One of the boys found some Scotch whisky in a cupboard. Everyone sampled it. Daniel took a couple of sips and told everyone he thought it tasted disgusting. Only one boy drank enough to be really drunk. Others drank small amounts and pretended to be drunk.

When Daniel was a junior in high school, his parents left him alone for a weekend for the first time. He immediately threw a party, which got out of hand. A wall was damaged, cigarettes were stubbed out on hardwood floors, and an outdoor deck was wrecked. Local police broke up the party. Daniel doesn't regret having the party even though his parents were furious. He was drunk at his own party: "I had to be. Otherwise I would have flipped out." In late adolescence, Daniel drinks about three times a month, and when he does, he drinks enough to affect his judgment.

Many of the stories I listened to were consistent with Daniel's account. From the very beginning, boys were primarily curious about the experience of being "under the influence," and they pursued this goal even when they found their first tastes of alcoholic beverages repellent. There is enough peer reputation involved that boys will sometimes pretend to be intoxicated when they aren't; or at least their friends suspect they are faking intoxication.

Even when boys postpone their first drinking experiences to later adolescence, they may harbor the same curiosity as younger boys to put themselves under the influence. Ross drank for the first time a few days after graduating from high school. He had been a member of the Student Awareness Program at his high school, which meant that he voluntarily abstained from using alcohol and drugs, and led discussions among middle school students about the hazards of substance use and abuse.

Once he had graduated, Ross wanted to discover what drinking was like before he went to college. He planned to do it at a friend's house where, for safety's sake, he could stay the night. Of the several age-mates at the friend's house, only three were drinking. Ross enjoyed himself. He was acting silly, and one of his friends followed him around writing down all the funny things he said, which annoyed him at the time but now he's glad to have the record. Two years later, he drinks about once a week; about once a month he drinks enough to affect his thinking.

John Donovan, a psychologist at the University of Pittsburgh who studies teen drinking, believes that peer influence is exaggerated as the cause of underage drinking. The main causes, he believes, are the general cultural acceptance of drinking, the observations a boy makes of drinking in his immediate environment beginning in early childhood, and the way drinking is addressed or ignored in family discussions as a boy is growing up.

In my conversations with boys, however, I found that peer influence appeared to be a strong contributing factor in most boys' introduction to drinking.

Certainly most of their drinking occurred in the company of peers, not adults. Students at Morgan's middle school were allowed to go home for lunch. One day in seventh grade, he and a few of his best friends all went to another boy's home for lunch. There were no adults present. They all poured themselves glasses of Manischevitz (sweet kosher wine). Most of the boys didn't finish their wine, but one of them finished his own and the remains in others' glasses. When the boys returned to school, the friend who had consumed the most acted drunk. Morgan believes he had taken enough to affect his behavior but that he was exaggerating his condition.

Some adolescents merely provide their peers with opportunities to drink, but others exert social pressure. When Ben was fourteen years old, he visited his older brother at college. His brother and some of his brother's friends decided it was their "duty" to get Ben drunk, and they did. Ben remembers thinking it was cool, but not at all his own idea. In late adolescence, he drinks moderately about twice a month, and enough to get drunk about twice a year.

The Well-lubricated Society

Most boys have been observing social drinking since early childhood. Susan Cheever gave one child's account of family cocktail hours in her memoir, *Note Found in a Bottle; My Life as a Drinker*: "I loved the paraphernalia of drinking, the slippery ice trays that I was allowed to refill and the pungent olives, which were my first childhood treat, and I loved the way adults got loose and happy and forgot that I was just a child."

Two-thirds of adults in the United States consume alcoholic beverages, many of them only occasionally, and a majority of them without causing known significant harm to themselves or others. Two-thirds doesn't mean everyone, but it is a substantial enough percentage to say that, among adults, drinking alcohol at least occasionally is normal rather than exceptional.

Many adult parties, ceremonial occasions, and business lunches are events where alcoholic beverages are served. In many families, the adults drink before dinner—and in some households before lunch also—and perhaps consume wine with their meals as well. The ubiquity of drinking is expressed in such folk humor as "Wherever four Episcopalians are gathered, there is sure to be a fifth." Adult consumption of alcohol is so common that people employ the words "drinking" or "drinks" to refer to alcoholic beverages; a group of beverages that might be consumed in place of alcohol have to be distinguished by adding the qualifier "soft."

Adult drinking in public is legal just about everywhere in the United States, although the sale and serving of alcohol is prohibited at certain times and places, and is subject to licensing and government regulation. If adults injure others while acting with impaired judgment or self-control from drinking alcohol, they may be held accountable, criminally or civilly or both, for the harm done. In some jurisdictions, adults can be prosecuted if they allow minors to drink in their homes or give them alcohol elsewhere; they are more liable to be prosecuted if the minors then injure themselves or others.

In addition to individual adults who abstain from drinking alcoholic beverages, there are large groups such as Mormons and Moslems who oppose on religious grounds the use of alcohol and other stimulants or depressants. Boys do have opportunities to see that drinking is optional, that it isn't practiced universally by adults. Unlike the consumption of drugs such as marijuana, cocaine, or heroin, which is illegal for everyone, adult and child alike, the consumption of alcohol is basically legal for adults across the country, and illegal in public places for everyone before their twenty-first birthdays. Many studies confirm, however, that a large proportion of adolescents, especially boys, have consumed alcohol long before they reach majority age.

According to a 1997 survey by the U.S. Department of Health and Human Services, between 8 and 9 percent of eighth graders had drunk alcohol within the past thirty days. There were about 9.5 million current drinkers between the ages of twelve and twenty, 4.5 million of whom could be classified as binge drinkers, and almost 2 million of whom were heavy drinkers—to all intents and purposes minors who are alcoholics. All of these statistics are extremely sobering, but I pay special attention to the binge drinkers. Some of the juvenile alcoholics have probably learned to function adequately even with a high level of consumption. But the binge drinkers are the ones who drink to such excess at parties or on other occasions that they often threaten themselves with alcohol poisoning, assault people, destroy property, and jeopardize the lives of others when they drive.

Seventy-five percent of twelfth graders in the Health and Human Services survey had drunk alcohol within the past year. Only a little more than 40 percent of all twelfth graders thought there was any great risk involved in heavy drinking. One study I consulted put the *median* age at which boys begin to drink at slightly over thirteen years; another study put the *average* age of first drink at twelve.

A 1995 Minnesota Department of Health survey showed that nearly a third of high school seniors statewide drank to a state of intoxication at least monthly, or had more than five drinks on a typical drinking occasion. A majority of boys surely think of drinking alcohol as something they are eventually going to do—like driving a car or having sex. The question is not so much whether as when, where, and what type of alcoholic beverage. Once they begin drinking, many adolescents participate in binge drinking, and some progress into alcohol addiction.

In the town where I live, there are eight schools that each combine the first eight grades. Graduates of all these schools converge on one high school campus for ninth grade. The town and school cooperate in providing full-time alcohol and drug counselors for the high school, an implicit admission that teenage drinking and drug use are serious and frequent problems. (Studies I've consulted indicate that a substantial number of students nationwide find ways to bring alcohol to school and consume it on school property.)

One counselor at our high school told me that over 90 percent of the students drink. It's a main way, she said, that kids overcome their discomfort in adjusting to this big, new, strange place. Drinking cuts through every clique and every status group. By the year-end holiday of their freshman year, many are falling apart. By the end of sophomore year, she judged, many have gotten a grip on their patterns of drinking, but I didn't find much reassurance in her estimate of the statistics. Obviously the high school doesn't invite or want the situation; it comes unbidden.

The lesser mass of a boy means that a given amount of alcohol will affect him faster and harder than it will affect most adults. As a story I picked up on the Internet made clear, even boys who are familiar with this general relationship between body mass and intoxication don't know how to apply it in actual situations:

> About a month ago, I had a rather difficult experience. I am a freshman in high school and had made plans with two girls in my class to go drinking with a few junior and senior boys. So I had planned, me and my 100 pounds, to have a drinking contest (shots of gin) with a 200 pound junior. I had drunk a few times, and I liked the way it made me feel. I thought it was fun! The boy I was to have a contest with had already smoked up a little. I knew he was gonna win. I had about three or four shots mixed with pink lemonade—I can't stand the taste straight—and I blacked out.
>
> I don't remember what happened next, but I was informed. The girls asked them to stop but the boys kept giving me more to drink. After I had about eight or nine shots I started throwing up. It was pretty bad after that. A friend called my parents who called 911, and I was rushed to the hospital in an ambulance. It was definitely the worst experience of my life. You may know how I feel and you may not, but it is really awful when your parents have no trust in you, and follow you around the house to make sure you aren't sneaking a quick drink or smoking up in a bathroom, especially since I only smoked up once, and they know only once. I will never have my same life back, and I will never have the freedom I once had!!

Motives

Adult motives for drinking include: easing discomfort or unease in social situations—drinking as icebreaking; providing solace for loneliness or boredom; inducing relaxation or relief from stress—drinking after work, for example; soothing the pain of episodic or chronic unhappiness at work or in family life or other relationships; allaying anxiety about sexual performance; enjoying the sensation or "buzz" a drinker may get from light to moderate drinking; satisfying the body's biological craving for a substance the person is addicted to; appreciating the acquired taste of the beverage itself—a distinctive beer or a prized wine; causing a feeling of release from inhibitions through getting "high"; and neutralizing inhibitions against aggressiveness and other antisocial behavior.

The conventional view is that men get drunk, and then when they are drunk and "don't know what they are doing," they become violent. My jazz colleague, Tony Pringle, told me once of a regular Saturday night gig he played at an English pub where it was expected the evening would end in a brawl. The evening-ending fight was so routine that the band played the same song, "Don't Go Way Nobody," when it broke out.

For some males, I believe there is a degree of intentionality involved in drinking and then provoking a fight, or in drinking and then initiating aggressive, uninvited sex. The drinking is counted on in advance to neutralize any inhibitions and then to provide an excuse: I didn't know what I was doing. Alcohol is very intimately associated statistically with criminal activity. It can function to allay the criminal's anxiety beforehand and to deliberately override his superego or conscience; it may be associated with his being excessively aggressive during the crime; and then afterward used as an excuse.

Curiosity about the experience of being high or drunk may motivate a boy's first consumption of alcohol, but even in adolescence boys may drink for any of the reasons adults manifest. Artemis, a college student, recalls that during the three months she dated Brian in their senior year in high school, he would sometimes be drunk but hide it so well that she couldn't tell for sure. "Brian is very shy, and he came to rely on alcohol as a means to overcome his shyness. I found out after we broke up that Brian wouldn't even call me for the first month we were going together without drinking first." Despite the history of alcoholism in his family, Brian could not be deterred in his drinking habits—or maybe *because* of the family history. He regarded himself as "stone cold sober" after drinking four beers, and would tell Artemis casually that he'd done a few shots of whisky by himself to prepare for later partying.

As males sometimes drink in order to fortify their nerve to pursue the sex they desire, so they may encounter girls who drink in order to override the reservations they feel about having sex. As Caroline Knapp wrote in her memoir, *Drinking: A Love Story,* "The first time Meg had sex, her best friend advised her: 'Just get drunk. It'll be easy.' So that's exactly what she did. She got drunk then, and she got drunk the next time and the time after that, and after a while the idea of having sex with a man without getting drunk first seemed pretty much impossible."

Drinking to alleviate loneliness or boredom is a well-known adult theme, but one should not discount its significance among adolescents. As one sixteen-year-old boy put it, "I don't do drugs, but a lot of my friends do. I do drink on occasion, but, hey, nobody is perfect. Parents tend to blame the media for these problems, but seeing a couple of cute frogs reading a Budweiser billboard is not going to make me want to drink. Boredom will, though. The main reason why we do these things is because we have nothing better to do. Movies and arcades are fairly expensive. Going to the mall isn't all that much fun because the security guards follow us around like we had trouble written on our foreheads. So what do we do? We go to a friend's house and drink or get high just to pass the time. Do discipline us when we get caught, but as a preventative, give us something to do."

To the list of motives for drinking that adults and adolescents may share, I would add a few others that are more characteristic of adolescents (or even preadolescents) than of adults. Drinking can be an act of rebellion by kids. They know it is a hot button to push. But just as some may wish to flaunt their drinking, many others, knowing what a hot button it is for adults, do their best to hide their drinking. Leif first drank beer in seventh grade at the home of a classmate whose Italian-American parents were accustomed to having children drink alcohol—mainly wine—in small quantities. The parents weren't home. His friend's older brother bought beer for a few boys. Leif drank enough to get sick. His friends tried to take care of him quietly so that his parents wouldn't learn of it; but they were unsuccessful. Leif endured a prolonged grounding.

Another motive of youthful drinking is to adopt a badge of faux maturity. Many boys like to pretend they are older than they are. Drinking for some is a pretend-to-be-adult activity.

More than is true of adults, I believe, boys also drink as deliberate risk-taking. They know that it is risky, although many feel that they are magically immune from the downside of risks. They have seen adults drink and drive without accidents—why can't they?

Drugs

"It was the summer after my freshman year in high school," Gary, now a freshman at Northwestern, said to me. "I had just finished adjusting to that hellish transition that comes with any major change in life. I was beginning to get into a new rhythm of living. I felt socially comfortable, reasonably confident in my maturity and decisionmaking ability. Until that summer, I had been completely against any form of substance abuse, from drugs to alcohol to cigarettes. Most of my friends were two or three years older than I, and well used to partying. I had grown quite used to hanging out with my friends when they got drunk and high. Many times I had an invitation to partake, always I refused.

"That certain summer evening felt different. I was feeling bold, rebellious, curious. I was beginning to get fed up with the 'just say no' propaganda. I felt no need to 'fit in.' I had spent all year trying to do that in other ways. I was not being pushed by my friends. I had had numerous conversations and debates relating to drug use, and they all knew my position well. I was simply . . . curious. I wanted to branch out, try something new.

It was a matter of exploring my world, not an instance of another world invading mine.

"Three friends and I piled into a van and drove to see the Allman Brothers. It was my first big-arena concert without adult supervision. I felt giddy and free. I had never seen anything like this before. Bikers and burnt-out hippies were there in abundance, but so were kids our age. New people, new clothing, new music, new style, new culture, new drugs . . . new everything! The whole atmosphere seemed to shout HAPPINESS! Let yourself go!

"The concert was a blast. We set up our blankets on the lawn overlooking the stage. I had already made up my mind—I was going to smoke pot. The sun began to set, the light grew dim, and the music started. The driver packed some nugs into his bowl, passed it around, and I inhaled . . .

"I didn't get high the first time, or the second or third. It took a while. I loved it. Every time after that, I smoked because I was with close friends and wanted to share an experience with them. Only once did I find myself developing a habit. I noticed the trend and stopped it. I tried alcohol and cigarettes as well, and as of now use the three occasionally. I am addicted to nothing except coffee, nor have I ever used marijuana to the point of addiction. For me, drug use is not the fiendish addiction of junkies, nor the mindless wasting of so many of my classmates. It is an occasional pleasure to be enjoyed among friends, and remains a subtle, yet exciting, part of my social life."

Gary's story reminds me that just as parental permission to spend the night after the prom at a hotel is an implicit permission to drink or use drugs and have sex, so parental permission to attend many popular music concerts in big arenas without chaperones is implicit permission to drink and use drugs.

The statistics on drug use by adolescents in the United States are as troubling as those on alcohol—both in terms of use and in perception of risk. From the 1997 Department of Health and Human Services survey: Fifty-four percent of twelfth graders have used illicit drugs at least once. The same is true of 47 percent of tenth graders, and a fraction less than 30 percent of eighth graders. Marijuana is the most widely used illicit drug in the United States and tends to be the first used by children and teenagers. Almost 6 percent of twelfth graders use marijuana daily. Slightly over 1 percent of eighth graders use it daily. Only 25 percent of eighth graders think there is any great risk involved in trying marijuana.

One of the drug counselors at our local high school says that, as with alcohol, over 90 percent of the students have tried marijuana. Its use is not by any means confined to kids doing poorly academically; many "top-of-the-line" kids come to her for consultation, she says. A large number consume alcohol and drugs on school premises, and many of them prefer marijuana to alcohol because it's easier to conceal.

Children and adolescents who do not like the taste of alcoholic beverages but want the experience of being under the influence can alter the taste with mixers, and some companies have facilitated matters by selling sweet-tasting coolers with plenty of alcohol in large containers. Smoking marijuana can't be sweetened up, but kids will persist through unpleasant first experiences, if Grant's story from tenth grade is representative: "I really wanted the experience. We all sat in a circle and I saw my first bong. I was intrigued and nervous—didn't want to betray my inexperience. I watched carefully, trying to work out the method. When the bong got to me, I did manage to take a hit, although my form was not good. I think I smoked out of it two or three more times. I remember getting light-headed in a very pleasant way. The world around me looked more vibrant. I had perma-grin. Somehow we ended up watching MTV. I lay on a couch and found out what happens when you smoke too much. I got clammy and nauseous. 'Give It Away' by the Red Hot Chili Peppers was on the TV. The sick feeling finally passed, but it was not pleasant. This experience did not turn me off the drug, though. It acted as a cautionary measure, showing me the cost of abuse as well as the pleasures of responsible use."

A majority of those who try marijuana do not go on to sample other drugs. But over 12 percent of eighth graders and 17 percent of tenth graders have tried stimulants such as amphetamines and methamphetamines at least once. Between 8 and 9 percent of twelfth graders have tried cocaine at least once.

Smoking cigarettes shouldn't be left out of a summary of addictive drugs. The side effects of cigarettes on concentration, memory, alertness, and ability to perform complex tasks may not be as great as with other drugs, but the longer range health risks are considerable. Nine percent of eighth graders smoke daily; 3.5 percent smoke a half-pack or more. By twelfth grade, the percent of daily smokers has climbed to 25; over 36 percent have smoked within the past thirty days. Of the 62 million Americans who smoke, over 4 million are kids aged twelve to seventeen.

Rules and Models

In Chapter 6 I told about a fellow pediatrician here in Boston, Nicholas Kriek, who grew up in South Africa—how his father told him at age twelve, after he had been involved in an incident of neighborhood vandalism, that he had to be accountable for his actions if he broke the law; his father was not going to rescue him. Nick remembers being surprised by that; he had thought of parents as people who came to your rescue no matter what. His own parents, Nick felt, were in many ways not particularly good models for him when he became a parent himself. But he remembers their emphasis, as poorly educated immigrants to South Africa, on his education. "They regarded the school system and teachers as being larger than life in character. I had the view as a kid that teachers were important and serious, an authority to be respected."

The time came when Nicholas Kriek's oldest son, Tommy, collaborated in some vandalism at the middle school, and Nick found himself sitting in the principal's office. She said the police would have to be notified. "If it's a police matter, then go to the police," Nick agreed. "Maybe he will learn a lesson." On the day of Tommy's court appearance, to his son's surprise, Nick did not accompany him because he had a long-standing engagement to present a paper in Washington, nor did he send a lawyer as some parents did. His son was learning something about accountability. But there were trying days to come for Tommy's parents.

"When Tommy went to high school, he got terribly involved in drugs and his schoolwork suffered. He had a terribly rebellious adolescence. He was never a problem at home. There, he was helpful and good-natured, but covertly defiant. When he was outside the house, he did his own thing. Neither my wife nor I grew up around drugs. In South Africa, getting caught using drugs was a felony offense. So I can tell you honestly that throughout that period we were bewildered and dazed. We asked ourselves over and over again, 'What did we do wrong, what are we doing wrong?' We were naive. Today, if there were an unexplained deterioration in a son's school performance, I would think first of all to look for drugs or alcohol, or both.

"Somehow among our circle of friends, one of the mothers discovered that our kids were doing a lot of marijuana and drinking as well. A meeting of several kids and their parents was called, and this horrific scene was laid out for us. The kids acknowledged what they were doing. The plan was to see if, as a parental group, we could help all of them. We met with a psychiatrist a few times. There was improvement, but Tommy did not stop using drugs.

"Approaching his senior year, Tommy got very interested in art and decided he wanted to go to art school in Maryland after graduation. No sooner had he arrived in Maryland than it was obvious he wasn't certain he'd made a good choice. He was quite depressed. I remember talking to him many times because I was quite concerned he might attempt suicide. In his first year there, he developed a burst appendix that caused life-threatening peritonitis. I got a call from a Baltimore emergency room asking permission to do surgery.

"The surgeon was marvelous. It turned out that his own son, an expert skier, had died in an avalanche. We had frank discussions of the challenges of raising our sons. When Tommy was better, the surgeon took him to a ball game. I know that my son admired him immensely as a human being, as a model. Tommy dropped out of art school after that year, worked as a waiter, moved in with some friends in Boston, and got very depressed again. But when he recovered his equilibrium, he decided to go to college. He had a very shaky first semester because he had lousy study habits. Then he just got stronger and stronger, graduated summa cum laude in three years, got a scholarship to Stanford and became a serious citizen. Now, with his new Ph.D., he's ready to teach philosophy.

"My boys—I think if you were to ask them about their dad, they would describe me as a moralist, as too moralistic. I have found thinking about morality essential to finding my own path in life—where to go, how to behave. Without it, I'm lost. If I've given my kids anything of value, it's that I've tried to set an example in my own behavior. You can't tell them one thing and do something different yourself. I know parents who make that mistake. If you want your kids to behave in a certain way, then behave that way yourself and there is a chance that they will think well of you and follow in that path."

Parents faced with sons in trouble over poor behavior or for drinking or taking drugs can veer to extremes. Some parents wish to dissociate themselves from misbehaving sons; they abandon them to their own devices, which is a very different thing from holding them accountable for what they have done but supporting them nonetheless. Other parents rush indiscriminately to their sons' defense in full confidence that there's no misbehavior for which a person can't escape the consequences if he has a good enough lawyer or an aggressive enough parent.

Recently I heard of a fourteen-year-old boy who was expelled from a private school for misconduct involving drugs. When he applied for admission to another private school, the school contacted his former school for academic records and comments on his overall performance. The old school forwarded the grades but refused to comment further; the boy's parents had threatened to sue the school if administrators divulged to anyone the cause of the boy's expulsion, or even that he had been expelled. It isn't hard to guess what a boy might infer from this: He can count on parental help to avoid the consequences of any delinquent behavior.

Many parents who face one or another of such behavioral crises will feel just as surprised, shocked even, as the Krieks felt. Unless parents remind themselves to look carefully into the culture their children are living in, they may blithely coast along assuming their children's adolescence will be very much like their own as remembered from twenty or more years earlier—until evidence surfaces that their children's lives are very different from what parents expected.

In the face of unexpected behavior by his sons, Nick Kriek did a number of things in exemplary fashion. He honored the laws and institutional rules about such things as vandalism, drinking, and drugs that circumscribed the boys' lives, making clear to them that they were accountable for their behavior if they were caught violating the rules. He didn't take the fence-straddling position that the laws and rules are ill-advised or too strict, therefore the issue is not whether one heeds the rules but whether one gets caught.

I mentioned to him the episode I describe in Chapter 18 of several high school seniors in our town who were caught with alcohol at the prom and excluded, as promised, from graduation ceremonies with their classmates. "I would like to think," said Nick, "that if my kid was one of those who transgressed knowing what the rules were, that we would be upset that something the whole family was looking forward to had been ruined, but we would say that the rules were known to everyone and the consequences have to be accepted."

With respect to drinking alcoholic beverages, there are different rules for adults than for minors. The reason for the variation in rules needs to be explained to kids—and can be explained in terms of the relative maturity needed to handle the effects of alcohol on the body and behavior, and the threat of addiction. But if kids observe their parents drinking to the point of intoxication or serving other adults enough alcohol that they become intoxicated, the moral authority of the adults, on this issue at least, is pretty badly compromised. Parents don't have to practice abstinence from alcohol to be effective models, but they do have to practice sobriety; and if they fall below that standard, to their children's knowledge, they should take the initiative in acknowledging their slip and its consequences for their being a good model.

Forewarned and Well-prepared

When I talked with the Melvins, I learned about another family that prizes clarity about rules. "Our boys (Ben and Ed are aged twelve and ten) know that we have expectations for their behavior," Patricia said. "We're not shy about letting them know. Many kids in this community are not really sure what their parents expect. Parents don't think they can put their foot down and say, 'I expect you not to drink alcohol on Saturday night.'" "We all make mistakes," George Melvin interjected. "I've told our kids on numerous occasions that they are going to make mistakes, and they have to be willing to admit to them. That's a crucial part of development."

George's viewpoint about both accountability and slips has a poignant background. His father died of alcoholism and was abusive when drunk toward George's mother and the children. George is a recovering alcoholic himself. Ben and Ed know the family history. "They know that my father, their grandfather, was not able to live a full life, not able to show that he loved people, not able to hold down a good job. I grew up with it as 'the big secret.' You really pay a big price for not talking about it." "Years ago," Patricia volunteered, "Ben said to me, 'Do you think I'm going to be like you, Mommy, and drink alcohol, or do you think I'll be like Daddy and have a problem with alcohol?' And I said, 'That's something we don't know. We do know that when a mom or a dad is an alcoholic, there is a greater chance that their child might have a problem.' Our kids know that they are at greater risk.

"George made a deliberate decision to be the man his father was not," Patricia remarked. "That was hard fought and hard won." "The kids are aware that we've made choices that our parents didn't make," George added. "I'm trying to say to them that you have to make choices. To us, the kids are top priority—teaching them that it's not about having a fancy car but about taking time to be with your family. That's basic stuff."

Patricia Melvin, who is a high school alcohol and drug counselor, pointed out the connections between alcohol and sexual experience among adolescents. "One of the things I do is teach a sexuality and health class at the high school. There was community support for it, and also community fanaticism about some of the topics we discuss. We let all the kids know that many kids have been drinking when they have their first sexual experience. We talk about how the sex might have been consensual, but would the person have made the same choice if he or she had not been drinking?"

As involved as she is in dealing with issues of sexuality, drinking, and drugs at the high school, Patricia Melvin still thinks the parental role is pivotal. "We can hire as many counselors as we want, but unless the families are behind us we will not get very far. We do run programs for parents through the school system, but often it's 'preaching to the choir.' At a PTA meeting I meet the parents who *do* know where their kids are on Friday and Saturday night—but not the parents who stopped having a curfew in tenth grade because the kids didn't like it and there was too much arguing about it. My greatest concern is that parents don't have any discussions with their kids before the problem hits them."

I asked Patricia what she thought about parents who allow kids to have parties with alcohol in their homes. "I think they sincerely believe they are providing a safety net for the kids," she replied. "They honestly believe they are doing a service by saying, 'You can come here, the keg is ready, and we will take the keys so you can't drive home.' My impression is that it's happening less than it used to. Many parents think the kids are going to drink anyhow, so there might as well be some safety built in. It's the same mindset as invented the designated driver—which is a way of saying that if the driver is reasonably sober, everyone else can get drunk. I agree that designated drivers are good for safety, but I think it's a poor overall message."

In her work with adolescents and young adults, Patricia Melvin emphasizes practical considerations: "Alcohol and drug issues are health issues with some fairly dramatic negative consequences. There are moral consequences, too. On all health issues I think in terms of the idea of moderation. Of course I see our society's ambivalence weaving through the issues of alcohol and drugs. I think it's very important to spell everything out—expectations, consequences, values, attitudes—so kids don't have to figure everything out for themselves." Her logic appeals to me. Let the morality flow out of information about what alcohol and drugs do to body and mind, and out of known potential consequences of impaired action and judgment, rather than beginning with a moral message that alcohol and drugs are bad, so "just say no." I believe adolescents respond to accurate information of obvious gravity better than to scare tactics.

When I asked George and Patricia how they were preparing their boys, who are on the edge of adolescence, to deal with its social pressures, they said they were aware that they were steering Ben and Ed away from an indiscriminate wish to be popular. "When I think of the 'cool kids' at even the elementary or middle school levels," Patricia says, "I think of kids who care more about what they look like, who wear designer labels. I think of a group of kids who will cut other kids to make themselves bigger. I think Ben is not comfortable with that kind of behavior. I don't think he wishes he was in this crowd or that. He has some friends who are thoughtful, nice kids, and he's happy with that. He doesn't do a lot of socializing on weekends. He's not talking about dating yet, but some of his classmates are. The kids that will be the partying kids in eighth or tenth grade, who will drink and smoke pot earlier—these are not the kids he gravitates toward, nor do they gravitate toward him. We've talked to the kids about how they only get to be kids once, and it should be fun, not high risk or high anxiety. I think the notion of letting them be kids as long as they can be is high up on my list of important things."

Two Families

The Krieks and the Melvins are both deeply attentive to the lives of their children. All four of them take with utmost seriousness their responsibility to model behavior as an intentional inspiration to their sons. All of them treat laws and rules about alcohol and drugs with respect and hold their sons accountable for behavior in violation of the rules. That said, the two families have approached adolescent drinking and drugs from very different backgrounds and mindsets. The Krieks were not mindful of the extent to which alcohol and drugs pervade adolescent social groupings, nor did they have any experience with drinking and drugs from their own adolescence to bring to bear on their sons' lives. Their sons were growing up in an environment in which a very large majority of students consumed both alcohol and drugs. Before they knew it, they were in the middle of a crisis with Tommy. It would have taken very carefully thought out parental strategies if the Kriek boys had gotten through high school without falling under the influence.

The Melvins were not hindered by naïveté. George knows from three generations of his family's history how much devastation addiction to alcohol can wreak. Patricia deals with the issues professionally every workday. She is particularly aware that pressure to use alcohol and drugs can vary considerably depending on what cliques and crowds a boy belongs to. In many adolescent groups, consumption of alcohol and/or drugs is virtually the price of admission. So the Melvins have family discussions and recite family history. Though the daughter of a minister, Patricia tends to her spirituality privately. It is George who takes the boys to church. The three males in the family are so engaged in the life of their congregation that Ben and Ed say it is their biggest support outside the immediate family and a further support for sobriety. With all their concern, however, the Melvins are not sure what lies ahead for Ben and Ed. "I remember our having a conversation about a year ago," George says to Patricia, "and I think I was more willing to say it is okay to let our boys be the odd one out; and you were the one saying, well, they've got to live with all these kids, so maybe we need to chill out a little bit. I don't know what adolescence will be like for them. Perhaps they will feel that Mom and Dad are a little too far off target."

The question of how much to monitor adolescents' activities is a delicate one. I remember when my daughter was in high school and invited to a party where, we ascertained, there were not going to be chaperones and were sure to be alcohol and marijuana. We told Mary Helen that she couldn't go, and she was not happy with our decision. But a couple of days later she said she was glad Carolyn and I had made the decision we did; she had heard that the party got very rowdy, and she knew she would have been uncomfortable. One of the things we can do for adolescents is stay in close contact with them, and, in the interest of protecting them, sometimes make decisions they might hesitate to make for themselves. They should be aware from frequent reiteration that we would as parents do everything possible to rescue them from situations where they feel endangered or pressured to act against their best judgment. I know this is a difficult balancing act, because the parent wants to be an ally, not a heavy-handed spoilsport. But the teenager's world is a dangerous place, which Joy Dryfoos captured in the title of her book, *Safe Passage: Making it Through Adolescence in a Risky Society*.

The best example of where a parent *doesn't* want to end up in relation to an adolescent comes from the boy I quoted earlier: his parents were following him around the house to make sure he didn't sneak a drink or smoke pot in the bathroom. The parent as policeman is not a happy role. Recently I saw an ad for an in-home drug test kit. If a parent mails an adolescent's urine and hair samples to the lab, a report will be issued within three days on traces of marijuana, cocaine, PCP, and heroin use—and, on request, no doubt for an extra charge, LSD and alcohol. "Parents can give their teen a reason to say no to drugs," the ad says: "'My parents drug test me.'" Mind-boggling.

The power of the youth drinking and drug culture is such that every strategy needs to be employed to help boys from getting entangled: early and continuing family discussions; clearly articulated family norms of respect for rules and laws regarding mind- and mood-altering substances; honest accountability for breaking the rules; parental modeling with respect to abstinence or moderation in consumption of alcohol and abstinence from illegal drug use; professional counseling as suggested by known problems within the family; monitoring of teens' activities, particularly in concert with other parents from their groups.

All of these techniques are needed to counter the capacity of these substances to affect adolescents' development adversely through habituation and addiction, through diversion and distraction from the central process of forming a personal identity, and by interfering with the making of good choices, the benchmark of character.

Yet for all the attention that has to be paid to the intrinsic and insidious effects of alcohol and drugs, that is not the main issue. Adolescents, like adults, drink and drug themselves to treat a wide variety of vicissitudes: boredom, loneliness, anger and resentment, anxiety, a sense of purposelessness, feelings of powerlessness, sexual frustration, and not having a useful enough role in society. If we could magically remove alcohol and drugs from adolescents' lives, those vicissitudes would scream even louder for attention; and if we would more forthrightly address these feelings and the social realities in which they are lodged, we would remove a fair amount of the incentive to resort to alcohol and drugs at appallingly young ages.

17

LATE ADOLESCENCE

Adolescence, as we saw earlier, is a stage rather than an age. The onset of the biological developments of adolescence can be separated by as much as several years from one boy to another. Yet there are some age-related events that are milestones in a boy's career, none more so that passing the required tests (written and road) and earning a first driver's license. In most states the minimum age is sixteen, and in many families the tests are taken by boys within a few days, or at most a few weeks, of their sixteenth birthdays because they have been secretly practicing as fifteen-year-olds. Having "wheels" makes such a difference in a boy's life that it is the ritual that separates early adolescence from late adolescence.

Charles McGrath, the editor of the *New York Times Book Review* reminisced recently about cars during his adolescence:

In the 50's and 60's, a car was more than a ride. It was a passport to freedom (even if freedom meant nothing more than cruising back and forth on the same well-traveled stretch of blacktop), and it was the embodiment of sexual possibility. Like many American boys of my generation, I grew up believing that automotive expertise and success with girls were intrinsically linked. . . . I could never afford a car of my own. When I went on dates, I had to borrow my father's. . . . The goal was not motion but rest: parking. My favorite spot was a reservoir not far from my house, where on any weekend night dozens of cars would be nestled, nose in, against the verge. There, with the radio playing softly and the window cracked down an inch or two to let in the summer breeze, we earnest young mechanics plied our trade, or tried to, kissing, stroking, petting—all in an effort to rev what we had been taught to think of as the notoriously balky female engine. Sometimes, in spite of our crude efforts, it did spring to life, with an ardor that startled us both, and sometimes, to tell the truth, it was we boys, scared, timid and clumsy, who needed jump starting. . . . Girls, it turned out, were not as different from us as we thought—except that most of them did not care about cars at all!

This milestone arrived for me in an unexpected fashion. As my sixteenth birthday approached, my father tossed cold water on any thoughts of independence I was harboring—and I was harboring quite a few. "A car is an instrument of death," he asserted with all the confidence one might expect from a chief justice of the Supreme Court. There was, on this issue, no appeal possible beyond my father's decision, and he promised that I wouldn't be allowed to drive until I was eighteen. Then, old enough to vote and to join the armed forces, I would in his eyes be old enough to drive.

I didn't take the ruling too personally because I knew that my behavior in early adolescence hadn't given my father any reason to think me less trustworthy behind the wheel than my peers. For all I knew, he was thinking of how much his car insurance premiums would jump with a licensed sixteen-year-old in the family.

There the matter rested until four months after my birthday, when my mother was admitted to a psychiatric hospital for the first time for treatment of disabling depression. Suddenly the prospect of my knowing how to drive soared in value. At my father's insistence, I took a crash course—no pun intended—at a Mount Vernon driving school, and then the two requisite tests. The written test was a piece of cake, but I was nervous about the road test. My examiner was nervous, too, as I recall. The vehicle was my mother's blue and white 1956 Plymouth with a stick shift. My father thought automatic transmissions were an unnecessary frill. What I worried about was that I might stall out the engine when I shifted gears using the clutch, or fail to do an acceptable piece of parallel parking. I managed not to stall and I aced the parallel parking; the state policeman testing me visibly relaxed. Along with my new chores as family chauffeur, I had some memorable experiences in the old Plymouth.

Diverging Tracks

By age forty, students of midlife and its now celebrated crisis have told us, most men have reached the highest plateau of their work lives or have a pretty clear idea what that highest plateau is going to be; the knowledge of career limitations itself is one of the stimulants of the midlife crisis. By age sixteen, analogously, most adolescent boys know which of three tracks they've chosen for the next five or more years. Many will finish high school and go on to college or some form of technical training. Many others will complete high school, find a job, and go to work, very likely living at home for a time until they acquire some experience and savings, then striking out on their own, perhaps marrying at a relatively early age. The smallest group—yet a substantial number—will drop out of school, perhaps find a job, probably at a low hourly wage, maybe drift into substance addiction or crime. The dropouts have the least promising prospects for adult life, and generally are aware of it.

About the time they get driver's licenses, boys who stay in school begin to take on paying jobs—after school, on weekends, or during holiday and summer breaks—that give them money of their own and a taste of what full-time employment might be like.

As my schoolteacher brother reminded me, every teenage boy has a job. It's called schoolwork, and it has a weighty overtime component called homework. Despite its lack of compensation, schoolwork is real work. It is demanding, it is more or less relentless, it is tiring, and it is constantly monitored and graded.

Those boys headed toward the tracks of education or stable work take advantage of the final spurts of development of the brain. One spurt occurs at age fifteen on average, and the other from age eighteen to twenty. These spurts appear to coincide with the best scores young males achieve on intelligence tests; they also appear to be associated with the refinement of abstract thinking, a prerequisite for mature and reflective thought. The only cognitive edge boys have over girls lies in spatial reasoning, not to be confused with the arithmetical part of mathematics. Boys display this edge before age ten, and it lasts right through adolescence.

Stephanie Coontz notes that two researchers in 1968 concluded that "readiness for adulthood comes about two years *later* than the adolescent claims and about two years *before* the parent will admit." Coontz thinks it likely the degree of miscalculation has increased on both sides since the late 1960s.

Two other variables that are getting more distant from each other are the average age of physical maturation and the average age of economic independence. The age at which boys can support themselves, let alone a family, has reached a new high in the past two decades. So there is a longer and longer period when adolescents are sexually mature and physically and mentally capable of adult work, but remain economically dependent.

As recently as 1940 about 60 percent of employed boys aged sixteen and seventeen worked in traditional settings such as factories, farms, or construction sites, where they labored alongside, and often as apprentices to, older men. By 1980 the percentage of boys so employed had dropped to 14 percent. The bulk of jobs available to boys are dead-end jobs such as in the fast-food business where they get relatively little adult mentoring and have few opportunities for significant advancement.

Teenagers with jobs are more likely than their unemployed peers to express cynical attitudes toward work, and to endorse unethical business practices; they are more likely to agree with statements such as "People who work harder at their jobs than they have to are crazy" or "In my opinion, it's all right for workers who are paid a low salary to take little things."

Earlier generations of boys may often have worked to help support their families, and that phenomenon is not unknown today. But to judge from the adolescents I interviewed in the past year, most work in order to earn money for their own consumption—to maintain their own cars and entertainment, some of their own clothes, and the expenses of dating. Many corporations have obviously targeted them as an enticing market with plenty of disposable income. This pressure to consume can take its toll on academic work and future opportunity. Adolescent boys frequently put in so many hours each week in wage-earning that they have no waking time left for homework; some of them fall asleep in classrooms out of sheer fatigue.

Delinquency

Nearly all adolescent boys, if asked directly and confidentially, will admit having been guilty of offenses of one sort or another besides driving violations: for example, under-age drinking, smoking marijuana, running away from home, petty theft, disorderly conduct, vandalism. A 1998 survey of 20,000 middle- and high-school students (both boys and girls) by the Josephson Institute of Ethics showed that 47 percent admitted stealing something from a store in the previous twelve-month period, up from 39 percent in a similar survey in 1966, with a quarter of the high school students saying they had committed store theft at least twice.

The report was released during National CHARACTER COUNTS! Week in October of 1998. The data showing very high levels of admitted stealing, lying, and cheating didn't seem to jibe with the respondents' self-image or with their perceptions of parental values. Ninety-one percent of the students said they were satisfied with their ethics and character. Almost as many believed that lying and cheating hurt character. Eighty-three percent said their parents always want them to do the right thing, no matter what the cost; only 7 percent believed that their parents would prefer them to cheat if necessary to get good grades.

Arrest data and adolescents' own testimony suggests that the incidence of minor crime rises in the early teenage years, remains high through the middle stage of adolescence, and declines toward the end of adolescence. The curve of the data reflects the waxing and waning of peer influence. As teenage boys spend more and more time with boys their own age, they succumb more frequently to peer pressure to commit illegal acts. As they become more selective about their friends in late adolescence, many of them resist activities that involve breaking laws.

Effective response to any act of juvenile delinquency depends on ferreting out the principal motive. Some transgressions are acts of aggression. Boys in groups may play off each other's aggressiveness and commit acts most of them would be incapable of—or at least far less capable of—if they were acting alone. Sometimes the aggressiveness is an expression of targeted resentment. When teenage boys disfigure the school walls with graffiti, it isn't hard to infer the object of their resentment.

Other acts of delinquency, however, seem to be acts of deliberate risk-taking more than aggression. Early experimentation with drugs and alcohol often has this motive. So, too, may petty theft—"Can I do this without being caught?" Within the dynamics of peer groups, members are often dared to commit illegal acts as proof of their masculine credentials. The less confident a boy is of his standing within the group, the more vulnerable he is to proposed tests of his daring.

Preadolescent children often display a strong sense—some of it innately temperamental, but some of it learned from protective parents and other adults—of caution about new and risky ventures. This caution dissolves in early adolescence as a boy further distances himself from his parents and other adults, sometimes deliberately flaunting his parents' sense of caution. But another factor here is that adolescent boys simply don't assess risks the way most adults do. Many boys have a sense of invulnerability to danger. "It can't happen to me" is a line many boys carry in their imaginations, while "It did happen to me" is an adult confession they may decline to heed.

For most teenagers, a brush with the law doesn't augur long-term antisocial behavior. However, boys who have many relatively minor encounters with the police are certainly at risk of becoming serious offenders. About 12 percent of violent crimes (homicide, rape, robbery, and assault) are committed by teenagers, overwhelmingly by boys. About 22 percent of property offenses (burglary and theft) are committed by teenagers, overwhelmingly by boys.

Some of the factors linked to adolescent delinquency are poor academic performance and low verbal ability, rejection by peers in earlier childhood, growing up in a home ridden with conflict, and close associations with other delinquent boys. Individual episodes of adolescent crime are replete with the judgment of bystanders: "I can't believe [Rick] would do a thing like that!" Gerald Patterson and his colleagues have done substantial research into the antecedents of youthful brushes with the law. One common pattern is of a boy growing up in a family beset with much internal conflict, where lax and inconsistent discipline leads to boyish con-duct problems, followed by academic failure and rejection by peers in middle childhood, culminating in the boy's joining a deviant peer group in which he is motivated to repeated antisocial behavior.

Sex

When I try to draw a profile of the sexual development and behavior of the later teenage boy, I am more than ever aware of the tension between statis-tics and individual cases. By age sixteen, many boys have developed active interpersonal sexual histories—either heterosexual or homosexual—but many others of their peers haven't had a date yet, and are relying on the media, fantasies, and masturbation for sexual pleasure; the specifics of counseling a boy's needs are going to vary considerably depending on where he stands in the range of sexual maturity and experience.

As recently as the 1970s, the division of males who had or had not had at least one experience of sexual intercourse by age eighteen was about even, with 55 percent on the experienced side. In twenty years the per-centage of boys with experience of intercourse by age eighteen has risen to 73 percent. Since the average age of first marriage for males in the United States is twenty-six, boys face on average a period of more than a decade between the onset of puberty (a process completed in about three years) and marriage.

Social and cultural factors might intervene to reverse the trend of early sexual intercourse for males, just as a rising tide of teenage pregnancies has recently been slightly reversed. But it is unlikely that a society can keep most of its males chaste through a decade during which they reach the apex of sexual drive and their attention is captured many times a day by sexual thoughts or images. It is not surprising at all that 93 percent of American males have had sexual intercourse before marriage, or that one of fifteen males fathers a child when he is still a teenager. Since 85 percent of teenage pregnancies are unintended, we can safely surmise that many of the children fathered by male teenagers are at best mixed blessings.

Who should teach adolescent males about sex, and what should they teach them? It is far easier to prescribe what kind of person should do the teaching than to know who that person might be in a given adolescent's environment. The teacher can be either a man or a woman who is knowl-edgeable about the information and wisdom to be transmitted, comfort-able with the subject of sex itself, and who does not bring a personal sexual agenda to the discussion.

If you ask teenagers today whom they most rely on for knowledge about sexuality, they say they look most to their parents, then to peers, then to schoolteachers, then to the media. Their parents—mothers significantly more frequently than fathers—acknowledge that they talk to their children about sex far more than their own parents talked to them about it. But they also indicate a good deal of discomfort about the responsibility and wish the schools would accept more of it.

Surveys make a good deal of the fact that despite all of the instruction about the physiology of sex, a large proportion of adolescent males don't understand much about fertility cycles in females. Some of the reticence of parents to be responsible for counseling their sons about sex is that they themselves have forgotten much of the relevant biology of reproduction, and don't want to discuss the experiential side of sex. The mark of this silence about experience is that many adolescents can't imagine their parents having sex; parental sex is either mysterious or even slightly repellent to them.

If we examine parental and school teachings, we find a predominant wish that adolescents would practice sexual abstinence, but that if they can't hold to that goal, they should at least avoid contracting sexually transmitted diseases, and avoid causing pregnancies. These concerns are undeniably important, given that a million teenage girls become pregnant every year (many of them to older than teenage males) and that 3 million teenagers are infected with a sexually transmitted disease each year.

What is missing in this approach is an acknowledgment or acceptance of the adolescent drive for pleasure. Adults have important interests, too, in avoiding sexually transmitted diseases and unwanted pregnancies; but these concerns take their place in the context of the attempt, through all of the complexities and frustrations involved, to have satisfying sex lives.

The formal and informal sexual education of boys, I believe, rarely pays sufficient attention to both the positive and the cautionary aspects of sexual engagement. There is no socially endorsed means of teaching an adolescent boy how to cope with the nervousness that typically affects a male with a first or a new sexual partner; how to control the impulsivity that accompanies sexual excitement; how and when to elicit assent by a partner to his sexual initiatives; how to communicate with a partner in order to discover—and care about—what gives *her* pleasure; how to reduce the manipulative and aggressive scripts in order to allow sexual activity to be more playful, more intimate, and more loving; how to heighten both the control and the pleasure of sex by making it more verbal, more articulate.

Despite what teenagers report about depending on parents and teachers for sexual information and advice, I believe they actually depend more on each other and on what they glean from a blizzard of media messages ranging from the sublime to the pornographic. Many boys are on their own, learning as they may from their peers, who often exaggerate and distort, and from erotic literature that often downplays the search for mutual pleasure in favor of mute, impulsive drives toward orgasmic relief by males pressing ever ahead to the next "base." Some males pass their entire sexual lives rarely experiencing the transformation of sexual excitement into mutual passion. Any romantic themes in the media are often vastly oversimplified. The line between reality and fantasy gets very blurred.

Adolescent discussions and media presentations (including movies, videos, talk shows, and sitcoms) need infusions of knowledge and insight that parents and teachers (and other concerned adults such as physicians, clergy, and lawyers) could effectively provide if they were willing to accept and honor, rather than to attempt to deny or proscribe or shame or riddle with fear, the adolescent's sexual drive.

One way boys reduce anxiety about the risk of sexual engagements is to consume alcohol or drugs. Their parents use this method on a wholesale basis, so it is not surprising that adolescents borrow the method. They may also thereby either reduce their capacity for performing sexually, or provoke sexualized aggression. (Not a few rapists appear to be trying to compensate for feelings of sexual inadequacy.)

In groups, adolescent males may give each other nerve that many of them would lack if relating individually to young women. The anthropologist Peggy Reeves Sanday has shown in disturbing detail how alcohol and pack behavior work together in some male college fraternity parties. In these situations, boys are free of the constraints of living with parents. (The same kind of events can happen with high school students when Mom and Dad go away for a weekend under circumstances that permit an unchaperoned teenage party in their house.)

Sanday interviewed some fraternity members and the girls they deliberately gang-assaulted. One male group described their objectives as "working a 'yes' out" of their dates. Their techniques included inviting dates from out of town who would not feel self-confident and protected in the unfamiliar environment, or inviting dates whose style of dress suggested they might be sexually receptive, or inviting dates of lower social-class standing who might feel they were winning acceptance at a higher social level. The dates were plied with alcohol until drunk or unresistant and then drawn into a bedroom. Sometimes the room designated for such sexual scenes had peepholes through which other members of the fraternity could watch. After the fraternity brother had sex with his date, he would leave the room and other brothers would take their turn, subduing or threatening the young woman to the extent necessary to achieve sexual compliance. Some college administrations are now concerned about the social dynamics, particularly the abuse of alcohol and sex, of male students living in unchaperoned groups and are taking steps to prevent such practices as Sanday has described.

Adolescent and Gay

A very small percentage of males discover themselves to be homosexual or bisexual as they grow up. For them, sexual maturation is a particularly demanding, sometimes hazardous, process; as many as a third are physically assaulted by gay bashers inside or outside their families before they complete adolescence.

Adults often exhibit a degree of amnesia about their sexual awakenings. For both heterosexual and homosexual boys, the experience of this awakening is something shared mostly with each other. Adults say very little about the experience itself. Every boy finds it mysterious, exciting, confusing, and frustrating. Many boys who will eventually have well-established heterosexual orientations have at least one homosexual experience as an adolescent, either with another boy or with a gay adult testing their orientation. As many as half of the males who eventually establish a homosexual orientation have experienced heterosexual sex, either during the period when they were uncertain of their inclinations, or as an attempt to adopt the predominant orientation, only to have it prove unsatisfactory to them.

Both heterosexual and homosexual males like to think of their orientations as destinies foreordained at birth, but it isn't quite that simple. Some adolescent boys, either because of the strong cultural preference for heterosexuality or because they were somehow sexually different then, establish heterosexual orientations in adolescence lasting into early or middle adulthood, and then change orientation and identify themselves as gay.

A sense of being "different" assails many homosexual males while they are still in elementary school. In some instances, this sense of differentness is mainly an internal perception, but in other instances a boy may be perceived by others to be different and singled out for teasing or taunting—at school or at home, or both—as lacking masculinity.

Researchers are very much divided on the origins of homosexual orientation. Perhaps tolerance of homosexuality would become a less divisive issue in our society if indisputable evidence could be found linking sexual orientation to genetic inheritance. No such evidence, no gay gene or heterosexual gene, has yet been clearly identified. There is some evidence that male homosexual orientation is more closely related to maternal than to paternal lineage, but even that evidence settles very little. The fact that identical male twins are more likely to share the same sexual orientation than are fraternal twins also suggests a biological component.

For every geneticist looking for a biological link, there is a behavioral expert offering an explanation involving the childhood experiences and environment of the boy. When I was growing up, homosexual orientation was often blamed on overprotective mothers who didn't encourage their sons to develop heterosexual relationships with their peers. More recently, cold and distant fathers have received much of the blame once heaped on too protective mothers: the homosexual boy, in this formulation, seeks the acceptance and love from other males that his father never offered him. As with the biological explanations, there is something plausible about the various behavioral explanations, but none has won acceptance as a comprehensive and solidly confirmed hypothesis.

For every biological or social scientist who has addressed the etiology of homosexuality, there are several moralists lamenting what they believe is the perversity of homosexual practice. Many of them base their intolerance of homosexuality on their reading of the Christian and Hebrew Bibles, but there is no more scholarly consensus about how to interpret the few biblical references to homosexuality than there is consensus among scientists about genetic or interpersonal factors. Such attitudes, however, are influential. The Boy Scouts of America, citing the organization's private rather than quasi-public standing, does not now permit acknowledged homosexuals to take positions of leadership or accept known homosexual boys as scouts.

A homosexual youth lives in a glass-house environment in which sexual orientation is exaggerated far out of its proper perspective in his life. A heterosexual boy is deeply affected by his sexuality, thinks about it, dreams about it, talks about it—especially with his peers—and expresses it in personal or interpersonal action. Yet his sexuality, central as it is to his identity and life, doesn't stimulate the same constant sense of vulnerability. He isn't teased in a hostile way about being heterosexual. Everyone makes so much of homosexuality that it's difficult for a gay adolescent to get his sexuality in proper perspective. Difficult, too, to anticipate where rejection will lie. Sometimes adolescent classmates are relatively tolerant and parents are completely intolerant.

There is enough uncertainty about parental response, linked to the need most adolescents have for continuing financial and emotional support from them, that parents are not generally the first recipients of male homosexual disclosure. Siblings or other peers are usually the first to hear. A large proportion—half or more—of gay adolescents do not disclose their orientation to parents until they have left home for college or other pursuits. Even so, most males anticipate a higher level of acceptance of the disclosure to parents than they receive. In one recent study, half of both mothers and fathers reacted to their college-age sons' disclosures of homosexuality with disbelief, denial, negative comments, or silence. Eighteen percent responded with acts of rejection including attempts to convert the son to heterosexuality or to cut him off financially and emotionally. Parents often feel guilty: What did I do wrong? It is indicative of the differences in relationships that mothers are usually informed face-to-face while fathers are as often informed in writing as in conversation.

Many issues young homosexual males confront are embedded in the life of Dan, a sixteen-year-old. He remembers feeling attracted to men as early as age five. When he was in fourth grade in California, he watched a gay actor on a talk show recount that getting turned on by Calvin Klein male underwear ads made him realize he was gay. "And I said, 'That's me, too,'" Dan recalled. "But I kept thinking, of course I'm straight. I'm going to grow up and have girlfriends and have kids. I began dating girls in fifth grade. In seventh grade, I dated a beautiful girl who kept pressuring me to have sex—she wanted to know what made me horny. What I realized was that there's a big difference between finding someone attractive and being attracted to them sexually and emotionally. That was when I knew that I was at least bisexual.

"The summer after seventh grade I came out to most of my friends that I was bisexual, and they were cool about it. There were other guys out at the high school, and some in the middle school, too. I was afraid of what everyone would think, and I didn't tell my parents. To deal with my anxiety I started using drugs—a lot of painkillers, some codeine.

"Just before eighth grade started, my parents moved separately to Connecticut." That year was Dan's worst year so far: "absolute hell."

"Immediately I was labeled a faggot, and I had never been called that before I moved. I would get punched and spat on by people passing in the hall. There were gay teachers who would get made fun of, and wouldn't respond. So I really didn't feel comfortable. If gay adults weren't safe from taunting, I certainly wasn't going to be safe."

I asked Dan how he explained the abuse by other students. "They're just not sure of themselves," he said. "A lot of them have grown up with a hatred of gays. I find that many guys are threatened by how comfortable I am with my sexuality. That's not to say they're gay, but they're questioning their own sexual confidence."

In ninth grade, Dan began sexual activity with men, some in their twenties, others in their thirties or older. He meets many of them in gay clubs. He also feels confident initiating contact with strangers in public, in stores, for example. He is diligent about safe sex and careful not to make himself vulnerable to sexual exploitation by drinking too much, but he has a considerable number of sexual contacts during a year. His sexual experience and self-confidence are beyond the reach of his gay, and also many of his heterosexual, schoolmates. Dan has had only two brief relationships with schoolmates. His insistence that boyfriends be as open as he about sexual orientation is too public for their comfort. Lacking heterosexual friends, he has no schoolmates he spends time with outside of school.

His family circumstances and his homosexuality have pushed Dan into a kind of premature adulthood. "I think of my father as my roommate," he said.

"Isn't that a lonely way to live?" I asked.

"I really enjoy my independence," he replied, "and there's no way I could go back to having a curfew."

The pronounced—but not as rare as one might think—detachment of Dan's parents from his life accentuates but doesn't define the consequences of Dan's homosexuality. The depression, the loneliness, and, indeed, the danger attendant to his sexual relationships is in part a consequence of homophobia, but his perception of his parents' preoccupations with their careers, his hypersexuality, and his self-destructiveness are themes in many boys' lives, whether or not they are gay.

There aren't many self-acknowledged male homosexuals in any high school class, and if their sexual orientation is considered socially unacceptable or even contagious by heterosexual age-mates, they will not have a very large pool of potential friends. Homophobia is exhibited by some women, but by and large it is a sentiment perpetuated by males in our society. It incites crude and cruel behavior in middle schools, and even more frequently in high schools.

Suicide

Among boys aged fifteen to nineteen, suicide ranks as the third most frequent cause of death. The suicide rate has been climbing slowly but steadily since the 1960s. The most frequent cause of death in this age group is accidents, many of them vehicular and many of them associated with alcohol, which does seem to justify my father's belief that the automobile is an instrument of death. The second most frequent cause is homicide, which reflects the distinctive access to firearms that adolescent males have in the United States.

There are some gender-based differences in adolescent suicide. Girls attempt suicide more frequently than boys, but boys complete the act more frequently than girls. Girls tend to employ passive methods such as drug overdoses that are less disfiguring and less certain to be lethal, while boys are apt to use more violent and certain methods such as hanging or shooting themselves. Boys don't typically commit suicide as an extreme reaction to a single precipitating event, even a great disappointment. Careful examination of individual cases shows that what appear to be immediate precipitating events are better seen as the culmination of a set of difficulties the boy has experienced over a substantially longer period of time. In a study of 154 adolescents who killed themselves, the researchers concluded that a sense of hopelessness was the most critical factor.

Suicide sets off such an intense and prolonged reaction among immediate family and friends that the question of whether they should have been able to prevent it is inevitably raised. Warning signals have been defined, including unusually stressful events in a boy's life, mood changes, disturbed sleep and eating patterns, statements suggesting despair, and even verbal mention of suicide. Only the last of these symptoms, however, is specifically predictive of suicide plans, and it may be a way of expressing despair rather than a forewarning. Parents of adolescents shouldn't generally regard themselves as on a chronic suicide watch.

What does matter is whether parents, teachers and other concerned adults consistently try to maintain close relations with adolescent boys. There are many reasons to do this besides suicide prevention. Adults who are close to kids and not disposed to deny the evidence before their eyes and ears will sense major mood shifts and can raise concerned inquiries or guide boys to professional help if the mood shifts seem beyond parental remedy. Sometimes a change of school or a new activity or expressions of interest and concern from other people will effectively counter a major downward mood swing. Adults who are relatively detached from their children may not notice signals of despair.

Some suicide *attempts* are social in nature—dramatic ways of showing how desperate and unhappy a person feels. Others reflect a person's ambivalence, a wish both to end it all and not to end it—but to have relief from the pain of despair.

Lives on Hold

There is a curve to adolescence that gives rise to optimism. At the beginning of puberty, most boys are reasonably obedient sons and schoolboys. As sexual maturation occurs, boys draw away from family intimacy. They experiment with sex, alcohol, tobacco, and perhaps other drugs. They excel in risk-taking. When they get their driver's licenses, their independence takes another quantum leap. They get jobs. They stay out late and sleep late every chance they get. They buy and wear clothes that irritate their parents. They adorn themselves with fancy haircuts and tattoos. The adults in their lives watch this process with a mixture of anxiety, fascination, and horror. The wisest of them repress some of their impulses to object, complain, worry aloud, or counsel without invitation.

Most of the sons, toward the end of high school, turn back toward more closeness with their families. As they begin to look ahead to college or full-time jobs, they see that family support is indispensable to their futures. Also, they see that they have already won considerable independence; the battle doesn't have to be rewaged every day. They have won space of their own that no one wants to take away from them.

And so all should be well, right? Family relations patched up again, high school graduation on the horizon, early adulthood in reasonable proximity. Yet it doesn't all feel right. I circle back to Stephanie Coontz and an observation she made almost in passing in *The Way We Really Are*: "It's not that we have more bad parents or more bad kids today than we used to. It's not that families have lost interest in their kids. And there is no evidence that the majority of today's teenagers are more destructive or irresponsible than in the past. [Perhaps the data cited in this chapter shows them to be a *little* more destructive and irresponsible.] However, relations between adults and teens are especially strained today, not because youths have lost their childhood, as is usually suggested, but because they are not being adequately prepared for the new requirements of adulthood. In some ways, childhood has actually been prolonged, if it is measured by dependence on parents and segregation from adult activities."

We have, to use Coontz's term, made adolescence too "roleless." We have designed educational structures for teenagers that many find boring, unlinked to any path to the adult world. We have neglected to give them any significant public space of their own. We have kept extending the amount of education needed to impress hiring institutions almost as a way of keeping late adolescents/young adults from competing in job markets before older adults want them to.

In addition, the facility of certain older teenagers for grasping the complexities of fast evolving technologies such as information science and "e-commerce" terrifies older adults who cannot absorb social and technological change as quickly. This may result in a kind of unconscious conspiracy to keep teenagers in limbo for quite a few years. They do not feel needed. Why should we be surprised if, in their separate subculture, they treat their boredom and comparative irrelevance with behavior adults don't admire?

The predominant approach to adolescence today is to balkanize the issues. Safer sex. Reduce crime. Just say no to alcohol and drugs. Indeed, these issues do develop lives of their own. But they must be seen in the context of what we believe adolescence to be. A redefinition of adolescence to give it serious and honored purpose would not fail to affect each of these issues.

18

ENABLING

In relation to adolescent development, the term "enabling" has a double edge. On the positive side, psychiatrist Stuart Hauser draws a distinction between "enabling" and "constraining" patterns of interaction in a family. Enabling interactions include explanation, problem-solving, and empathy. Constraining interactions are distracting, devaluing, or judgmental of a family member's behavior or opinions. Laurence Steinberg writes of Hauser's work and related research by others:

> Not surprisingly, adolescents who grow up in homes in which the family tends to interact in enabling ways score higher on measures of psychological development than do those who grow up in relatively more constraining families.
>
> One recent study found as well that adolescents' needs for autonomy can be especially frustrated when their parents form strong coalitions with one another. Rather than viewing attachment and autonomy as opposites, these studies of family interaction indicate that the path to healthy psychological development during adolescence is likely to combine the two. In other words, adolescents appear to do best when they grow up in a family atmosphere that permits the development of individuality against a backdrop of close family ties. In these families, conflict between parents and adolescents can play a very important and positive role in the adolescent's social and cognitive development, because individuals are encouraged to express their opinions in an atmosphere that does not risk severing the emotional attachment.

Some parents might consider individuality strivings by an adolescent to be categorically a challenge to family ties, but Steinberg suggests—correctly, I believe—that the adolescent needs the support of family ties as he explores individuality and independence. Likewise, parents might believe that open conflict between themselves and adolescents is unmistakably a sign of broken family bonds. Again, not necessarily so. The adolescent profits from a certain amount of conflict with parents, particularly when parents have the wisdom to make clear that the conflicts do not threaten the basic bond between them.

Enabling Trouble

I shall return to this positive concept of enabling later in the chapter, but first I want to refer to another use of the term "enabling" that has emerged in the literature about human personality. Here enabling is used to indicate behavior that tolerates, sometimes ignores or denies, or even promotes self-destructive patterns of behavior by another person. In this chapter, I want to keep both definitions of enabling in view.

A neighbor told me that if I was interested in boys and character, I should look into a recent episode in the suburban town where I live, just outside Boston. In the spring of 1998, the neighbor reminded me, both local and Boston newspapers reported an incident that began with drinking at the senior prom and spilled over to the high school graduation ceremony three days later. I called the high school headmaster, Bob Weintraub, whom I had never met before, and asked him to tell me what had happened at the prom and afterward.

"The kids know that possessing alcohol or drugs at school is an expellable offense," he began. "We reemphasize school policy at prom time because we know it's a big issue. We would rather not have any tragedies in the community. Every student picking up a ticket to the prom signed a written contract acknowledging that he or she could not participate in graduation ceremonies if caught using, or even in possession of, drugs or alcohol at the prom or party after the prom.

"At the graduation rehearsal, one of the deans and I repeated the terms of the contract. We said it several times. We also said we knew some of the seniors weren't present for the rehearsal, so their friends should remind them of the agreement."

"Have you had any violations of the rule in the past?" I asked.

"There usually are one or two kids who violate the rules of the prom," Weintraub said, "and we just send them home. Again, this year, a boy walked in drunk and fell down. Some of the other staff took him off to a room to tend to him. When they asked him where he had been drinking, he said there was a lot of booze on a bus that some seniors had rented for the night. About fifty kids allegedly had rented the bus, and one of the kids had signed for it. It was a private bus company. No parent had signed off on it. They rode in the bus from our town over to the town where the prom was taking place. I understand they took a rather circuitous route and spent about forty-five minutes on the road, drinking a lot.

"Once the senior told us there was more booze on the bus, the issue was no longer what to do, but how to do it. The prom was in its mid to late phase, but all the students were still there. With other staff members, I located the bus. The driver didn't want to let us on, but we just said, 'Get out of the way.'

"In the middle of the aisle was a huge plastic garbage pail already one-third full of empty bottles—Seagram's and the like—and beer cans. We searched the backpacks in which the seniors had packed casual clothes for the after-prom party, and took a dozen of them off the bus because they contained significant amounts of alcohol. The confiscated bottles and cans covered a large table top the next day. Quarts of vodka, quarts of rum, lots of stuff. Most of it hadn't been opened yet. It was to be drunk after the prom. I was stunned. You know, after the warnings and knowing the kids for a long time, I'm still stunned by it all.

"All of a sudden there was a second bus there. The two drivers moved all the kids' packs that we hadn't confiscated onto the other bus. They obviously were trying to eliminate any kind of liability they might have incurred. The kids came back and saw a bunch of us standing there. They started whispering to each other, knowing they'd been discovered. I told them to get on the bus so I could talk to them, which they eventually did, but it was a very upsetting scene.

"They weren't obviously drunk—we had already sent home the one or two who were. They were in formal clothes with their dates. And they were in no mood to listen to me. A couple of them became self-appointed lawyers, telling me I had no right to search the bus because it was private. My colleagues couldn't believe the abuse they gave me. You know . . . 'Get off the bus' . . . 'Get out of here' . . . some nasty obscenities.

"'This isn't working,' I said to myself. So I negotiated with a couple of the senior boys. Off the bus and away from the rest of their peers, they were very reasonable. They said, in effect, okay, we're not happy about this, but you warned us and we got caught, so whatever happens is fair. 'I don't need your clothing,' I said, 'but you have to identify whose stuff this is, and then I'll take the booze and you take the packs and clothing.' Most of them came and claimed their packs, and I took their names. Two of the packs went unclaimed. I put all the alcohol in the trunk of my car.

"There were nine seniors—seven boys and two girls—among the ten students identified by us as having alcohol in their packs. The prom was on Thursday night. Friday morning other staff members and I called the nine seniors' parents and asked them to bring their kids to a meeting at the high school on Saturday morning.

"Graduation was to take place on Sunday. Some of the parents asked me over the phone if I'd made a decision about what I was going to do, and, if so, why we needed to have a meeting. 'Because I don't want to do this over the phone,' I said. 'I want to talk to you. This is a big issue.'

"The meeting lasted four hours. I ran the meeting by myself, but I had all of the major administrators of the school system with me, and the complete support of the school committee and the town selectmen. The parents of the nine had met together on Friday night and developed a strategy that all fifty-five seniors on the bus had been drinking, so none of them should be allowed to attend graduation. If I accepted their argument, they thought, I wouldn't have the nerve to keep that many kids away from graduation ceremonies.

In my opening statement, I said: I have evidence on nine seniors. I am not so naive as to think only nine had been drinking or were going to. But I only have evidence on nine. I'm not going to ignore the rule because I don't have evidence on forty other suspects. I understand the pain this brings to them and to their families."

"How did they take your position?" I wondered.

"The tone of the meeting was up and down. There were both civil and ugly moments with the parents. Some of the parents are lawyers, so the group didn't have to bring outside lawyers to represent them. But the anger was very deep, and some parents did throw expletives at me. The seniors who accepted accountability on Thursday night had changed by Saturday morning. To their families they had become heroic figures, martyrs.

"My job involves handling many disciplinary situations. For example, I've handled three expulsions of boys this year—one for weapon possession, one for assaulting a teacher, one for selling drugs on the school campus. One of the things I say from time to time, reflecting on my job, is that 'No.' is a complete sentence. In our town, for many parents, 'no' is not a complete sentence. It is supposed to be the first word of a process that leads to a compromise solution. Why not, the parents asked on Saturday morning, let the kids come to graduation and do some community service? I told them that community service is something everyone should do. I know it's much used by the courts in place of other punishment, but it usually goes along with other punishment.

"Despite the fact that their kids had signed written contracts about alcohol and the prom, the parents still tried to argue that I hadn't been very, very, very, very clear about the rules. Yes, I said to them, I was very, very,

very, very, very clear. But they hated it that they had no power because their kids had disregarded the contract.

"They went crazy because it was going to be a public humiliation for them. You're not punishing our son, they said, you're punishing our family."

"How did the parents evaluate your handling of the situation on prom night?" I asked.

"I think all of the parents acknowledged that I did the right thing in confiscating the booze. Begrudgingly, but they did. Some of them acknowledged that their children had done the wrong thing. But they didn't want the penalty. One story within the story says it all. By way of background, everyone—parents and school staff—pitches in to help prepare the party after the prom; it's a great community event.

"On Thursday afternoon, one of the senior class mothers helping to set up for the party came over to the superintendent of schools and the cochairs of the school committee, who were also doing their bit, and said, 'I just want to congratulate Bob Weintraub on the great job he's doing, taking such a strong stand against drugs and alcohol.'

"A few hours later I busted her son as one of the nine seniors caught with alcohol in their backpacks. Her son had two quarts of hard liquor. He was one of the boys who helped me negotiate a reasonable solution to the standoff in the bus. What is scary is that he told me his parents knew he was taking the alcohol to the prom, and told him to drink in moderation. When I spoke with his mother about the Saturday morning meeting, I said, 'I have a tough question to ask you. Your son told me you knew he had those two quarts, and that you told him to drink in moderation. Is that true?' There was silence at the other end of the line. Finally she said, 'Sandy's sobriety is *his* responsibility.'"

I couldn't help uttering a murmur of dismay.

"That's a true story," Weintraub said, "and it's not the only example of that kind of behavior I could cite. I believe that some of the parents must have bought the alcohol for the kids. One of the kids caught with alcohol on the bus had a party at his house during the school year that practically destroyed the house. Another of the boys wrote to our local paper after the story broke, saying he couldn't believe he was being punished in this way for one thing. But his school disciplinary record just for his senior year shows he's been in trouble from day one—fighting, being incredibly disrespectful to teachers, things like that.

"In addition to projecting onto me a lot of anger they were feeling toward their sons or themselves, the parents were also in heavy denial. I was about five minutes into my opening statement at the Saturday morning meeting, and had already made it clear that the nine would be barred from graduation ceremonies, when a parent raised his hand and said, 'Bob, can you just tell us what you're going to do and be finished with this?' And I said, 'I thought I was clear, but I can say it again. The kids are not going to be participating in the ceremony.' The same exchange happened with three more parents. They weren't listening.

"Toward the end of the Saturday meeting, the nine seniors went off with some alcohol and drug counselors, leaving me alone with the parents. We worked out an agreement with all of the families that the students would receive from one to ten individual counseling sessions—we have a very good drug and alcohol prevention program—and then receive their diplomas at some unspecified date.

"Saturday night, the mother I referred to before, who knew her son was going to break the rule, called me to say that maybe we should give the nine seniors their diplomas soon since they had made a commitment to counseling. I said I was flexible about the timing. 'They've earned their diploma,' I said. 'Their diploma is not the issue.' 'Okay, that's good, Bob,' the mother said, 'Let's talk about the diploma on Monday.' I said, 'Monday, after graduation's over? Fine.'

"Sunday night the nine excluded seniors and their parents came to graduation and sat in the audience out on the athletic field. They were very disruptive, the parents as much as the kids. They were shouting and harassing. During my talk, two of the senior boys who were excluded from the ceremony came forward and threw their caps and gowns at the stage, to the cheers of their parents. It was a miserable, miserable time. It ruined everything.

"After the ceremony was over, the mother I've referred to and another parent came over to me on the field. She was enraged to a level I have never seen in anyone before. She had her finger in my face, and she was shaking, and her face was about to explode in rage. 'Bob, you just don't get it,' she said. 'If you don't give them their diplomas right now, you're going to have a riot on your hands, and we're going to destroy this place.'

"There were police with me who heard her. 'I think she's really threatening you,' one of them said. 'You seem to think this is going to be okay, but we're nervous about it.' For some reason I didn't feel in danger. 'I already told you the diplomas are not a big issue for me,' I said to the two enraged parents. 'The issue for me is getting some help for the kids. But I have to find out whether I can get the diplomas. Right now they're locked in the safe.'

"The three plainclothes police insisted on staying by my side. A few minutes later, the superintendent of schools and I and the deans of students, accompanied by the police, walked up the steps of the high school between the glaring nine seniors and their parents. The atmosphere was just electric with anger. One by one the students were admitted to my office, received a diploma, and walked out to be cheered in the corridor by the other students and all the parents. I felt like I was in an Ionesco play."

Walking the Walk

The complicity of parents in the problems of their kids doesn't have to involve anything as dramatic as drinking at the prom.

"I have some examples at school," Bob Weintraub says, "where parents are influenced by their kids in a way that's not helpful to the kids. Attendance, for example. Too many parents call their kids out and make excuses for them. Kids say they don't feel well—with no convincing evidence—or have to study for a math test, and parents take them out of school. Grades, another example. If the kid doesn't get a good grade, parents are often in the teacher's face saying the child deserves a better grade.

"I think there's a generally critical environment about educators. I can't remember one example from my own school years of my parents talking negatively about teachers or coaches; but I think it's very common in our town for parents to criticize educators, and I don't think that's helpful to kids. When things are going well for the student, teachers are respected, and when things are not going well, teachers become the enemy, regardless of the family's social class. This is a very diverse town. The seniors who got in trouble at the prom came mostly from affluent families. As you know, I'm not interested in squashing freedom of speech or openness; that's not what this is about. This is about the impact of what you say in front of kids.

"Parents are not vigilant about the parties their kids go to. There's lots of drinking and drugs going on at parties—mainly parties that lack adult supervision. And because parents don't want their kids to be social isolates, they let them go and tell them to be good. It comes down to the fact that many parents talk a good talk, but when it comes down to their very own child, they refuse to walk the walk.

"I'm not about to cast anyone off into the tundra for making a mistake or three. That's not why I am in this work. I understand all that. But I do think it's critical to hold kids accountable for their behavior. If you don't, they get very confused, and they push it until they do something tragic. So that's where it's at for me: getting parents to acknowledge that being strict is good, that saying 'no' to kids is okay. Even if it's painful in the short term, it's really good for the long term. And the short term, by the way, lasts for about six hours. If there's pain, it's over and you move on. When I penalize kids, we usually have a better relationship the next day than we did before, because the kids know exactly where I stand.

"Some people say to me, 'Oh, Bob, you can't have it both ways. You can't be friends with these kids and then be their disciplinarian. And I say, 'Excuse me. You don't see what I do in this school in terms of discipline. I think most of the students will say that I'm nice, I'm a friendly person, but don't cross the line or else you're in deep trouble. I have a history of taking violations to the school community in a very serious manner."

I believe the point Weintraub is making here is another example of the point made at the beginning of the chapter. Some people assume that the disciplinary mode has to be harsh and unfriendly, and that the school administrator ultimately responsible for discipline should present a stern, seemingly unfriendly presence to students to buttress his authority; but Weintraub is taking the correct position that one can be firm, fair, and friendly without contradiction.

In Weintraub's account—and in other true stories in this book—there are examples of families where there has been an inversion of power. The boy is controlling and manipulating his parents rather than his parents providing a framework of regulation, communication, and support for the boy. By caving in and defending their children's wrongdoing, they are enabling it, and neglecting to encourage responsibility. This phenomenon cuts across all social classes. Pascal Lehman in Chapter 1 mentions a classmate whose affluent parents "act afraid of him."

Mechanisms of Defense

What makes parents so vulnerable to being enablers of their sons' misbehavior? Psychological mechanisms of defense can be contributors. Faced with the prospect of unpleasant reality, the self, the ego, has astonishing capacity at times to deny what to others may be fairly obvious. Bob Weintraub referred to two defense mechanisms—denial and projection—in his conversation with me. His knowledge of these mechanisms surely helped him to understand how to cope with this crisis without losing his poise and fair judgment. I want to refer to two other defense mechanisms, too—displacement and overidentification.

Parents who understand these mechanisms can sometimes interpret the behavior of their sons and spouses more sensitively and respond more appropriately. But a strong cautionary note needs to be sounded, too. Defense mechanisms are just that—they allow us to hold ourselves together in the face of unpleasant and even frightening feelings, impulses, or realizations. One doesn't simply strip them away, or challenge them. It's better not to understand the concepts at all than to misunderstand them and use them as weapons—as in, "There you go again, using denial to wiggle out of a jam." That can force an even worse response.

A person using denial, for example, may resort in the face of threat to a more primitive and aggressive self-protection strategy, such as projection. People who have grown up in so-called "alcoholic families" know that breaking the code of silence imposed by denial may provoke verbal or physical violence. This is another reason that it is always well to keep in mind seeking the aid of mental health professionals or groups like Alcoholics Anonymous. Their useful guidance can be helpful, and it's often in the process of counseling that parents develop insight about where these reactions are coming from—one's relationships with one's own parents, for example—and what needs to be done to change them.

I think it's important to add that sometimes it's necessary for parents themselves to get professional help to change. I'm a great believer in timely therapy with a psychologist or social worker for parents in the interest of their better understanding themselves and helping their kids, and a great skeptic about simply referring the child for treatment for *his* ostensible problem.

Parent groups, run by informed professionals, can also help immensely. It becomes clear that you're not the only person with an important problem, and you can share insights and strategies, and seek and find support as you struggle through the complexities of addressing your child's provocations.

Feeling guilt over a child's misbehavior may motivate parents to respond inappropriately—trying to defend themselves rather than deal thoughtfully with the child. The parent may wonder: What did I do wrong? If I'd raised my son the right way, he wouldn't have done what he is accused of doing. The fault must be mine. What should I do? The pain, the conflict, is just too much to bear. If a parent can get an accusation dismissed, then the guilt diminishes. Easy rationalizations—"Boys will be boys" or "You're making too much of this" will do for starters. But if soft diversionary tactics don't work, some parents attack the accusation with every weapon at their command. Parental guilt turns parents into unlicensed lawyers, and teachable moments into adversarial situations. The son who doesn't understand what's going on in his parents' heads may take their tactics at face value, and conclude that he is indeed the victim of malicious prosecution.

Because of the very poised response of Bob Weintraub to the senior drinking crisis at his school, I think there was little opportunity for the parents to employ the defense mechanism known as *projection*. Projection involves attributing to another person in the situation the feelings we harbor ourselves. So, again, a parent might be angry toward a son for embarrassing the family, but elects—again, unconsciously—to project feelings of anger to someone like Bob Weintraub. If Weintraub, then, expresses anger for the disrespectful way some of the seniors responded to his exposure of their drinking plans, the parent can zealously defend the son from Weintraub's anger—but really, from the parent's own anger projected onto the headmaster. But Bob Weintraub didn't give that defense mechanism an opening. At the final faculty meeting of the year at his school, one of the teachers stood up and said, "Bob went through this really difficult process showing an incredible amount of respect for everyone, and that wasn't easy because he wasn't always respected, and I just want to congratulate him." All the faculty stood and cheered.

Another defense mechanism is *overidentification*. Some parents meld so completely with the lives of their sons that everything the son suffers is felt by the parent as an experience of the parent's own. A son's successes may be treated by his parents as though they were successes of their own; accusations by others of misbehavior by the son may be perceived by the parent as a personal attack on the parent himself.

The more public a son's successes or errant behaviors become, perhaps the stronger a parent is tempted to overidentify, and, with respect to errant behavior, to behave in a way that might seem out of character compared to the parent's usual conduct. A parent need not—should not—cease to be supportive of a son who has gotten himself in trouble. Being supportive includes being empathic and tending to the stress the son is experiencing. But the parent need not abandon his own values and adopt his son's way of viewing the situation. Doing so lessens the parent's opportunity to be a healing force—perhaps even to support a son in acknowledgment of wrongdoing and the penalty or restitution flowing from it, and then to help him move on to the next phase of his life.

The boys I talked to in the course of preparing this book constitute mostly a well-parented population who have coped successfully with all the stages of their lives. Quite a number of them, however, have had brushes with disciplinary action at school or with law enforcement authorities. There they find even in childhood and adolescence that others identify with them differentially depending on their social class (expressed in dress and comportment, and in family status) and race. Bob Weintraub has already referred to occasions when courts seem to treat affluent kids' misbehaviors lightly.

One boy I talked to mentioned this episode: "During ninth grade I started stealing, like a lot. In February of that year I got caught shoplifting and actually went to court. The people there were totally biased. I went in with a tie. The others were mainly black kids. The prosecuting attorney was like, I'll take care of you because you're not like this guy over here, this scum. They recommended to the judge that it not go on my record, but I bet that's not how the others got treated. It's not like I stole a thousand dollars' worth of merchandise. It was petty theft, but, still, they bent the rules. Like, look at my privilege."

Another defense mechanism is known as *displacement*. I suspect there were elements of displacement in the reactions of some of the parents in the story Bob Weintraub told. The parent, upon learning that a senior son has been excluded from high school graduation for possessing alcohol at the prom, feels embarrassed and humiliated for its effect on the family reputation.

The parent is angry. The son would appear to be the appropriate object of his or her parental wrath. But something stands in the way of the parent expressing anger toward the son. Perhaps the parent also feels guilty about the son's misbehavior. Or perhaps the parent overidentifies with the son. The sticky thing about defense mechanisms is that various combinations of them can coexist in a single parental reaction. In any case, the parent might direct toward someone else—displace—the anger that logically would be directed toward the misbehaving son . Someone else might be a high-school headmaster.

The Dangers of Denial

The most widespread and supple of the mechanisms of defense is denial. Denial has been much publicized in the 1990s as a defense mechanism frequently employed by people addicted to alcohol or drugs; the same literature has targeted the families and associates of addicts as "enablers" because they tolerate rather than challenge evidence of addiction, maybe even protect addicts from others who would challenge them. Denial is a convenient defense in many other situations. An example is the well-publicized story of Alex Kelly.

In 1983, when he was a high school student in Darien, Connecticut, Alex and three other boys began a series of burglaries of neighbors' houses. They used the money to buy drugs. Eventually they were caught; Alex pleaded guilty to nine burglaries as a juvenile offender, and was sentenced to a maximum of thirty-five months in a juvenile detention institution where he entered a drug rehabilitation program. To his more rebellious contemporaries, Alex was "cool." A young journalist who grew up in Darien remembers: "People who knew about this at the time said, 'Yeah, that's crazy. This guy is crazy.' But they said it with a touch of admiration, like, this is *real* rebellion. A lot of people staked their rebellion on being associated with Alex Kelly rather than doing the things he did."

Sixty-eight days after Alex was sent away, he was released on probation by a judge who found him essentially rehabilitated. For a year, Alex made the judge look prescient. He studied himself onto the academic honor roll, starred on the football team, captained the wrestling team, and warned other students about drug abuse. Some called him "the comeback kid." His principal says, "He was the charming All-American boy. 'With it,' as the kids say. He was in the inner circle, an accomplished athlete, lots of things that kids want to be."

Then Alex was arrested again in February, 1986. A seventeen-year-old Darien girl told the police that Alex offered to drive her home from a party, drove instead to a deserted country club parking lot, and raped her. Police were already investigating the complaint of another sixteen-year-old girl, who said that Alex had offered her a ride home four days earlier and choked and raped her. Both girls claimed that Alex threatened them with repeat rape or even death if they told anyone of his sexual assaults.

Alex's father, in a 1996 ABC *Turning Point* documentary narrated by Forrest Sawyer, recalled the moment he heard of the arrest. "I got a telephone call from the police department, so I dropped everything and ran down there."

Forrest Sawyer: "Did it ever cross your mind that it was possible?"
Alex's father: "No."
Forrest Sawyer: "Not once?"
Alex's father: "No. I know Alex. To this day there's no question in my mind."
Forrest Sawyer asked Alex's mother: "Why would two young girls come forward and accuse a young man of rape under similar circumstances?"
Alex's mother: "Good question. Unbelievable. I don't believe it."

Alex's high school principal told Forrest Sawyer that she first heard of the arrest of Alex in a telephone call from the chief of police. "He said to me, 'We have come *this* close to two possible murders this week.'" Sawyer reported her words to Alex's parents: "*This* close . . . to two murders."

Alex's father: "It's got to be one of the most irresponsible things I've ever heard for a chief of police to ever say . . . if that is the truth. Irresponsible!"
Forrest Sawyer: "There were, according to the two alleged victims, threats of murder."
Alex's father: "I don't believe that."

Concerned that Alex's presence at school while he awaited trial would cause anxiety and distraction, the school administration graduated him in absentia a month after his arrest and forbade him to return. Alex noted that "All of these people that were so supportive and so behind me—they did all they could to, like, take credit for what I was doing. But the second any sort of rough times came, any allegations, they just jumped off."

A few days before he was to go on trial for the second of the alleged rapes, Alex Kelly jumped bail, flying to Europe with a ten-year passport in hand. Ten years later, with capture virtually certain, Alex turned himself in, was extradited to the United States, and went on trial. The first trial ended in a deadlocked jury. At a second trial, Alex was found guilty and sentenced to twenty years in prison. The judge rationalized the severe sentence not on the flight to Europe but on the nature of the crime and on Alex's lack of remorse.

Probably none of the parents whose stories have been told in this chapter were motivated principally by concern for their own or their family's reputations. What stirred them was the urge to protect and support their sons.

The parents of Alex Kelly were said to have had greater hopes for Alex's success than for his two brothers. Alex was to be the star of the family, and he showed considerable promise of fulfilling these expectations. There wasn't anything the family wouldn't do to enable Alex to be a success. The burglaries conviction was a trouble sign apparently largely ignored in the glow of his sports achievements and his academic record. Alex's arrest on two different rape charges was a stunning blow to him and to his family.

One can feel compassion for them—the family's hopes collapsed as swiftly as a house of cards—while believing that denial and flight simply delayed a resolution of wrongdoing. Alex will be middle-aged before he leaves prison. One of his two brothers died of an overdose of drugs while Alex was hiding out in Europe. The only way the family seemed to be able to survive these tragic changes of fortune was through denial: Alex still protesting his innocence, his parents still believing him.

Parents sometimes believe they are showing unconditional love when they really are exhibiting mechanisms of defense—denial, displacement, overidentification, and the like. We can't any of us be simply objective in our evaluation of others' behavior; our hopes and expectations inevitably are going to be entangled to a degree with our perceptions of what is going on. But there is no reason to be confused in principle. Loving a son does not require denying his wrongdoing; his wrongdoing never justifies ceasing to love him.

Positive Enabling

While one might expect single parents to confront unique challenges in nurturing good values and behavior in their sons, one of the families who demonstrated positive ways of supporting character as sons grow up was a divorced mother and her fifteen-year-old son.

When I asked the mother, Marilyn Bendix, about her situation, she said, "I always correct the term 'broken home' when I hear it applied to a family like ours. Brett lives in a 'fixed home.' In many ways, his dad is a wonderful person, but in the family he was very self-centered, resentful of any time I spent on anything else, even Brett. And he was an alcoholic. There were incidents of drunk driving. I'm the adult child of an alcoholic, so I know the problems an alcoholic brings to a family. When Brett was four, I could already see evidence of his becoming an enabler for his dad. I decided then to get a divorce, even though I had been married for sixteen years. It was very awkward and uncomfortable. It took Brett's dad a few years to forgive me for divorcing him, and to stop drinking.

"Brett has told me that one of his only memories of living in our old house is peeking through the upstairs banister into the foyer below and watching us starting to fight—though our fights were never physical. My goal as a single parent is to provide Brett with a safe and peaceful environment. In fact, our life is a little sheltered from typical family dynamics. There is no sibling rivalry, my attention goes nowhere else, I'm here at his beck and call. In some ways that's unnatural, and in some ways he's definitely spoiled.

"There have been times when it was very difficult for Brett not to have his father here. I remember as early as day care when they had a 'father's day' and Brett couldn't deal with all those boys and their dads. For me, it has been hard in some respects to be the mother and the father. In other respects it's much easier to be the one making all the decisions.

"My main job is supporting Brett. I work my job around his schedule as much as I can. I have to work, but I make sure that I am home every night. I go to his sports games. When he was little, I would throw balls to him. I'm the one that took a baseball in the leg."

Marilyn is aware of the contribution male mentors can make to a boy growing up with a single mother—not to underestimate the contribution they can make to boys living with both parents. One of Brett's mentors has been a coach Marilyn and Brett met when Brett was playing in the Pop Warner football league. The romance didn't last between Marilyn and the coach, but the friendship among them all did endure.

"He was really nice," Brett says, "and I think from coaching football he really had an interest in being involved in kids' lives. He would stop by and take me to a sports store, and he actually got me involved in taking pictures. Different interests than my mom. He told me things not to do and stuff like that. One time my friend and I had a campfire in the woods and we got in trouble with the police. I didn't know what I had done wrong, and he told me." The downside of the Pop Warner league was that the coach prescribed large numbers of pushups and other exercises before their musculature could support it. Brett developed osteochondritis and now can't fully extend his elbows. His once promising development as a pitcher in the town baseball league is on hold for an indefinite period. "I love to pitch," says Brett, "but I guess I'll just have to work on another specialty. For example, I went to kicking class for football."

"It amazes me," says Marilyn, "that Brett doesn't have to find blame for this situation. I backed over our cat once with the car by accident and killed it. Brett told me later that it wasn't anyone's fault. He's very fortunate to have the ability to be accepting of things that he can't really have any control over. He also has an amazing amount of compassion that I would like to take credit for, but he had it too early for me to take the credit. He's always had a sense of people's feelings. As a little two-year-old, he never let me kill an insect. I had told him that 'you should never kill a living thing,' and he said to me, 'that's a living thing, too.'"

The single child of a single parent can certainly tempt the parent to zealous protectiveness that some kids might read as overprotectiveness. "When you are a single parent, I think you have more love for the single child," says Brett. "For example, some of my friends will be gone for the whole day without calling home and I have to call every two hours. So I think she feels closer because she needs me to call so much and stuff like that." But Marilyn's need for closeness is something that Brett can reciprocate. "I tell my mom way more things than my friends would tell their moms."

Brett's life is full of the cliques and crowds that I discussed in Chapter 15 as the center of the adolescent's social life. His mixed crowd consists of about thirty peers, six or seven of them girls, all of them interested in athletics. They hang out at each other's houses. "There isn't much to do in this town; that's why I think some of the older kids turn to drinking," Brett suggests. Marilyn is naturally concerned about Brett and drinking, but when she brought up the subject recently Brett said to her, "Mom, how could you think I would drink? That's what separated you and Dad."

The girl Brett likes most is not in his crowd. "My group are kind of the 'cooler' group, and she's not considered 'cool.' I told one of my friends, and he told me that if I really liked her it shouldn't matter just because she's not in our group. I liked another girl from second grade until this year. I'll probably like her all my life, but she's not possible anymore. She's way too gorgeous—out of my league." "Would you be comfortable going outside your group to date a girl you like?" I asked. "I would want to," he replied, "but I don't think I would have the guts. None of my friends would care. They might joke around, but they're just kidding, I know that. But I don't think anything will happen this year. As we get older, I think everybody will be more in the same group. I think we'll always be tight, but the guys might start seeing girls from other groups and bring them into our group. That's happened before."

Brett Bendix's life is a model of the right kind of enabling. It begins with a parent who has made a resolute decision to put parenthood first in her life, even though that commitment has led her, without complaint or self-pity, through divorce to single parenthood. Mother and son have excellent communication. All of the elements of enabling stressed by Hauser—empathy, explanation, and problem-solving—are richly present in their descriptions of their lives. I particularly admire their ability to explain their lives as well as to describe them in terms of feelings or incidents. Her protestations to the contrary, I'm sure that Marilyn had a great deal to do with nurturing Brett's early capacity for empathy. He has already had some valuable experience with a mentor and will undoubtedly attract more mentors in the future. The crowd Brett belongs to is the kind of athletic, 'cool' crowd in which boys often adopt a macho veneer in adolescence, hiding their uncertainty and stifling their capacities to be sensitive. But Brett, thanks in large part to articulate and attentive parenting, has a very distinct sense of who he is—and isn't yet—as a boy on the threshold of late adolescence.

19

CHEATING

There are several situations in which boys are frequently tempted to cheat—in sports, for example, or in their after-school employment—but I've elected to look mainly at academic cheating because academic work is the equivalent in a boy's life to his parents' jobs. A student who habitually cheated in his schoolwork might find it less guilt-provoking to cheat in his adult work than he would if he had gone through school with academic integrity.

Boys are familiar with cheating well before they are tempted to practice it academically. They may have observed it or done it in family life—cheating in games in order to win, for example—or in play groups. They may have heard parents boast of successful cheating—on expense accounts or tax returns. Cheating is rife in adult life, from white-collar business fraud to falsified research data.

My brother, Henry, is a high school social studies teacher. It was thus natural for me to turn to him first for information on academic cheating by boys today. According to Henry, cheating is prevalent in high school. He told me about a boy he observed using a crib sheet during the first exam of the past school year. Henry reacted with obvious enough indignation that the rest of the class immediately knew of the transgression and teased the student mercilessly for weeks. The academic penalty for the student was to get a grade of zero to begin the year's grading.

In Henry's school, there is no established school policy on cheating penalties—maybe a sign in itself that the school as an institution is uncertain how to deal with cheating. Each teacher has to use his own judgment. There is no written school code of academic and social behavior, nor are students regularly reminded of standards of behavior. It is assumed that "everyone knows" cheating is not permitted.

The happy fallout of the story is that Henry's student responded to the cheating exposure by buckling down to work; by June he was near the top of the class despite having his initial grade of zero averaged in. He became an exemplary student, not only successful in tests but impressive in classroom discussions.

Others might regard the embarrassing public exposure as contributing to the boy's change of direction, but Henry believes he would just as surely have changed course if Henry had handled the episode firmly but more discreetly—in other words, without shaming the boy publicly. Henry regrets his outburst when he discovered the crib sheet. It is better, he says, not to embarrass students deliberately. Peer status is everything to kids, he believes. The last thing a student wants is to be uncool. Though Henry didn't say so, perhaps what classmates considered socially uncool in this situation was that the student got caught, not that the student had attempted to cheat. A boy who cheats today does so as a member of a society in which appearances are often judged more harshly than underlying social realities. Adultery, for example, is reported by survey research to be a prevalent type of cheating. There is little evidence of public concern about adultery if it is effectively kept secret.

Every boy has to sort out for himself a set of inconsistent social cues that he is given beginning in childhood. One cue is that cheating is wrong, but other cues include the obvious fact that some people think it is more wrong than others do, that society as a whole regards some forms of cheating as morally worse than others, and that sometimes people are more scornful of getting caught than of the cheating offense itself. I don't think it is too exaggerated to say that there is a culture of dishonesty coexistent with a culture of integrity in our society. A boy who is tempted to cheat has many precedents from the culture of dishonesty to use as justification when he elects to cheat. Fortunately, he also has exposure to the culture of integrity that espouses good choices.

Another student came to see Henry late last year to ask about his grade average. Henry consulted his grading book and pointed out that the student had failed to turn in some written assignments, a factor that, if not remedied, would adversely affect his final grade. The student hurried off to complete the missing work. Then he went a step further. He graded the assignments himself (very highly) and tried to slip the papers into Henry's desk. Unwittingly, he used a different color of ink than Henry ever uses, so the cheating strategy was exposed.

Reactions to cheating can be intemperate and have unpredictable consequences. A female high school teacher spoke about getting caught cheating in an English lit course during her freshman year in college. She had plagiarized a published critique of a work for one of her reports, and her professor recognized the passages and knew their source.

The dean suspended her for a semester. He said of her cheating, "You've done well, but not well enough. We suspect you've done this kind of thing in all your classes." His suspicious accusations were untrue. She was deeply affected by the way a single incident had provoked a wholesale condemnation of her character.

The eighteenth-century philosopher, Jean Paul Richter, commented: "If a child tells a lie, tell him that he has told a lie, but don't call him a liar. If you define him as a liar, you break down his confidence in his own character." I think his is profoundly wise advice. What the dean did to the student was to generalize her single offense and call her a cheater. She might have withdrawn from an academic career, or she might have developed a deep resentment of his unfair characterization of her and resolved to cheat more skillfully. Fortunately, this student resolved to clear her reputation. After serving her suspension, she returned to the same college, graduated with honors, and now counsels all her high school students on the potential consequences of cheating. Her story is sobering, but is her experience the final word on cheating? How prevalent is cheating, and is it best handled with a punishment-as-deterrent policy?

Why Do Students Cheat?

Who's Who Among American High School Students surveyed 3,210 "high achievers" in 1997. Eighty-eight percent judged cheating to be "common" among their peers. Seventy-six percent confessed they themselves had cheated. Compare this figure to the results of a national sample of college students in the 1940s, only 20 percent of whom admitted to cheating in high school when questioned anonymously. The students queried in 1997 ranked copying someone else's homework as the most frequently practiced form of cheating (65 percent of the cheaters); cheating on a quiz or test next most often (38 percent); consulting a published summary in lieu of reading the book, third (29 percent); and plagiarizing published work, fourth (15 percent). "Every single day I see cheating, a lot, in every single class I'm in," says a high school freshman from Madison, Connecticut. "They ask to see someone's homework, they write things on their hands or bring in little cheat cards to hold in their laps. It's bad."

Another type of academic cheating appears to have increased significantly in the past few decades. When William Bowers surveyed 5,000 college students in 1963, 11 percent admitted to collaborating with other students on work that was assigned to be done individually. Donald McCabe and Linda Trevino partially replicated Bowers's study in 1993 at some of the same colleges and found 49 percent admitting to the same kind of forbidden collaboration. My brother Henry's policy, when he discovers evidence of collaboration on work that was assigned to be done individually, is to grade the work on its merits, then divide the grade by the number of collaborators.

The odds of getting away with academic cheating appear to be heavily in the cheater's favor. Ninety-two percent of the confessed cheaters surveyed by *Who's Who* said they had never been caught. As we shall see, temptation to try cheating may be encouraged by the uncertain application of penalties: from severe to nothing at all. The prevailing attitude of a majority of students about cheating is that "it's not a big deal."

"They are driven cheaters," says the high school teacher I've mentioned who was suspended from college for cheating. "They do it for grades, not because they're lazy or stupid or don't know the material. It's sad, you see, because they're so driven to have a high grade-point average so they can get into their first-choice college. I hate it, because they lose interest in learning. I tell their parents that it's okay if they get a B. It's more important to be a well-rounded, interested, bright kid. But that's a hard sell."

When Henry and I were schoolboys, the students who were believed to have the strongest incentive to cheat were the students in danger of failing. Is the primary incentive now to get into the college of one's choice? A Chicago area mother reflected the grade pressure recently when she complained bitterly to a teacher upon her son's receiving a B instead of the desired A. The grade, the mother argued, could make the difference between her son's "getting into Northwestern or having to settle for Northeastern." While one might give her credit for knowing how to turn a phrase, she doesn't appear ready to settle for a "well-rounded, interested, bright kid" who gets B's.

Eighty percent of high school students share the belief that college is the door to a successful career, and they may believe as well that the better the college, the better the chances of success later on. Only about 50 percent of the students in high school today will actually go on to college, but about 80 percent of middle school and high school students say they intend to go to college. While there are many ways to define success, and not all of them go through college, it's easier to see that later in life than it is as a teenager.

About 20 percent of high school students are in some kind of serious alienation from the educational system at any given time, surveys suggest. They are working too many hours in paid employment to cope with schoolwork, or they have been devastated by drugs or alcohol or crime, or they are distracted by psychiatric or severe family problems, among the more common reasons. What this means is that almost everyone except the alienated student is pushing toward the door to college. In that kind of environment, the temptation to cheat to get the coveted admission or scholarships must be very powerful indeed.

The self- and family-induced pressure to get into the "right" college is not unlike the pressure many adults feel as they try to balance their economic and social class aspirations with the realities of their incomes. When they sit down to subtract from disposable income what they owe in taxes, the temptation to cheat a little here and there, or a lot, is very powerful.

Bill Brashler, a journalist, decided to compare high school statistics on cheating to seventh-grade attitudes and practices by interviewing several classes of bright students selected for magnet programs. The seventh graders, especially the boys, were quick to tell him their methods. How they wrote information relevant to tests on shoe soles or wrists. How they covertly used pocket calculators when it was forbidden. How the class brain signaled correct answers to the others. Their methods were more traditional than the technique of some high school boys I read about who wrote crib sheet information on the underside of their baseball cap brims until their high school teacher said all such hats had to be worn backward during exams.

They all cheated, the seventh graders said, on tests, on homework, on reports. One of their teachers laughed off their talk as exaggeration, as a way of being cool. Only a few of them, he insisted, cheated as much as they all claimed. But why did they all claim to cheat?

The simple desire to take the easy road is sometimes advanced as the basic reason that students cheat. My brother says that in almost thirty years of teaching he has never ceased being surprised how many students "just never studied." So there would appear to be a certain portion of the student body disposed from the beginning to take the easy path: book reports off the Internet, for example. A mother writing to an Internet bulletin board provides a perfect example:

> My 15-year-old son had an English paper due on *Great Expectations*. When I didn't see him working on it, I gave him a gentle reminder. 'Don't worry Mom,' he told me. 'My paper's going to be great.' And it was. In fact, it was so great that I became suspicious. I called up the file on our computer and discovered that he had downloaded the paper from the Internet! I was shocked. Even more shocking was my son's attitude when I confronted him with cheating. He didn't see it that way. 'Everyone cheats, Mom,' he said. Is he right? What can I say to get through to him?

There certainly is a sizable pool of teenagers who resent the cheating going on around them for making it more difficult for them to succeed honestly. But other testimony, including that of my brother Henry, sounds plausible to me. Students, on the whole, are very tolerant of other students' cheating. The statistics, after all, indicate that only somewhere between a fifth and a third have the right to claim that they don't cheat. My guess is that the incentive in the majority of cases is to get a better grade, either to keep from failing or to build a superior academic record to facilitate getting into college; cheating as an easier path than actually doing the work would also be a motive, but one made all the more accessible by the prevalence of cheating for other reasons.

Of those who don't cheat in order to get better grades than they could get on their own, some certainly are collaborating with cheaters by giving them assistance—letting cheaters copy their homework or look at their papers during exams, for example. So they are endorsing cheating and contributing to it, even though they aren't benefiting from it. The mother of an eighth grader found giving answers to others during a test argued that his *giving* did not constitute cheating; only *receiving* information was cheating, she said, as she accused the teacher of pursuing a vendetta against her son.

There may be some social benefit for the bright collaborator in a system in which cheating is widespread. For the "brain" to give others the opportunity to copy his work, thus leveling the academic playing field to some extent, would be viewed as a "cool" thing to do in some schools. A bright student who refused to assist other students asking for collaboration in cheating might be ridiculed or excluded from high-status cliques and crowds.

Attitudes Toward Cheating

Early in his career, long before he had become an icon of American architecture, Frank Lloyd Wright was so desperate to acquire a commission that he showed his potential client one of Louis Sullivan's great buildings in Chicago and claimed that he, Wright, was its architect. He got the commission. I think of Wright whenever I'm tempted to assume that it's the untalented who cheat, or that cheating will surely corrupt talent.

Of the three parties most interested in the outcome of a high school cheating incident—the accused student, the teacher (and the school administrators behind him or her), and the parents, each has a different perspective. The alleged pressure that leads to cheating is attributed by most high school students to their parents, to their peers, and sometimes to their own personal calculations.

The overwhelming testimony of high school students is that when a student is caught cheating, the teacher, out of sympathy, misguided or not, or out of desire to avoid personal confrontation with the student or his parents, often looks the other way. Many instances of exposed cheating are not followed up. The teacher knows that even the most blatant case may provoke hassling by parents, administrative hearings, maybe an override decision by the principal, or even litigation. For whatever reason, most of the time there is no penalty. Consequently, there is little general deterrence based on fear.

In some instances, I'm sure, the disinclination of the teacher to pursue evidence of cheating is based on sympathy for students trying to cope in a grade-oriented system. My brother has a high school teacher colleague who, when he is teaching a class drawn from a low-achiever track, deliberately leaves the room for a few minutes during each test so that the students can swap answers. He rationalizes this action on the basis that those students need "all the help they can get." So, in certain respects, the status quo pits students and teachers as allies against the grading system.

In times now gone by, a teacher could afford without risk to judge each case of cheating on its merits, meting out either punishment or exemption. These days, however, teachers are often judged on the overall performance of their classes, compared, when feasible, to standards set on a statewide or nationwide basis. Teachers now have incentive to collude with students' cheating in order to make it appear that the teacher has been successful in raising class performance to an acceptable level.

In 1995 the Academic Decathlon team from a Chicago high school compiled a tremendous score on the six-hour written examination that is the basis of the competition, and it appeared the school had won the coveted state title. But elation soon turned to dismay when evidence of cheating turned up. With the collusion of the faculty mentor, the team had prepared ahead of time, using a stolen copy of the exam questions. "It was such a good team," the principal remembers ruefully. "A dream team. They didn't have to win it all. It would have been wonderful if they had finished tenth or twelfth in the state. We'd have been so proud. Instead they went right down the tubes. It was gut-wrenching." The school hasn't fielded a team since then.

Parents may swing back and forth from a parental role in which they are interested in remedying their sons' cheating, to overidentifying with their sons. A father whose eighth-grade son had been suspended for cheating, said that he supported the suspension; but, he said, if the suspension caused any permanent blemish on his son's school record, or if the matter were made public in such a way as to harm his son's reputation, he would immediately switch passionately to his son's defense.

Educational Testing Services, known worldwide for its standard entrance examinations for colleges and universities, recently proposed a national public service campaign against cheating, especially in test-taking in schools. The rationale for the campaign cited the same kind of statistics I've cited above concerning the prevalence of academic cheating. The plan targeted nine- to twelve-year-olds in public schools as a group to be taught individual values such as honesty, integrity, and responsibility. Though I think there are flaws in the proposal, I applaud attempts to raise the level of national awareness of character issues.

One theme of the proposal emphasized individual competition: "Children need to understand that tests are a part of life—whether it be your turn at bat or a spelling quiz. Each is a test, and each requires practice. . . . In order to prepare themselves for winning, children need to understand that winning requires doing, and doing requires learning. If a child hasn't learned to swing a bat, he won't hit the ball." As the proposal concluded, at another point, "Cheating undermines integrity and fairness at all levels. It leads to weak life performance and corrodes the merit basis of our society."

Another theme of the proposal emphasized the intrinsic value of learning, though not without getting learning, values, and success intertwined: "Children must know that learning, knowledge, values and ethics are more important in assuring moral character *and success*, than just getting by or getting a grade." (Italics mine.) If only individual children would adopt the view that it is learning that matters, and that cheating obscures lack of learning, it is suggested, all will be well. There is a degree of contradiction between these two themes. A college student newspaper essay quoted in the Educational Testing Service proposal identifies the contradiction without knowing how to resolve it. For some students, the essay says,

> the desire to secure the best grades has become a paramount force that drives their education. With so much emphasis placed on outcomes in our society something is lost along the way. The learning process becomes overshadowed by the final outcome. . . . Grades, rather than education, have become the major focus of many students entering universities today. Their goals become simple: get in, survive, get the grade, and get out.

Why target nine- to twelve-year-olds in a campaign about cheating? It is in the middle school years (sixth or seventh through eighth or ninth grades, depending on where a particular school system makes the divisions) that grading gets emphasized in many American schools; there are schools that do not give numerical or letter grades for achievement until the sixth or seventh grade. It is in the middle school years that widespread cheating is first noticed, and the phenomenon intensifies in high school.

Researchers at the University of Kentucky studied cheating patterns among almost three hundred middle school students. Forty percent of the students admitted to cheating. "Cheaters thought the purpose of school is to compete and show how smart you are," says the main author of the study. "To them, what's most important is doing better than others and getting the right answers."

Defining cheating as an individual moral issue for a meritocracy carries a barely hidden ideology with it; and that ideology, of course, is as open to moral scrutiny as is the issue of cheating itself. The implication of pure meritocracy is that everyone should take the test honestly, and the (perhaps relatively few) winners should reap the coveted rewards, and all the losers should accept the verdict and make do with the scraps that are left over. The tracking system in many middle and high schools begins early in life to assign kids their probable destinations in the meritocracy.

Is it any wonder that adolescents try to rig the system to their own benefit and that they often do it in collaborative ways that suggest collective solidarity as much as individual self-interest? As Robin Stansbury wrote in the *Hartford-Courant*,

> Jake Raphael was sitting quietly in his sixth-period foreign language class at West Hartford's Hall High School last year when his teacher passed out a weekly quiz—a quiz Raphael had already obtained the answers to. It happened quickly earlier that morning, as students shuffled between classes. Another student, who had taken the test earlier, shoved the copied exam into Raphael's outstretched hands. He wasn't the only student given an advance copy of the test. Most of the students in the afternoon session had seen the quiz by the time the class began. Raphael, now a senior, said he debated with himself for only a minute that morning before deciding to memorize the quiz. And as he sat at his desk, the perfectly completed quiz sheet before him, Raphael said he had no remorse.

One way to evaluate a school is to analyze how it emphasizes two different modes—a learning mode or a selection mode. The latter mode emphasizes the selection, mainly through grading, of the students who are the brightest. There is certainly a very substantial overlap between good grades and the amount of learning that has occurred. Sometimes, though, real learning occurs but it isn't fully reflected in the grading system. In other instances, grades bestowed indicate more learning has occurred than is true. Cheating would account for some of this disparity, but not all of it. Favoritism by teachers accounts for some of it, too.

For the learning mode to fulfill its promise, I think a society has to establish hope for every student that diligent and honest effort will be re-

warded with attractive continuing opportunities in life, no matter how
well his results stack up against the grades of the best students. It is too
idealistic to argue that learning is its own reward, because you can't expect
kids growing up not to make decisions based heavily on how their choices
might take them toward a satisfying career.

A learning mode would naturally take into consideration the many factors that can adversely influence an individual student's capacity: a difficult temperament; emotional problems such as depression; neurological
problems such as ADD/ADHD or dyslexia; health problems that affect vision or hearing; distracting, sometimes abusive, family situations; social
barriers such as racial, ethnic, or class prejudice; the amount of family
support available; and the quality of instruction both technically and temperamentally. A learning-based system tries to take account of all these
factors, because only in doing so can the potential of the student be max-
imized. Merit or grading systems, I believe, show less incentive to try to
make the playing field as level as it can be for all.

Every school is a mixture of both these modes. The teachers that most
high school students remember with highest affection are the teachers
who inspired them to learn, often by teaching a subject with notable bril-
liance and enthusiasm, but many times also by showing acute sensitivity
to the particular needs of students. But most middle and high schools are
dominated by the grading system, and the evidence of it is the prevalence
of cheating.

When learning is most highly valued, there is little incentive to cheat.
When grades matter most, cheating rises as students begin to use every
available means to increase their class ranking, or be seen as helpful to
friends when they offer work to copy. Thus we may think of cheating as a
social phenomenon induced by grading pressure at least as much as it is a
phenomenon of individual character failure. The grading pressure is generated by the culture and personified by many parents. We can see resistance to this pressure when better students give worse students their
homework to copy—by far the most common form of school cheating.
This is too massive a phenomenon to be dismissed individual by individual; it amounts to social resistance by the young. Collaborative academic
cheating is, in its way, an odd expression of altruism among adolescents at
the same time that it is a deceitful breaking of rules.

Who Loses with Cheating?

The literature on cheating is surprisingly inconclusive on what constitutes
its moral offense. Some writers, viewing academic cheating as a "victim-
less" act, argue that the damage is mainly self-inflicted. The cheater ap-

pears to know more, or be more competent, than is actually the case. A weakness is being papered over, and sooner or later it will harm the cheater when he can't perform as expected at a higher academic level, or professionally, and is made to suffer the consequences.

This argument—that cheating harms the cheater—is learning-based in a grading-dominated environment. When grades are the defining element and the competition is intense, many students will employ every means they can to stay afloat as long as they can. The very prevalence of academic cheating suggests to cheating students that their bubble of deception might never burst.

Others writers view cheating as a form of stealing. Academic cheating does involve stealing recognition and grades that are undeserved, and that others are earning meritoriously. Cheating is always fraudulent, and shows disrespect for the people directly affected by it. In academic cheating, fellow students are the ones treated disrespectfully by cheaters. What keeps the issue of respect from powerfully deterring student cheaters is that they often don't stop to think of other students as being hurt. Their focus is on cheating as an issue between the cheater and the faculty and administration. In an analogous case, people who file false tax returns don't think of themselves as hurting their neighbors who are reporting accurately; the tax cheaters think of it as an issue strictly between themselves and the government or the IRS. Or, again, people who make false insurance claims don't think of themselves as raising everyone else's insurance rates; they regard their cheating as an issue between them and the insurance company. This blindness to the consequences of cheating for one's peers is, I believe, very widespread.

Patricia Hersch has described a forum in which several bright high school seniors were asked to comment on the hypothetical situation of a college basketball star back on campus, exhausted, after performing well in a game, and looking forward to the next night's game when a professional scout would be watching him. But tomorrow he also has a calculus test in a course he must pass to keep his scholarship. Should he study as best he can and give it a try; hire a tutor and study most of the night in order to get a passing grade; or get the answer key to the exam, memorize it, then rest up for the game? There was nearly unanimous agreement that the student athlete should cheat. "Ethically, I would cheat," says an honor student. Only one boy, named Jonathan, disagrees: "We have to take responsibility for our actions and if he screwed up, it is his problem and he has to accept the consequences. If he cheats, it is not taking responsibility. If he stays up all night studying, he does."

Theft as the essence of cheating is particularly stressed in academic honor codes, for there the student has the double responsibility of being beyond reproach himself in the integrity of his academic work, and also of coming forward to accuse anyone whom he sees cheating; in fact, he is guilty of a violation of the code if he knows of cheating by others and does not report it to the judicial system.

A professor of business at the University of Kansas has built an honor code and other deterrents into his sophomore course with an enrollment of three hundred to four hundred students. Each student is assigned a seat. A dozen or so vigilant teaching assistants patrol blocks of fifty seats. At the bottom of each test are two statements with signature lines by them. One statement says: "I have not received nor given unauthorized aid during this exam. I have not observed any other students receiving or giving such aid." The other says, "I cannot in good faith sign the above statement."

To get credit for the exam, every student has to sign one of the statements. If it is the second one, he gets an interview with the professor; most of those who sign the second statement think that others may have been looking at their answers. The teaching assistants also always compare the exams of people sitting side by side. Only about 5 percent of the class get caught bucking this very vigilant system.

There is some evidence that cheating occurs less under honor code systems than other codes. It is unclear whether the honor code promotes superior character formation where it is employed. Punishment is much surer and harsher, and more evenly applied, when it is based on a proven violation of an honor code; in addition to the penalty, which might well rise to the level of expulsion, there is dishonor or shaming for the person found guilty of cheating. The environment where an honor code is in effect doesn't tolerate cheating to the extent it is tolerated in most high schools.

Cheating and Trust

Even where cheating goes unnoticed, I believe it deeply affects relationships because the perpetrator knows he is violating someone's trust, and therefore can't be candid about acts that, if known, would deeply affect the relationship. The cheater is always holding something back, and people sensitive to human interaction can often sense it. Adulterers, for example, may have taken great pains to hide their infidelity, but something about their behavior often sends a signal to their partners, who may not know precisely what is wrong, but know something has shifted in the relationship.

Perhaps we are not quite as trusting, on the whole, as some of our ancestors were. Many business deals were once closed with an oral agreement followed by a handshake as a seal of trust. Those days are long gone. Now we like to have everything in writing—an estimate for every project, a warranty for every appliance, a printed insurance policy for every risk, a waiver of liability for every responsibility we undertake. The degree of our trustfulness in many situations can be measured by the length of the written contracts involved. Where trust lags, people entering contracts, or their lawyers in their behalf, want to specify the consequences of every possible thing that could go wrong.

Erik Erikson, in his delineation of the eight developmental stages a person passes through from birth to elderly age, saw the emergence of a sense of basic trust as the central issue of an infant's first year of life; this sense, he said, is nothing less than the ontological source of faith and hope in a person. Development of trust is concentrated in the relationship between mother and child. The child has very little capacity to give, so trust is established by the trustworthiness of the mother to give to him, and she can do that, Erikson suggests, only if she is in a wholesome relationship to both her infant and her culture. This is not just a private transaction. The culture, and its degree of nurturing and reliability, is a participant in the process.

If the infant fails to develop trust, he falls into basic mistrust.

> One cannot know what happens in a baby, but direct observation as well as overwhelming clinical evidence indicate that early mistrust is accompanied by an experience of 'total' rage, with fantasies of the total domination or even destruction of the sources of pleasure and provision; and that such fantasies and rages live on in the individual and are revived in extreme states and situations.

Even in preschool years, trust comes to have a deep mutuality. It cannot endure unless a boy has an essential trustfulness of others and a matching sense of his own trustworthiness. One cannot survive without the other. No one gets through childhood without some disappointments in the quality or reliability of care received, so no boy is completely trusting; no one completes childhood without disappointing his family or others through some acts of dishonesty or irresponsibility, so no boy is completely trustworthy.

We fear for the welfare of any child who is completely trusting; his gullibility may make him too easily the victim of exploitation. But I fear that gullibility is not as often the plight of the child as is mistrust. Sadly, the landscape is littered with parents, particularly fathers, who are regarded by their sons with mistrust because of too many broken promises, missed appointments, failed expectations.

One way of nurturing trust is protecting the reliability and truthfulness of one's word in the sense conveyed by the phrase "keeping your word." When boys begin to experiment with telling little lies, the best approach, I believe, is not to try to stigmatize lying as bad, but to explain, with examples, that lying erodes trust. "What would you feel if I told you every night that your supper is ready, but when you came into the kitchen there was no food ready to eat? Pretty soon you wouldn't believe me. You need to know that I'm telling the truth, even if I'm tempted not to. I need to know that you're telling the truth, even if you're tempted not to."

Another way of instilling trust in a boy is to fulfill his basic material and emotional needs in a dependable way. This can lead to many possible disagreements as to what is "basic." Family meetings, beginning with preschoolers and lasting through teenage years, are almost indispensable opportunities for exploring how needs are being met or allegedly not met. Many children's requests based on their own emergent values that the parent may not share, are dismissed with the statement: "You don't need that." At least, the subject should be aired, reasons given, decisions explained. Parents should also articulate what they feel they need from their children materially (a few household responsibilities, perhaps) and emotionally. If parents don't express the need for emotional giving from their children, their children may not observe these needs on their own.

Boys very much need to learn early in childhood that incidents of lying and cheating are wrong, but that they are subject to repair and redemption. When deterrence is the main motive in dealing with academic cheating, redemption takes a back seat because the school authority wants the student to believe that he continues under a cloak of suspicion and mistrust.

A sense of basic trust may develop between siblings, but it isn't inevitable, given the desire of many children to protect fiercely their relationships with parents and therefore to see siblings as rivals. Boys may find it easier to develop basic trust with siblings when all have become adolescents or adults, and no longer feel as competitive with each other.

The sense of basic trust between mother and infant can, in childhood and later, be elaborated in a variety of relationships of varying moral value. When boys go off to school, opportunities exist both for trust between peers and trust between students and those teachers willing to be mentors. Now a boy can begin to develop trustful relations outside the family. In the course of his school years, a boy begins to see that various persons in his environment are making bids for mutual trust and that it is not easy to fulfill all of them. His parents may assume that the issue of trust is something to be worked out principally at home. His peers may be asserting the primacy of trust among classmates. His teachers will be asking for trustworthiness in his academic work and school behavior.

A boy will sometimes experience these claims as conflicting. Parents can help him to sort out these conflicting bids for trust, showing him that where there is conflict there is a moral problem to be solved; so, for example, a boy might maintain trust with his classmates but not to the extent of participating in academic cheating, because cheating would violate his trustworthiness with the teacher.

The existence of trust among peers does not guarantee that the group will pursue entirely admirable purposes. Boyhood and adolescent gangs value trust within the group very highly, and often ritualize its importance. The activities of a gang are usually a mixture of legitimate mutually supportive activities and antisocial activities. The biologically based aggressiveness of males can be elevated in a group of mutually trusting boys. Even on the playground, boys may bond in groups that treat other boys and girls badly. So trust will be invited in the service of a variety of pursuits, some of them laudable and some of them lamentable.

The great leap in trust possible in adolescence or later adulthood is for an individual to become trustworthy individually—even when it is not reciprocated. Trust has to be reciprocal in infancy or the infant develops basic mistrust. In childhood, trust is still basically reciprocal in the service of many ends of varying value. But an individual can decide to strive for general trustworthiness. Such an individual would choose not to cheat in financial matters, taxes, or professional responsibilities because he couldn't do so without breaking trust with someone, maybe someone he doesn't even know.

I believe males get to this highest level of trustworthiness only when they are inspired to it by encountering someone who embodies it. It is a level of character that is much more effectively caught than taught.

20

PLAY AND SPORTS

On a Saturday afternoon a few months ago, a visiting junior league football team of middle-school-age boys dealt a loss to a team from a suburb not more than twenty miles from where I live. The score was not close. The home team was winless for the season, which didn't improve the mood of the parents and other locals who had gathered to watch and to cheer if the game gave them any opportunity.

It seemed to the hometown crowd that the officiating was faulty. The head coach for the home team was ejected from the game for challenging a referee's decision. The local announcer broadcast obscenities directed at the officials over the public address system during the game, for which behavior he was barred from the announcer's booth for the remainder of the season.

In the parking lot after the game, there was a noisy confrontation between the teams and their followers. Bottles were thrown by the hometown crowd toward the visitors. Eventually, parents of the visiting team charged, the assistant coach of the home team deliberately accelerated his car toward a thirteen-year-old visiting player, forcing him to jump quickly aside to escape being hit. The local chief of police described the altercation as "stupid" and "inappropriate," but he also felt that the news media blew it out of proportion.

As we shall see, deciding what constitutes judicious proportion is not a simple matter where sports are concerned. But it isn't hard to find examples of the injudicious. Richard Lapchick of Northeastern University has told of going to see his twelve-year-old son's first hockey game. The son's team lost by one goal. After the game another of the fathers came into the locker room, yanked his son up off the bench where he was sitting, and yelled: "You fucking son of a bitch; if you'd hit that guy against the wall you wouldn't have lost this game."

What Is Play?

Before boys can walk, they display a capacity to play, and before they begin school they will be old enough in some communities to participate in organized sports. Their behavior will be scrutinized in reference to standards of behavior we refer to as sportsmanship. But what is play, and what are sports? The latter are perhaps easier to define: They are games of physical activity with rules that define the terms of engagement, the roles and limits on the players, and what players need to do to win.

A good definition of play can be found in a much quoted paper by Kenneth Rubin and his colleagues. They describe play as having five necessary characteristics. It is *intrinsically motivated*, pursued for the sheer satisfaction it offers. This aspect most distinguishes play from work, for even when work is intrinsically pleasurable, it is also extrinsically motivated: to earn income, to enhance status, to support a household, among other motivations. Certain activities, however, can begin as work and develop into play, and vice versa. The transition can occur in both directions, and a specific event may switch back and forth several times.

Play is also, by definition, *freely chosen* by the participants. Fergus Hughes, who has written incisively about play, recalls a first grader named Scott who had no interest in competitive sports but was pressured by both parents to join a school soccer team. The games caused Scott so much anxiety that he could scarcely eat his supper on the eve of a game. Even gentle pressure, Hughes believes, can move activity outside the realm of play.

Play must be *pleasurable*, or it isn't play. This criterion raises some difficult questions about group activities when what purports to be sport consists of someone enjoying making someone else miserable. Patricia Hersch observed some seventh-grade boys who play in the same kind of junior football league I mentioned at the beginning of the chapter:

> At the field, the kids bound out of the car, happy to see their teammates. They talk about the past weekend's game, where they crushed their opponent. Chris is still giddy with success: 'I got into a fight with a center and that was the best time I ever had—I was talking so much trash, we were crushing Springfield—the center started crying and he was swinging at my helmet with bare hands.' It's controlled violence, Chris and Brad explain. 'If you get run over, blocked or something like that, you want to get back. The same thing happened at Lake Braddock—I cut-blocked this guy and he said, "Come on, [obscenity], try again." So I did it again,' says Chris. 'That part of the game is fun to me,' adds Brad. 'I like the talking part, but at the end of the game you come together and you shake hands and say good job and that

resolves the problem. So in that period of time you can be mean and violent and dangerous. And then it's over.'

Is what Chris and Brad were doing—trash-talking to inflame an opponent and disrupt his concentration, which is common in professional, college, and high school sports, and cut-blocking, which is a type of block apt to injure an opponent's legs—the kind of pleasure that passes the standard of constituting play? Obviously male drives to establish dominance hierarchies and to test an opponent's response to physical aggression are an inevitable component in contact sports even when played by young boys, and in other sports as well.

But do we really want to say that an activity, even if it intentionally causes displeasure or injury to another player, is still play because it gives the inflicter pleasure? When a boy plays fairly to win, and succeeds, he may cause the loser displeasure, but that is somewhat incidental, and not inevitable, in a competitive game; it's possible to lose and feel satisfied if you've tried hard and been treated with respect by your opponent.

A fourth characteristic of play is its *symbolic* aspect. There is an element of make-believe. Another way of saying it is that play has a nonliteral aspect. Baking an actual cake may be fun, but it is work that happens to be fun; playing house and baking a pretend cake is play; building an imaginary house with Lego is play.

Finally, play has to be *actively engaged in* by a person—physically or psychologically or both. A boy who is indifferent to what he is doing and what is going on about him is not at play. By the same token, I suppose, a fan who is completely, vicariously caught up in watching a game might be thought of as being at play. He is stressing the symbolic aspect of the experience. He might be concentrating on who is winning, on rooting for someone, in which case his association with play is borderline; or he may be enjoying the skill of players, in which case his activity is more closely related to play. But watching is unlikely ever to be the equivalent of playing.

This five-part definition of play offers guidelines for understanding boys' activities. If a parent realizes that he is pressuring a son into participating in a sport, and the son clearly doesn't enjoy it and wouldn't pursue it without the pressure, the parent might be inspired to think: What is going on here? Is my son having any pleasure *playing* this game or is he being forced against all of his inclinations to *work* to realize his parents' dreams? Or a parent can use such a definition to gauge when an activity has ceased to be play, and tactful adult intervention might be in order.

Parents can also use this definition to monitor their own play with their children. That such play is important to a boy's development seems beyond doubt. Physical play, including what we call roughhousing, begins in early infancy, peaks in most children's experience between the ages of one and four, and diminishes gradually. My grandson Noah, a fledgling toddler, is very fond of a shortly-before-bedtime game of running and getting caught—quite a few times in a row. Several studies have shown that children rated as popular by their teachers are the most likely to have parents who have engaged in regular physical play with them. Children who are popular with their peers are more likely to engage in high levels of physical play with them, while rejected children seem to engage in physical play with more reluctance.

Hughes suggests that self-control is among the skills developed by boys in physical play with parents.

> Since play of this sort is usually intensely stimulating, the child is highly aroused, and, more importantly, the high arousal level must be sustained for the duration of the play. When the play is over, however, the child is admonished to 'settle down.' Thus the player learns to become intensely engaged with another person, to stay engaged, and to disengage when the activity comes to an end.

Hughes also believes this kind of activity may help a child to read the emotional states—happiness, fright, sadness, and so on—of others as they are expressed or mimed in play, and to express his own emotions effectively with facial expression and gesture.

Play is the most characteristic activity of children when they aren't eating or sleeping or doing assigned chores. It isn't all physically vigorous. Reading and being read to can be play. Conversation can be play. Playing a musical instrument can be play—should be play, unless the child feels pressured into it. As a boy matures, work intrudes more and more into his daily life; school is defined as a place of work interrupted by play periods. As folk wisdom puts it, "All work and no play makes Jack a dull boy," but most schoolboys think their play periods are too brief. The adult "workaholic" is a person who has allowed work to overwhelm his personal life to the virtual disappearance of play. Average folks try to find ways to interrupt work with moments of play; even crumpling paper into a ball and sending it to the wastebasket via an air hook worthy of Kareem qualifies as play.

Play, as defined above, is an appetite of lifelong significance for a healthy male. Many adult hobbies other than conventional sports can be forms of play—woodworking or gardening, for example. Sexual experience often involves times of play for the male who doesn't turn it into work, as is acknowledged in speaking of foreplay and afterplay. All work and no play makes Jack Senior a dull boy, too.

The Development of Play

Boys play long before organized sports come into their lives. My concern in this chapter is chiefly with the adolescent, but a few words are in order about the childhood activities that precede sports and sportsmanship. All of the issues apparent in adolescent sports have surfaced in rudimentary form much earlier in childhood.

Infants begin to play even in the first half-year of life. Students of child development have taken pains to distinguish the activity of play from the activity of exploration. Exploration comes first, logically. Perhaps early exploration is the precursor of what a person will eventually regard as work. When the environment is, at least in some ways, unfamiliar, the infant tries to figure it out. His attention is intense, his heartbeat steady, his demeanor serious and often somewhat cautious. His way of exploring an object he can grasp—smelling it, putting it in his mouth, rubbing it against his skin—can look almost ritualistic.

Play is more relaxed and joyful than exploration. The infant will continuously repeat activities such as sucking or grasping that give him pleasure; he will bang on his high chair in the latter half of his first year because it amuses him or it appears to amuse someone else, or both. He loves to put things into other things and take them out again. By the time he is a year old, he might turn a game of pushing aside a pillow to find the toy hidden under it into a game of simply repeatedly pushing aside the pillow—the means becomes an end in itself.

During his second year, a boy begins to show a preference to play with more than one object at a time; he begins to realize the proper function of objects—balls to be rolled or thrown, blocks to be stacked and knocked over; and he begins symbolic play—for example, using any available material or toy at hand as make-believe food to feed to his stuffed animal. In general, a boy's play will be more sophisticated when he is interacting with an adult than when he is playing alone.

Until a child is about twenty months of age, the mother is the principal adult playmate of American children. Parents in two-parent homes share play activities about equally for the next year; after that, fathers initiate more play periods with preschoolers than mothers do. Mothers spend more time with them, but the fathers specialize more in playtime. There is a culturally defined division of labor here, with mothers specializing in some aspects of child care and fathers specializing in other aspects, including play. Fathers do more roughhousing, and they also are more inclined to direct the child's play activities. Mothers are more likely than fathers to follow the child's lead and to emphasize the instructional possibilities in the child's play.

Research in Sweden and in an Israeli kibbutz did not show the mother-father differences observed in the United States, so these patterns are by no means universal. There is a point to emphasize here. Some writers on raising boys are currently emphasizing fathers' roles, especially in play, suggesting that there is a correlation between extensive father-involvement in a boy's upbringing and his later success academically and professionally. The implication of this is gloomy for boys raised by a single mother. The more likely truth is that boys thrive on certain play elements in their lives, including a lot of play that is physically active. If fathers don't provide it, others can, with comparable consequences for a boy's wellbeing. By "others" I mean mothers or hired child care or relatives, or older siblings who've been shown how to do it with proper supervision. A playmate, someone to play with regularly, is deeply meaningful for a child.

In the inclination of males to be directive in their play with children, we see a trend that we will come to later. It isn't females, predominantly, who have built the elaborately overorganized system of sports for boys in the United States, mimicking professional sports with uniforms, leagues, intricate scheduling, commercial sponsors, media coverage, maintenance of performance records, selection of all-stars, seasons leading to playoffs, and enormous emphasis on competitiveness and winning. While both fathers and mothers engage in their sons' competitions vicariously, it is mostly men who have imposed many of the extrinsic values of their occupations on what should be intrinsically pleasurable children's play, and who bear much of the responsibility for this invasion of childhood. I should add, however, that I have also seen mothers screeching in fury or triumph at ball games.

Two-year-olds have the advantage of greater mobility and language development. Still lacking fine motor skills, they may enjoy the look and feel of play materials more than the things they may create with them. Their most typical play is solitary, or else onlooker play in which they watch another child nearby.

Three-year-olds show that they are identifying with adults more than two-year-olds do. They are better able to wait their turn, share, and cooperate. They are becoming interested in making things they can show to others. To say it another way, two-year-olds are more interested in process, three-year-olds are becoming interested in results. Blocks aren't any longer just for stacking; they can be made by the three-year-old into buildings and bridges that loosely represent the actual world. There is an expansion of fantasy in their play and blurring of the distinction between fantasy and reality.

By the age of four, a boy's advancing fine motor skills usually affect his choice of playthings. His increasing sociability enables him to make quite elaborate plans with playmates for their play projects. Five-year-olds, having begun to show signs of logical thinking, reflect a stability in their play missing in most younger boys. Adults see them as more malleable and co-operative than younger boys, and they are more willing to share play materials and take turns with their peers. The expansion of fantasy in the three-year-olds is being countered with a move back to realism by the five-year-olds.

The social development of children's play was analyzed as early as the 1930s by Mildren Parten. As two-year-olds, she noted, children engage mostly in solitary play and onlooker play. When circumstances promote it, children of that and later ages will often display parallel play—children playing separately at the same activities in the same place and at the same time. Three-year-olds, to some extent, but four-year-olds even more, display associative play: Each child is doing his or her own thing, but there is sharing, lending of toys and materials, and taking turns. Four-year-olds begin to demonstrate cooperative play where two or more children engage in play in which participants have to fulfill complementary tasks toward a common goal. Once that begins most of the issues grouped under the umbrella of sportsmanship exist in recognizable form. Researchers today believe Parten underestimated the capacity of children as young as a year and a half to play cooperatively, and they don't attribute social immaturity to solitary play to the extent Parten did; but they still use her typology.

In sociodramatic play, older preschoolers often imitate the adults in their lives and unwittingly reveal a good deal of how they perceive their home lives. They express their urgent needs and also express impulses that might be frowned upon if expressed directly—aggression, for example, or curiosity about the human body as dramatized in "playing doctor." This kind of play also permits role reversal, as when a child who feels relatively helpless about something in real life may play a make-believe role with greater power in that situation.

Children tend to seek out same-sex playmates as early as age two. When playing with male peers, boys show more exploratory zeal, and they also are likely to engage in forms of play that are traditionally gender-typed. An argument can be made for encouraging a mixture of same-gender and cross-gender play, since the latter mitigates against gender stereotyping.

Play is a central part of group day care, with, studies show, mixed findings as to how beneficial the experience may be. The experience can stimulate social maturity in a boy, but it may also stimulate displays of aggression and resistance to adult direction. The degree of variation in quality from one day-care environment to another makes it difficult to generalize.

Similarly, exposure to television has a mixed effect on children's play. Excessive exposure to television can inhibit the quality of play of normally imaginative children; but children who are relatively unimaginative may be stimulated by watching the more intellectually stimulating children's programs such as *Mr. Rogers* and *Sesame Street.*

There is now little question that many boys—some very powerfully—are affected by violence on the television they watch. The average child in the United States between ages five and fifteen witnesses about 13,000 killings, most of them dramatized but occasionally an actual death. The effects of watching violence are both direct and indirect. More exposure leads to more violent behavior, to a greater tolerance of violence, to a view of the world as a mean and dangerous place where violence is warranted because it's normal. Boys with an early propensity to aggression feed on violence in the media and use it to organize and stimulate their behavior. The advent of interactive computer games does seem to represent a quantum leap beyond passively watching others commit mayhem and murder on the screen, because in many computer games the player becomes a participant in the unfolding action and commits dramatized violence himself. That is worrisome enough in public arcade machines but more sobering when one knows that millions of kids are playing in the privacy of their homes with parental consent.

Less than deserved attention is given, in my view, to the influence on boys of violence in televised sports. Dramatized violence within the story line of a film or comic book is usually set in a moral context, admittedly often in a simplistic way, but there is some attempt to justify the violence within the good guys/bad guys formulas. But sports violence doesn't have that context. Attempts to injure the opposing quarterback, hockey brawls, beanballs and dugout-emptying, spitting on officials, flagrant fouls in basketball, none of this has even a shred of moral justification. A sports contest is between our guys and the other guys, not between the good guys and the bad guys. Yet boys grow up watching their elders respond approvingly or indifferently to injuries to the "others" in broadcast sports.

One view prevalent in the United States is that aggressive contact sports such as professional football, hockey, and boxing act as a catharsis for the release of hostile energy by athletes and spectators, thus reducing incentives by the people caught up in them to revert to crime or domestic violence. But, as Myriam Miedzian points out in *Boys Will Be Boys*, "An exhaustive study of heavyweight prizefights held between 1973 and 1978 and subsequent homicide statistics revealed that U.S. homicides increased by 12.46 percent directly after heavyweight championship prizefights. The increase was greatest after heavily publicized prizefights."

The philosopher Sissela Bok takes the analysis a step further in her recent book *Mayhem: Violence as Public Entertainment.* The long tradition
of cathartic spectator violence, she notes with bloody examples, extends
back to the Roman amphitheater where violence was used to entertain
and also to encourage in spectators an acceptance of official violence in
the conquests and administration of the empire.

No one today is nailed to a crucifix and mauled by a Caledonian bear
before a screaming throng. Yet the effect of viewing violence in organized
sports may still encourage the expression and acceptance of violence in
other forms. We risk boys' making use of violence in contexts other than
sport: toward intimates, and in antisocial acts committed by individuals
or groups. Violence, I'm afraid, does appear to breed violence, and the
forum in which it is most frequently bred outside the home is on the field
of sport.

The games of the schoolboy with their often elaborate rules become
fiercely competitive. It isn't quite enough to play for the thrill of the action. The point is also to win. Some psychologists believe that these competitive activities fail to qualify as play as defined at the beginning of this
chapter, and that play as an activity declines swiftly in boys' lives once
competitive games with rules establish dominance in free activity time. It
is true that competition and the goal of winning introduce an (often ru-
inous) extrinsic element into these activities, but it is also true that these
activities have many moments in which all of the defining elements of
play appear to be in effect. Still, the aggressive behavior and tension generated by the drive to win spoil the experience for many boys. The National Alliance for Youth Sports says that 45 percent of children have been
called names and insulted while playing sports (the number may be low,
judging from the anecdotes I have already offered) and that 70 percent of
children have stopped playing competitive sports by age thirteen because
all the fun has gone out of it.

Boys' play, Stanley Greenspan points out in *Playground Politics*, is often
more assertive and competitive than girls', and boys are encouraged by
their parents to win, and sometimes kidded or chastised if they fail.
Greenspan gives a nice example:

> Eight-year-old Michael and his dad are each racing a remote-control car.
> The competition is fierce. Each competitor is trying to navigate his car
> around the couch and under chairs to the finish line. Michael's car crosses
> the finish line first. Dad says, 'You beat me. You're the winner!' and claps
> loudly at Michael's victory.
>
>   On the other hand, Dad and Michael's 10-year-old sister, Ashley, are play-
> ing Junior Scrabble. Ashley has been getting lots of pieces, and she has

spelled out more words than her father. But Dad downplays Ashley's interest in competing and winning.

'Dad, I spelled out six more words than you!' Ashley says excitedly.

'Those are good words, honey,' Dad says calmly.

'But I beat you!' Ashley says in frustration.

'Honey,' says Dad, 'that's very nice, but remember, it's just a game.'

The function of play changes in fundamental ways from the preadolescent to the adolescent. While the schoolboy was intensely preoccupied with belonging to a peer group, the adolescent begins to single out other individuals with whom to develop close friendships. In these relationships, communication is valued and practiced. Mere preference for the same play activities isn't as sufficient a basis for friendship as it once was; adolescents are looking for complementary personalities.

So for the adolescent play begins to be less structured than it was for the preadolescent. Much of it consists of "hanging out" together, watching television and videos, listening to music, going to dances and parties. There is decreased interest in games with rules. There is a gradual decrease in the number of different play activities engaged in per week. Having a good time becomes less defined as *doing* something with friends, more defined as *being* together, enjoying time of one's own.

Organized team sports continue to enjoy intense commitment among adolescent males, but for a declining number of them. As the more athletically talented are selected and rewarded with status and recognition, the less talented or committed drop out. Yet another way to look at the decline in numbers of males committed to organized sports is that they have turned to activities, as I've just indicated, that promote less structured hanging out with more intense relationships as the goal.

Organized Sports

From early childhood through middle childhood to adolescence, organized sports play a role in the lives of many children, having increased in popularity among children decade by decade in recent history. Thirty million school-age children participate in organized sports in the United States. They play twenty-five different kinds of sports, directed by a volunteer army of 4.5 million coaches and 1.5 million administrators. Four-year-olds can sign up for midget hockey, six-year-olds for Little League baseball. Eleven- and twelve-year-olds often spend 40 percent of their free activity time engaged in organized sports.

For boys, organized sports offer plenty of instruction, comparatively high quality equipment, community recognition, institutionalized self-esteem for those who do well, and a ready-made social group. In communities where boyhood sports are very highly organized, a boy may feel that he has little choice but to participate if he wants to feel deeply attached to his peers; everyone he wants to pal around with is playing team sports. Parents often view these activities as ways of keeping boys' free time occupied so they won't get into trouble inventing activities on their own.

Coaches and parents often assert that participation in organized sports contributes to self-esteem, particularly among boys who are more likely than girls to define themselves in terms of athletic accomplishment. Not unexpectedly, several researchers have found a positive relationship between successful athletic participation and a child's self-esteem *as an athlete*. But rather than thinking of a boy as having a single global self, it is probably more appropriate to think of a set of self-images. His self-image as an athlete may be high based on his successful participation in the local soccer or football league, but this self-confidence may not be equaled by his self-image as a student or as a member of his class or family. However, it is also true that athletic achievement in organized sports rewards more boys with community recognition than any other activity, and that star athletes enjoy as high, or higher, status among peers as any other adolescent group.

Does participation in organized sports contribute, as is often claimed, to a boy's character by promoting such values as former United States Senator and New York Knickerbocker forward Bill Bradley recently enumerated in *Values of the Game*: passion, discipline, selflessness, respect, perspective, courage, leadership, responsibility, resilience, and imagination? Brenda Bredemeier and David Shields interviewed high school and college students—some of them athletes, some not—asking them to comment on the moral dimension of athletic and nonathletic situations. For example, they asked what the interviewee thought a football player should do if asked by his coach to try to injure a key player on another team.

What the researchers found was that both athletes and nonathletes believed a different and lower set of moral principles applied to sporting events than applied to ordinary everyday events. There was a high level of agreement that in everyday life one should try to be considerate, but in sports, because of the emphasis on winning, one needn't be very concerned about others. They found, as Hughes reports, that: "People who have the greatest interest in highly aggressive contact sports, or have participated in them for the longest amounts of time, tend to score lower on tests of moral reasoning. . . . Athletes who do earn high moral reasoning scores are the least willing to display hostile aggression during a game."

Michael Messner, a sociologist, once interviewed Jack Tatum, an Oakland Raiders linebacker whose tackle in one game broke Darryl Stingley's neck, leaving him paralyzed. "When I first started playing," Tatum told Messner, "if I would hit a guy hard and he wouldn't get up, it would bother me. (But) when I was a sophomore in high school, first game, I knocked out two quarterbacks, and people loved it. The coach loved it. Everybody loved it."

In boys' organized sports, coaches have immense influence. As Michael Oriard, who played football through school years and then for Notre Dame and the Kansas City Chiefs reported, "From the fourth grade into my first year as a professional, I was to look to my coaches as figures of wisdom and authority whose pronouncements were gospel and whose expectations of me were to be met at whatever cost." The coaches are teachers and strategists, but just as much they are motivators; some use rather bizarre methods to provoke the level of enthusiasm they desire in a team. A high school coach in Wisconsin gave a "Hit of the Week" award to the player who appeared from analysis of game films to have made the most vicious hit on an opposing football player. Another coach from Iowa painted a chicken gold to represent the rival "Golden Eagles" and had his team kick it around the field to "get the Eagle."

A phenomenon referred to as "doubling" often takes place in organized sports whereby the players conform to a frame of mind and a moral code imposed by an authoritarian coach. The players have implicitly abandoned responsibility for their own actions to the direction of coaches and public sentiment. Thus a player who in ordinary situations is well-mannered and friendly may become extremely aggressive and callous about inflicting injuries when he is within the team culture.

Part of the equation is that the player is also supposed to be indifferent to his own injuries; but he may remain anxious about being injured himself. The sight of football players kneeling together in prayer in a stadium after a game in which they have often tried to injure others suggests the irony that afflicts sports where competitive values have overwhelmed other values. One lineman in the 1999 Super Bowl, Denver Broncos guard Mark Schlereth, has had twenty-two operations for sports injuries—seventeen times on his knees—and will have a twenty-third a week after the game. "No doctor in his right mind would ever pass me for a physical if his job were on the line," Mark says, "but this is the NFL. If they want you to pass the physical, you will pass the physical." In fact, some teams have given him physicals and turned him down based on the findings. But one of the best teams signed him. He can't bend over to putt a golf ball, and he can't crawl on the floor to play with his kids, but he's still going to put his body on the line in the Super Bowl.

Brenda Bredemeier measured the attitudes of high school and college basketball players toward intentionally hurting their opponents on the court. Boys more than girls were inclined to endorse such acts, and older, experienced athletes more than novices.

Something akin to "doubling" also occurs between players or teams, and officials. Officials are as human as players. Players seldom perform without error in contests, and officials make mistakes of judgment and observation. But more and more, teams cede all moral responsibility to the officials. If officials make errors that everyone acknowledges, few players or coaches from the side that has benefited volunteer to correct the situation. It is usually considered the prerogative of the players in officiated contests to accept as unearned blessings the benefits of officiating errors. In many sports it is the habit of players and coaches who believe an official has made an error to their disadvantage to react in extravagant accusatory fashion.

Failure to display aggressiveness and self-abandonment desired by coaches and teammates subjects adolescent athletes frequently to suggestions that they are feminine or homosexual. Ira Berkow once reported in the *New York Times* that the men's basketball coach at the University of Indiana Bobby Knight "put a box of sanitary napkins in the locker of one of his players so that the player would get the point that Knight considered him less than masculine." Dave Meggyesy, a former football player, says "this sort of attack on a player's manhood is a coach's doomsday weapon. And it almost always works, for the players have wrapped up their identity in their masculinity, which is eternally precarious for it not only depends on not exhibiting fear of any kind on the playing field, but is also something that can be given and withdrawn by a coach at his pleasure." Without doubt, this denigration of the feminine contributes to the potential for male athletes to be manipulative and exploitative in their relationships with real females.

The Decline of Play

The intrinsic delight of play certainly has been overwhelmed by extrinsic considerations in much of the organized sports we see for boys in the United States. As collegiate and professional sports have become an ever larger entertainment industry, swamping amateurism or making it a subsidized sham in sport after sport, organized sports have become talent selection systems feeding the ranks of high school and college teams and rosters as a prelude to the eventual recognition of the small number of players who will prosper in professional competitions. The premise is statistical. The more boys that try to master a given sport, the more likely it is that those with superior natural talent and trainability will be identified. Even given as large a pool of children as the United States has to draw upon, there remain sports in which American athletes consistently do poorly in international competition compared to athletes from much smaller countries where those sports are emphasized.

Organized sports make those who fail at the early levels feel unwarrantedly discouraged, and it makes many of those who succeed exaggeratedly self-regarding. The system is very steeply pyramidal in every sport. Few of the elementary, middle school, and high school "stars" will excel in collegiate sports, and few of those who play college varsity sports will find a professional career awaiting them.

Clearly organized sports excite the upward social mobility strivings of many families who see athletic prowess in their sons as a talent that will pull the entire family into greater prominence and security. The values that are being reinforced in organized sports are not so much the traditional values of "sportsmanship" but the core values of a society that has made sports into a business: individual competitiveness; a facade of self-confidence; the demonstration of earnest effort; a provisional willingness to bear pain and injury for the greater good of the company, yet an apprehension that loyalty is pretty much a one-way street, not to be reciprocated if the company loses confidence in the value of the individual; indifference to those who lose out in competition; willingness to be aggressive and to injure others in the interests of one's team.

Dave Meggyesy puts the best possible face on it when he says that "football represents the core values of the status quo, and coaches and school administrators want players to win adherence to these values, not only on the football field but also in their private lives." But it is hardly surprising that for every Bill Bradley there are several prominent athletes being prosecuted for drug violations and sexual assaults, being pursued, despite seven-figure salaries, for nonpayment of alimony and child support or in paternity suits. Beyond the misbehavior of individual athletes there lies an undercurrent of corruption among the administrators and officials of organized sports. The recent Olympics scandals show how this reaches to the top echelons.

An observer can't help but note the irony that the sports into which most boys are organized are not, by and large, the games they will play as adults. They are organized in largest numbers into baseball, football, soccer, hockey, and basketball. As adults they will watch these games in large numbers, but they won't play them. And not just because they've lost the physical skills to play them enjoyably. I suspect they don't play adult basketball and baseball because such games were ruined for them as kids. They remember them as tense and conflictual, so they trade them in for golf, hiking, jogging, swimming, fishing—trying to recover activities that might be playful for them.

In my own childhood and youth, I played far more music than sports. But I asked a contemporary of mine what he remembered of the games of our summers and after-schools and weekends. Here is what, in essence, he said: What organized sports has substantially displaced was an informal network of neighborhood or interneighborhood activities that boys organized themselves. What we used to call "pickup games." The old way offered less instruction, and the equipment was less adequate, so boys had to invent game sites in yards and streets and share equipment. There was little, if any, community recognition outside the group and their families. No status, but plenty of fun. We'd play until we were tired, and then we'd sit around and talk, and then maybe get up and play some more.

Since neighborhood sports were self-governed, boys themselves dealt with all the issues of fair play, and I have no doubt that the process was more educational from a character standpoint than many boys find in organized sports today. Leaders always emerged. They were the ones whom everyone expected to be in charge of a side or team, and to choose its members. Leaders were always among the best players but weren't necessarily the very best; they were, however, natural leaders whose influence we instinctively recognized and honored. Rules were kept as simple as possible because the players had to interpret and implement them, and no one wanted a game to break down over a rules controversy. There were arguments about how specific plays were to be governed by the rules—heated arguments at times—but everyone knew the process had to come to consensus.

Boys who didn't fit in were gradually excluded until they came to understand what stood between them and inclusion, and made an accommodation acceptable to the other boys. Generally it wasn't talent or the lack thereof that kept anyone on the sidelines. I don't remember any boys getting excluded because they were untalented. Anyone who played with obvious intent to injure others was eased out. Chronic whiners were eased out because the games were meant to be fun, and a good whiner could take the euphoria out of a game very rapidly.

The best games were those with evenly matched sides and close scores; then everyone felt good at the end, because with a lucky break here or there the game could credibly have gone the other way. If a game got one-sided, it usually ended sooner because it ceased to be enough fun. Left to their own devices, boys can develop impressive neighborhood conventions of sportsmanship.

Sportsmanship

In my conversations with boys, sports came up over and over again. In Chapter 18, I referred to Brett. His yard and the street outside the fence were full of his contemporaries who had come over to play when I arrived to talk with him and his single mother. Talking with him reminded me of the patterns of my childhood. Some days the kids (mostly boys, but—unlike my childhood days—also some girls who like sports) congregate at Brett's house, other days at the home of another member of the crowd.

Neighborhood play needs parental attention and involvement that organized sports delegate to coaches and managers. The logistics of organized sports lead to a lot of parents standing on the sidelines watching others work with their kids, waiting to take them home again. I saw a fine kind of parent-child interaction when I visited Evan and his mother. She is a single mother who works, so Evan, an only child in early adolescence, usually gets home a couple of hours before his mother; he immediately checks in with her by telephone.

One of their main sports issues is the trampoline in the backyard. The rule Margaret and Evan have agreed to is that no one uses the trampoline unless she is at home. Another rule is that other kids can't come into the house to play while his mother is at work. Evan volunteered that the issue is one of safety. "Do your friends ever want to jump on the trampoline when your mother is at work?" I asked him. "Yeah," he replied. "One guy keeps asking and asking, and he gets mad, but I keep saying no. Sometimes he waits until my mom arrives, and then he wants me to ask permission right away; and I tell him to let her have a breather." (Evan and his mother, incidentally, are right to be concerned. Trampolines caused 249,000 accidents, and the annual frequency of injury doubled, between 1990 and 1995; they are now among the leading causes of childhood injury.) Evan and Margaret also appreciate what he has gained from his relationships with coaches in organized sports. "One of my coaches," Evan says, "was always encouraging when people made mistakes. He'd say things like 'We'll get them next time' and 'You can do it.'"

The values that we associate with sportsmanship—including the thoughtfulness and regard for safety articulated by Evan—are inestimably valuable aspects of male character. They imply attainment of an admirable civility or courteousness, regard both for rules and for the welfare of everyone playing the game, self-control when something upsetting or frustrating has occurred, a capacity to win without overvaluing the victory, and to lose without taking it overly to heart, and a sense of proportion that focuses much of the time on the sheer pleasure of the game.

The question is: Where does sportsmanship come from? Bill Bradley suggests that the several values we refer to collectively as sportsmanship come from the game itself. He played collegiate basketball at Princeton where, with luck, there might be a player with potential to star as a professional once in a decade or a generation. What Princeton had was a remarkable coach, Pete Carril, who taught his intelligent squad to play a very deliberate, controlled style that enabled them to perform well against—and often beat—teams with much more natural talent but far less discipline. In his years with the New York Knicks, Bradley played with a similarly intelligent and disciplined team. Times change, however, and his old team, the Knicks, have been negotiating, while I've been writing this chapter, a contract with a professional player of undisputed talent who has been under suspension for several months for assaulting the coach of his former team during a practice session, choking him and threatening to kill him.

The chapter on responsibility in Bradley's *Values of the Game* has the subtitle, "No Excuses—None." It is an interesting tack because sports post-mortems are as rife with lame excuses as those in any other kind of human endeavor; and the ability to take responsibility for one's actions when they haven't turned out well is a benchmark of character. Bradley gave an example from which he drew the subtitle of the chapter.

> The coach who gets across the importance of punctuality introduces order into many a young life. . . . On Red Holzman's teams, there were few rules, but they were rigid. His attitude was 'No excuses—none!' If you weren't on the bus at the designated time, it left without you. If you didn't make the plane, you paid your own way. If you were late for practice, even two minutes late, you were fined. The result was that most of us turned up early. Even if you were late because of circumstances clearly beyond your control, you got no sympathy or credit. 'Sure, Bill, I know your mother's cousin called with an emergency that your mother's nephew couldn't take care of,' Holzman used to say, 'and it rained on the highway and made it slick, after the earthquake damaged the bridge, but still you're fined.' He smiled and I paid up.

To me, the example doesn't point the way to exemplary character at all. This is not what taking responsibility or refusing to make excuses for oneself is about.

Bradley recalls a rule for which no exception was ever granted—a rule that was worthwhile but hardly worth making into the eleventh commandment: Thou shalt be punctual. Suppose, to underline the shallowness and rigidity of the rule, we turn the story around and have Bill Bradley, arriving punctually for practice, report to Holzman, "Boy, the roads were a sheet of ice this morning and I had no tread on my tires. I drove seventy miles an hour to get here, spun out twice, ran three cars off the road and roared past an accident where it looked like they needed some help. But I got here on time." And Red Holzman smiles and says, "That's my boy."

The values of sportsmanship—including a suppleness to make wise choices in demanding circumstances—are values that boys bring to sports as much as, or more than, they learn from sports. The characterological difference between a Bill Bradley and a Latrell Sprewell, the choker traded to the Knicks, was established long before either got a contract to play professional basketball, or even college ball.

The development of these values begins in the first years of a boy's life as his play is influenced by interaction with his parents and other adults, and with siblings. Those first experiences in the delight of play, accompanied by the inevitable tensions of sharing and cooperating with others, stand behind a boy as he begins to participate in schoolyard play with a peer group. There such factors as dominance hierarchies, individual aggressiveness, and group prejudices continually threaten the integrity of play as we've defined it in this chapter. Sportsmanship, in a sense, consists of a set of values and techniques to keep human nastiness from ruining play.

The ambiguity of organized sports for boys is that they often confusingly support both sides of the equation. Sportsmanship is always given lip service in youth sports, and often there is some substance to it; but at the same time there is support for nastiness: overaggressiveness, demonizing the opponent, deliberately injuring others, taking foolish risks, and exaggerating the significance of winning. Each boy can assimilate what pleases him. If a boy demonstrates superior talent in organized sports, but also displays behavior that is offensive, his behavior is sometimes tolerated in order to keep his talent available to the team.

For these reasons, I view sportsmanship as something a boy more likely brings to the sport than vice versa. Sports can support the development of a boy's character, or they can degrade it. Because of the prominence of athletes in the social hierarchies of teenagers, and the number of young male athletes who offend against others, girls in particular, I think we need to impose some rules about who is allowed to play in organized sports.

Any serious antisocial behavior should prompt a serious and careful review of a boy's suitability for what has to be seen as an unelected leadership position. If his values and choices suggest that he will use his prestige and power to exploit others, he should probably be barred from organized sports until, through a process of education, noncompetitive athletics, community service, and counseling, he is able to demonstrate values of respect and fairness that would serve him well under the stress of competition. Drawing him into organized sports as a rehabilitative gesture because he will learn "sportsmanship" there places unwarranted expectations on those sports. The exemplary coach certainly exists who can take a troubled boy and guide him into a U-turn. But I believe there are many other coaches who will exacerbate the flaws.

The particular relevance of sportsmanship to adolescence is that boys are working then on their own identity, refining the values they will carry into adulthood. Only a minority are still playing organized sports in late adolescence. For this minority, the experience may not even be of neutral value in their moral development—it may actually impede moral development. What remains of crucial value for every adolescent boy is that he makes time for play that nurtures closeness, communication, self-reflection, the euphoria triggered by physical exertion, dreaming, and sheer, unbridled pleasure.

21

Giving Back

In 1994 the environmental club at a high school in Wheaton, Illinois, began transforming sixty acres of land near the school to be prairie again. The school provided funding for materials, the right grasses and wildflowers, and the students provided the labor. In biology classes the students had learned that only a tenth of 1 percent of the land remained natural prairie in their state, which had once been largely prairie. The students hoped that wildlife would be drawn to the sixty-acre plot when prairie vegetation was restored. Some neighbors objected that wildlife would bring disease, and dissenting students at the high school thought the funds should be put to different and, in their eyes, better use; but the club persisted, and within a year a similar prairie restoration project was initiated at the public school in a nearby town.

About the same time a young student at the University of Pennsylvania, Brian Fan, was founding Penn Musicians Against Homelessness, a consortium of student musicians who played classical music concerts and donated the proceeds to local charities benefiting the poor. From raising money the consortium expanded its activities to include hands-on renovating of low-income family houses and giving free instrumental music lessons to underprivileged kids.

Idealism

In a book edited by John Bartlett for student activists telling them how to organize, plan, and proceed effectively, I noted that most of the stories, including the foregoing two, were of activities explicitly or implicitly critical of the larger society of adults and their stewardship of the world. Most projects dealt with environmental issues or the ramifications of poverty and powerlessness. You aren't taking proper care of the Earth, these pro-

jects say, and you aren't taking proper care of the people of the Earth. •
Some of the projects were more "in your face" than others, but they all
were meant to rally adolescents in behalf of good causes and, often,
against the forces that made the cause necessary. Thus they put many
adult onlookers in the quandary of being at once admiring of the idealism
and defensive about its prophetic sting. The accusatory aspect of adolescent idealism doesn't distinguish it from adult idealism, of which, thank
goodness, some remains alive and well. But other adults don't dismiss
adult idealists as cavalierly as they often dismiss adolescents, though they
do sometimes accuse adult idealists of never having "grown up" (growing
up, in this context, means adopting varying degrees of "realism" and cynicism about what is feasible). In any case, adults need to be aware of the
attitudes, defensive and dismissive as well as celebratory, that they bring to
the subject of youthful idealism.

Teenage idealism doesn't get as much press as teenage misbehavior, and
there may not be quite as many idealistic enterprises as misbehaviors, but
there is an impressive amount of the former. Yet the subject of youthful
idealism can't be written up, or written off, with some applause and the
hope that there should be more of it. Even idealism has its skeptics among
prominent theoreticians of human personality.

Anna Freud wrote to Robert Coles in 1972 warning against what she believed was a habit "to idealize idealism in the young" of that time. Her appraisal flies in the face of the view many of us had and have that the
idealism of the 1960s and early seventies made it a brighter and more spir-
ited time, though not without its disappointments and tragedies. Don't we
who were there remember the decade as remarkably different from the
comparative mean-spiritedness and individualistic materialism of the
1990s? By the late 1960s, however, the hopeful enthusiasm of the decade
was in retreat. The Great Society initiatives in civil rights, education, and
human welfare were about to dissolve in corrosive disagreements about
foreign policy.

Freud's questioning of the integrity of the 1960s was consistent with her
much-quoted summary of adolescence in her most influential book, *The
Ego and the Mechanisms of Defense*:

> Adolescents are excessively egoistic, regarding themselves as the center of the
> universe and the sole object of interest, and yet at no time in later life are
> they capable of so much self-sacrifice and devotion. They form the most
> passionate love relations, only to break them off as abruptly as they began
> them. On the one hand, they throw themselves enthusiastically into the life
> of the community and, on the other, they have an overpowering longing for

solitude. They oscillate between blind submission to some self-chosen leader and defiant rebellion against any and every authority. They are selfish and materially minded and at the same time full of lofty idealism. They are ascetic but will suddenly plunge into instinctual indulgence of the most primitive character. At times their behavior to other people is rough and inconsiderate, yet they themselves are extremely touchy. Their moods veer between light-hearted optimism and the blackest pessimism. Sometimes they will work with indefatigable enthusiasm and at other times they are sluggish and apathetic.

The mind loves these deft plays of opposites, perhaps because we know that all our personalities contain opposing elements that we can't entirely reconcile. There is something insightful that she is writing, and yet there is also exaggeration in it, even caricature. The oppositional elements she has noted in the adolescent aren't necessarily more dramatic than the range of behavior one can note in younger children or in adults. Her portrait, to the extent it holds up, does so only in general.

My contemporaries exhibited the contrasting attributes of selfish materialism and lofty idealism as adolescents, but both were not usually prominent in the same kids. Some of my peers were very attached to their own possessions and security, then and now; others were idealistic then, and many of them have retained a significant amount of idealism as we live through our fifties together. To be sure, the wholehearted adult idealists I know today have a depth of sensibility well beyond the reach of less experienced adolescents.

On the whole, fewer of my contemporaries during adolescence developed as strong an adherence to some authority (political or religious) as many of them have developed in adulthood. I wish I could say that being rude and inconsiderate to others, but touchy about oneself, was a specialty of adolescents, but I have seen it manifest in too many younger children and adults to think it other than a widespread human characteristic.

My sense of caution about generalizations isn't meant to dismiss every comparative statement. Even assuming egotism as a human phenomenon from childhood to senior citizenship, there may be variations by age groups. Fergus Hughes has described two characteristics specific to adolescent egocentrism. One goes by the name of "imaginary audience," by which is meant that the exquisite self-consciousness of teenagers derives partly from their notion that everyone is watching them, and partly from their tendency to think that what is of personal interest to them must certainly be of equal interest to others.

Adolescents are often shocked to discover that their passion for a particular cause is not shared by other people; in fact, most people may be totally indifferent to an issue that an adolescent may be ready to die for. . . . Adults are likely to realize that their interest in themselves is probably not shared by others. Adolescents often feel that other people are as interested in them as they are in themselves.

Hughes's other aspect of adolescent egocentrism is known as "the personal fable." It refers to "the belief that one is unique and that no one could possibly share or understand one's thoughts and feelings." Both these aspects reflect the relative isolation of the adolescent from the sensibilities of adults. A certain naïveté among adolescents is inevitable and, so long as it is not exploited—for example, adolescent female egocentrism sexually exploited by older males—it is not undesirable. The freshness and crispness one finds in adolescent viewpoints is due in part to the fact that adolescents haven't been fully exposed to all the challenges and disillusionments awaiting them in the adult world. As Hughes notes, their misperception of uniqueness sometimes makes adolescents, believing themselves impervious to danger, take risks that many older people would shy away from; and in this respect they need to be protected from their impulses. But otherwise adolescent egocentrism is something for parents to take into consideration but not try to tear down just because it is sometimes unrealistic.

The terrible burden idealism has to carry is that many people believe it either has to be pure or else it is worthless. If the motives or strategies of the idealist can be shown to be in any way impure, then the idealist's project can be dismissed; or so many critics maintain. How did this very extreme definition of idealism infect the thinking even of Anna Freud? Perhaps our very concept of idealism is formed at the age when it first flourishes, in adolescence. That would account for the lack of acknowledgment of ambiguity in much discussion of idealism, despite the fact that there is virtually nothing in human experience that is free of ambiguity.

Because the discussion of idealism is so freighted with perfectionism, I want to introduce a substitute term, "giving back." At the beginning of his life, a boy is completely dependent on what others are doing for him. His principal mode is receiving. There is an exchange of sorts in most cases between him and his family, because he gives pleasure just by being. His parents feel rewarded simply to have a child.

But over the course of his life, a boy with strong character will sooner or later confront the question of when he is going to begin to give back in return for all he has received. Understanding the concept of giving back begins when a boy learns how to participate in caring for himself and his family. In childhood he may begin to give back through such means as performance of household chores, but if these are assigned rather than volunteered it is likely that a boy will come to associate being "responsible" with being "dutiful." Many parents assign chores as a way of promoting responsibility, rather than teaching the underlying meaning of responsibility: giving back. I haven't met many boys who regard chores with gratitude—"Gee, Mom, can I take out more garbage?" A fair number of boys negotiate agreements with parents whereby their chores are paid for, lessening the sense that anything is being voluntarily contributed to the functioning of the household, and furthering the notion that any act should provide a financial benefit rather than a social one.

Adolescence is the first phase of life when most boys have to confront seriously the question of what they want to make of their lives and why. One of the icons of this process is the fabled "personal essay" that many colleges require of high school students as part of the application process. Who are you? the applications ask. Why should we choose you over someone else to be a student here? These would be challenging questions at any age.

Taking Care

Well before adolescence and the necessity to write my own personal essay, I faced a family situation that raised questions of how much responsibility I could shoulder within my family. My earliest memory of my mother is of her flaming red hair, ever the beacon for a toddler to locate her in a crowd. I know now that I was fortunate to have all of my preschool years with my mother before she had her first episode of mental illness. She was a devoted and affectionate mother, so we had a basis of well-demonstrated mutual love before she began to withdraw into self-preoccupation. Between bouts of illness she continued to be a loving mother. My wife, Carolyn, has found in her work as a clinical psychologist that some children can be burdened with extremely difficult situations at home, but if there is just one person—not necessarily even a member of the child's immediate family—who openly adores the child, a resilience inside the child to cope can be built on that single saving relationship; it may enable the child to have a more positive than despairing view of life. My mother was part of the situation asking me as a child to give back, but she was also the adoring adult during my early childhood.

The depth of my mother's despair when she was ill, and the way she made my father the principal target of her anger, was more than he could

handle. As is true of many men, he took flight from an angry woman instead of working through the anger to some level of understanding. All of
our relatives lived at least an hour away by car, so our relations with them
atrophied. We were on our own, and my father was distancing himself
emotionally from my mother's chronic illness and her moods.

What psychologists refer to as "parentification" developed at the center
of my outlook as a young schoolboy. I felt deeply responsible, as a parent
would, for the care of my brother and sister. I believe it made a lasting difference that I took on this parental (with many elements of "mothering")
role as a boy. I bore up, doing much of the household management in the
stoic manner boys were supposed to assume toward duty, and seldom
complained. But I also felt overwhelmed; no one was checking on my feelings when my mother was incapacitated. The balance of giving and receiving had shifted far more toward giving than is typical of the childhood
of many boys. Parental support and encouragement was unpredictable in
my life, and I was trying to do what was expected of me, yet often feeling
inadequate.

I came from a conventional family of the 1940s. Most of the nurturing
of children of both genders was done by females. Most of the child sitters
were females. Most of the schoolteachers who took over daytime management of boys' lives at age six were females. Boys grew up expecting that females would provide for most of their needs. No boy's needs get answered
completely or all of the time, but on balance boys learned to turn to
women with expectation of a positive and generous response.

This relationship between boys and nurturing females might be expected to yield boys who are comfortable with females as they grew up.
But one has to take into account that ours is a gender-polarizing culture.
While boys were being nurtured by females, they also were being taught
that males are very different from females. Boys of my generation saw
plenty of evidence that females were responsible for boys' happiness, but
they were also being set up to conclude that females were perhaps responsible for any unhappiness they felt.

My father chose to distance himself from my mother, but many of his
male contemporaries were aggressive toward females in their households.
A paramount issue in raising boys today is finding ways to prevent their
growing up disposed to treat females, even the caring women in their
lives, badly. Some males never feel called to *give back* the nurturance they
have received from females. Instead, many take out on women all the frustrations they feel from a host of sources.

My own situation, as that of many boys in homes with illness or hard-
ships suffered by their mothers, helped me avoid the mindset of many
men that women exist principally to tend to males' needs.

What Motivates Idealism?

The way I thought of my family responsibilities changed when I became an adolescent. Then it was more: How can I balance my responsibility to take care of my family with my responsibility to myself and my independence? Can I ever become independent if I have to raise my younger siblings and care for an ailing mother without much help from an ever more detached father? The need to deal with my own identity formation was running headlong into my seemingly never ending family responsibilities.

Fortunately for the family, I went to college in New Haven, Connecticut, only about forty miles from our family home in Mount Vernon, New York. It was relatively easy to go back and forth, and I did so countless times. My senior research project at Yale on jazz piano style was not completed (though I had done enough to satisfy my professors) until several years after I graduated because my mother suffered another hospitalization that year, and by then I was handling such arrangements for her myself.

Looking back at that period and at my undergraduate decision to major in my first passion, music, but to take all the courses required for eligibility for medical school, I see that my idealism wasn't grounded in general philosophical principles or global observations, but in very specific intentions. My sense of inadequacy in being able to care for my mother played a very central role in my decision to study medicine. As a physician, conceivably, I could help her more than I had been able to assist her when I was a child and adolescent. In medical school, I noted that the motivation of many of my classmates seemed to be grounded in health crises in their particular family histories. I also observed that many of my classmates exhibited no idealism or sense of giving back at all. Medicine for them was being on the take; they were determined to acquire the status and income and other perks promised for doctors; they are practicing today alongside their (imperfect) idealistic classmates.

Idealism, like other character strengths we treasure and foster in ourselves, is in dynamic tension within us with its very opposites. And under stress, we are vulnerable to become the very opposite of what we aspire to.

In *The Ego and the Mechanisms of Defense*, Anna Freud says "it remains an open question whether there is such a thing as a genuinely altruistic relation to one's fellowmen, in which the gratification of one's own instinct plays no part at all, even in some displaced and sublimated form." She put the question to Robert Coles for his answer. "I was hard put to answer her categorically; I tried to sift and sort, to evade a blunt yes or no. But finally I decided, after looking over many pages of summary notes, that I would vote with those who see sin everywhere." I believe his reply is one of those moments when philosophy trumps psychology—even though the philosophy is being provided by a psychologist! If you ask a perfectionistic question, you deserve an ambiguous answer. All the young idealists he had ever gotten to know well, Coles thought, were struggling with motives that included envy, ambition, rivalry, pride, and condescension, yet they kept to their enterprises in spite of the struggle.

In the powerful chapter on "Young Idealism" in his *The Moral Life of Children*, Coles writes at length about a young man in his twenties whom he interviewed many times in the 1970s. One of four sons of a New England judge, Harvard educated, this young man had settled into being a community organizer for the poor, mostly blacks, in a town in Georgia; and despite entreaties from his friends that he was masochistic and had a martyr complex, he was sticking to his work. As he said to Coles on one occasion:

> My mother, who taught me a lot of the 'idealism' I'm supposed to have (she was always telling us 'idealism is important'), *my mother* is the one who wrote me a letter a year ago and told me she was praying for me, in church, that I 'find myself,' and that I 'get a regular job.' I wonder what Jesus said, listening to her prayers! I felt like writing her back and asking her if Jesus ever held 'a regular job'—or ever 'found Himself.'

The young man was definitely not confusing *himself* with Jesus; he was very aware of his longings for better clothes, foreign travel, maybe just one air conditioner for Georgia summers, and for the girlfriends who found his circumstances too challenging to stay in a relationship with him.

Is idealism at least partly a cover for something less worthy? Is it impure, mixed with less noble motives? The answer is yes. As seen in adolescence, is it a passing phase? The answer, I believe, becomes yes unless the person is aware of the struggle between wanting to give idealistically and wanting to get other things, and regularly confronts the conflict between these desires. Is it a vocation for the few or a possibility for many? So long as idealism is defined perfectionistically, it is a vocation only for a few, but if it is defined more subtly, it is an option for anyone anytime.

The True Self

There are two other concepts that I believe bear on the discussion of idealism and giving back. One is the image of the true self as Alice Miller has written of it, and the other is the concept of reciprocity.

The concept of the true self comes out of Miller's experience as a psychotherapist. The true self is not an ideal self—far from it, as Miller shows in this passage from *The Drama of the Gifted Child*:

It is one of the turning points in therapy when the patient comes to the emotional insight that all the love she has captured with so much effort and self-denial was not meant for her as she really was, that the admiration for her beauty and achievements was aimed at this beauty and those achievements and not at the child herself. [Substitute boyish bravado and sports accomplishments for beauty, and this passage applies equally to boys.] In therapy, the small and lonely child that is hidden behind her achievements wakes up and asks: 'What would have happened if I had appeared before you sad, needy, angry, furious? Where would your love have been then? And I was all these things as well. Does this mean that it was not really me you loved, but only what I pretended to be?

The surface self that many people admire is in certain ways a false self. It is mortifying at first to a person to see what lurks under the surface from childhood. But there is enormous relief when the true self can express pain and grief, and give up the pretense always to be good, understanding, self-controlled, obedient, and without needs; it is good when these admirable but not fully representative qualities need not be the sole basis for self-respect.

The relation of this discussion of the true self to idealism is fairly obvious. If a boy's idealism is an expression of an admirable but false self that hides his true self with its grittier components, the idealism itself is part of an illusion and unlikely to endure. Thus it is all the more important that young idealists learn to recognize and struggle with the mixture of desires and motives we all have. It is this struggle that gives the true self some breathing room.

Reciprocity

Robert Coles recounts an interview he had with Dorothy Day of the Catholic Worker Movement that gets to the very heart of idealism. She said that lots of young people came to help run the Movement's "hospitality houses" in New York City expecting to find Dorothy Day "pure as a fresh snowfall, and always sweet-talking, and full of love for everyone I see." What they found, she said, was a woman who often got angry with her coworkers, with the people they were befriending, and with herself. She was indeed a direct, sometimes vinegary, woman.

And so it is a favor these people (the needy) are doing us by coming here and taking from us what we have to offer. This is not easy for some young people to understand: the reciprocity of giver and receiver, the two sides of the same coin, the help the helpless offer to the helpers. But when a young vol-

unteer—on leave from a college, maybe—does begin to see what that means
(the giving to us by those who are down-and-out, and supposedly with
nothing to give anyone), then it's a real breakthrough for the young man or
the young woman. A *spiritual* breakthrough.

Dorothy Day described the sequence many of the young idealists went
through as they worked with her. They began by thinking they were sacrificing their own interests for the sake of someone else. They often attributed their idealism to the way they were raised. It took them quite a
while to stop looking at others and look at themselves. Then they found
themselves getting annoyed because the people they were helping weren't
more grateful—blessing the idealists as wonderful, wonderful people.
They were expecting to be rewarded for their good deeds more than appeared to be happening. Finally it dawned on them that they were feeding
people—not feeding dependency in others to make themselves feel virtu-
ous—and being fed in return.

Reciprocity is a remarkable human invention. It is everywhere to be
seen in social interaction. A friend does me a favor. I tuck into my mind
an intention to reciprocate, to find some comparable way to help him in
the near future. Reciprocity is not a law, and it is seldom realized in perfect equilibrium, that is, exactly as much given back as was received. In the
human life cycle, there is an evolving natural imbalance. In the first stages
of life, a boy needs a great deal of care and has a very limited capacity to
give back care to anyone, though he honors those who care for him by fix-
ing their images indelibly in his mind. In the last stages of a normal life
span, there is apt to be another period during which a man generally
needs a great deal more care than he is able to give to anyone else. But in
between those early and late stages, there are decades in which the potential to give back is very great, perhaps as great as, or greater than, the need
to receive. Over the course of a lifetime, the balance struck can be a gen-
uine equilibrium if the person grasps the principle and adopts it.

As Dorothy Day or any of the young male idealists Robert Coles interviewed would testify, giving creates an obligation but not a demand. It
doesn't work—though it's tried often enough in family and other social
interactions—to say, "Look what I've done for you. Now what are you
going to do for me?" Reciprocity doesn't flourish when it's buttressed by
an appeal to guilt or even duty; the person being asked to give something
back may do so, but not without some underlying feeling of resentment
that becomes part of the true self.

Most of us, I believe, can get to the kind of understanding of reciprocity articulated by Dorothy Day only in stages. Inevitably we will begin
with idealistic projects that make us feel good, and also feel superior. But

even that is a start. Moreover, the example can lead others to follow. One mother of five children in New Canaan, Connecticut, volunteered herself and her children to help clean a disabled person's house. Many of her children's friends who heard of the activity asked to be included the next time. She hadn't planned there to be a next time, but the knowledge of others eager for giving-back projects spurred her to found Kids Care Club; by the end of 1997 there were a hundred more such clubs in thirty states: many kids taking early steps in giving back.

When boys who have benefited from early participation in giving back projects, and therefore have a base for youthful idealism, reach adolescence, they face the tension between idealism and individual success as measured in acquired possessions and professional status. The pull of acquisitiveness and self-concern is very strong. Nevertheless, even for the rich and powerful, fulfillment remains elusive.

> Over the last few years, however, psychological researchers have been amassing an impressive body of data suggesting that satisfaction simply is not for sale. Not only does having more things prove to be unfulfilling, but people for whom affluence is a priority in life tend to experience an unusual degree of anxiety and depression as well as a lower overall level of well-being. Likewise, those who would like nothing more than to be famous or attractive do not fare as well, psychologically speaking, as those who primarily want to develop close relationships, become more self-aware, or contribute to the community.

Alfie Kohn cites some of the studies behind this generalization, and cautions that what is known refers more to correlations of goals or statuses and self-evaluation than to solidly demonstrated causes and effects.

The correlations Kohn reports do not surprise me—they mainly confirm impressions many of us have from our life experience. But even if they are further refined into causes and effects, and shown to be generally true for humankind, I doubt that the power of acquisitiveness and personal ambition would be culturally tempered by such findings alone. Aphorisms such as "Money is the root of all evil" have spawned more bad jokes than cultural revolutions, so I don't hold out great hopes for "Money as the root of unhappiness."

Yet I am immensely optimistic about idealism, about giving back, and even about reciprocity. The psychological issue has to do with transforming our view of the world and our place in it. If in the giving we come to see ourselves not as superior beings but as individuals who share a common humanity on a common planet, we become different people. I am convinced from my experience and that of others in the Peace Corps that notwithstanding the variety of motivations that took us to West Africa, after two years we all were tremendously different.

When I hear current news from our old Peace Corps delegation, "Upper Volta One," as it was called, I am always fascinated to note virtually everyone's involvement with one or another kind of community or charitable work. The magic of the legislation establishing the Peace Corps was that it imagined the volunteers would return to enrich the United States with their knowledge and insight about life in the nonindustrial world. What the authors of the legislation could not have foreseen is that most volunteers returned as different human beings.

Adolescent males stand at a pivotal point of huge consequence. Left to their own devices, they will see their main challenge as one of achieving independence, particularly from their families of origin. Yet if they commit single-mindedly to ambition and acquisition (supported often in this pursuit by well-intentioned parents), they launch themselves into a life in which self-indulgence, even in the guise of professional attainment, will be the means and the end. No matter how successful they are, those males will always be affected by forces beyond their control: by their own unintended errors; by the merited or unmerited ill will of colleagues, superiors, and competitors; by the unpredictable trajectories of marketplaces and technologies; or by unexpected capitulations of body and mind to pressure. Without grasping what they are doing, they will fight their own feared dependency by exploiting those who are dependent on them.

Throughout this book, we have seen that the most important character issue for males is to learn how to avoid exploiting others (females, younger males, subordinates, competitors, strangers who get in their way) with their physical, social, and cultural power. The will to exploit is fueled more by fear of dependencies, by weaknesses, than by superior strength; the genesis of exploitation in weakness makes it all the more virulent and difficult to change

The great challenge for young men is to temper rather than cultivate the power imperatives that lie close to the biological core of being male. As the political commentator Walter Lippmann wrote in A Preface to Morals, "In all the great moral philosophies from Aristotle to Bernard Shaw, it is taught that one of the conditions of happiness is to renounce some of the satisfactions which men normally crave."

The age-old way to achieve happiness is to seek reciprocity wherever it is available—in marriage, in parenthood (where the helpless child can, paradoxically, by his very being give as much as he receives), at work, or at play. Giving back and reciprocity are the most powerful bulwarks against the urge to be exploitative. The foundations of admirable character lie in a boy's realistic sense of himself as a human being. He will never be perfect, and he is what he is because others have given to him. With such knowledge comes the possibility of fulfillment, and of character that will continue to be strengthened by choosing to do right, and, after failure, to do better the next time.

NOTES

Chapter One: What Is Character?

4   E. Canin, *For Kings and Planets* (New York: Random House, 1998).

13   W. Gallagher, *Just the Way You Are: How Heredity and Experience Create the Individual* (New York: Random House, 1997).

13   S. Chess and A. Thomas, *Know Your Child: An Authoritative Guide for Today's Parents* (New York: Basic Books, 1987), 22–24.

14   S. Chess and A. Thomas, *Temperament Theory and Practice* (New York: Brunner/Mazel, 1996).

15   W. B. Carey, "Enriching Pediatric Practice with Temperament Concepts," *Developmental-Behavioral News* (newsletter of the Section on Developmental and Behavioral Pediatrics of the American Academy of Pediatrics) 6 (1997), 5–7.

15   W. B. Carey with M. Jablow, *Understanding Your Child's Temperament* (New York: Macmillan, 1997).

15   S. I. Greenspan, *The Growth of the Mind and the Endangered Origins of Intelligence* (Reading, Mass.: Perseus, 1996).

16   J. Kagan and N. Snidman, "Temperamental Factors in Human Development," *American Psychologist* 46 (1991), 856–862.

18   R. Coles, *The Moral Intelligence of Children.* (New York: Random House, 1997), 194.

19   U. Bronfenbrenner, "The Bioecological Model from a Life-Course Perspective: Reflections of a Participant Observer," in P. Moen, G. H. Elder, Jr., and K. Luscher, eds., *Examining Lives in Context* (Washington, D.C.: American Psychological Association, 1995), 599–618.

19   U. Bronfenbrenner, *The Ecology of Human Development: Experiments By Nature and Design* (Cambridge, Mass.: Harvard University Press, 1989).

Chapter Two: The Roots of Character

20   C. M. Newberger, "The Cognitive Structure of Parenthood: Designing a Descriptive Measure," *New Directions for Child Development* 7 (1980), 45–67.

24   B. S. Zuckerman and S. Parker, "Teachable Moments: Exploring the World," *Contemporary Pediatrics* 14 (1997), 50.

29   United States Census Bureau (1999). *Marital Status and Living Arrangements. Current Population Survey. Living Arrangements of Children Under 18 Years Old: 1960 to Present.* Washington: Department of Health and Human Services (Internet Release Date: January 7, 1999).

30   M. Robinson, "Family," in M. Robinson, ed., *The Death of Adam: Essays on Modern Thought* (Boston: Houghton Mifflin, 1998), 91–92.

32   S. Coontz, *The Way We Really Are: Coming to Terms with America's Changing Families* (New York: Basic Books, 1997), 62–63.

33   J. R. Gillis, *A World of Their Own Making: Myth, Ritual and the Quest for Family Values* (Cambridge, Mass.: Harvard University Press, 1997).

33   J. Belsky, cited in D. Blum, *Sex on the Brain: The Biological Differences Between Men and Women* (New York: Viking Penguin, 1997), xx–xi.

35   Associated Press, "Boy, 5, Helps Jail Father." Boston Globe (October 24, 1998), A7.

38   J. R. Harris, *The Nurture Assumption: Why Children Turn Out the Way They Do?* (New York: Simon and Schuster, 1998).

38   H. Gardner, "Do Parents Count?" Review of J. R. Harris, *The Nurture Assumption: Why Do Children Turn Out the Way They Do? New York Review of Books* 45(17) (1998), 22.

Chapter Three: Infants and Toddlers

43   Blum, *Sex on the Brain*, xviii.

43   **brain size** J. P. Rushton and C. D. Ankney, "Brain Size and Cognitive Ability: Correlations with Age, Sex, Social Class, and Race," *Psychonomic Bulletin and Review* 3 (1996), 21–36.

43   R. Lynn, "Sex Difference in Intelligence and Brain Size: A Paradox Resolved," *Personal and Individual Differences* 17 (1994), 257–271.

43   M. Gurian, *The Wonder of Boys* (New York: G. P. Putnam's Sons, 1996).

44   **gender difference in brain function** H. L. Wagner, R. Buck, and M. Winterbotham, "Communication of Specific Emotions: Gender Differences in Sending Accuracy and Communication Measures," *Journal of Nonverbal Behavior* 17 (1993), 29–53.

44   R. C. Gur, B. E. Skolnick, and R. E. Gur, "Effects of Emotional Discrimination Tasks on Cerebral Blood Flow: Regional Activation and Its Relation to Performance," *Brain and Cognition* 25 (1994), 271–286.

44   U. Dimberg and A. Ohman, "Behold the Wrath: Psychophysiological Responses to Facial Stimuli," *Motivation and Emotion* 20 (1996), 149–182.

44   **male hormones in behavior** J. R. Udry, J.O.G. Billy, N. M. Morris, T. R. Groff, and M. H. Raj, "Serum Androgenic Hormones Motivate Sexual Behavior in Boys," *Fertility and Sterility* 43 (1985), 90–94.

44   D. Kimura, "Sex Differences in the Brain," *Scientific American* (September 1992), 119–125.

44   J. Archer, "Testosterone and Aggression," in M. Hillbrand and N. J. Pallone, eds., *The Psychobiology of Aggression* (New York: Haworth Press, 1996), 3–35.

44   J. A. Harris, J. P. Rushton, E. Hampson, and D. N. Jackson, "Salivary Testosterone and Self-Reported Aggressive and Pro-Social Personality Characteristics in Men and Women," *Aggressive Behavior* 22 (1996), 321–331.

44   C. T. Halpern, J. R. Udry, B. Campbell, and C. Suchindron, "Relationships Between Aggression and Pubertal Increases in Testosterone: A Panel Analysis of Adolescent Males," *Social Biology* 40 (1993), 8–24.

44   B. Schaal, R. E. Tremblay, R. Soussignan, and E. J. Susman, "Male Testosterone Linked to High Social Dominance but Low Physical Aggression in Early Adolescence," *Journal of the American Academy of Child and Adolescent Psychiatry* 35 (1996),1322–1330.

45   J. Archer, "Sex Differences in Social Behavior: Are the Social Role and Evolutionary Explanations Compatible?" *American Psychologist* 51 (1996), 909–917.

45   D. C. Geary, *Male, Female: The Evolution of Human Sex Differences* (Washington, D.C.: American Psychological Association, 1998).

45   N. Eisenberg, R. A. Fabes, M. Nyman, J. Bernzweig, and A. Pinuelas, "The Relations of Emotionality and Regulation to Children's Anger-Related Reactions," *Child Development* 65 (1994), 109–128.

45   N. Eisenberg, R. A. Fabes, G. Carolo, A. L. Speer, G. Switzer, M. Karbon, and D. Troyer, "The Relations of Empathy-Related Emotions and Maternal Practices to Children's Comforting Behavior," *Journal of Experimental Child Psychology* 55 (1993), 131–150.

46   D. N. Stern, *The Interpersonal World of the Infant: A View from Psychoanalysis and Developmental Psychology.* (New York: Basic Books, 1985).

47   J. S. Bruner, *Actual Minds: Possible Worlds* (Cambridge: Harvard University Press, 1986).

47   J. Kagan, *The Second Year of Life: The Emergence of Self Awareness* (Cambridge: Harvard University Press, 1981).

47   T. B. Brazelton, *Touchpoints: Your Child's Emotional and Behavioral Development* (Reading, Mass.: Perseus, 1994).

48   **empathy** C. Zahn-Waxler and M. Radke-Yarrow, "The Origins of Empathic Concern," *Motivation and Emotion* 14 (1990), 107–130.

48   B. Klimes-Dougan and J. Kistner, "Physically Abused Preschoolers' Responses to Peers' Distress," *Developmental Psychology* 26 (1990), 599–602.

49   Chess and Thomas, *Know Your Child*, 51.

49   M. H. Bornstein and M. E. Lamb, *Development in Infancy: An Introduction,* 3rd ed. (New York: McGraw-Hill, 1992).

50   **parental response** M. F. Small, *Our Babies, Ourselves: How Biology and Culture Shape the Way We Parent* (New York: Anchor Books, 1998). 73–75 crying R. G. Barr, "The Enigma of Infant Crying: The Emergence of Defining Dimensions," *Early Development and Parenting* 4 (1995), 225–232.

50   T. B. Brazelton, "Crying in Infancy," *Pediatrics* 29 (1962), 579–588.

50   P. H. Wolff, "The Causes, Controls and Organization of Behavior in the Neonate," *Psychological Issues* 5(1)(1966).

53   Metropolitan Diary, *New York Times* (October 19, 1998).

53   M. Schwartzman with Judith Sachs, *The Anxious Parent: Freeing Yourself from the Fears and Stresses of Parenting* (New York: Simon and Schuster, 1990).

Chapter Four: Male Connection and Emotion

56   K. Lorenz, *King Solomon's Ring* (New York: Harcourt Brace Jovanovich, 1952).

56   Lorenz, K. *The Foundations of Ethology* (New York: Simon and Schuster, 1981).

56   J. Bowlby, *Maternal Care and Mental Health* (Geneva: World Health Organization, 1951), 158.

56   J. Bowlby, "An Ethological Approach to Research in Child Development" (Lecture to the British Psychological Society, 1957), in J. Bowlby, *The Making and Breaking of Affectional Bonds* (London: Tavistock, 1979), 25–43.

      J. Bowlby, *Attachment and Loss,* vol. 1: *Attachment* (New York: Basic Books, 1969).

58   S. Chess, "Developmental Theory Revisited," *Canadian Journal of Psychiatry* 24 (1979), 101–102.

62   K. Parnell, "Toddler Interaction in Relation to Mothers and Peers" (Ph.D. diss., Boston University, 1991).

62   J. Gleason, "Sex Differences in Parent-Child Interaction," in S. Phillips, S. Steele, and C. Tanz, eds., *Language, Gender, and Sex in Comparative Perspective* (Cambridge: Cambridge University Press, 1989), 189–199.

62   R. Fivush, "Exploring Sex Differences in the Emotional Content of Mother-Child Conversations About the Past," *Sex Roles* 20 (1989), 675–691.

62   J. Kuebli, S. Butler, and R. Fivush, "Mother-Child Talk About Past Emotions: Relations of Maternal Language and Child Gender Over Time," *Cognition and Emotion* 9 (1995), 265–283.

62   **gender differences in emotion**   L. R. Brody and J. A. Hall, "Gender and Emotion," in M. Lewis and J. M. Haviland, eds., *Handbook of Emotions* (New York: Guilford Press, 1993), 447–460.

62   C. Z. Malatesta and J. M. Haviland, "Learning Display Rules: The Socialization of Emotion Expression in Infancy," *Child Development* 53 (1982), 991–1003.00–00

62   D. Botkin and S. Twardosz, "Early Childhood Teachers' Affectionate Behavior: Differential Expressions to Female Children, Male Children, and Groups of Children," *Early Childhood Research Quarterly* 3 (1988), 167–177.

62   D. W. Birnbaum and W. L. Croll, "The Etiology of Children's Stereotypes About Sex Differences in Emotionality," *Sex Roles* 10 (1984), 677–691.

63   R. T. Hare-Mustin and J. Maracek, "The Meaning of Difference," *American Psychologist* 43 (1988), 455–464.

Chapter Five: Word Magic

65   S. H. Fraiberg, *The Magic Years: Understanding and Handling the Problems of Early Childhood* (New York: Charles Scribner's Sons, 1959), 107.

Chapter Six: Discipline and Punishment

74   D. Orentlicher, "Spanking and Other Corporal Punishment of Children By Parents: Overvaluing Pain, Undervaluing Children," *Houston Law Review* 35 (1998), 147–185.

76   P. Greven, *Spare the Child*: The *Religious Roots of Physical Punishment and the Psychological Impact of Physical Abuse* (New York: Knopf, 1991).

80   M. A. Straus, *Beating the Devil Out of Them: Corporal Punishment in American Families* (San Francisco: Jossey-Bass, 1994).

80   M. A. Straus, D. B. Sugarman, J. Giles-Sims, "Spanking by Parents and Subsequent Antisocial Behavior of Children," *Archives of Pediatrics and Adolescent Medicine* 151 (1997), 761–767.

81   M. A. Straus, "New and More Definitive Evidence About the Benefits of Avoiding Corporal Punishment" (paper presented at the World Congress of Sociology, Montreal, Quebec, August 1, 1998).

80   W. T. Greenough, C. S. Wallace, A. A., Alcantara, B. J. Anderson, N. Hawrylak, A. M. Sirevaag, I. J. Welier, and G. S. Withers, "Development of the Brain: Experience Affects the Structure of Neurons, Glia, and Blood Vessels," in N. J. Anastasiow and S. Harel, eds., *At-Risk Infants: Interventions, Families, and Research* (Baltimore: Paul H. Brookes, 1993), 173–185.

80   H. J. Neville, "Neurobiology of Cognitive and Language Processing: Effects on Early Experience," in K. R. Gibson and A. C. Peterson, eds., *Brain Maturation and Cognitive Development: Comparative and Cross-cultural Perspectives* (New York: Aldine DeGruyter, 1991), 355–380.

82   S. Pinker, *How the Mind Works* (New York: W. W. Norton, 1997).

82   J. Gilligan, *Violence: Our Deadly Epidemic and Its Causes* (New York: G. P. Putnam's Sons, 1996).

84   **effects of parenting styles** D. Baumrind, "Child Care Practices Anteceding Three Patterns of Preschool Behavior," *Genetic Psychology Monographs* 75 (1967), 43–88.

84   D. Baumrind and A. E. Black, "Socialization Practices Associated with Dimensions of Competence in Preschool Boys and Girls," *Child Development* 38 (1967), 291–327.

84   L. Kuczynski and G. Kochanska, "Function and Content of Maternal Demands: Developmental Significance of Early Demands for Competent Action," *Child Development* 66 (1995), 616–628.

84   **development of sense of right and wrong** G. Kochanska, N. Aksan, and A. L. Koenig, "A Longitudinal Study of the Roots of Preschoolers' Conscience: Committed Compliance and Emerging Internalization," *Child Development* 66 (1995), 1752–1769.

84   E. Turiel, *The Development of Social Knowledge: Morality and Convention* (New York: Cambridge University Press, 1983).

84   E. Turiel and M. Killen, "Morality: Its Structure, Functions, and Vagaries," in J. Kagan and S. Bloom, eds., *The Emergency of Morality* (Chicago: University of Chicago Press 1988).

84   **moral understanding** J. G. Smetana and J. L. Braeges, "The Development of Toddlers' Moral and Conventional Judgements," *Merrill-Palmer Quarterly* 36 (1990), 329–346.

85   J. E. Grusec and J. J. Goodnow, "Impact of Parental Discipline Methods on the Child's Internalization of Values: A Reconceptualization of Current Points of View," *Developmental Psychology* 30 (1994), 4–19.

Chapter Seven: Preschoolers

90   **motor development** B. J. Cratty, *Perceptual and Motor Development in Infants and Children,* 3rd ed. (Englewood Cliffs, N.J.: Prentice-Hall, 1986).

90   M. A. Roberton, "Changing Motor Patterns During Childhood," in J. R. Thomas, ed., *Motor Development During Childhood and Adolescence* (Minneapolis: Burgess, 1984), 48–90.

91   **childhood memory** R. Fivush, C. Haden, and S. Adam, "Structure and Coherence of Preschoolers' Personal Narratives Over Time: Implications for Childhood Amnesia," *Journal of Experimental Child Psychology* 60 (1995), 32–56.

91   M. K. Mullen, "Earliest Recollections of Childhood: A Demographic Analysis," *Cognition 52* (1994), 55–79.

91   **mathematical reasoning** M. S. Strauss and L. E. Curtis, "Development of Numerical Concepts in Infancy," in C. Sophian, ed., *Origins of Cognitive Skills: The Eighteenth Annual Carnegie Symposium on Cognition* (Hillsdale, N.J.: Erlbaum, 1984), 131–155.

91   H. M. Wellman, S. C., Somerville, and R. J. Haake, "Development of Search Procedures in Real-life Spatial Environments," *Developmental Psychology* 15 (1979), 530–542.

91   C. F. Gallistel and R. Gelman, "Preverbal and Verbal Counting and Computation," *Cognition* 44 (1992), 43–74.

92   D. C. Geary, *Children's Mathematical Development* (Washington, D.C.: American Psychological Association, 1994).

92   **intelligence** B. Hayslip, "Stability of Intelligence," in R. J. Sternberg, ed., *Encyclopedia of Human Intelligence,* vol. 2 (New York: Macmillan, 1994), 1019–1026.

92   **music training** F. K. Rauscher, G. L. Shaw, L. J. Levine, E. L. Wright, W. R. Dennis, and R. L. Newcomb, "Music Training Causes Long-term Enhancement of Preschool Children's Spatial-Temporal Reasoning," *Neurological Research* 19 (1997), 2–8.

92   **learning optimism** K. K. Burhans and C. S. Dweck, "Helplessness in Early Childhood: The Role of Contingent Worth," *Child Development* 66 (1995), 1719–1738.

92   **assessing emotions** R. A. Fabes, N. Eisenberg, M. Nyman, and Q. Michealieu, "Young Children's Appraisals of Others' Spontaneous Emotional Reactions," *Developmental Psychology* 27 (1991), 858–866.

92   J. Cassidy, R. D. Parke, L. Butkovsky, and J. M. Braungart, "Family-Peer Connections: The Roles of Emotional Expressiveness Within the Family and Children's Understanding of Emotions," *Child Development* 63 (1992), 603–618.

92   P. W. Garner, D. C. Jones, and J. L. Miner, "Social Competence Among Low-Income Preschoolers: Emotion Socialization Practices and Social Cognitive Correlates," *Child Development* 65 (1994), 622–637.

93   S. A. Denham, D. Zoller, and E. Couchoud, "Socialization of Preschool-
        ers' Emotion Understanding," *Developmental Psychology* 30 (1994),
        928–936.

93   J. Dunn, J. Brown, C. T. Somkowski, and L. Youngblade, "Young Chil-
        dren's Understanding of Other People's Feelings and Beliefs: Individual
        Differences and Their Antecedents," *Child Development* 62 (1991),
        1352–1366.

93   L. M. Youngblade and J. Dunn, "Individual Differences in Young Chil-
        dren's Pretend Play with Mother and Sibling: Links to Relationships
        and Understanding of Other People's Feelings and Beliefs," *Child De-
        velopment* 66 (1995), 1472–1492.

93   **self-esteem** D. J. Stipek, S. Rechhia, and S. McClintic, "Self-Evaluation
        in Young Children," *Monographs of the Society for Research in Child De-
        velopment* 57(1) (1992).

93   **self-control** B. E. Vaughn, C. B. Kopp, and J. B. Krakow, "The Emer-
        gence and Consolidation of Self-Control from Eighteen to Thirty
        Months of Age: Normative Trends and Individual Differences," *Child
        Development* 55 (1984), 990–1004.

93   **delayed gratification** W. Mischel and N. Baker, "Cognitive Appraisals
        and Transformations in Delay Behavior," *Journal of Personality and So-
        cial Psychology* 31 (1975), 254–261.

93   **verbal expression of feelings** A. Bandura, "Social Cognitive Theory of
        Moral Thought and Action," in W. M. Kurtines and Gewirtz, eds.,
        Handbook of Moral Behavior and Development, vol. 1 (Hillsdale, N.J.:
        Erlbaum, 1991), 45–103.

94   **gender stereotyping** A. C. Huston, "Sex-typing," in E. M. Hetherington,
        ed., *Handbook of Child Psychology,* vol. 4: *Socialization, personality, and
        social development,* 4th ed. (New York: Wiley, 1983), 387–467.

94   M. L. Picarielo, D. N. Greenberg, and D. B. Pillemer, "Children's Sex-Re-
        lated Stereotyping of Colors," *Child Development* 61 (1990), 1453–1460.

94   C. L. Martin, L. Eisenbud, and H. Rose, "Children's Gender-Based Rea-
        soning About Toys," *Child Development* 66 (1995), 1453–1471.

94   S. L. Bem, "Genital Knowledge and Gender Constancy in Preschool
        Children," *Child Development* 60 (1989), 649–662.

96   **sociodramatic play** R. J. Coplan, K. H. Rubin, N. A. Nox, S. D. Calkins,
        and S. L. Stewart, "Being Alone, Playing Alone, and Acting Alone: Dis-
        tinguishing Among Reticence and Passive and Active Solitude in Young
        Children," *Child Development* 65 (1994), 129–137.

97   D. J. Elkind, *The Hurried Child: Growing Up Too Fast, Too Soon* (Read-
        ing, Mass.: Perseus, 1989).

98   J. Trelease, *The Read-Aloud Handbook,* 4th ed. (New York: Penguin,
        1995).

98   T. Kump, quoting J. Trelease, "How to Avoid Reading Roadblocks," *Parenting Magazine* (November 1998), 254.

101   **television and preschoolers** J. P. Murray, "The Impact of Televised Violence," *Hofstra Law Review* 22 (1994), 811.

Chapter Eight: Sharing

108   U. Bronfenbrenner, Bessie Sperry Memorial Lecture, Judge Baker Guidance Center, Boston, Mass., June 5, 1984.

109   M. Drucker and G. Block, *Rescuers: Portraits in Moral Courage in the Holocaust* (New York: Holmes and Myer, 1992), 118.

110   V. G. Paley, *You Can't Say You Can't Play*, (Cambridge, Mass.: Harvard University Press, 1992).

Chapter Nine: Curiosity

117   T. B. Brazelton, *Neonatal Behavioral Assessment Scale*. Clinics in Developmental Medicine, No. 50. (Philadelphia: Lippincott, 1973).

117   M. H. Klaus and P. H. Klaus, *Your Amazing Newborn* (Reading, Mass.: Perseus, 1998).

118   H. F. Harlow, M. K. Harlow, and D. R. Meyer, "Learning Motivated By a Manipulation Drive," *Journal of Experimental Psychology* 40 (1950), 228–234.

118   I. Eibl-Eibesfeldt, *Ethology: The Biology of Behavior* (New York: Holt, Rinehart, and Winston, 1970), 242.

120   J. Lear, *Open Minded: Working Out the Logic of the Soul* (Cambridge, Mass.: Harvard University Press, 1998).

120   E. J. Anthony, "Risk, Vulnerability, and Resilience: An Overview," in E. J. Anthony and B. J. Cohler, *The Invulnerable Child* (New York: Guilford Press, 1987), 19.

123   C. W. Snow, *Infant Development,* 2nd ed. (Upper Saddle River, N.J.: Prentice-Hall, 1988), 180.

123   L. S. Vygotsky, *Mind in Society* (Cambridge, Mass.: Harvard University Press, 1978).

123   M. Montessori, *The Absorbent Mind* (New York: Holt, Rinehart, and Winston, 1949).

124   A. Phillips, *The Beast in the Nursery: On Curiosity and Other Appetites* (New York: Pantheon, 1998), *xv*.

126   R. Sapolsky, "Why Eighty-Year Olds Don't Wear Tongue Studs," *The New Yorker* (March 30, 1998), 57–72.

127   C. P. Cavafy, "Ithaka," in C. P. Cavafy, *Collected Poems,* trans. E. Keeley and P. Sherrard (Princeton: Princeton University Press, 1992), 36. Reprinted by permission of Princeton University Press. Copyright 1992 by Edmund Keeley and Philip Sherrard.

Chapter Ten: Schoolboys

129   **physical growth** R. M. Malina and C. Bouchard, *Growth, Maturation, and Physical Activity* (Champaign, Ill.: Human Kinetics, 1991).

129   M. G. Fischman, J. B. Moore, and K. H. Steele, "Children's One-Hand Catching As a Function of Age, Gender, and Ball Location," *Research Quarterly for Exercise and Sport* 63 (1992). 349–355.

130   **obesity** L. H. Epstein, J. McCurley, R. R. Wing, A. Valoski, "Five-year Followup of Family-based Treatments for Childhood Obesity," *Journal of Consulting and Clinical Psychology* 55 (1990), 661–664.

130   S. L. Gortmaker, A. Must, J. M. Perrin, A. M. Sobol, W. H. Dietz, "Social and Economic Consequences of Overweight in Adolescence and Young Adulthood," *New England Journal of Medicine* 329 (1993), 1008–1012.

132   R. L. Roberts and C. J. Aman, "Developmental Differences in Giving Directions: Spatial Frames of Reference and Mental Rotation," *Child Development* 64 (1993), 1258–1270.

132   **self-evaluation** D. J. Stipek, S. Recchia, and S. McClintic, "Self-Evaluation in Young Children," *Monographs of the Society for Research in Child Development, 57*(1) (1992).

132   S. Harter, "Issues in the Assessment of the Self-Concept of Children and Adolescents," in L. LaGreca, ed., *Through the Eyes of a Child* (Boston: Allyn and Bacon, 1990), 292–325.

133   D. J. Stipek and D. MacIver, "Developmental Change in Children's Assessment of Intellectual Competence," *Child Development* 60 (1989), 521–538.

134   H. Gardner, *Multiple Intelligence: The Theory in Practice* (New York: Basic Books, 1993).

135   G. D. Heyman, C. S. Dweck, and K. M. Cain, "Young Children's Vulnerability to Self-Blame and Helplessness: Relationships to Beliefs About Goodness," *Child Development* 63 (1992), 401–415.

136   H. W. Marsh and P. J. Gouvernet, "Multidimensional Self-Concepts and Perceptions of Control: Construct Validation of Responses by Children," *Journal of Educational Psychology,* 81 (1989), 57–69.

136   **gender assumptions** P. J. Turner and J. Gervai, "A Multidimensional Study of Gender Typing in Preschool Children and Their Parents: Personality, Attitudes, Preferences, Behavior, and Cultural Differences," *Developmental Psychology* 31 (1995), 759–772.

136   **self-esteem** C. S. Dweck, "Self-Theories and Goals: Their Role in Motivation, Personality, and Development," in R. Dienstbier, ed., *Nebraska Symposia on Motivation,* vol. 36 (Lincoln, Neb.: University of Nebraska Press, 1991), 199–235.

136   **differences in perspective-taking** R. L. Selman, *The Growth of Interpersonal Understanding* (New York: Academic Press, 1980).

136   R. S. Siegler, *Children's Thinking,* 2nd ed. (Englewood Cliffs, N.J.: Prentice Hall, 1991).

136   H. S. Sullivan, *The Interpersonal Theory of Psychiatry* (New York: Norton, 1953).

136   **biological change** J. Tanner, "Sequence, Tempo, and Individual Variation in Growth and Development of Boys and Girls Aged Twelve to Sixteen," in J. Kagan and R. Coles, eds., *Twelve to Sixteen: Early Adolescence* (New York: Norton, 1972).

136   A. Petersen and B. Taylor, "The Biological Approach to Adolescence: Biological Change and Psychological Adaptation," in J. Adelson, ed., *Handbook of Adolescent Psychology* (New York: Wiley, 1980).

136   **friendship** D. Buhrmester and W. Furman, "The Development of Companionship and Intimacy," *Child Development* 58 (1987), 1101–1115.

136   J. G. Parker and S. R. Asher, "Friendship and Friendship Quality in Middle Childhood: Links with Peer Group Acceptance and Feelings of Loneliness and Social Dissatisfaction," *Developmental Psychology* 29 (1993), 611–621.

136   G. P. Jones and M. H. Dembo, "Age and Sex Role Differences in Intimate Friendships During Childhood and Adolescence," *Merrill-Palmer Quarterly* 35 (1989), 445–462.

138   National Research Council, Institute of Medicine. *Child Care for Low-Income Families: Summary of Two Workshops* (Washington, D.C.: National Academy Press, 1995).

139   H. Rodman, D. Pratto, and R. Nelson, "Child Care Arrangements and Children's Functioning: A Comparison of Self-Care and Adult-Care Children," *Developmental Psychology* 21 (1985), 413–418.197–199divorceE. M. Hetherington, "The Role of Individual Differences and Family Relationships: Children's Coping with Divorce and Remarriage," in P. A. Cowen and M. Hetherington, eds., *Family Transitions* (Hillsdale, N.J.: Erlbaum, 1991), 165–194.

139   J. S. Wallerstein and J. B. Kelly, *Surviving the Break-Up: How Children and Parents Cope with Divorce* (New York: Basic Books 1980).

139   E. M. Hetherington and W. G. Clingempeel, "Coping with Marital Transitions: A Family Systems Perspective," *Monographs of the Society for Research in Child Development* 57(2–3) (1992).

140   C. M. Buchanan, E. E. Maccoby, and S. M. Dornbusch, "Caught Between Parents: Adolescents' Experience in Divorced Homes," *Child Development* 62 (1991), 1008–1029.199–2

140   **prejudice** A. B. Doyle and F. E. Aboud, "A Longitudinal Study of White Children's Racial Prejudice As Social-Cognitive Development," *Merrill-Palmer Quarterly* 41 (1995), 209–228.

Chapter Eleven: Honesty

143   P. Fitzgerald, "The Preacher's Life," *New York Times*, February 22, 1998. Review of I. Klima, *The Ultimate Intimacy*, trans. A. G. Brian (New York: Grove Press, 1988).

144   **Piaget** Siegler, *Children's Thinking*, 33–34.

145   S. H. Cath, "Divorce and the Child: 'The Father Question Hour?'" in S. H. Cath, A. R. Gurwitt, and J. M. Ross, eds., *Father and Child: Developmental and Clinical Perspectives* (Boston: Little, Brown, 1982), 470-479.

148   S. Bok, *Lying: Moral Choice in Public and Private Life* (New York: Random House, 1978).

148   T. H. Johnson, ed., *The Poems of Emily Dickinson* (Cambridge, Mass.: Harvard University Press, 1951).

155   Coles, *The Moral Intelligence of Children*, 34–51.

Chapter Twelve: Self-control

159   W. Moyers, "John Henry Faulk: Humorist," in W. Moyers and A. Tucher, ed., *A World of Ideas, II: Public Opinions from Private Citizens* (New York: Doubleday, 1990), 254–255.

161   J. E. Brody, "Battered Women Face Pit Bulls and Cobras," *New York Times* (March 7, 1998), C7.

161   N. Jacobson and J. Gottman, *When Men Batter Women* (New York: Simon and Schuster, 1998).

164   Chess and Thomas, *Know Your Child*, 172–175.

165   S. Bezirganian and C. Cohen, "Sex Differences in the Interaction Between Temperament and Parenting," *Journal of the American Academy of Child and Adolescent Psychiatry*, 31 (1992), 790–801.

166   D. Goleman, *Emotional Intelligence: Why It Can Matter More Than IQ* (New York: Bantam, 1995). 81.

167   Y. Shoda, W. Mischel, and P. K. Peake, "Predicting Adolescent Cognitive and Self-Regulatory Competencies from Preschool Delay of Gratification," *Developmental Psychology* 26 (1990), 978–986.

168   J. L. Collier, *Louis Armstrong: An American Genius* (New York: Oxford University Press, 1983), 34–45, 243–249.

174   (ADD/ADHD) W. Carey, *Developmental-Behavioral News* (Newsletter of the Section on Developmental and Behavioral Pediatrics), American Academy of Pediatrics (Fall 1998).

175   M. Vonnegut, "Why Attention Deficit Disorder Shouldn't Get All the Blame," *Sunday Focus, Boston Globe* (November 2, 1998).

175   National Institutes of Health Consensus Statement, *Diagnosis and Treatment of Attention Deficit Disorder* (Bethesda, Md.: Office of Medical Applications of Research, National Institutes of Health) 16(2) (November 16–18, 1998).

176   R. A. Barkley, *ADHD and the Nature of Self-Control* (New York: Guilford, 1997), *ix*.

Chapter Thirteen: Teasing and Bullying

184   R. Kayton, "Help Your Child Cope with Teasing," *Washington Parent Magazine,* n.d., at www.washingtonparent.com/articles/9711/teasing. html.

186   D. M. Ross, *Childhood Bullying and Teasing: What School Personnel, Other Professionals and Parents Can Do* (Annapolis Junction, Md.: American Counseling Association, 1996).

188   B. Thorne, *Gender Play: Girls and Boys in School* (New Brunswick, N.J.: Rutgers University Press, 1993), 77.

192   J. Mitchard, "With Friends Like These . . . ," *Parenting* (December/ January 1999), 105.

193   R. A. Hawley, *Boys Will Be Men: Masculinity in Troubled Times* (Middlebury, Vt.: Paul S. Eriksson, 1993), 86–92.

194   **bullying** L. Bennett and S. Fineran, "Sexual and Severe Physical Violence Among High School Students: Power Beliefs, Gender, and Relationship," *American Journal of Orthopsychiatry* 68 (1998), 645–652.

194   L. Sjostrom and N. Stein, *Bully Proof: A Teacher's Guide on Teasing and Bullying for Use with Fourth and Fifth Grade Students* (Wellesley, Mass.: Wellesley College Center for Research on Women, 1996).

195   D. Olweus, *Bullying at School* (Oxford: Blackwell, 1993).

196   L. Grinspoon, ed., "Aggressive Children and Their Self-Esteem," *Harvard Mental Health Letter* 14 (1998), 3.

196   J. N. Hughes, T. A. Cavell, and P. B. Grossman, "A Positive View of Self: Risk or Protection for Aggressive Children?" *Development and Psychopathology* 9 (1997), 75–94.

197   **violence prevention program** M. Feldman, J. Kral, Z. Obeid, S. Respass, B. Coleman-Miller, and D. Prothrow-Stith, *Peace By Piece: A Violence Prevention Guide for Communities* (Boston: Harvard School of Public Health, 1998), 42.

200   F. H. Frankel, *Good Friends Are Hard to Find: Help Your Child Find, Make and Keep Friends* (Indianapolis, Ind.: Perspectives Press, 1996).

201   B. Porro, "The Nonsexist Classroom: A Process Approach," in E. M. Sheridan, ed., *Sex Stereotypes and Reading* (Newark, Del.: International Reading Association, 1982).

201   K. Karkau, "Sexism in the Fourth Grade," in M. Guttentag and H. Bray, eds., *Undoing Sex Stereotypes: Research and Resources for Educators* (New York: McGraw-Hill, 1976).

201   R. Best, *We've All Got Scars: What Boys and Girls Learn in Elementary School* (Bloomington, Ind.: Indiana University Press, 1983).

Chapter Fourteen: Early Adolescence

203   C. Quintana, "Riding the Rails," in "Being 13," Special Photography Issue, *New York Times Magazine* (May 17, 1998), 66.

204   L. Steinberg, *Adolescence,* 4th ed. (New York: McGraw-Hill, 1996), 23–60.

204   **growth patterns** Tanner, "Sequence, Tempo, and Individual Variation," in Kagan and Coles, *Twelve to Sixteen*, 5.

205   L. Steinberg, "The Impact of Puberty on Family Relations: Effects of Pubertal Status and Pubertal Timing," *Developmental Psychology* 23 (1987), 451–460; and "Reciprocal Relation Between Parent-Child Distance and Pubertal Maturation," *Developmental Psychology* 24 (1988), 122–128.

206   Peterson and Taylor, "The Biological Approach to Adolescence," in Adelson, *Handbook of Adolescent Psychology*, 129.286–290pubertyB. Goldstein, *Introduction to Human Sexuality* (Belmont, Cal.: Star, 1976).

207   **adolescent moods** C. Buchanan, J. Eccles, and J. Becker, "Are Adolescents the Victims of Raging Hormones? Evidence for Activational Effects of Hormones on the Moods and Behavior At Adolescence," *Psychological Bulletin* 111 (1992), 62–107.

208   "Being 13," *New York Times Magazine,* 66.

208   **cliques** N. Livson and H. Peskin, "Perspectives on Adolescence from Longitudinal Research," in Adelson, *Handbook of Adolescent Psychology*, 47–98.

208   T. G., Power and J. Shanks, "Parents As Socializers : Maternal and Paternal Views," *Journal of Youth and Adolescence* 18 (1989), 122–128.

208   J. Youniss and R. D. Ketterlinus, "Communication and Connectedness in Mother- and Father-Adolescent Relationships," *Journal of Youth and Adolescence* 16 (1987), 191–197.

210   B. Speicher-Dubin, "Relationships Between Parental Moral Judgment, Child Moral Judgment and Family Interaction: A Correlational Study," *Dissertation Abstracts International, 434* (1982), 1600B.

210 E. M. Cummings and A. W. O'Reilly, "Fathers in Family Context: Effects of Marital Quality on Child Adjustment," in Lamb, *The Role of the Father in Child Development*, 49–65.

210 N. Radin, "Childrearing Fathers in Intact Families I: Some Antecedents and Consequences," *Merrill-Palmer Quarterly* 27 (1981), 489–514.

210 R. W. Blanchard and H. B. Biller, "Father Availability and Academic Performance Among Third Grade Boys," *Developmental Psychology* 4 (1971), 301–305.

210–211 K. Norris, "Infallibility," in K. Norris, *Amazing Grace: A Vocabulary of Faith* (New York: Penguin Putnam, 1998), 369–370.295–3

211 L. Steinberg, "Transformations in Family Relations At Puberty," *Developmental Psychology* 17 (1981), 833–840.

211–212 **relations with parents** R. Larson and M. Richards, *Divergent Lives: The Emotional Lives of Mothers, Fathers, and Adolescents* (New York: Basic Books, 1994).

212 C. A. Hosley and R. Montemayor, "Fathers and Adolescents," in M. P. Lamb, *The Role of the Father in Child Development*, 3rd ed. (New York: John Wiley and Sons, 1997), 162–178.

212 J. Santrock, "Relation of Type and Onset of Father-Absence to Cognitive Development," *Child Development* 43 (1972), 455–469.

212 J. M. Bailey, D. Bobrow, M. Wolfe, S. Mikach, "Sexual Orientation of Sons of Gay Fathers," *Developmental Psychology* 31 (1995), 124–129.

213 S. T. Hauser, B. K. Book, J. Houlihan, S. Powers, B. Weiss-Perry, D. Follansbee, A. M., Jacobson, and G. G. Noam, "Sex Differences Within the Family: Studies of Adolescent and Parent Family Interactions," *Journal of Youth and Adolescence* 16 (1987), 199–220.

213 G. Patterson, B. DeBaryshe, and E. Ramsey, "A Developmental Perspective on Antisocial Behavior," *American Psychologist* 44 (1989), 329–335.

213 Sullivan, *The Interpersonal Theory of Psychiatry* (New York: Norton, 1953).

213 A. O. Harrison, M. N. Wilson, C. J. Pine, S. Q. Chan, and R. Buriel, "Family Ecologies of Ethnic Minority Children," in G. Handel and G. G. Whitchurch, eds., *The Psychosocial Interior of the Family* (New York: Aldine DeGruyter, 1994), 187–210.

213 J. Youniss and J. Smollar, *Adolescent Relations with Mothers, Fathers, and Friends* (Chicago: University of Chicago Press, 1985).

213 E. E. Maccoby, "Men and Women As Parents," in E. E. Maccoby, *The Two Sexes: Growing Up Apart, Coming Together* (Cambridge, Mass.: Harvard University Press, 1998), 255–286.

214 J. G. Dryfoos, *Safe Passage: Making It Through Adolescence in a Risky Society* (New York: Oxford University Press, 1998).

215 United States Department of Health and Human Services, "Youth Risk Behavior Surveillance—United States, 1995," *Morbidity and Mortality Weekly Report* (September 17, 1996), 45:SS–4.

215 J. Fox, *Trends in Juvenile Justice,* (Washington, D.C.: U.S. Department of Justice, Bureau of Justice Statistics, 1996), 2.

215 J. Dryfoos, "The Prevalence of Problem Behaviors: Implications for Programming," in R. Weissberg, T. Gullotta, R. Hampton, B. Ryan, and G. Adams, eds., *Healthy Children 2010: Enhancing Children's Wellness* (Thousand Oaks, Cal.: Sage, 1997), 17–46.

216 J. Keith and D. Perkins, *13,*

216 *Adolescents Speak: A Profile of Michigan Youth* (E. Lansing, Mich.: Community Coalitions in Action, Michigan State University, 1995).

217 M. Rutter, "Young People Today: Some International Comparisons on Patterns of Problems, Education, and Life Circumstances," in *Preparing Youth for the 21st Century* (Washington: D.C.: Aspen Institute, 1996), 25.

217 W. Pollack, "Hamlet's Curse: Depression and Suicide in Boys," in W. Pollack, *Real Boys: Rescuing Our Sons from the Myths of Boyhood* (New York: Random House, 1998), 303–337.

218 P. F. Gjerde, J. Block, and J. H. Block, "Depressive Symptoms and Personality During Late Adolescence: Gender Differences in the Externalization and Internalization of Symptom Expression," *Journal of Abnormal Psychology* 97 (1988), 475–486.

219 R. A. Barkley, *ADHD and the Nature of Self-Control,* 18–19.

Chapter Fifteen: Identity and Friendship

221 E. H. Erikson, *Childhood and Society,* 2nd ed. (New York: W. W. Norton, 1963).

222 A. Nin, *The Four-Chambered Heart,* cited in G. W. Goethals and D. S. Klos, *Experiencing Youth: First-Person Accounts,* 2nd ed. (Lanham, Md.: University Press of America, 1986), 340.

227 E. H. Erikson, *Identity: Youth and Crisis* (New York: W. W. Norton, 1968).

228 D.C. Dunphy, "The Social Structure of Urban Adolescent Peer Groups," *Sociometry* 26 (1963), 230–246.

229 R. E. Muuss, *Theories of Adolescence,* 6th ed. (New York: McGraw-Hill, 1996), 52.

229 R. B. Cairns and B. D. Cairns, *Lifelines and Risks: Pathways of Youth in Our Time* (Cambridge: Cambridge University Press, 1994).

230 J. G. Parker and S. R. Asher, "Friendship and Friendship Quality in Middle Childhood: Links with Peer Group Acceptance and Feelings of

Loneliness and Social Dissatisfaction," *Developmental Psychology* 29 (1993), 611–621.

232   K. A. Urberg, S. M. Degirmencioglu, J. M. Tolson, K. Halliday-Scher, "The Structure of Adolescent Peer Networks," *Developmental Psychology* 31 (1995), 445–460.

234   A. Mastoon, *The Shared Heart: Portraits and Stories Celebrating Lesbian, Gay, and Bisexual Young People* (New York: William Morrow, 1997), 36.

Chapter Sixteen: Alcohol and Drugs

239   J. Donovan and R. Jessor, "Structure of Problem Behavior in Adolescence and Young Adulthood," *Journal of Consulting and Clinical Psychology* 53 (1985), 890–904.

240   S. Cheever, *Note Found in a Bottle: My Life As a Drinker* (New York: Simon and Schuster, 1998).

241   United States Department of Health and Human Services, *Drug Use Survey Shows Mixed Results for Nation's Youth.* Report of the 23rd annual Monitoring the Future Survey. Posted on the Internet December 20, 1997, at www.hhs.gov.

241   Prevention Resource Center, Minnesota Department of Public Health. Interview of Jean Funk, Project director, by Julia Jergensen-Edelman, posted on the Internet by sci@gartland.com (1998).

243   C. Knapp, *Drinking: A Love Story* (New York: Dell, 1996), 83.

244   J. Gans, *America's Adolescents: How Healthy Are They?* (Chicago: American Medical Association, 1990).

245   L. Johnston, J. Bachman, and P. O'Malley, *Monitoring the Future: Questionnaire Responses from the Nation's High School Seniors, 1993* (Ann Arbor, Mich.: Institute for Social Research, 1994).

246   U.S. Department of Health and Human Services, *Youth Risk Behavioral Surveillance—United States, 1995*, 45:ss–5.

253   Dryfoos, *Safe Passage.*

Chapter Seventeen: Late Adolescence

254   C. McGrath, "Autoerotic," *New York Times Magazine* (July 5, 1998), 50.

256   Coontz, *The Way We Really Are,* 14.

257   **adolescent attitudes** L. J. Stone and J. Church, *Childhood and Adolescence: A Psychology of the Growing Person* (New York: Random House, 1968), 30.

257   Josephson Institute of Ethics, "1998 Report Card on the Ethics of American Youth," posted on the Internet October 19, 1998 (Josephson

Institute of Ethics, Publications Department, 4640 Admiralty Way, #1001, Marina del Rey, CA 90292–6610).

257   **arrest data** United State Department of Justice, *Crime in the U.S.: Uniform Crime Reports* (Washington, D.C.: U.S. Government Printing Office, 1995).

258   **risk-taking** Dryfoos, *Safe Passages.*

258   G. R. Patterson, B. D. DeBaryshe, E. Ramsey, "A Developmental Perspective on Antisocial Behavior," *American Psychologist* 44 (1989), 329–335.

259   **adolescent sexual experience** Steinberg, *Adolescence,* 408–420.

259   Alan Guttmacher Institute, *Sex and America's Teenagers* (New York: Planned Parenthood Federation, 1994).

260   S. B. Kinsman, D. Romer, F. F. Furstenberg, and D. F. Schwarz, "Early Sexual Initiation: The Role of Peer Norms," *Pediatrics* 102 (1998), 1185–1192.

261   R. Kaufmann, A. Spitz, and L. Strauss, "The Decline in United States Teen Pregnancy Rates, 1990–1995," *Pediatrics, 102* (1998), 1141–1147.

         C. Stevens-Simon and D. Kaplan, "Teen Childbearing Trends: Which Tide Turned When and Why?" *Pediatrics 102* (1998), 1205–1206.

         M. D. Resnick, P. S. Bearman, R. W. Blum, K. E. Bauman, K. M. Harris, J. Jones, J. Tabor, T. Beuhring, R. E. Sieving, M. Shew, M. Ireland, L. H. Bearinger, and R. Udry, "Protecting Adolescents from Harm: Findings from the National Longitudinal Study on Adolescent Health," *Journal of the American Medical Association* 278 (1997), 823–832.

         R. Garofalo, R. C. Wolf, S. Kessel, J. Palfrey, R. H. DuRant, "The Association Between Health Risk Behaviors and Sexual Orientation Among a School-Based Sample of Adolescents," *Pediatrics* 101 (1998), 895–902.

261   P. R. Sanday, *Fraternity Gang Rape* (New York: New York University Press, 1990).

262   **homosexual adolescence** R. C. Savin-Williams and K. M. Cohen, *The Lives of Lesbians, Gays, and Bisexuals: Children to Adults* (New York: Harcourt, Brace, and Company, 1996).

         R. C. Savin-Williams and L. M. Diamond, "Sexual Orientation As a Developmental Context for Lesbians, Gays, and Bisexuals: Biological Perspectives," in N. L. Segal, G. E. Weisfeld, and C. C. Weisfeld, eds., *Uniting Psychology and Biology: Integrative Perspectives on Human Development* (Washington, D.C.: American Psychological Association, 1997), 217–238.

263   **disclosure of sexual orientation** R. C. Savin-Williams, E. M. Dube, "Parental Reactions to Their Child's Disclosure of a Gay/Lesbian Identity," *Family Relations* 47 (1998): 7–13.

R. C. Savin-Williams, "The Disclosure to Families of Same-Sex Attractions By Lesbian, Gay, and Bisexual Youths," *Journal of Research on Adolescence* 8 (1998), 49–68.371–372adolescent suicideB. Guyer, M. F. MacDorman, J. A. Martin, K. D. Peters, and D. M. Strobino, "Annual Summary of Vital Statistics—1997," *Pediatrics* 102 (1998), 1333–1349.

D. K. Curran, *Adolescent Suicidal Behavior* (Washington, D.C.: Hemisphere, 1987).

R. Wetzel, "Hopelessness, Depression, and Suicide Intent," *Archives of General Psychiatry* 33 (1976), 1069–1073.

267   Coontz, *The Way We Really Are,* 14.

Chapter Eighteen: Enabling

269   S. Hauser, B. Book, J. Houlihan, S. Powers, B. Weiss-Perry, D. Follansbee, A. Jacobson, and G. Noam, "Sex Differences Within the Family: Studies of Adolescent and Parent Family Interactions," *Journal of Youth and Adolescence* 16 (1987), 199–220.

269   Steinberg, *Adolescence,* 168.

269   **adolescent autonomy** S. Vuchinich, R. Vuchinich, and B. Wood, The interparental relationship and family problem solving with preadolescent males. *Child Development* 64 (1993), 1389–140.

280   Kelly, interviewed by Forrest Sawyer, *Turning Point,* American Broadcasting Company, broadcast April 9, 1996.

281   W. Glaberson, "Alex Kelly, Convicted Rapist, Accepts a Plea Deal in a Second Case from 1986," *New York Times* (December 24, 1998), A18.

Chapter Nineteen: Cheating

287   J. P. Richter [pseud. Jean Paul] (1763–1825), quoted in I. Weiss and A. D. Weiss, eds., *Reflections on Childhood: A Quotations Dictionary* (Santa Barbara, Cal.: ABC-CLIO, 1991), 204.

287   **prevalence of cheating** University of Kansas Office of University Relations, "How Prevalent Is Cheating?" Internet posting (1996) quoting David Shulenburger, vice chancellor for academic affairs; Beverly Sypher, associate professor of cummunication studies; Tim Shaftel, associate dean of liberal arts and sciences; Jordan Haines, distinguished professor of business; Paul Krouse, Who's Who publisher and founder; Lawrence Sherr, Chancellors Club teaching professor of business administration; and graduate teaching assistant Jim Danoff-Burg, at www.kurelatn@kuhub.cc.ukans.edu.

287   J. Johnson, S. Farkas, and A. Bers, *Getting By: What American Teenagers Really Think About Their Schools* (New York: Public Agenda, 1997), 29.

D. L. McCabe and W. J. Bowers, "Academic Dishonesty Among Males in College: A Thirty Year Perspective," *Journal of College Student Development* 35 (1994), 5–10.

D. L. McCabe and L. K. Trevino, "Individual and Contextual Influences on Academic Dishonesty: A Multicampus Investigation," *Research in Higher Education* 38 (1997), 379–396; "What We Know About Cheating in College: Longitudinal Trends and Recent Developments," *Change* 28 (1996), 28–33; and "Academic Dishonesty: Honor Codes and Other Contextual Influences," *Journal of Higher Education* 64 (1993), 522–538.

289   W. Brashler, "So Smart They Cheat: In Today's Moral Climate, Should Students be Held Accountable for Abandoning Honesty?" *Chicago Tribune Magazine* (April 12, 1998), 18–19.

292   Educational Testing Services, *To Sound the Alarm: Cheating Has Consequences. A Campaign Proposal for "Commitment 2000,"* presented to The Advertising Council, Inc., June 18, 1998 (Princeton: Educational Testing Services, 1998).

293   E. Anderman, T. Griesinger, and G. Westerfield, "Motivation and Cheating During Early Adolescence," *Journal of Educational Psychology* 90 (1990), 84–93.

293   R. Stansbury, "When the Ends Justify the Means," *Hartford Courant* (March 2, 1997).

295   P. Hersch, *A Tribe Apart: A Journey Into the Heart of American Adolescence* (New York: Fawcett Columbine, 1998), 99.

297   Erikson, *Identity*, 82.

Chapter Twenty: Play and Sports

300   B. MacQuarrie, "Youth Football Game Turns Ugly—in Parking Lot," *Boston Globe* (October 17, 1998), p.1.

301   K. H. Rubin, G. C. Fein, and B. Vandenberg, "Play," in P. H. Mussen, ed., *Handbook of Child Psychology*, 4th ed. (New York: John Wiley and Sons, 1983), 693–774.

301   F. P. Hughes, *Children, Play, and Development*, 2nd ed. (Needham Heights, Mass.: Allyn and Bacon, 1995).

301   Hersch, *A Tribe Apart*, 138.

304   **parent/child play** M. E. Lamb, A. M. Frodi, C. P. Hwang, M. Frodi, and J. Steinberg, "Effects of Gender and Caretaking Role on Parent-Infant

Interaction," in M. E. Lamb, ed., *Nontraditional Families* (Hillsdale, N.J.: Erlbaum, 1982).

305 K. Sandqvist, "Sweden's Sex-Role Scheme and Commitment to Gender Equality," in S. Lewis, D. N. Izraeli, H. Hottsmans, eds., *Dual-Earner Families: International Perspectives* (London: Sage, 1992).

305 A. Sagi, M. E. Lamb, R. Shoham, R. Dvir, and K. S. Lewkowica, "Parent-Infant Interaction in Families on Israeli Kibbutzim," *International Journal of Behavioral Development* 8 (1985), 273–284.306M.

306 M. Parten, "Social Play Among Preschool Children," *Journal of Abnormal and Social Psychology* 28 (1933), 136–147.

306 **day care environments** K. H. Rubin, T. L. Maioni, and M. Hornung, "Free Play Behaviors in Middle- and Lower-Class Preschoolers: Parten and Piaget Revisited," *Child Development* 47 (1976), 414–419.

307 A. R. Somers, "Violence, Television, and the Health of American Youth," *New England Journal of Medicine* 15 (1976), 811–817.

307 D. M. Zuckerman and B. S. Zuckerman, "Television's Impact on Children," *Pediatrics* 75 (1985), 233–240.

307 Commission on Youth and Violence, *Violence and Youth: Psychology's Response* (Washington, D.C.: American Psychological Association, 1993).

307 G. Slaby and G. R. Quarfoth, "Effects of Television on the Developing Child," in B. W. Camp, ed., *Advances in Behavioral Pediatrics* (Greenwich, Conn.: Johnson Associates, 1988), 225–266.

307 D. Phillips, "The Impact of Mass Media Violence on U.S. Homicides," *American Sociological Review* (August 1983), 560–568.

307 M. Miedzian, *Boys Will Be Boys: Breaking the Link Between Masculinity and Violence* (New York: Doubleday, 1991), 198.

308 S. Bok, *Mayhem: Violence as Public Entertainment* (Reading, Mass.: Perseus, 1998).

308 Personal communication, Lisa Licata, Vice President, National Alliance for Youth Sports, 2050 Vista Parkway, West Palm Beach, FL 3341. www.nays.org

308 **decline in play** M. E. Ewing and V. Seefeldt, "American Youth and Sports Participation: Why They Participate, Why They Quit, How They Feel About Winning, How Motivations Differ, What Adults Can Do" (North Palm Beach, Fla.: Athletic Footwear Association, 1990).

308 S. I. Greenspan, *Playground Politics: Understanding the Emotional Life of Your School-Age Child* (Reading, Mass.: Perseus, 1993), 32.

310 B. Bradley, *Values of the Game* (New York: Workman Publishing Company, 1998).

310 B. J. Bredemeier, M. R. Weiss, D. L. Shields, B. Cooper, "The Relationship of Sport Involvement with Children's Moral Reasoning and Aggression Tendencies," *Journal of Sport Psychology* 8 (1986), 304–318.

310   B. J. Bredemeier and D. L. Shields, "Game Reasoning and Interactional Morality," *Journal of Genetic Psychology* 147 (1986), 257–275; and "Moral Growth Among Athletes and Nonathletes: A Comparative Analysis of Males and Females," *Journal of Genetic Psychology* 147 (1986), 7–18.

311   M. Messner, "When Bodies Are Weapons: Masculinity and Violence in Sport," *International Review of Sociology of Sport,* August 1990. Cited in Miedzian, *Boys Will Be Boys,* 199.

311   B. Ryan, "Cut Blocker: Facing His 23rd Operation, Broncos Guard Mark Schlereth Is Still Going Strong," *Boston Globe* (January 28, 1999), C1.

311   B. J. Bredemeier, "Moral Reasoning and the Perceived Legitimacy of Intentionally Injurious Sport Acts," 1985.

312   I. Berkow, "The High Priest of Hoop Hysteria," *New York Times* (May 14, 1988), 53.

312   D. Meggyesy, *Out of Their League* (Berkeley, Cal.: Ramparts Press, 1970).

315   S. Gilbert, "Home Trampoline Injuries Double," *New York Times* (March 3, 1998), C7.

315   G. A. Smith, "Injuries to Children in the United States Related to Trampolines, 1990–1995: A National Epidemic," *Pediatrics* 101 (1998), 406–412.

316   Bradley, *Values of the Game,* 121–122.

Chapter Twenty-one: Giving Back

319   J. W. Bartlett, ed. *The Future Is Ours: A Handbook for Student Activists in the 21st Century* (New York: Henry Holt and Company, 1996).

320   R. Coles, *The Moral Life of Children* (Boston: Houghton Mifflin Company, 1986), 157.

320   A. Freud, *The Ego and the Mechanisms of Defense* (New York: International Universities Press, 1936).

321   Hughes, *Children, Play, and Development,* 106.

325   Freud, *The Ego and the Mechanisms of Defense.*

326   Coles, *The Moral Life of Children,* 157.

327   A. Miller, *The Drama of the Gifted Child* rev. ed. (New York: Basic Books, 1997).

327   Coles, *The Moral Life of Children,* 191–196.

329   D. Spaide, "Growing a Giver," *Parents* magazine (November 1997), 203.

329   A. Kohn, "In Pursuit of Affluence, At a High Price," *New York Times* (February 2, 1999), D7.

330   W. Lippman, *A Preface to Morals* (New York: Macmillan, 1929), 156.

BIBLIOGRAPHY

Ackerman, D. *A Natural History of Love.* New York: Vintage Books, 1995.

Anthony, E. J., and B. J. Cohler, eds. *The Invulnerable Child.* New York: Guilford Press, 1987.

Badinter, E. *XY: On Masculine Identity.* New York: Columbia University Press, 1995.

Baker, M. *Sex Lives: A Sexual Self-Portrait of America.* New York: Simon and Schuster, 1994.

Barkley, R. A. *ADHD and the Nature of Self-Control.* New York: Guildford Press, 1997.

Bee, H. *Lifespan Development.* 2nd ed. Reading, Mass.: Addison-Wesley Educational Publishers, 1998.

Benkov, L. *Reinventing the Family: The Emerging Story of Lesbian and Gay Parents.* New York: Crown Publishers, 1994.

Berk, L. *Child Development.* 4th ed. (Needham Heights, Mass.: Allyn and Bacon, 1997.

Blankenhorn, D. *Fatherless America: Confronting Our Most Urgent Social Problem.* New York: HarperCollins Publishers, 1995.

Blum, D. *Sex on the Brain: The Biological Differences Between Men and Women.* New York: Viking, 1997.

Bok, S. *Lying: Moral Choice in Public and Private Life.* New York: Vintage Books, 1979.

_____. *Mayhem: Violence as Public Entertainment.* Reading, Mass.: Perseus, 1998.

Bornstein, M. H., and M. E. Lamb. *Development in Infancy: An Introduction.* 3rd ed. New York: McGraw-Hill, 1992.

Bowlby, J. *Attachment and Loss.* Vol. 1: *Attachment.* New York: Basic Books, 1969.
_____. *The Making and Breaking of Affectional Bonds.* London: Tavistock, 1979.

Bradley, B. *Values of the Game.* New York: Workman Publishing Company, 1998.

Bronfenbrenner, U. *The Ecology of Human Development: Experiments By Nature and Design.* Cambridge, Mass.: Harvard University Press, 1989.

Cairns, R. B., and B. D. Cairns. *Lifelines and Risks: Pathways of Youth in our Time.* Cambridge: Cambridge University Press, 1994.

Carey, W. B. *Understanding Your Child's Temperament.* New York: Macmillan, 1997.

Cath, S. H., A. R. Gurwit, J. M. Ross, eds. *Father and Child: Developmental and Clinical Perspectives.* Boston: Little, Brown, 1982.

Cheever, S. *Note Found in a Bottle: My Life As a Drinker.* New York: Simon and Schuster, 1998.

Chess, S., and A. Thomas, *Know Your Child: An Authoritative Guide for Today's Parents.* New York: Basic Books, 1987.

———., *Temperament Theory and Practice.* New York: Brunner/Mazel, 1996.

Coles, R. *The Moral Intelligence of Children.* New York: Random House, 1997.

———. *The Moral Life of Children.* New York: Houghton Mifflin, 1991.

Coontz, S. *The Way We Really Are: Coming to Terms with America's Changing Families.* New York: Basic Books, 1997.

Cowan, P. A., and M. Hetherington, eds. *Family Transitions.* Hillsdale, N.J.: Lawrence Erlbaum, 1991.

Crain, W. *Theories of Development: Concepts and Applications.* 3rd ed. Englewood Cliffs, N.J.: Prentice Hall, 1992.

Damon, W. *The Moral Child: Nurturing Children's Natural Moral Growth.* New York: The Free Press, 1988.

Delpit, L. *Other People's Children: Cultural Conflict in the Classroom.* New York: The New Press, 1995.

Diessner, R., ed. *Sources: Notable Selections in Human Development.* Guilford, Conn.: Dushkin/McGraw-Hill, 1997.

Dryfoos, J. G. *Safe Passage: Making It Through Adolescence in a Risky Society.* New York: Oxford University Press, 1998.

Eibl-Eibesfeldt, I. *Ethology: The Biology of Behavior.* New York: Holt, Rinehart, and Winston, 1970.

Elkind, D. J. *The Hurried Child: Growing Up Too Fast, Too Soon.* Reading, Mass.: Perseus, 1989.

Elium, J., and D. Elium, *Raising a Son: Parents and the Awakening of a Healthy Man.* Berkeley, Cal.: Celestial Arts, 1994.

Erikson, E. H. *Childhood and Society.* 2nd ed. New York: W. W. Norton, 1963.

———. *Identity: Youth and Crisis.* New York: W. W. Norton, 1968.

———. *Young Man Luther: A Study in Psychoanalysis and History.* New York: W. W. Norton, 1962.

Federal Interagency Forum on Child and Family Statistics. *America's Children: Key National Indicators of Well-Being.* Washington, D.C.: Office of Management and Budget, 1997.

Finnegan, W. *Cold New World: Growing Up in a Harder Country.* New York: Random House, 1998.

Fisher, H. E. *Anatomy of Love: The Natural History of Monogamy, Adultery, and Divorce.* New York: W. W. Norton, 1992.

Fraiberg, S. H. *The Magic Years: Understanding and Handling the Problems of Early Childhood.* New York: Charles Scribner's Sons, 1959.

Frankel, F. H. *Good Friends Are Hard to Find: Help Your Child Find, Make and Keep Friends.* Indianapolis, Ind.: Perspectives Press, 1996.

Furstenberg, F. F., and A. J. Cherline, *Divided Families: What Happens to Children When Parents Part.* Cambridge, Mass.: Harvard University Press, 1991.

Gallagher, W., *Just the Way You Are: How Heredity and Experience Create the Individual.* New York: Random House, 1996.

Gardner, H. *Multiple Intelligence: The Theory in Practice.* New York: Basic Books, 1993.

Garvey, C. *Play.* Cambridge, Mass.: Harvard University Press, 1977.

Gauvin, M., and M. Cole, eds. *Readings on the Development of Children.* 2nd ed. New York: W. H. Freeman and Company, 1997.

Geary, D. C. *Male, Female: The Evolution of Human Sex Differences.* Washington, D.C.: American Psychological Association, 1998.

Gilligan, C. *In a Different Voice: Psychological Theory and Women's Development.* Cambridge, Mass.: Harvard University Press, 1982.

Gilligan, J. *Violence: Our Deadly Epidemic and Its Causes.* New York: G. P. Putnam's Sons, 1996.

Gillis, J. R. *A World of Their Own Making: Myth, Ritual and the Quest for Family Values.* Cambridge, Mass.: Harvard University Press, 1996.

Goethals, G. W., and D. S. Klos, *Experiencing Youth: First-Person Accounts.* Lanham, Md.: University Press of America, 1986.

Goleman, D. *Emotional Intelligence: Why It Can Matter More Than IQ.* New York: Bantam, 1995.

Greenspan, S. I. *Playground Politics: Understanding the Emotional Life of Your School-age Child.* Reading, Mass.: Perseus, 1993.

_____. *The Challenging Child: Understanding, Raising, and Enjoying the Five "Difficult" Types of Children.* Reading, Mass.: Perseus, 1995.

_____. *The Growth of the Mind and the Endangered Origins of Intelligence.* Reading, Mass.: Perseus, 1997.

Greenspan, S. I., and S. Wieder. *The Child with Special Needs.* Reading, Mass.: Perseus, 1998.

Greven, P. *Spare the Child: The Religious Roots of Physical Punishment and the Psychological Impact of Abuse.* New York: Knopf, 1991.

Gurian, M. *A Fine Young Man: What Parents, Mentors and Educators Can Do to Shape Adolescent Boys Into Exceptional Men.* New York: Penguin Putnam, 1998.

_____. *The Wonder of Boys: What Parents, Mentors and Educators Can Do to Shape Boys Into Exceptional Men.* New York: G. P. Putnam's Sons, 1996.

Hamer, D., and P. Copeland, *Living with Our Genes: Why They Matter More Than You Think.* New York: Doubleday, 1998.

Hamill, P. *A Drinking Life: A Memoir.* Boston: Little, Brown, 1994.

Harris, R. H., and M. Emberly. *It's Perfectly Normal: Changing Bodies, Growing Up, Sex, Sexual Health.* Cambridge, Mass.: Candlewick, 1994.

Hawley, R. A. *Boys Will Be Men: Masculinity in Troubled Times.* Middlebury, Vt.: Paul S. Eriksson Publisher, 1993.

Hersch, P. *A Tribe Apart: A Journey into the Heart of American Adolescence.* New York: Fawcett Columbine, 1998.

Hughes, F. P. *Children, Play, and Development.* 2nd ed. Needham Heights, Mass.: Allyn and Bacon, 1995.

Karr-Morse, R., and M. S. Wiley, *Ghosts from the Nursery: Tracing the Roots of Violence.* New York: Atlantic Monthly Press, 1997.

Kimmel, M. S., ed. *Men Confront Pornography.* New York: Crown Publishers, 1990.

Klaus, M. H., and P. H. Klaus, *Your Amazing Newborn.* Reading, Mass.: Perseus, 1998.

Knapp, C. *Drinking: A Love Story.* New York: Dell Publishing, 1996.

Leach, P. *Children First: What Our Society Must Do—and Is Not Doing—for Our Children Today.* New York: Alfred A. Knopf, 1994.

Lear, J. *Open Minded: Working Out the Logic of the Soul.* Cambridge, Mass.: Harvard University Press, 1998.

Lefkowitz, B. *Our Guys: The Glen Ridge Rape and the Secret Life of the Perfect Suburb.* Berkeley: University of California Press, 1997.

Lewis, M. *Altering Fate: Why the Past Does Not Predict the Future.* New York: Guilford Press, 1997.

_____. *Clinical Aspects of Child Development.* Philadelphia: Lea and Febiger, 1971.

Lewis, M., and J. M. Haviland, eds. *Handbook of Emotions.* New York: Guilford Press, 1993.

Ludtke, M. *On Our Own: Unmarried Motherhood in America.* New York: Random House, 1997.

Maccoby, E. E. *The Two Sexes: Growing Apart, Coming Together.* Cambridge, Mass.: Harvard University Press, 1998.

Mash, E. J., and R. A. Barkley, eds. *Treatment of Childhood Disorders.* New York: Guilford Press, 1989.

Mastoon, A. *The Shared Heart: Portraits and Stories Celebrating Lesbian, Gay, and Bisexual Young People.* New York: William Morrow and Company, 1997.

Miedzian, M. *Boys Will Be Boys: Breaking the Link Between Masculinity and Violence.* New York: Doubleday, 1991.

Merrens, M. R., and G. G. Brannigan, *The Developmental Psychologists: Research Adventures Across the Life Span.* New York: McGraw-Hill, 1996.

Miller, A. *The Drama of the Gifted Child: The Search for the True Self.* Rev. ed. New York: Basic Books, 1997.

Muuss, R. E. *Theories of Adolescence.* 6th ed. New York: McGraw-Hill, 1996.

Newcombe, N. *Child Development: Change Over Time.* 8th ed. New York: HarperCollins College Publishers, 1996.

Olweus, D. *Bullying at School.* Oxford: Blackwell Publishers, 1993.

Paley, V. G. *You Can't Say You Can't Play.* Cambridge, Mass.: Harvard University Press, 1992.

Phillips, A. *The Beast in the Nursery: On Curiosity and Other Appetites.* New York: Pantheon Books, 1998.

Phillips, L. *The Girls Report: What We Know and Need to Know About Growing Up Female.* New York: The National Council for Research on Women, 1998.

Pinker, S. *How the Mind Works.* New York: W. W. Norton, 1997.

Plotkin, H. *Evolution in Mind: An Introduction to Evolutionary Psychology.* Cambridge, Mass.: Harvard University Press, 1998.

Pollack, W. *Real Boys: Rescuing Our Sons from the Myths of Boyhood.* New York: Random House, 1998.

Reiss, A. J., and J. A. Roth, eds. *Understanding and Preventing Violence.* Washington, D.C.: National Academy Press, 1994.

Sameroff, A. J., and R. N. Emde. *Relationship Disturbances in Early Childhood: A Developmental Approach.* New York: Basic Books, 1989.

Sanday, P. R. *Fraternity Gang Rape: Sex, Brotherhood, and Privilege on Campus.* New York: New York University Press, 1990.

Siegler, R. S. *Children's Thinking.* 2nd ed. Englewood Cliffs, N.J.: Prentice Hall, 1991.

Small, M. F. *Our Babies, Ourselves: How Biology and Culture Shape the Way We Parent.* New York: Anchor Books, 1998.

Snow, C. W. *Infant Development.* 2nd ed. Upper Saddle River, N.J.: Prentice Hall, 1998.

Schwartzman, M., and J. Sachs. *The Anxious Parent: Freeing Yourself from the Fears and Stresses of Parenting.* New York: Simon and Schuster, 1990.

Silverstein, O., and B. Rashbaum. *The Courage to Raise Good Men.* New York: Penguin Books, 1994.

Slaby, R. G., W. C. Roedell, D., Arezzo, and K. Hendrix. *Early Violence Prevention: Tools for Teachers of Young Children.* Washington, D.C.: National Association for the Education of Young Children, 1995.

Sober, E., and D.S. Wilson. *Unto Others: The Evolution and Psychology of Unselfish Behavior.* Cambridge, Mass.: Harvard University Press, 1998.

Steinberg, L. *Adolescence.* 4th ed. New York: McGraw-Hill, 1996.

Stern, D. N. *Diary of a Baby.* New York: Basic Books, 1990.

_____. *The Interpersonal World of the Infant: A View from Psychoanalysis and Developmental Psychology.* New York: Basic Books, 1985.

Straus, M. A. *Beating the Devil Out of Them: Corporal Punishment in American Families.* San Francisco: Jossey-Bass, 1994.

Tannen, D. *You Just Don't Understand: Women and Men in Conversation.* New York: Ballantine Books, 1990.

Thomas, R. M. *Comparing Theories of Child Development.* 3rd ed. Belmont, Cal.: Wadsworth Publishing Company, 1992.

Thorne, B. *Gender Play: Girls and Boys in School.* New Brunswick, N.J.: Rutgers University Press, 1993.

Trelease, J. *The Read-Aloud Handbook.* 4th ed. New York: Penguin, 1995.

Turecki, S. *The Emotional Problems of Normal Children: How Parents Can Understand and Help.* New York: Bantam Books, 1994.

Turiel, E. *The Development of Social Knowledge: Morality and Convention.* New York: Cambridge University Press, 1983.

Weiss, I., and A. D. Weiss, eds. *Reflections on Childhood: A Quotations Dictionary.* Santa Barbara, Cal.: ABC-CLIO, 1991.

Weiss, R. S. *Staying the Course: The Emotional and Social Lives of Men Who Do Well At Work.* New York: The Free Press, 1990.

Weissbourd, R. *The Vulnerable Child: What Really Hurts America's Children and What We Can Do About It.* Reading, Mass.: Perseus, 1996.

Wells, J., ed. *Lesbians Raising Sons.* Los Angeles, Cal.: Alyson Books, 1997.

Wolfe, A. *One Nation, After All: What Middle-class Americans Really Think About God, Country, Family, Racism, Welfare, Immigration, Homosexuality, Work, the Right, the Left, and Each Other.* New York: Viking, 1998.

Wolff, R. *Sports Parenting: Encouraging Your Kids on and Off the Field.* New York: Pocket Books, 1998.

Zoldbrod, A. P. *Sex Smart: How Your Childhood Shaped Your Sexual Life and What to Do About It.* Oakland, Cal.: New Harbinger Publications, 1998.

INDEX

ABOUT THE AUTHOR

Eli Newberger, M.D., a leading figure in the movement to improve the protection and care of children, is renowned for his ability to bring together good sense and science on the main issues of family life. A pediatrician and author of many influential works on child abuse, he teaches at Harvard Medical School and founded the Family Development Program at Children's Hospital in Boston. From his research and practice he has derived a philosophy that focuses on the strength and resilience of parent-child relationships, and a practice oriented to compassion and understanding, rather than blame and punishment. He lives in Brookline, Massachusetts with his wife Carolyn, a developmental and clinical child psychologist.